MARLOWE

A CRITICAL STUDY

BY

J. B. STEANE

CAMBRIDGE UNIVERSITY PRESS

Published by the Syndics of the Cambridge University Press
Bentley House, 200 Euston Road, London NW1 2DB
American Branch: 32 East 57th Street, New York, N.Y.10022

© Cambridge University Press 1964

Library of Congress Catalogue Card Number: 77-121363

ISBNS
0 521 06545 3 hard covers
0 521 09623 4 paperback

First published 1964
Reprinted 1965, 1970, 1974

First printed in Great Britain by
Spottiswoode, Ballantyne & Co. Ltd, London and Colchester
Reprinted in Great Britain by
Alden & Mowbray Ltd at the Alden Press, Oxford

CONTENTS

iii

To my
Father and Mother †

PREFACE TO THE PAPERBACK EDITION

This is a reprint, not a new edition. So the text has to remain largely unaltered in spite of the author's reluctance, like Caesar's with the crown, to lay his fingers off it. The book was not published until 1964, Marlowe's centenary year; but it had been completed by 1961, and much of it was written several years before that. In ten years one's mind changes; style too; and also one's sense of what is important in presentation. Writing this book afresh now would probably involve renunciation of the more colloquial features of its style, and some of its modern references and comparisons; and there would certainly be more detailed textual references. In that matter, at least, it has been possible to improve the original somewhat for this edition: the bibliography is fuller, as well as containing mention of publications dating from 1962 onwards, and the footnotes carry more detail. I have also added a short note at the end of Chapter 5 to record a comment on new criticism; and on p. 373 I set out the reasons for my partial change of mind about *Edward II*.

Inevitably, the book still cannot attend with more than a passing reference to the more recent work on Marlowe which would have influenced it, in some instances quite strongly, had it been known to me at the time. Douglas Cole's book[1] and the essays in the *Tulane Drama Review*[2] are the prime examples in written work; the Prospect Theatre's production of *Edward II*[3] was an outstanding experience in the theatre. Even so, the main observations and arguments would remain the same in essence, and the intervening decade has, if anything, only widened the gap between the Marlowe of this book and the Marlowe of what one can almost call the new orthodoxy. For, since Professor

[1] D. Cole, *Suffering and Evil in the Plays of Christopher Marlowe* (Princeton, 1962).
[2] *Tulane Drama Review* (Marlowe Issue) (VIII, 4, 1964).
[3] First produced at the Edinburgh International Festival 28 August 1969 (directed by Tony Robertson).

v

Battenhouse's study of *Tamburlaine*[1] appeared in 1941, with its view of Marlowe as one who 'differs from his Protestant contemporaries . . . not in his moral outlook but only in his ability as an artist', much modern scholarship has put its weight behind a qualified acceptance of this opinion. Mr Cole's learned and devoted study has supported it, and so in a different way has David Bevington's, with its stress upon Marlowe as a craftsman working within the conventions of his time.[2] I am afraid that my own dissent has simply to be reaffirmed. Re-reading Battenhouse is to find again that Marlowe has been tricked into line with his contemporaries, and that basic poetic and dramatic qualities have been disregarded when they run contrary to the thesis. The kind of Marlowe who emerges from these studies in fact seems to me to be incompatible with a qualitative, critical reading of the poetry (there is a tell-tale phrase in Douglas Cole's discussion of Faustus' speech to Helen, when he says 'clearly this is not just poetry').[3]

So in the face of this growing body of opinion, presenting a 'Christian' Marlowe, 'detached' and conventional, it may be as well, if only for variety, that a 'reactionary' voice is again raised (some American reviewers of the original seemed so surprised, that one felt it was as if grandfather had spoken up from the arm-chair in which he was supposed to be quietly and peacefully crossing the bar). It only remains to thank those readers and reviewers whose corrections and suggestions have now been incorporated in the book, and my publishers for their continued care and patience.

J. B. S.

1970

---

[1] R. Battenhouse: *Marlowe's Tamburlaine: a Study in Renaissance Moral Philosophy* (Nashville, 1941), p. 177.

[2] D. M. Bevington, *From Mankind to Marlowe* (Harvard, 1962).

[3] Cole, *op. cit.*, p. 222.

PREFACE

I would like to express my gratitude to several kind friends, notably Mr H. E. M. Crowle whose collaboration in discussions and in criticism of first drafts has been invaluable. Any good ideas in the book may well be his, and the particularly bad ones almost certainly occur in parts he was unable to read. Generous and necessary help over the Latin translations was given me by my colleague, Mr W. J. H. Robson. His enthusiasm for Lucan was luckily at hand, and with it went much practical and tireless scholarship. Mr Edward Greenfield and the late A. P. Rossiter are two other begetters. The one has been a constant stimulus to critical work both in conversation and by example; and to the other, my supervisor at Cambridge, I owe a debt I can hardly measure but can at least in some degree acknowledge by quotation from his work in these pages.

My greatest debt is one which the book appears almost to repudiate. Quotations from critics and scholars 'in the field' are so often made for purposes of disagreement, that one seems to be at perpetual war with the very people who have made the present work possible. The long studies by Boas, Levin, Greg and others are constant sources of information and understanding. Then, for one writing a book, possibly the most unnerving experience is to read work published and virtually buried in the quarterlies. So much scholarship is most likely worth a great many critical 'perceptions' (and I have kept before me as a sort of *memento mori* T. S. Eliot's sentences on these matters, as well as a passage in Erich Heller's *The Ironic German* (page 101), which argues the dangers and limitations of 'close criticism'). Nevertheless it has seemed to me that

vii

what Marlowe has lacked, in the great amount written about him, is criticism that has the poetry as its centre of interest, looking inwards to the art as something to be appreciated with enjoyment and judgment, rather than outwards to the life, times, background and abstracted thought. This book is offered principally as an attempt to supply that need.

LONDON   J. B. S.
July 1962

NOTE

Marlowe quotations are taken from the edition of his works by C. F. Tucker Brooke (Oxford, 1910).

Part I

I

MARLOWE'S LIFE:
FACTS AND THEORIES

AT THE HEART of any discussion about Marlowe's life is the knowledge we have of his death. He was killed on 30 May 1593, at the age of twenty-nine, in circumstances which have exercised scholars, preachers, playwrights, novelists and gossips to an extraordinary degree. An early version of what happened survives in Thomas Beard's *Theatre of Gods Iudgements*, published in 1597. He tells that 'in London streets as he purposed to stab one whome hee ought a grudge vnto with his dagger, the other party perceiuing so auoided the stroke, that withall catching hold of his wrest, he stabbed his owne dagger into his owne head, in such sort, that notwithstanding all the meanes of surgerie that could be wrought, hee shortly after died thereof'. His death was 'an horrible and fearefull terrour to all that beheld him', what they saw being a man who 'cursed and blasphemed to his last gaspe, and together with his breath an oth flew out of his mouth'. Writing a year later, Francis Meres (*Palladis Tamia*) adds that he was 'stabd to death by a bawdy Seruing man, a riuall of his in his lewde loue'. More authentic, as it turns out, is an account by William Vaughan in *Golden Grove* (1600): 'At Detford, a little village about three miles distant from London, as he meant to stab with his ponyard one named Ingram, that had inuited him thither to a feast and was then playing at tables, he quickly perceyuing it, so auoided the thrust, that withall drawing out his dagger for his defence, hee stabd this Marlow into the eye, in such sort that his braines comming out at the

3

daggers point, hee shortlie after dyed.' So the story grew, embellished from time to time over the three centuries of its currency. Marlowe, it seemed, was killed in a tavern brawl, his loose living and lewd loving being somehow involved.

Nineteenth-century scholarship supplied one further piece of information, though it later proved to be inaccurate. In 1820 James Broughton, who had read the account of Marlowe's death in Vaughan, saw that the place-name provided a lead for some literary detection. He accordingly wrote to the vicar of St Nicholas Church, Deptford, asking whether he could trace any reference to the event in the burial register. In this way the name of Marlowe's killer was thought to have been found. '1st June 1593,' the Minister quoted, 'Christopher Marlow, slaine by Ffrancis Archer.' But Francis Archer remained a mystery; nor, for many years, did it seem to help matters when it was discovered that the vicar had misread the surname, which was not Archer at all, but Frezer. Then in 1925 Dr Leslie Hotson published the findings of one of the most famous and exciting pieces of literary research. Working in the Public Record Office in Chancery Lane, he noticed the name Ingram Frizer mentioned in the Calendar of Close Rolls. He was immediately certain, he says, that this was the man who killed Marlowe, the 'Ingram' of Vaughan's account being the Christian name (everyone appears to have made the contrary assumption) and the burial register's 'Francis' being a mistake. Dr Hotson went on to reason that if Marlowe had been murdered, there must have been legal proceedings. He tried Inquisitions Post Mortem, criminal records, and the Rolls of Assizes on South-Eastern Circuit, but found nothing. Then he thought of pardons, and in the index to these documents read an entry which triumphantly confirmed his hunch. The queen did in fact grant

4

a pardon to Ingram ffrisar for killing in self-defence. The
date was 28 June. If the pardon was in existence, so very
probably was a copy of the coroner's inquest on the basis
of which the pardon was granted. This too Dr Hotson
found.

It tells how, on 30 May, four men 'met together in a
room in the house of a certain Eleanor Bull, widow; &
there passed the time together & dined & after dinner were
in quiet sort together & walked in the garden belonging
to the said house until the sixth hour after noon of the same
day & then returned from the said garden to the room
aforesaid & there together and in company supped'. These
men were 'Christopher Marlowe, Ingram Frisar, Nicholas
Skeres and Robert Poley'. 'After supper the said Ingram
& Christopher Morley were in speech & uttered one to the
other divers malicious words for the reason that they could
not be at one nor agree about the payment of the sum of
pence, that is, le recknynge, there.' Quite suddenly Marlowe
attacked Frizer. He had been lying on a bed and Frizer
had been sitting at a table with his back to Marlowe, his
dagger 'at his back'. Marlowe seized this and with it gave
the other man 'two wounds on his head of the length of
two inches & of the depth of a quarter of an inch'. Frizer
could not get away, the document explains, because Skeres
and Poley were sitting on either side of him. 'In fear of
being slain' Frizer struggled with his attacker for possession
of the dagger, and 'with the dagger aforesaid of the value
of 12d. gave the said Christopher then & there a mortal
wound over his right eye of the depth of two inches & of
the width of one inch'. Of this wound Marlowe 'then &
there instantly died'.

But, as several writers were quick to maintain, there are
some odd things about this account. One of them is the
behaviour of the other two men. Perhaps when they saw

Marlowe get up from the bed and draw Frizer's dagger they decided they had best keep out of the way. Perhaps when Marlowe dealt Frizer these two head wounds they were too paralysed to move, for it seems that their continued presence cut off Frizer's retreat. Perhaps Marlowe and Frizer were great powerful fellows while Skeres and Poley were bony starvelings, but at any rate they seem to have done little towards parting the combatants. Again, it was clearly a bad mistake on Frizer's part to present his weapon and his back to the man with whom he had just been arguing; it would be uncharacteristic too, for Frizer appears to have been a shrewd, active person, living a life of contention and sharp practice in London and then preserving himself for another twenty-two years or so as a gentleman (and churchwarden) at Eltham. Active of course he must have been, to grapple with Marlowe so successfully when he had just been wounded in the way the coroner's report describes. But the blow with which he killed Marlowe raises still more questions. Dr S. A. Tannenbaum, in 1928, with a good deal of expert backing objected that the wound as described could not have caused instant death but only a coma; to have the effect stated in the report it would have had to be six or seven inches deep, and the force needed to inflict such a wound would be very considerable indeed. In several respects, then, the account is not altogether convincing.

It may be an entirely unconnected fact that when Marlowe was killed, a warrant was out for his arrest. On 18 May, the Privy Council ordered its representative 'to apprehend and bring him to the Court in his Companie'. They thought it probable that he would be staying with Thomas Walsingham at Chislehurst. What they wanted with him is not known: a summons to appear before the Council was not always as serious a matter as it sounds. But it can hardly be another unconnected fact that a few days before the writ was issued, Thomas Kyd, under arrest and torture, had denounced Marlowe for holding atheistical and treasonable opinions. In a letter to Sir John Puckering, the Lord Keeper, Kyd makes some general remarks about his character and with ostensible reluctance particularises some of his 'monstrous' views. The first he recalled was the most salacious: 'He wold report St John to be our savior Christes *Alexis*. I cover it with reverence and trembling that is that Christ did loue him with an extraordinary loue.' Then apparently Marlowe had scoffed at Kyd's intention of writing a poem about the conversion of St Paul: he said it would be 'as if I shold go write a book of fast & loose, esteeming *Paul* a Jugler'. He also made a joke about the Prodigal Son which was supposed to show that he did not understand the story to be a parable. Finally he held that 'things esteemed to be donn by devine power might haue as well been don by observation of men'. Possibly more interesting than 'marlowes monstrous opiniouns' is the picture that Kyd paints of his character. He was 'intemperate & of a cruel hart'; 'it was his custom when I knewe him first & as I heare saie he contynewd it in table talk or otherwise to iest at the devine scriptures gybe at praiers, & stryve in argument to frustrate & confute what hath byn spoke or wrytt by prophets & such holie menn'; and these opinions 'he wold sodenlie take slight occasion to slyp out as I & many others in regard of his other rashnes in attempting soden pryvie iniuries to men did ouerslypp thogh often reprehend him for it'. To such a man, it may well be argued, one would not present one's back and one's dagger.

Kyd had been arrested on 12 May after a government raid on the rooms of various persons suspected of libel and sedition. Some papers had been found in his chamber denying the divinity of Jesus, and Kyd had defended himself by asserting that they belonged to Marlowe. Marlowe, he said, had shared the room with him 'twoe yeares synce', and these papers had, unknown to him, got shuffled in with some of his own. It was very probably these allegations and others made subsequently under torture that caused the Privy Council to send for Marlowe on the 18th.

Kyd's testimony is vivid and dramatic but, unfortunately, not beyond suspicion. The wretched man no doubt had the fear of gallows, rack, pillory and branding-iron before his eyes, and he knew that Marlowe was dead. This is clear from his letter to Puckering. It is undated, but the last sentence (which contains, incidentally, the only political reference) reads: 'He wold perswade with men of quallitie to goe vnto the k[ing] of *Scotts* whether I heare *Roydon* is gon and where if he had liud he told me when I sawe him last he meant to be.' That he did not live may have been lucky for Kyd: *les morts ont tort*. Kyd certainly emerges here playing some very unenviable roles: Uriah Heep ('in discharge of dutie both towardes god your lordships & the world thus much haue I thought good brieflie to discover in all humblenes'), Eric 'or *Little-by-Little*' ('as in hatred of his life & thoughts I left & did refraine his companie'), Pecksniff ('that I shold loue or be familier friend with one so irreligious were verie rare . . . besides he was intemperate & of a cruel hart, the verie contraries to wch, my greatest enemies will saie by me'), or a gutter-press reporter ('I cannot but with an agreved conscience think on him or them'—'them' being the opinions which he goes on to report). The desperation of the grovelling (and he is servile, even for those days of necessary sycophancy) weakens the credibility of his charges.

But such evidence as we have goes to support them. Another testimony was handed in to the authorities, probably on 2 June, denouncing 'the opinion of one Christopher Marly Concerning his damnable Judgment of Religion, and scorn of Gods word'. This was signed by one Richard Baines, possibly a member of the Middle Temple who had come before the Privy Council himself some years previously (Dr Boas gives the relevant facts in his *Christopher Marlowe*, 1940, pp. 245–50). The note repeats some of Kyd's accusations in a form sufficiently close to support them, yet sufficiently different to make any association seem unlikely.[1] Marlowe is said to have argued that the Bible is historically wrong: Adam is supposed by Christians to have lived 'within 6 thowsand yeares' whereas writers of other civilisations tell of times long before that. He attacked both Old and New Testaments. Moses was a clever man who had been brought up among the sorcerers of the Egyptian court, and had learnt the tricks of the trade too well for them. It was easy for him to impress the Hebrews, who were simple, ignorant people. He (a representative figure from the Old Testament) was a fraud, and so was Jesus. 'If the Jewes among whome he was borne did Crucify him theie best knew him and whence he came.' Religion served its purpose amongst primitive peoples ('the first beginning of Religioun was only to keep men in awe'), but now it was a laughable institution (the Sacrament 'would have bin much better being administered in a Tobacco pipe'); it was moreover based on a badly written book. He himself could devise a much better religion if he tried, and in the meantime 'all they that love not tobacco & Boyes were fooles'. These were opinions which he was constantly voicing: 'almost into every Company he Cometh he perswades men to Atheism willing them not to be afeard of bugbeares and hobgoblins, and utterly scorning both god and his ministers'. Baines says

---

[1] The full text of the Baines note is given in Appendix I below.

that he will back his accusations with 'the testimony of many honest men', and the note ends with a further sting in its tail: 'He saieth likewise that he hath quoted a number of Contrarieties oute of the Scripture which he hath given to some great men who in Convenient time shalbe named.' It is high time, Baines considers, 'that the mouth of so dangerous a member may be stopped'. He did not have long to wait.

There is a good deal to be discussed here, but it would be natural to ask first what kind of a life it was which led to the violence and scandal of this death.

It began in Canterbury in 1564. The father was a shoemaker, living in fairly comfortable conditions. He was a freeman, a bondsman and a parish clerk. The mother, Catherine Arthur, came from Dover, and married the twenty-one year-old John Marlow in 1561. There were plenty of children, four sons and five daughters, though not all survived childhood. The girls married Canterbury tradesmen and there is no record of any Marlowe other than Christopher travelling beyond his native city. Christopher's distinction among Marlowes begins with his scholarship to the King's School. Close by the cathedral and the cloisters, its antiquity guaranteed by the Norman staircase, King's is one of the earliest of foundations. It was reorganised by Henry VIII (the 'king' in question), and his statutes provided for the education of 'fifty poor boys' (which seems very quickly and characteristically to have been interpreted as a relative term). Marlowe joined the school when he was nearly fifteen, the maximum age for entrance, and left in the following year, 1580, on a Matthew Parker scholarship to Corpus Christi, Cambridge. Both of his scholarships suggest that some unusual quality about him was recognised. King's took him late in his school career: he had probably come to their special notice, or they would have filled the vacancy with a boy who could enjoy it longer and whom they could educate from an earlier age. And John Parker, the archbishop's son, awarded him his scholarship to Corpus after he had been less than two years at the school. But if academic promise had been diagnosed, it was not fulfilled with any marked success. When Marlowe took his M.A. in 1587, he had achieved no particular acclaim as a scholar. He had, moreover, clearly decided not to follow the intentions behind the Parker scholarships, for he did not take holy orders.

On the other hand, it is quite evident that he did more than merely drift through these six years. Much of the learning found in the plays derives from books in the college library, and in any case the mind and temperament that produced these plays are lively and passionate. We also have information about one respect in which Marlowe's university career was notably distinguished: he was at first refused his degree and then granted it at the intercession of the Queen's Council. This was another of the discoveries of Dr Hotson, and was due again to one of those deductions which occurred to no one for a few centuries and now look obvious enough. If Marlowe's name was spelt in so many different ways by his contemporaries (Marley, Morley, Marlin and Merlin for instance), then may it not well be that references to the poet lie around under our very noses, unidentified because of the unfamiliar appearance of 'Marlor' or 'Malyn'? A case in point, Dr Hotson suggested, was an entry in the Privy Council register, dated 29 July 1587. This is under the names of the Lord Archbishop, Lord Chancellor, Lord Treasurer and Mr Controller, who urged the university authorities not to oppose 'Christopher Morley' in the degree he was to take next commencement. There had been rumours, the entry explains, that he had gone to Rheims 'there to remaine'.

No such thing, however: in fact, he had 'behaued him selfe orderlie and discreetlie wherebie he had done her Majestie good service, and deserued to be rewarded for his faithfull dealinge'. The rumours were to be silenced, for 'it was not her Majesties pleasure that anie one emploied as he had been in matters touching the benefitt of his Countrie should be defamed by those that are ignorant in th'affaires he went about'.

The implications of this document have been discussed and tested pretty thoroughly (an interesting account is given in Dr Boas's book).[1] The probability is that Marlowe had come to the notice of those who ran the secret service, and had been sent to Rheims, where the English Catholics had their seminary. In 1581, the Government had issued a proclamation 'recalling her Majesty's subjects which under pretence of studies do live beyond the seas both contrary to the laws of God and of the realm, and against such as do receive or retain Jesuits and massing priests, sowers of sedition and of other treasonable attempts'. It was a nervous decade. The martyrdom of Edmund Campion and the execution of Mary Stuart were symptoms, and the Armada was the culmination of fears which its defeat did not remove. Laws against the Catholics were tightened, and the English Catholics at home and abroad became still more urgently one of Secretary Walsingham's first cares. To send a young man over to Douai or Rheims 'under pretence of (Catholic) studies' was an obvious step for the secret service to take. But the young man in question might often find that his difficulties did not end with his return to England. In Marlowe's case, the University authorities, strict on religious conformity, seem to have heard rumours of recusancy, and their consequent hostility would have been the reason for his appeal for support from

[1] *Christopher Marlowe* (Oxford, 1940), pp. 21-7.

the Privy Council. Few Cambridge men can have secured
their degree by pulling quite such well-connected strings.
Few also are the men who have made quite such an immediate
success on coming down from their university.
Marlowe took his degree in July 1587 and it seems very
likely that by November *Tamburlaine* had been produced
in London, Part 2 as well as Part 1. This dating is implied
by a letter which also suggests one reason for the play's
popularity. In the fifth act of Part 2, the Governor of
Babylon is hung in chains and shot on his own walls. In a
performance referred to in Philip Gawdy's letter home,
dated 16 November, the actor 'missed the fellowe he aymed
at and killed a chyld and a woman great with chyld forthwith
and hurt an other man in the head very sore'. If this sort
of thing could happen, anything might. Another kind of
excitement is made vividly apparent by the indignation of
Greene's preface to *Perimedes* published in 1588. In a
famous passage, Greene attacks those who 'set the end of
schollarisme in an English blank-verse'. Although he says
'I speake darkely, gentlemen,' the target is in little doubt:
'such impious instances of intollerable poetrie, such mad
and scoffing poets, that haue propheticall spirits as bred of
Merlins race'. To make assurance surer, he suggests that
he himself is to be congratulated on not writing verses
which 'jet upon the stage in tragicall buskins, everie word
filling the mouth like the Faburden of Bo-Bell, daring God
out of heaven with that Atheist *Tamburlan*'. Like many
dealers in righteous indignation, Greene makes the object
of his attack sound unusually interesting. We today know
well how a little judiciously publicised denunciation will
stimulate popular interest, and the Elizabethans were quite
up to this. In Sir Roger Wilbraham's journal we hear of a
printer who could not sell one of his publications, but
'caused a preacher in his sermon to inveigh against the

vanity thereof; since which it hath been six times under press, so much was it in request'. Greene is hardly likely to have intended assistance of this sort, but a reputation for 'daring God out of heaven' is not one that the London public was likely to ignore.

So with *Doctor Faustus*. A short but vivid glimpse of the early audiences at that play is afforded by a sentence in Thomas Middleton's *Black Book* (1604). Here the story-teller, 'the light-burning sergeant Lucifer', goes at midnight to Pict-hatch, the celebrated 'vaulting-house'. The bawd's husband comes 'puffing out of the next room'. 'His eyebrows jetted out like the round casement of an alderman's dining-room, which made his eyes look as if they had been both damned in his head; for if so be two souls had been so far sunk into hell-pits, they would never have walked abroad again.' And 'he had a head of hair like one of my devils in Doctor Faustus when the old theatre cracked and frighted the audience'. Middleton was writing one of those devil-comedies which, with the *Faustbook* behind them, had become popular. He was casting an amused yet impressed eye back to those less sophisticated days when the Theatre was the theatre and the devil a fearful but fascinating thing to find there. The tradition is mediæval, and often in the mediæval plays (as often in *Doctor Faustus*) the devils provide the fun. They enlivened the Moralities with fireworks (Belial in *The Castle of Perseverance* had 'pypis in his handis and in his eris and in his ers', all containing gunpowder); and the chief devil fairly clearly has the star-part ('I com, with my leggis under me' says Titivillus on his arrival in *Mankind*, and if ever a stage-entry called for a round of applause this does). In the Miracle plays, the devil had his temporal representatives, and for perhaps two centuries ears rang to the sound of 'Pilats vois' and that of the Herod who could hardly be out-Heroded and who raged in the streets of Coventry. But this is no straightforward comedy or entertainment: 'Here the Evil One and the bully Tyrant belong together to the comedy of the terrifying-grotesque, and hilarity touches hysteria. In ages of faith it is all very well to *know* that the horned and black-faced monster is only Black Will showing his "lightnesse and maistrye"; but there is no being absolutely *certain* that he has not become possessed.'[1] This is exactly what *did* in fact seem certain to the audience at a performance of *Doctor Faustus* in Exeter. The account conveys the uncanny feeling of the moment so that even we, who have sent bugbears and hobgoblins to the right-about, can share something of the supernatural shiver:

As a certain number of Devels kept everie one his circle there, and as Faustus was busie in his magicall invocations, on a sudden they were all dasht, every one harkning other in the eare, for they were all perswaded there was one devell too many amongst them; and so after a little pause desired the people to pardon them, they could go no further with this matter; the people also understanding the thing as it was, every man hastened to be first out of doores. The players (as I heard it) contrarye to their custome spending the night in reading and in prayer got them out of the town the next morning.

Many plays have no doubt alarmed and 'frighted' their audiences, few their actors.

Faustus, *Tamburlaine* and *The Jew of Malta* were all exceptionally popular. Their appeal was felt in more wholesome ways and at more subtle levels than are represented here; but the plays are now a complex hunting-ground for scholars and we forget that they were once, amongst other things, sensational stage-shows for ordinary people. Like the others, *The Jew of Malta* had the great actor Edward Alleyn in a role which gave him plenty of scope, and again the play involves the attraction of the repulsive ('We needs

[1] A. P. Rossiter, *Drama from Early Times to the Elizabethans* (London, 1950), p. 64.

must love the lowest when we see it,' says Aldous Huxley). The grotesque and murderous Jew and the faceless Christians around him inhabit a sordid world. But at least it is an exciting one, and the play ran for a record number of performances, often bringing in fifty shillings a time.[1] Equally sordid and a good deal more depressing (because more realistic for one thing) is the world of *Edward II*, but we do not hear of this play's enjoying a similar popularity. Marlowe's short career remains one of the most spectacular the theatre has known; and play-writing was certainly not his whole life during these years.

He spent a certain amount of time violating the Queen's Peace. In 1592 he was bound over by Sir Owen Hopton, having been reported by two constables of Shoreditch. Three years earlier he had been arrested and imprisoned for his part in a case of homicide. This was the Bradley affair, and most of our knowledge here is due to the researches of Mr Mark Eccles.[2] The document which he discovered describes a fight between 'Christoferus Morley' and 'Willelmus Bradley'. The latter was an innkeeper's son who in the summer of that year had applied for legal protection against three men, one of whom was the poet Thomas Watson. This same Watson appeared in Hog Lane as Marlowe and Bradley were fighting, and at the sight of him Bradley, with a fine sense of the dramatic, cried 'Arte thowe nowe come then I will haue a boute wth thee'. So he did, but with tragic consequences, for Watson killed him. This, the jury found, was in self-defence, but the verdict did not prevent Watson from going to Newgate for five months. Marlowe went also and within a fortnight had found two men to stand as sureties for him (one of

---

[1] *The Massacre at Paris* may have done better still: at one performance the takings were £3. 14*s*.

[2] M. Eccles, *Marlowe in London* (Cambridge, Mass., 1934).

them was a lawyer called Kitchin who seems to have had professional relations with Henslowe and the Mermaid, and who was accused of a similarly violent assault in 1594).

A picture of the man begins to emerge with the strange, patchy vividness of a crackly phonograph cylinder through which we can *just* hear some great singer: the impression is so very vivid that we tend to forget that what we have is only a small part of the truth. Thus some hint of Marlowe's wilder moments comes down to us and we may think that we can talk of his temperament and personality on the basis of it. John Bakeless is one amongst the many biographers of Marlowe who confidently do so. The man Kitchin, for instance, is said to have been 'of a temperament akin to Marlowe's'.[1] But the assumptions (however unimportant) seem almost absurdly rash: attacks, fights and troubles with the law were by no means uncommon, and the diversity of people concerned in such matters is usually more striking than the similarity. The biographer seems to be on such confident, intimate terms that one wonders if he would recognise this 'most reckless spirit in all that turbulent age' if he could have met Marlowe in the street. The most savage critics are often the mildest of men in normal day-to-day encounters—everyone knows this un-expectedness and contradictoriness of human beings. Yet again we are told that even at Cambridge 'the fiery spirit of the youthful Marlowe was already in fierce rebellion against every restriction of any kind whatsoever'.[2] Marlowe probably did read Machiavelli and certainly did not take holy orders; and he did make Faustus say that he would like to provide fine clothes for the university scholars whom the statutes dressed with austerity. But this is not necessarily evidence of 'fierce' rebellion, and it is

---

[1] J. Bakeless, *Christopher Marlowe* (London, 1938), p. 161.
[2] *Op. cit.*, p. 52.

not against 'every restriction' (even 'of any kind whatsoever'). The claim to a personal familiarity with 'Kit Marlowe' is in fact frequently excessive. Biographical material provides one or two glimpses of a few hours in a few days. The glimpses may be as clear as crystal, and generalising from them as futile as crystal-gazing.

Another of the glimpses we have of Marlowe's life during these years in London concerns his relations with Sir Walter Raleigh and the 'School of Night'. Again one is tempted by picturesque notions based on Elizabethan rumour and modern conjecture. There is evidence, certainly, of an association between some men of independent mind and distinguished reputation, Raleigh being chief amongst them. But the idea of a 'school' may be misleading. The term derives from two texts, both of questionable value. The first is in an English summary of the Jesuit Robert Parsons's *Responsio ad Edictum Elizabethae*: 'Of Sir Walter Rawleys school of Atheisme by the waye, & of the Conjurer that is M[aster] thereof, and of the diligence vsed to get yong gentlemen of this schoole, where in both Moyses, & our Sauio^r, the olde, and the new Testamente are iested at, and the schollers taughte, amonge other thinges, to spell God backwarde.' Parsons was answering an attack on him made by the queen herself, and he did so by fiercely attacking her chief councillors. He was an ingenious, indefatigable and bold man, but hardly a disinterested witness. The other text is the famous one from *Love's Labour's Lost* (IV. 3):

> *King.* By heauen! thy Loue is blacke as Ebonie.
> *Berowne.* Is Ebonie like her? O wood devine!
> A wife of such wood were felicitie.
> O, who can give an oth? where is a booke?
> That I may sweare, Beautie doth beautie lacke,
> If that she learne not, of her eye to looke:
> No face is fayre, that is not full so blacke.

King. O paradox! Blacke is the badge of Hell,
The hue of dungions and the Schoole of night;
And beauties crest becomes the heauens well.

The King's lines are usually quoted out of context, and in isolation it is easier to believe that they carry a reference to Raleigh's 'school of atheism' (the play being seen partly as a satire on the 'school', and Armado, the fantastical Spaniard, being Raleigh himself). The 'school of night' is said to be 'Shakespeare's nickname'[1] and so indeed it may be, but taking the lines in context I am not at all convinced. There is no pointing towards this meaning, which would be an irrelevance in the lines, and the general sense is clear without invoking this interpretation. The joke, if it is one, is oddly and ineffectively placed; and if it is in fact a reference to the 'atheism' of Raleigh's circle, one might expect to find the atheism figuring elsewhere in the satire, which it does not.[2]

The 'school', however, seems to have become history. In Trevor-Roper's *Historical Essays*, Raleigh is 'the patron . . . of the disquieting "School of Night" . . . [and] of the atheist Marlowe' (p. 104). In Philip Magnus's book on Raleigh we learn that 'the popular name for that circle was "The School of Night"' and that one of its members was 'Thomas [*sic*] Marlowe, the playwright'.[3] Sometimes it is even described as Raleigh's 'club'; and we have a picture of Raleigh puffing away judicially at his pipe, the 'greate blasphemer' Thomas Allen tearing up the Bible to dry his tobacco, while Harriot the scientist denied the resurrection of the body (Marlowe agreeing with him, Chapman feeling rather out of it), the Wizard Earl Northumberland brooding moodily on his alchemy, until Matthew

---

[1] See the revised Arden edition (editor Richard David) for full documentation here.
[2] On Raleigh and the school see Peter Ure, *The Pelican Guide to English Literature*, vol. II, p. 145.
[3] P. Magnus, *Sir Walter Raleigh* (London, 1956), p. 61.

Roydon with some 'comicke invention' made everybody laugh, whereupon they set about arranging the next meeting. Perhaps indeed it was a little like that; or, more seriously, perhaps there was an esoteric but coherent body of doctrine. But the evidence for such organisation of meetings and thought is not very strong.

Evidence for contacts and unorthodoxies, however, is. Kyd, for instance, speaks of Marlowe's associations with Harriot, William Warner (the author of *Albion's England*), and Roydon. The earl of Northumberland became a patron of Harriot, who is associated with Raleigh by both Parsons and Baines. Marlowe, says the Baines note, claimed that 'one Heriots being Sir W. Raleighs man' could do more than Moses, who was 'but a Iugler'. The Baines note had also mentioned a Richard Chomley who admitted to having become an atheist at Marlowe's persuasion. This same Chomley was arrested shortly after Marlowe's death, with accusations of treason and atheism against him. A document called *Remembraunces of wordes and matter against Richard Cholmeley* includes the following article: 'Hee saieth & verily beleueth that one Marlowe is able to shewe more sounde reasons for Atheisme then any devine in Englande is able to geue to prove devinitie & that Marloe tolde him that hee hath read the Atheist lecture to Sᴿ Walter Raliegh & others.'

This statement probably gives the clearest picture we have of a 'school' and also one of the most vivid glimpses of Marlowe as a man. But again the testimony comes from that underworld of plots and counter-plots, where there is every temptation and inducement to involve others—particularly when Rumour lies at hand, as Raleigh says, 'without Witness, without Judge, malicious and deceivable'. Perhaps inevitably, the evidence for the atheism of Raleigh and his group usually sounds from the pipe of Rumour, 'blown by surmises, jealousies, conjectures'. Surmise as to the application of Baines's remark (Marlowe's association with 'some great men who in convenient time shalbe named') piped in Raleigh's direction. And plenty of jealousy engendered in his days of greatness was about in the early nineties to keep him in disfavour. In March 1594, a Commission of Inquiry began to investigate these rumours at Cerne Abbas near Sherborne Abbey, Raleigh's country seat. The charges of atheism could not be upheld, but amongst all the false trails and mere silliness there does occur evidence that Raleigh would probe and question in places where mere acquiescence was the comfortable and conventional thing. At supper, we learn on good authority, he began to question a clergyman, Ralph Ironside, about the nature of the soul. No one had been able to make him understand what it was, he said, and 'neither coulde I learn heitherto what god is'. But how serious Raleigh was in this discussion, or how disingenuous and teasing, we cannot know. His published works are those of a devout and God-fearing man. Also those of a man well acquainted with sceptical thought:

Man . . . that hath so short a time in the World, as he no sooner begins to learn, than to dye; that hath in his memory but borrowed knowledge; in his understanding nothing truly; that is ignorant of the Essence of his own Soul, and which the wisest (If Aristotle be he) could never so much as define, but by the Action and Effect telling us what it works (which all men know as well as he) but not what it is, which neither he, not any else doth know but GOD that created it (For though I were perfect, yet I know not my soul, saith Job). Man, I say, that is but an Idiot in the next cause of his own life, and in the cause of all actions of his life: will (notwithstanding) examine the Art of GOD in creating the World. . . . He will disable Gods power to make a World, without matter to make it of. He will rather give the Motes of the Air for a cause; cast the work on necessity or chance; bestow the honour thereof on Nature; make two powers, the one to be the Author of the Matter, the other of Form; and lastly, for want of a workman, have it Eternal.[1]

Here Raleigh speaks with the sober conviction of his three-score years; but his mind may well have gone back to a period, twenty years earlier, when he himself was testing belief with more respect for the sceptical faculty than he shows here.

If Marlowe did indeed 'read his atheist lecture' to Raleigh, what form did it take? There are other references, besides Chomley's, to the existence of anti-religious writings by Marlowe. Thomas Beard, whose *Theatre of God's Judgment* (1597) contains an account of his death quoted already, says that Marlowe 'not only in word blasphemed the Trinitie, but also (as it is credibly reported) wrote bookes against it, affirming our Saviour to be but a deceiver, and Moses to be but a conjurer and seducer of the people, and the holy Bible to be but vaine and idle stories, and all religion but a device of pollicie'. Vaughan's *Golden Grove* has a similar reference. More interesting are the remarks of Simon Aldrich, a Kentishman and a Cambridge scholar, who told Henry Oxinden 'that Marlowe was an Atheist and wrote a book against the Scriptures, how that it was all one man's making; and would have printed it, but it could not be suffered to be printed'. He also speaks of a Mr Fineaux of Dover (another scholar of Corpus Christi), who 'learnd all Marlo by heart & divers other bookes'.

P. H. Kocher[2] believes that this 'atheist lecture' and the 'Marlo' which Thomas Fineaux learned by heart were probably the same thing, and that through the Baines note we can reconstruct them. 'Baines seems to be taking notes either direct from a manuscript written by Marlowe or from

---

[1] Raleigh, Preface, *History of the World*.   [2] *Christopher Marlowe: A Study of his Thought, Learning and Character* (N. Carolina, 1946), Ch. III.

some lecture which he delivered.' Kocher claims, and I
think demonstrates, 'an essential unity of design', showing
how the accusations in the note can be grouped so as to
summarise a broad and coherent attack on religion. He is
able, by reference to other writers who had made similar
points, to suggest how the various items may have been
developed. Summarising his case, he writes of Marlowe:

He became one of the spokesmen of a tendency. For free thought
was stirring in England in a vague, unorganised way during the
last fifty years of the century. Underneath the intonations of the
orthodox writers, one can hear it rising, this mutter of revolutionary dissidence. But in Marlowe we can see the quintessence
of it drawn together and revealed . . . For revolutionary impact
and scope it [the Baines note] stands alone, an extraordinary
document in the history of English free thought.

The very fact that these ideas were in the air means that
they lay at hand for Baines to attribute to the man he was
accusing. But in its fullness, and taken with the rest that
comes down to us about Marlowe's life, the note looks
more like truth than fiction; and if true, it is important.

I think Kocher overstates, however, when he calls it the
'master key to the mind of Marlowe'. He can say so because
he also believes that 'criticism of Christianity appears in all
the biographical documents as the most absorbing interest
of his life. And likewise in his plays it is the most anxiously,
skilfully and passionately reiterated theme of dramatization.'
The first statement seems unacceptable because 'all the
biographical documents' are still not sufficient for us to
pronounce on the 'absorbing interests of his life', and in
any case many of them (the Council's note to the college
authorities, the account of the Bradley affair, and the
coroner's inquest on Marlowe's death, for instance) have
nothing directly to do with religion. The claim that such
criticism is the most purposeful common concern of the

plays seems to me also untrue: I think that man's nature, its potentialities and limitations, has that place.

But Kocher's, virtually alone amongst the theories about Marlowe's life, is a soundly based and valuable idea. There remains, of course, plenty of opportunity for theories which cannot be so described. Many questions still tempt imaginative replies. Was he a government agent? Thomas Walsingham was his friend and patron, and Francis Walsingham was chief of the security service. If so, was he murdered so that government secrets should not come to light in any public trial? The other men at Deptford had suspicious records and had associations with the Walsinghams too. Was he, perhaps, murdered at the instigation of the Raleigh set or of certain other 'great men' who feared being dragged into the scandal of an inquiry into atheism? Was he indeed not killed at all, as Calvin Hoffman urges, but spirited across to Europe to write Shakespeare's plays and die a good old man? Did he possibly survive the trouble at Deptford only to be killed five years later by Ben Jonson?[1] Or was the hand that struck the fatal blow really—Will Shakespeare's?[2]

In such matters, sense and speculation are readily borne aloft by fantasy and folly. But at least it can be said that so much imaginative interest and scholarly endeavour testify to some strange thing about this short life that began four hundred years ago and this small body of works all of them written in less than a decade. In his essay on Dickens, George Orwell says: 'When one reads any strongly individual piece of writing, one has the impression of seeing a face somewhere behind the page.' The interest in Marlowe's biography is really a search for a face, and the intensity of the search bears witness to the individuality of the

---

[1] W. G. Zeigler, *It Was Marlowe* (1895).
[2] Clemence Dane, *Will Shakespeare* (1922).

writing. What kind of face emerges from the biography? Perhaps that of a bold, even heroic man, as Kocher sees him ('Into every Company he cometh he perswades men to Atheism willing them not to be afeard of bugbeares and hobgoblins'). The Baines note unwittingly speaks for his courage and in a sense his encouragement of others: 'the heir', says Kocher, 'of all the ages of protest against Christianity and a voice for the inarticulate and nameless of his own day'. Or perhaps it is the face of a violent man with an unusual capacity for arousing dislike: 'his other rashness in attempting sudden privy injuries to men' is not (if true) a particularly amiable characteristic. Kyd also refers to 'my lord', probably Lord Strange, who never could 'endure his name or sight'. Greene hated him so much that his publisher, Henry Chettle, had to censor some references in the manuscript of his *Groatsworth of Wit*; yet plenty of venom remains in the accusations of atheism and 'pestilent Machiauilian pollicie', and Chettle himself hints fairly plainly that he had little time for Marlowe as a man. Possibly the face that inspired so much dislike was also one which drew admiration and affection, for there were some to speak well of him after his death. Notably Drayton, whose lines in *Of Poets and Poesy* make perhaps the best epitaph a poet has had (though it would be interesting to know whether his enthusiasm was personal as well as literary):

> Neat *Marlow* bathed in the *Thespian* springs
> Had in him those braue translunary things,
> That the first Poets had, his raptures were,
> All ayre, and fire, which made his verses cleere,
> For that fine madnes still he did retaine,
> Which rightly should possesse a Poets braine.

All of these faces look out in turn from behind his writings: the bold and independent; the mean and sadistic;

and the face lit with a rare light of inspiration and strength. But what also emerges from the works is something one does not see in the biography: a restless, conflicting, unstable spirit; and this probably generated the intensity which is most valuably and characteristically Marlovian. It also probably contributed more than anything else to the tragedy of his life and the limitations of his writing.

Part II

THE PLAYS

2

'THE TRAGEDIE OF DIDO'

WRITING in 1919, T. S. Eliot said that he thought *Dido* an underrated play. A hint by the Eliot of those days is likely to have had more influence than a whole book by most critics, but here is an exception, for *Dido* seems to be valued little more now than it was then. John Bakeless says that it is 'in itself of no more interest to modern readers than *The Massacre at Paris*, and Elizabethan readers seem to have felt much the same about it'.[1] Since that sentence was written, interest in *The Massacre at Paris* has grown along with interest in the Elizabethan-Machiavellian, but *Dido* has remained largely where it was, read infrequently and little esteemed.

This is a pity, for Marlowe put much of the best of himself into it. It has weaknesses enough to prevent a successful stage revival, and there are limitations in the enthusiasms and sympathies, the qualities of mind. But the energy and fire shine out brilliantly, in a more admirable way than in *Tamburlaine* and without the destructive bitterness of the other works. 'Energy is eternal delight': some element in Marlowe's energy evidently perverted the working of Blake's equation in himself (*Edward II* does not testify to eternal delight). But energy remains the quality that most often impresses, and in *Dido* it is found in its best form: a vigorous delight, a rare expression of enthusiasm and relish for the realms of gold, pride in man's stature, respect for his sorrows and loyalties, and a glorying in romantic love which is certainly immature compared with *Antony*

[1] *Op. cit.*, p. 255.

29

and Cleopatra, yet fine enough to make that comparison the natural and only one. There is good reason, in fact, to believe that Shakespeare, probably with other Elizabethan readers, had some time for the play after all.

Points of association between the stories of *Antony and Cleopatra* and *Dido* have occurred to readers before now. They have obvious similarities: Aeneas torn between Italy and Carthage, Dido left alone; famous lovers of heroic stature and a whole world involved in their love. But these would hardly be worth mentioning if it were not for more fundamental connections. As in Shakespeare's play there is a sense of the immensity of creation and of human beings proportionate to it, so in Marlowe's, poetry makes the universe the lovers' stage, and the lovers actors great enough to fill it. In both plays the cosmic note is struck early:

> *Cleo.* I'll set a bourn how far to be belov'd.
> *Ant.* Then must thou needs find out new heaven, new earth.
> (*Antony and Cleopatra*, I. 1)

And Jupiter to Ganimede:

> Why are not all the Gods at thy commaund
> And heauen and earth the bounds of thy delight? (30–31)

Before this, Ganimede has lodged a complaint against Juno, and Jupiter promises that another time she shall hear from him about it:

> I vow, if she but once frowne on thee more,
> To hang her meteor like twixt heauen and earth,
> And bind her hand and foote with golden cordes. (12–14)

In the violence of its poetic leap and its pleasure in humiliation the passage is thoroughly Marlovian and not at all Shakespearean. But though Shakespeare paints his own backcloth, he uses the same vast canvas.

'I am fire and air' says Cleopatra, and Drayton's words about Marlowe come to mind:

> His raptures were
> All ayre and fire.

This is true of *Dido* above all the other plays. Venus tells how Juno

> Made *Hebe* to direct her ayrie wheeles
> Into the windie countrie of the clowdes. (56–7)

She speaks of 'the starres surprisde', and the waves which 'threat our Chrystall world'. The imagery works together as a unity, making for an excitement and enthusiasm which is more than the excitement of the 'high astounding term' in itself and for its own sake. It is the setting made for man: the magnificence which the world offers to the human being great enough to take it. Aeneas is such a man. Achates' first speech establishes him as 'propertied' in this godlike manner:

> Doe thou but smile, and clowdie heauen will cleare,
> Whose night and day descendeth from thy browes. (155–6)

Ascanius, his son, is similarly invested with majesty, but by Jupiter himself:

> . . . bright *Ascanius*, beauties better worke,
> Who with the Sunne deuides one radiant shape,
> Shall build his throne amidst those starrie towers,
> That earth-borne *Atlas* groning vnderprops:
> No bounds but heauen shall bound his Emperie,
> Whose azured gates enchased with his name,
> Shall make the morning hast her gray vprise,
> To feede her eyes with his engrauen fame. (96–103)

Jove's eloquence does not on this occasion carry away his audience, the sceptical and sharp-tongued Venus: one of the play's strengths is that it is not intoxicated by its eloquence (as I think is true of *Tamburlaine*) but maintains an awareness of the mundane and the humorous. Nevertheless it is a fine eloquence: there is a splendid pride in man, and a glamour preserved from vulgarity by the poise and dignity of the hyperbole.

The vast canvas darkens in Iarbas' description of the oncoming storm. He sees it as an enchantress who has power to

> ... diue into blacke tempests treasurie,
> When as she meanes to maske the world with clowdes.
>
> (1064–5)

Later, in his prayer, Iarbas appeals to a god evoked as lord of a vast creation:

> Eternall *Ioue*, great master of the Clowdes,
> Father of gladnesse, and all frollicke thoughts,
> That with thy gloomie hand corrects the heauen,
> When ayrie creatures warre amongst themselves.
>
> (1098–1101)

Dido too evokes this ominous upper-world, but only to dismiss it:

> Not bloudie speares appearing in the ayre,
> Presage the downfall of my Emperie,
> Nor blazing Commets threatens *Didos* death.   (1323–5)

It is in lovers' infiniteness and her 'man of men' that the universe has its validity and splendour:

> If he forsake me not, I neuer dye,
> For in his lookes I see eternitie,
> And heele make me immortall with a kisse.   (1327–9)

Aeneas is deified in Dido's wonder: 'Now lookes *Æneas* like immortall *Ioue*.' Strongly present is the feeling that her lover, like Cleopatra's, is 'past the size of dreaming'. And with it goes the sense that 'the nobleness of life is to do thus':

> Heauen enuious of our ioyes is waxen pale,
> And when we whisper, then the starres fall downe,
> To be partakers of our honey talke.   (1258–60)

A play with lines like these does not need to ask the indulgence of its readers, modern or Elizabethan. But however recognisably fine such passages are in quotation, the fact that makes a Shakespearean comparison not impertinent is that they work together as Shakespearean dramatic poetry does to make a unified work of art. The imagery is not an embroidery or an ornament, but the substance of the creation, the dramatist's essential means of expression; and even in Elizabethan drama this Shakespearean working is not common.

These examples of the love poetry might represent the play as justifying in its emotional force the saying of the old Nurse: 'If there be any heauen in earth, tis loue.' Love, moreover, is shown as the delight of the gods, and heaven within heaven itself. Jupiter woos Ganimede with Ovidian fervour, quoting the thirteenth poem of the first book of *Amores*, the lines spoken in anguish by Faustus. In Marlowe's complete translation they are over-compressed by the demands of the couplet:

> But heldst thou in thine armes some *Cephalus*
> Then wouldst thou cry, stay night and runne not thus.
>
> (I. 13. 39–40)

But here Jupiter's reference is closer to *currite noctis equi* and the whole passage is alight with Marlovian air and fire:

> Whose face reflects such pleasure to mine eyes,
> As I exhal'd with thy fire darting beames,
> Haue oft driuen backe the horses of the night,
> When as they would haue hal'd thee from my sight. (24–7)

Jove has the power to do what all lovers have wanted to do. But for the rest he woos like Marlowe's Passionate Shepherd ('. . . if thou wilt be my loue'). Ganimede flirts prettily: a jewel for his ear and a fine brooch for his hat will satisfy him—

> And then Ile hugge with you an hundred times. (48)

Jupiter's love-making sets the erotic mood of the play, and prepares for the more normal love-making of Dido and Aeneas (though here too is a kind of perversion, for as Ganimede is wooed by Jove so is Aeneas by Dido—the initiative and driving passion are hers). Marlowe also plays a short scherzo-like variation on the theme of love in the scene between the Nurse and Cupid (IV. 5). The Nurse believes that Cupid is Ascanius and has been told to take him away from the court to her house. She entices him with promises of all kinds of delights and Cupid asks to be carried. His spell begins to work on the old woman as it worked on Dido, and it makes a strange comedy, faintly pathetic and cruel but both amusing and moving in its grotesque way. Cupid attracts partly by the easy-going nonchalance which he has in common with Ganimede:

> *Cupid.* Nurse I am wearie, will you carrie me?
> *Nurse.* I, so youle dwell with me and call me mother.
> *Cupid.* So youle loue me, I care not if I doe. (1386–8)

Lewdness begins to mutiny in the matron's bones, and the suppleness of inflection makes good opportunities for the actor:

> That I might liue to see this boy a man!
> How pretilie he laughs, goe ye wagge,
> Youle be a twigger when you come to age.
> Say *Dido* what she will I am not old . . . (1389–92)

'Twigger' is a picturesque term: a vigorous, prolific breeder (as of a ewe), or in slang 'an unchaste or lascivious person'. The nurse determines to get a husband 'or els a louer', but Cupid has the mercilessness of his youth and exclaims 'A husband and no teeth!' This brings her to earth, and there follows a speech in which she moves to and fro in a way not unlike the indecision of 'Now Faustus must thou needes be damnd'. The speech contains the panegyric quoted above:

> . . . O sacred loue,
> If there be any heaven in earth, tis loue.   (1397–8)

And there is a sad awareness of time and of what it brings us to:

> A graue, and not a louer fits thy age:
> . . . My vaines are withered, and my sinewes drie,
> Why doe I thinke of loue now I should dye?   (1401–5)

Cupid could answer that question but he merely says 'Come Nurse', and with a cruder comic turn the scene ends. It is an interesting piece: very Marlovian in its exposure of discomfited woman, its rather hard comedy, and its dramatising of a hither-and-thithering indecision, apparently the working of 'will' but drily observed by the fate which has determined it, the whole grotesquely parodying the similar disturbance in Dido herself.

Cupid, on his mother's instructions, has touched and conquered Dido as he did the Nurse. He wheedles, sings and flirts, while Iarbas looks on with impotent irritation. The spell begins to work, pulling Dido from her superior position of majestic security and aloofness, so that at one moment the erotic disturbance impels her towards Iarbas and at the next her former indifference to him turns to positive dislike. The transition is well represented:

> . . . his lothsome sight offends mine eye,
> And in my thoughts is shrin'd another loue:
> O *Anna*, didst thou know how sweet loue were,
> Full soone wouldst thou abiure this single life.   (691–4)

She hymns Aeneas' beauty in a lyrical passage which is more

genuine in its eroticism and less conventional than it at first looks:

> Ile make me bracelets of his golden haire,
> His glistering eyes shall be my looking glasse,
> His lips an altar, where Ile offer vp
> As many kisses as the sea hath sands. . . .   (719–22)

Dido is imagining their embrace, his hair round her wrists as she runs her hand through it, and their looking into each other's eyes as they kiss. She recognises the unmaidenliness of her imaginings, and is afraid of a power beyond her control:

> O here he comes, loue, loue, give *Dido* leaue
> To be more modest then her thoughts admit,
> Lest I be made a wonder to the world.   (728–30)

Disguising her passion, she woos Aeneas in images where the suppressed eroticism finds expression:

> Ile giue thee tackling made of riueld gold,
> Wound on the barkes of odoriferous trees,
> Oares of massie Iuorie full of holes,
> Through which the water shall delight to play. (750–3)

The erotic is subtly present as in Enobarbus' description of Cleopatra in her barge:

> The Windes were Loue-sicke with them, the Owers were Siluer,
> Which to the tune of Flutes kept stroke, and made
> The water which they beate, to follow faster;
> As amorous of their strokes.   (II. 2.)

Dido's own longings are transferred to the 'wanton Mermaides' who shall court Aeneas with sweet songs,

> Flinging in fauours of more soueraigne worth,
> Then *Thetis* hangs about *Appolloes* necke.   (765–6)

When, in the storm, Aeneas at last realises the truth about Dido's love, her happiness is vigorously and movingly expressed; but her real triumph—and the apotheosis of love in the play—occurs when Aeneas' first attempt to leave her is thwarted:

Æn. O *Dido*, patronesse of all our liues,
      When I leaue thee, death be my punishment.
      Swell raging seas, frowne wayward destinies,
      Blow windes, threaten ye Rockes and sandie shelfes,
      This is the harbour that *Æneas* seekes,
      Lets see what tempests can annoy me now.
Dido. Not all the world can take thee from mine armes. (1261–7)

This is the peak of Dido's fortune, for love is her whole world. But it is not the whole world to Aeneas, nor is it the play's only concern.

The male world is very unlike Dido's. The lines quoted above come from the only passage where Aeneas responds as passionately as Dido woos. For the rest he merely accepts, gratefully enough, what is offered him. Dido is always aware of that part of his desires which lies beyond her: it is represented in her mind by 'a forraine land calde Italy'. To her (as to Marlowe's Edward II) the kingdom matters nothing beside her love:

      . . . let rich Carthage fleete vpon the seas,
      So I may haue *Æneas* in mine armes.   (1340–1)

But although her 'ticements' make him forget Italy for a time, Aeneas still has a life outside her arms. At the beginning of Act V he is planning to build 'a statelier Troy': his ambitions find an outlet here, as very quickly they are directed by Hermes to 'raise a new foundation to old Troy' in that foreign land which Dido so dreads. In three perfunctory lines he protests his sorrow:

      Witness the Gods, and witnes heauen and earth,
      How loth I am to leaue these *Libian* bounds,
      But that eternall *Iupiter* commands. (1488–90)

But the tragedy of these lovers who do not 'love so alike that . . . none can die' is felt in Dido's lines:

> Why look'st thou toward the sea? the time hath been
> When *Didos* beautie chaind thine eyes to her. (1521-2)

To chain the eyes is not enough: Aeneas is never shown to feel about Dido with the intensity of his passionate love for Troy. Even his emotional life has not been fully involved. For the woman the emotional life is everything, while the man looks towards the sea, to a world beyond.

Dido, then, like *Antony and Cleopatra*, is a play of two worlds, inimical to each other. The luxuries and enchantments of Carthage are 'ticements' (for this is, as Mr Levin notes, the recurrent word[1]), and 'Nobilitie abhors to stay'. Achates echoes this:

> This is no life for men at armes to liue,
> Where daliance doth consume a Souldiers strength.
> (1183-4)

He advises Aeneas to 'banish that ticing dame' from his thoughts but Aeneas knows the strength of Dido's hold over him and expresses it in superb erotic hyperbole:

> Come backe, come backe, I heare her crye a farre,
> And let me linke thy bodie to my lips,
> That tyed together by the striuing tongues,
> We may as one saile into *Italy*. (1177-80)

Here is the tension of the drama, and one is aware of it throughout in small things as well as great. When, for instance, Ascanius is found, he has been

> Eating sweet Comfites with Queene *Didos* maide,
> Who euer since hath luld me in her armes. (1455-6)

In a sense it is what they have all been doing: as Achates says,

> . . . wanton motions of alluring eyes
> Effeminate our mindes inur'd to warr. (1185-6)

Ascanius has been enticed by Venus with spangled feathers,

[1] Harry Levin: *The Overreacher* (1954), p. 34.

sugar-almonds, a silver girdle and golden shafts. He sleeps amidst

> sweete smelling Violets,
> Blushing Roses, purple *Hyacinthe*   (613–4)

it is lotos-land where men are spellbound as children and all are enticed into forgetfulness.

But Aeneas comes from the world beyond and goes back to it. Very unlike this downy paradise is the strife and harshness of reality as represented by his narrative of the fall of Troy. There is indeed a connection between the two worlds: Dido, 'that ticing dame', curses Helen, 'that ticing strumpet'. But the foreignness of the narrative to the world of Dido's court and to the language of the love scenes is defined significantly by her other reaction:

> Trojan, thy ruthfull tale hath made me sad:
> Come let vs thinke vpon some pleasing sport,
> To rid me from these melancholly thoughts.   (596–8)

Dido and her court are escapist enticements. They have their charms, and in the delights of love their validity and magnificence. But between them and the other world there is a tension which the play makes felt, not simply in the story it tells, but with a wealth of dramatic and poetic interlinking, which like the unity of imagery is essentially Shakespearean.

Much, then, is exuberance and delight which would justify the things often said (unjustifiably) about *Hero and Leander*: Marlowe is in 'a holiday mood', 'in a world of imagined deliciousness where all beauty is sensuous and all sensuality is beautiful'.[1] But though there is 'anger, shame and rage' in this as in *Hero and Leander*, it is not so much in the final tragedy that one is made aware of the darker side

---

[1] C. S. Lewis: *English Literature in the Sixteenth Century, Excluding Drama* (Oxford History of English Literature, vol. III), 1954, p. 486.

of life, nor in Iarbas' frustrations, as in Aeneas' tale of
Troy. Here is a nightmare of violence and humiliation, an
extreme realism penetrating or perhaps intensified by what
Eliot called a characteristic of 'hesitating on the edge of
caricature'. Aeneas lists the horrors he saw in a series of
quick sketches, savage and vivid as Goya's etchings of the
Peninsular War:

> Yong infants swimming in their parents bloud,
> Headles carkasses piled vp in heapes,
> Virgins halfe dead dragged by their golden haire,
> And with maine force flung on a ring of pikes,
> Old men with swords thrust through their aged sides,
> Kneeling for mercie to a Greekish lad,
> Who with steele Pol-axes dasht out their braines. (488–94)

Brutal and pathetic is the description of Hector as he
appeared to Aeneas (in Virgil this is a dream, but in
Marlowe's nightmare world it is reality):

> His armes torne from his shoulders, and his breast
> Furrowd with wounds, and that which made me weepe,
> Thongs at his heeles, by which *Achilles* horse
> Drew him in triumph through the Greekish Campe.
>
> (498–501)

Another Goyesque sketch is that of Pyrrhus'

> ... band of Mirmidons
> With balles of wilde fire in their murdering pawes. (512)

The assonance of 'Mirmidons ... murdering' and the
animal ferocity ('pawes') of the herd intensify the lines, and
reflect their savagery upon the blood-drunk Pyrrhus. But
the climax of the narrative is in the account of Priam's
murder. Priam and Hecuba, he 'foulding his hand in hers',
falling on the ground before the altar, are depicted with a
poignant tenderness violated by Pyrrhus' careless brutality:

> He with his faulchions poynt raisde vp at once,
> And with *Megeras* eyes stared in their face. (524–5)

Virgil's Priam challenges Pyrrhus and taunts him with degeneracy, contrasting him with his father Achilles, but Marlowe's laments and pleads for life:

> *Achilles* sonne, remember what I was,
> Father of fiftie sonnes, but they are slaine,
> Lord of my fortune, but my fortunes turnd,
> King of this Citie, but my *Troy* is fired,
> And now am neither father, Lord, nor King:
> Yet who so wretched but desires to liue?
> O let me liue, great *Neoptolemus*.   (528–34)

'Stylised rhetoric' is a pejorative term but as factual description partly justified, for these lines have the ritual rocking to-and-fro of lament (as caught by Shakespeare in the mourning queens of *Richard III*). What follows is more savage, and again has no equivalent in Virgil (indeed the whole speech is the work of a man who has made his Virgil so thoroughly and imaginatively his own, that his version of the story is virtually independent of its source):

> *Æn.* Not mou'd at all, but smiling at his teares,
>   This butcher whil'st his hands were yet held vp,
>   Treading vpon his breast, strooke off his hands.
> *Dido.* O end *Æneas*, I can heare no more.
> *Æn.* At which the franticke Queene leapt on his face,
>   And in his eyelids hanging by the nayles,
>   A little while prolong'd her husbands life:
>   At last the souldiers puld her by the heeles,
>   And swong her howling in the emptie ayre,
>   Which sent an eccho to the wounded King:
>   Whereat he lifted vp his bedred lims,
>   And would haue grappeld with *Achilles* sonne,
>   Forgetting both his want of strength and hands,
>   Which he disdaining whiskt his sword about,
>   And with the wind thereof the King fell downe:
>   Then from the nauell to the throat at once,
>   He ript old *Priam*.   (535–51)

This is the essential Marlowe as much as are the air and fire of the Carthaginian raptures. The savage sketches of greatness humiliated and violated scream out amongst the romance and enchantments of Dido's court:

> We sawe *Cassandra* sprauling in the streetes,
> Whom *Aiax* rauisht in *Dianas* Fane,
> Her cheekes swolne with sighes, her haire all rent.
>
> (569–71)

The realism of the last line and the indignity of the first—'sprauling'—are in themselves an image of the violation. In Cassandra sanctity is defiled as is reverend age in the king and queen: Priam's hands struck off as he holds them in prayer, Hecuba pulled by the heels and swung howling by the soldiers, the famous pair carelessly and brutally raised up at the point of Pyrrhus' sword. This fierce picturing of indignity and humiliation is, for better or worse, one of Marlowe's most distinctive contributions. The nearest comparisons are probably with satirists: possibly the Jonson of *Volpone*, where the dignified lawyer grovels and foams in a simulated fit, and the proud merchant cuckolds himself and prostitutes his wife for 'the dumb god' riches; possibly in Swift or Aldous Huxley. But Marlowe 'on the edge of caricature' is here without humour and without moral purpose. Goya's 'Désastres' denounce war, and even Goya has been suspected of being fascinated by the brutality which he also detested. Marlowe's pictures arouse the emotions of pity and horror but do not direct them to anything beyond their immediate cause. What is shown evokes a strong response, but it is essentially an emotional response, enthusiastic, horrified, pitiful, erotic or sadistic, as the case may be. Intellect and moral sense must, of course, be involved in some degree; but in as far as such reactions can be purely emotional, these are.

The play does not, however, live perpetually on the heights of romantic love and epic heroism. It contains

some of the most human and humane of Marlowe's writing.
The two scenes in which Aeneas appears before his meeting
with Dido are moving at this less exalted level. Aeneas'
first speech, it is true, gives encouragement to his men in
eloquent but conventional rhetoric; it is also a paraphrase
of Virgil, closer than most of the verse. Achates' reply, however, is more interesting, beginning in the same lofty tone,
but developing movingly towards the humane and practical:

> Though we be now in extreame miserie,
> And rest the map of weatherbeaten woe:
> Yet shall the aged Sunne shed forth his haire,
> To make vs liue vnto our former heate,
> And euery beast the forrest doth send forth,
> Bequeath her young ones to our scanted foode.
>
> (157–62)

It is notoriously difficult to combine the heroic and the
prosaic, and this scene has given critics opportunity to
substantiate their complaints that Marlowe lacks a sense of
humour, while making it clear by their smiling that they
do not. The line

> Gentle *Achates*, reach the Tinder boxe   (166)

is commonly cited for tolerant derision. It is certainly funny
staring out of the page like that amongst mighty lines and
lofty phrases. But this is not quite fair. The work is a play,
written for the stage. It is natural to forget this because
so much of it has been static, but now there is movement
and the mood of the writing changes accordingly. Aeneas
and his followers have come to this strange land; Aeneas
gives his men encouragement and Achates replies with
sober faith for the future and begins to take stock of the
situation. He mentions their prime need, which is food,
and this makes the boy Ascanius speak of his hunger:

> Father I faint, good father giue me meate.   (163)

Aeneas turns to the problem of finding food:

> Alas sweet boy, thou must be still a while,
> Till we haue fire to dresse the meate we kild:
> Gentle *Achates*, reach the Tinder boxe,
> That we may make a fire to warme vs with,
> And rost our new found victuals on this shoare. (164–8)

The line is not particularly funny in context, I think. In fact the episode has a naturalness and truth which is in no way at odds with the earlier verse.

> Hold, take this candle and goe light a fire,
> You shall haue leaues and windfall bowes enow
> Neere to these woods, to rost your meate withall:
> *Ascanius*, goe and drie thy drenched lims . . . (171–4)

The passage tells 'the whole truth' which, as Aldous Huxley maintained,[1] tragedy does not often do.

At the beginning of Act II, Aeneas stands with Achates and Ascanius outside the walls of Carthage, and is overcome by the memories of Troy which the city stirs in him. His mind is imaginatively shown as tormentedly possessed by what it recognises as illusion:

> *Achates* though mine eyes say this is stone,
> Yet thinkes my minde that this is *Priamus*:
> And when my grieued heart sighes and sayes no,
> Then would it leape out to giue *Priam* life:
> O were I not at all so thou mightst be. (319–23)

---

[1] 'The Twelfth Book of the *Odyssey* concludes with these words: "When they had satisfied their thirst and hunger, they thought of their dear companions and wept, and in the midst of their tears sleep came gently upon them" . . . In any other poem but the *Odyssey*, what would the survivors have done? They would, of course, have wept, even as Homer made them weep. But would they previously have cooked their supper, and cooked it, what's more, in a masterly fashion? Would they previously have drunk and eaten to satiety? And after weeping, or actually while weeping, would they have dropped quietly off to sleep? No, they most certainly would not have done any of these things. They would simply have wept, lamenting their own misfortune and the horrible fate of their companions, and the canto would have ended tragically on their tears. Homer, however, preferred to tell the Whole Truth.' ('Tragedy and the Whole Truth,' in *Music at Night*.)

The passion is enforced by the almost unremitting punch of the monosyllables, and the very Marlovian violence of the verb 'leape'. Ascanius is bewildered and tries to comfort his father:

> Sweete father leaue to weepe, this is not he:
> For were it *Priam* he would smile on me.   (330–1)

The naïveté of the couplet is risky but not a misfire. The dramatic effect of the scene is to prepare for the great speech. We are made to realise the emotion which Troy calls up in Aeneas and his followers, and we do ourselves begin to share it, helped by the reiteration of the proper names, culminating in Aeneas' cry:

> O *Priamus*, O *Troy*, oh *Hecuba*!   (400)

When Dido commands him to describe the fall of Troy she does it with little imagination or sympathy, having only the curiosity of one who has heard several versions and now has the opportunity to hear an authentic account. We feel for Aeneas in this, and the violence of his reference to the memory as something which

> . . . like pale deaths stony mace,
> Beates forth my senses from this troubled soule   (410–11)

registers as truth and not as a mere figure of speech. What then has to be noted, as Aeneas begins his narrative, is the control and unexaggerated, restrained diction of all the first part, in which there is indeed (as Hamlet says) 'no matter in the phrase, that might indite the Author of affectation'. It is admirable both in itself and in the heightened passion it allows the rest of the speech.

In these scenes, then, tenderness and humanity extend the play's range; and there is a further extension in the incidental comedy and passages of relaxed lyricism. The scene which follows Aeneas' narrative contrasts with the brutality and suffering described there, and does in fact provide the diversion which Dido asks for. Venus lays the sleeping Ascanius in a grove 'amongst greene brakes' and speaks a lullaby over him. The whole passage is akin to the fairy world of *A Midsummer Night's Dream*:

> Sleepe my sweete nephew in these cooling shades,
> Free from the murmure of these running streames,
> The crye of beasts, the ratling of the windes,
> Or whisking of these leaues, all shall be still,
> And nothing interrupt thy quiet sleepe,
> Till I returne and take thee hence againe.　　(629–34)

The verb 'whisk' occurred about eighty lines previously, when it described Pyrrhus' sword felling King Priam; it has now modulated to the sound of blown leaves. This is very much a poetic 'port after stormy seas'. A similar piece of pretty lyricism is the Nurse's 'ticing' of Cupid to her house, which presents something like an Elizabethan version of the modern birthday-card rustic garden idyll, except perhaps in the lively relish of

> a siluer streame,
> Where thou shalt see the red gild fishes leape. (1380–81)

The tone then hardens almost immediately, with the sardonic humour of Cupid's games with the Nurse. The quick shifts of mood and tone are very characteristic—of an author too unstable, I think, to succeed in dramatising this essentially tragic story as a tragedy.

And, of course, the play, for all its fine and interesting qualities, is not a successful tragedy. Elizabethan and modern practice demonstrates that a tragic effect may be strengthened rather than harmed by comedy, and the comedy of the Nurse scene, for instance, is not responsible for the failure here, though neither is it well placed to prepare for a tragic fifth act. Nor is Dido's heroic status seriously affected by the comic spectacle of her subjection to Cupid's spell (a comedy resembling Hero's 'the more she striv'd the deeper was she strooke'). What does jeopardise the tragedy before the start of the fifth act is the treatment of the gods. In other hands, the gods as *dramatis personae* in such a context would be darkening powers, baleful and menacing; but with Marlowe they are merely part of the exuberant power-play. The prologue in Olympus has set the stage for comedy. Jupiter has been seen cajoling a cheeky, teasing Ganimede ('I am much better for your worthless loue . . .'), who paints a lively picture of a very substantial Juno:

> She reacht me such a rap for that I spilde,
> As made the bloud run downe about mine eares.   (7–8)

Jupiter rises to his full height at this: 'By *Saturnes* soule, and this earth threatning haire . . . I vow . . .'. This amuses Ganimede, who would 'bring the Gods to wonder at the game', like a crowd in a fairground. These gods are petty childish humans who have all the worlds to play with. They are not, I think, seen by the *author* as childish. He gives no hint of critical burlesque: he is probably offering them in a high-spirited, deliberately 'outrageous' manner, enjoying the freedom which their power and exuberant sports, desires and enmities gives to the imagination. 'Come *Ganimed*, we must about this geare'[1]: Jupiter's last words in the play are an engagingly casual, over-the-shoulder reference to the stuff of the tragedy, but they hardly induce a tragic tone. Nor are they sufficient to give a sense that men to the gods are 'as Flies to wanton Boyes', though

---

[1] 'Geare': stuff in deprecatory sense, rubbish, matter, affair, cf. Lightborne, 'So now I must about this geare' (*Ed. II*, 2487). It could also mean 'organs of generation', cf. Marlowe, *Elegy* I. vi. 36.

there is more than a touch of wanton boyhood about this father of the gods.

Only an exceptionally fine fifth act could have made successful tragedy with these things working against instead of preparing for it. The last act of *Dido* is in fact its great weakness, and the last scene quite fatal. The rapid succession of suicides calls for the parody it and its kind got in 1730 when Fielding's *Tom Thumb* burlesqued the English tragedy.[1] Dido throws herself into the flames; Iarbus enters running and kills himself after three lines of speech; and Anna commits suicide after another ten.

Dido's last aria is the greatest glory of Purcell's *Dido and Aeneas*, but Marlowe rises to nothing comparable. The mere facts of Dido's death, the relics and curse for example, are of course impressive in themselves. It is also a very Marlovian death (compare 'Tongue curse thy fill and dye'), and the terms of the speech are those of the play ('And now ye Gods that guide the starrie frame'). Marlowe may even have been well-advised when he left the curse in Latin: there is a mystery and solemnity in the utterance, and an impressive neatness in *littora littoribus contraria* not easy, though probably not impossible, to render as effectively in English. But his being content merely to quote Virgil shows him not to be taken up, involved in the material, as he had been in Aeneas' narrative. The impression throughout is that he is in too much of a hurry: doing

---

[1] *Tom Thumb*, with its six deaths in as many lines, parodies *The Rival Ladies* with its chain of lovers linked in death. Fielding's note (rather more heavy-handed than his comedy) implies a fair critical comment: 'Nor do I believe our victories over the French have been owing to anything more than to those bloody spectacles daily exhibited in our tragedies, of which the French stage is so entirely clear'. *Tom Thumb* does not know of *Dido* but it applies at other points, e.g., 'Whence flow those tears fast down thy blubbered cheeks?': cf. 'And wofull *Dido* by these blubbred cheekes'. Or the encounter of Glumdulca and King Arthur: *Glum.* 'What do I hear?' *King.* 'What do I see?' *Glum.* 'Oh.' *King.* 'Ah.': cf. *Dido.* '*Æneas*'. *Aen.* 'Dido'.

a job, no more. But his Dido is in a similar hurry. Her preparations, frantic in their suddenness and determination, are also business-like in a way which withdraws (at any rate) classical dignity from the scene:

> *Iarbus*, talke not of *Æneas*, let him goe,
> Lay to thy hands and helpe me make a fire . . .   (1691-2)

Again Marlowe is telling 'the whole truth' in the characteristic Elizabethan manner, which cares nothing for the proprieties and appears barbarous to the neo-classic. This Elizabethan manner was one of the things which Dryden reformed when he wrote his neat and tidy Antony and Cleopatra play. The Cleopatra of *All for Love* could not hop forty paces through the public street any more than she would call for a helping hand in laying the fire: she is a perfect model of the tragic-heroic, and has as much life as Dido's right arm or the Shakespearean Cleopatra's little finger. Shakespeare's play passes what is to our minds perhaps the ultimate test of its poise and assurance in making tragedy outside the limits of the conventionally heroic. But Marlowe cannot achieve any raising of the character or heightening of the seriousness corresponding to Cleopatra's last act. This is what he would have had to do to succeed in the tragedy, and it is asking a great deal of him. As it is, the feeling in this last scene is that the tragedy is all in the rough-and-tumble of life. The ending (the antithesis of the death of Edward II) has at least nothing depressingly passive about it. The energy has at least an outlet: Aeneas goes to Italy to 'raise a new foundation to old *Troy*', and Dido dies energetically, piling on the wood, stage-managing the whole affair, vengeful and cursing.

What Marlowe had in him here was the energy to experience keenly a variety of sensations—of wonder and ecstasy as well as pain and horror. But for all the gorgeous panoply of power, relished in this play as in *Tamburlaine*, there is no real sense of dignity in life or the possibility of a tragic dignity in the loss of it.

The reading of *Dido* can still, however, be a great pleasure, and the weak fifth act by no means justifies the critical neglect of the whole play. Nor do most of the criticisms commonly made. Derision of '*Achates*, reach the Tinder boxe' and similar 'false touches' or 'lapses of taste' is, as I have argued, probably obtuse and certainly disproportionate. Michel Poirier says that a few of Marlowe's details 'display a faulty taste: such are the appearance of the old toothless nurse fidgeting with love at the sight of Cupid, or the ridiculous account of Pyrrhus'.[1] Perhaps they do, but they are so essentially Marlovian as to call for more consideration than this. They link with so much in his work that the whole sensibility is in question, not an incidental failure of 'taste'. One may dislike a great deal in the 'whole sensibility' and still find it interesting and moving to study. But the examples Poirier gives seem to me to be some of the most characteristic manifestations of this sensibility, and neither they nor their author can be understood if they are to be dismissed as incidental lapses. The criticism is too light and superficial to help towards a judgment of Marlowe, and has too little appreciation of the strength of what it criticises to help the understanding. For his word 'ridiculous', Poirier has some support: the nineteenth-century editor Bullen, for instance, used it— and it is a judgment that belongs more to his century than to ours. Eliot's essay has intervened, and the lights it provided seem sufficiently recognisable as such to call for some critical adjustment.

Similarly, reference to Eliot's term 'caricature' might

---

[1] M. Poirier, *Christopher Marlowe* (London, 1951).

have prevented Philip Henderson's criticising as 'precious' these lines of Aeneas:

> Her siluer armes will coll me round about,
> And teares of pearle, crye stay, Æneas, stay.[1] (1201–2)

Marlowe himself is critically aware of the 'precious' in poetry. Dido speaks of 'The water which our Poets terme a Nimph' and having used the convention attacks it scornfully: 'The water is an Element, no Nimph' (1353). But in any case, Aeneas here is caricaturing deliberately. His tone is knowing and ironical: he is exaggerating what Dido's response will be when she learns that he is leaving her, and he uses the conventions of contemporary love poetry for his purpose. This is one example of the curious critical reluctance to give credit for any subtlety. Kocher concedes 'It is even possible that Marlowe's scene of Dido changing her mind back and forth between Iarbas and Aeneas is meant to show a comic mutability, but one cannot be sure.' The mutability obviously *is* comic, whatever its intention, while the grotesquely comic parallel with the Nurse and the more sophisticated one with Hero suggest that the scene in *Dido* is partly comic in intention too.

Dido is sometimes written off because it is, in John Bakeless's words, 'nothing but a re-writing of the first part of Virgil's *Aeneid*'. Poirier says that one-third of the lines translate or expand Virgil.[2] But this is extremely misleading: 'expand' is a term admitting some breadth of interpretation,

---

[1] P. Henderson, *Marlowe* ('Men and books') (London, 1952).

[2] This is documented in a thesis published in 1930 by T. M. Pearce of the University of New Mexico. Mr Pearce claims that over one-third of the lines are 'a literal carry-over or close paraphrase of Virgil's Latin'. Of these, 194 are 'straight translations' and 420 are 're-expressed'. I have not seen this study and may well have missed several of the 420 when making the comparison myself. But what impressed me then was the way the imagination built on the *Aeneid*, until the last act, making the story its own in a bold and unpedestrian adaptation. It is most unfortunate if writers use Mr Pearce's conclusions to give the impression that the play is a piece of hack-work.

but I would say that not more than one-seventh or one-eighth of the play follows Virgil with any closeness. In that I do not, for instance, count much of Aeneas' narrative, where Marlowe is telling the same story as Virgil but for the most part very differently.

Nor do I follow the argument that *Dido*, containing many lines which resemble others by Marlowe, is therefore an early work, these lines being first drafts of what was later to be improved. An obvious example is this, from IV. 4, a scene which contains many echoes or (as they are called in the gramophone world) pre-echoes:

> It is *Æneas* frowne that ends my daies:
> If he forsake me not, I neuer dye.
> For in his lookes I see eternitie,
> And heele make me immortall with a kisse.   (1326–9)

The famous 'perfected' version of the last line is in Faustus' address to Helen:

> Sweete *Helen*, make me immortall with a kisse.   (1330)

There seems to me little to choose between them, and it is not so much the quality of the line that makes me ready to believe the *Dido* version was indeed the first, as the fact that in *Dido* there is so much inspiration elsewhere. It seems altogether more likely that such a line would germinate there, where poetic energy and ardour are most abundant.

This abundance is not at all exhausted by the considerable number of quotations already made. There are, for example, a good many fine lyrical passages where the action is static, as in an operatic aria. Venus has a speech starting like a lyric in a Dowland song-book: 'Disquiet Seas lay downe your swelling lookes' (122). The 'calmie cheere' is reflected by the heavy regular beat of the lines. At other points, the disquiet seas are represented in alliterative verse which buffets about like the tides it describes:

> But of them all scarce seuen doe anchor safe,
> And they so wrackt and weltred by the waues,
> As euery tide tilts twixt their oken sides:
> And all of them vnburdened of their loade,
> Are ballassed with billowes watrie weight. (222–6)

Near the end of the play, Dido's delirium is felt and intensified in the sea-sickening extremities of

> See see, the billowes heaue him vp to heauen,
> And now downe falles the keeles into the deepe.
> (1660–61)

Another fine and subtle effect occurs as Venus, imagining Aeneas' troubles at sea, compares his present perils with those of Troy, from which he has just escaped:

> Poore *Troy* must now be sackt vpon the Sea,
> and *Neptunes* waues be enuious men of warre . . .
> And *Æolus* like *Agamemnon* sounds
> The surges, his fierce souldiers, to the spoyle:
> See how the night *Vlysses*-like comes forth . . . (64–70)

The mystery of the last line, quiet after the hissing onomatopœia before it, completes a piece of poetic double-exposure: one picture is superimposed on another, the Trojan image reappearing in Aeneas' narrative. That narrative is the most finely sustained speech in Marlowe. The restrained language and unforced movement of the first section are doubly impressive on account of the strength of feeling which we know is being controlled. Bitterness grows as Aeneas feels the irony of the Trojans making a breach in their own walls to admit the horse:

> These hands did helpe to hale it to the gates. (465)

The ludicrous, impotent anger is felt in the monosyllables (the sort of emphasis with which Horatio says 'These hands are not more like') and in the alliteration. Marlowe's alliteration is nearly always purposeful, as in the desperation of

> Yet flung I forth, and desperate of my life,
> Ran in the thickest throngs. (505–6)

The alliteration performs analogous action, as it does in Chaucer's *Knight's Tale*: 'he thurgh the thikkeste of the throng gan threste', where the tongue forces itself through the barricade of consonants. But imagination is always alight in this speech. Here, for instance, it catches the descent of the Greeks from the horse, vividly bringing to mind the disaster already imminent and inevitable as it shows the faces of the destroyers:

> Then he vnlockt the Horse, and suddenly
> From out his entrailes, *Neoptolemus*
> Setting his speare vpon the ground, leapt forth,
> And after him a thousand Grecians more,
> In whose sterne faces shin'd the quenchles fire,
> That after burnt the pride of *Asia*. (477–82)

*   *   *

This dramatic poetry is not negligible, and was not in its own time. It is true that the only evidence of its having been performed is on the title-page of the Quarto: 'played by the Children of her Maiesties Chappell'; and the only evidence of its not having been totally neglected is in the work of Shakespeare—the attention of 'which one', however, 'must . . . o'erweigh a whole theatre of others'.[1] This 'evidence' is naturally questionable. Here it derives from the one unquestionable but not very impressive fact— that in reading *Dido* I have been repeatedly struck by what seem to me likenesses to Shakespeare. The value and significance of such observations is not a thing one can be confident about and it has certainly led critics into strange

[1] *Hamlet*, II. 2.

capers often enough. However, I am myself convinced of these things: that Shakespeare had a copy of *Dido* or knew it well, that the memory remained with him as late as *The Tempest*, and that few contemporary plays moved him more than this.

The only indisputable point of contact is the lines on Pyrrhus and Priam in the Player's speech in *Hamlet*:

> *Pyrrhus* at *Priam* driues, in Rage strikes wide:
> But with the whiffe and winde of his fell Sword
> Th'vnnerued Father fals. (II. 2)

This is close to Marlowe's lines:

> Which he disdaining whiskt his sword about,
> And with the wind thereof the King fell downe.
>
> (548-9)

Out of context the lines are laughable and Shakespeare is sometimes represented as burlesquing them in *Hamlet*. Incidentally the Quarto of *Dido* reads 'wound' for 'wind'. J. P. Collier was the first to conjecture 'wind',[1] unless one accepts Boas's comment that 'Shakespeare is in a sense the first emendator'.[2] 'Wound' is surely better: more brutal and original in usage, and not so uneasy a hyperbole. But in any case the suggestion for the lines in *Hamlet* is quite clearly present in *Dido*: it does not occur in Virgil and another common source is unlikely. The description of Pyrrhus 'horridly Trick'd With blood' is like Marlowe's

> At last came *Pirrhus* fell and full of ire,
> His harnesse dropping bloud . . . (508-9)

It is also the beginning of the climax in Aeneas' narrative and would be a natural place for Hamlet to begin his quotation.

The Player's speech (*Hamlet*, II. 2) is an essay in a style remote from that of the play itself, and the dramatic purpose

---

[1] MS. notes in copy of Dyce's edition of Marlowe's plays.
[2] Boas, *op. cit.*, p. 57.

of this remoteness is clear and justification enough for it. There is irony in Hamlet's 'loving' so bloodthirsty a piece, and a further irony in that at one point the 'hellish *Pyrrhus*', who

> . . . like a Newtrall to his will and matter,
> Did nothing,

is an image of Hamlet himself. The last line ('Did nothing') is emphasised by its metrical incompleteness. Shakespeare is in fact writing his own speech with specific dramatic intentions, and he is neither parodying Marlowe (for parody—as opposed to irony—would be out of place in a speech which so moves Hamlet and the Player) nor emulating him (for the style is not really Marlovian). But he did have some features of Marlowe's narrative in mind, and probably took, in introducing the passage, an opportunity to pay some tribute to a play he admired.

The piece Hamlet refers to 'was never acted, or if it was, not above once, for the play I remember pleased not the million'. That is the sort of remark one would expect to have specific reference, and when he says 'one Speech in it I cheefely lou'd, twas *Æeneas* Tale to *Dido*', he may be taken to identify as Marlowe's the 'excellent play', in which that speech is indeed the most memorable. The other terms of Hamlet's praise may not apply specifically to *Dido*: Shakespeare is listing dramatic virtues probably for their own sake, as later he lets Hamlet express his ideas about acting. But as even the most cautious and least romantic of readers will allow that those views may well be Shakespeare's own, so I think that here also Shakespeare may be speaking through the character in a way unusual with him.

This would be a mere article of faith if it were not for the number of times Shakespeare comes to mind as one reads *The Tragedie of Dido*. Two associations with *The Tempest*, for instance, occur within ten lines, and there are others within the same scene. Venus has watched over Aeneas' sea-sorrows as Prospero and Ariel looked after Alonso's ship.

> *Venus.* And for thy ships which thou supposest lost,
> Not one of them hath perisht in the storme,
> But are ariued safe not farre from hence.　　(235–7)

Spiritlike, Venus disappears from sight and Aeneas says:

> But thou art gone and leau'st me here alone,
> To dull the ayre with my discoursiue moane.　　(247–8)

Aeneas has just described the violence of the storm ('euery tide tilts twixt their oken sides'). In *The Tempest* (I. 1) Shakespeare is describing a similar violence, and it appears that, a few lines later, what Coleridge called 'the hooks and eyes of the memory' have functioned to bring forward fragments of Marlowe's play:

> *Prospero.* But are they (*Ariel*), safe?
> *Ariel.*　　　Not a haire perishd:
> On their sustaining garments not a blemish,
> But fresher then before: and, as thou badst me,
> In troops I haue dispersd them 'bout the Isle:
> The Kings sonne haue I landed by himselfe,
> Whom I left cooling of the Ayre with sighes,
> In an odde Angle of the Isle, and sitting
> His armes in this sad knot.

The other ships, Ariel reports, are returning to Naples:

> Supposing that they saw the Kings ship wrackt,
> And his great person perish.

In the *Dido* scene, Venus stands aside, watching them at their task and commenting with compassion and thoughtfulness, as Prospero looks on the labours of Ferdinand. Achates looks around with the eyes of Gonzalo and Adrian:

> The ayre is pleasant, and the soyle most fit
> For Cities and societies supports.　　(178–9)

Compare *The Tempest*, II. 1:

> The ayre breathes vpon vs here most sweetly.
> Heere is euery thing aduantageous to life.

and Gonzalo's Utopian commonwealth. And, of course, this is the scene (and the part of it) where there is the talk of 'Widdow *Dido*' and 'this *Tunis*' which, as Gonzalo points out to the wondering Adrian, 'was *Carthage*'.

In the third act of *The Tempest* Miranda is confused by the conflict of love and modesty within her. She weeps, she says,

> At mine vnworthinesse, that dare not offer
> What I desire to giue; and much lesse take
> What I shall die to want. (III. 1)

In this first love scene between Ferdinand and Miranda, Prospero observing them unseen and noting how Miranda is caught ('Poore worme thou art infected'), Shakespeare's memory 'hooked onto' the meeting of Dido and Aeneas in the cave, where they think they are free agents but are in fact 'in a net'. Aeneas asks what Dido 'may desire and not obtaine'. She replies:

> The thing that I will dye before I aske,
> And yet desire to haue before I dye. (1004–5)

Miranda's conflicting emotions have recalled Dido's, and the reminiscence, whether conscious or not, has caught the sense of Marlowe's first line and the antithetical expression of the couplet.

Many scattered associations occur as one reads *Dido*.

> With thy gloomie hand corrects the heaven
> When ayrie creatures warre amongst themselues,
> (*Dido*, 1100)

> Corrects the ill Aspects of Planets euil . . .
> . . . But when the Planets
> In euil mixture to disorder wander . . .
> (*Troilus and Cressida*)

Music 'that calles my soule from forth his liuing seate' (*Dido*, 1048); 'that sheepes guts should hale soules out of mens bodies' (*Much Ado about Nothing*—note the Marlovian verb 'hale').

> Tut, I am simple, without mind to hurt,
> And haue no gall at all to grieue my foes   (*Dido*, 826)

> But I am Pigeon-Liuer'd, and lack Gall
> To make Oppression bitter.   (*Hamlet*[1])

'Stay not to answere me' (*Dido*, 1210); 'Stay not to answer me' (*Julius Caesar*, II. 4)—both spoken by anxious women. 'A winters tale' (*Dido*, 969).

But above all *Dido* suggests *Antony and Cleopatra*. Here it is not so much a matter of local similarities or general resemblances of plot but essentially of a similar 'feel' in the substance of the poetry. Marlowe's imagery here is very like Shakespeare's. Caroline Spurgeon's account of the imagery in *Antony and Cleopatra* clearly suggests the Marlovian: 'The group of images in *Antony and Cleopatra* which, on analysis, immediately attracts attention as peculiar to this play, consists of images of the world, the firmament, the ocean and vastness generally.'[2] Miss Spurgeon has noted elsewhere that in Marlowe such images are particularly abundant, but although she has included *Dido* in her charted calculations there is no reference to it in the text. Wolfgang Clemen, also neglecting *Dido*, writes of the imagery of *Tamburlaine* in terms similar to those Miss Spurgeon used of *Antony and Cleopatra*: Tamburlaine reaches 'for the stars and elements as if they were playthings, traversing (in his imagination) the immeasurable vastness of the firmament with ease . . . Only the world of imagery offered the requisite gigantic proportions'.[3] There is not much

---

[1] *Hamlet*, II. 2. 580–1 (immediately following the Aeneas speech).
[2] C. Spurgeon, *Shakespeare's Imagery and What it Tells us* (Cambridge, 1935).
[3] W. Clemen, *The Development of Shakespeare's Imagery* (London, 1951).

reason to associate *Antony and Cleopatra* with *Tamburlaine*, the subjects being so different. But with *Dido* the subject offers every reason, and it is very natural that Shakespeare's mind should have caught up memorable snatches of Marlowe's music.

There is, then, this feeling of kinship between the two plays, and I have given some examples and analysis in the opening pages of this chapter. There are also local points, which show that *Dido* was retained in that part of Shakespeare's mind which was active most in the writing of *Antony and Cleopatra*. Aeneas' beauty is such that 'the people swarme to gaze him in the face' (706), as they do for female beauty in Shakespeare:

> The Citty cast
> Her people out vpon her . . .
> . . . th'ayre; which but for vacancie,
> Had gone to gaze on *Cleopater* too. . . .　　(II. 2)

The likenesses between Dido's wooing ('Ile giue the tackling made of riueld gold') and Enobarbus' description of the barge are clear enough, both in the words and their erotic working. I think it is also probable that the assonance of 'Mirmidons, With balles of wilde fire in their murdering pawes' (511–12) in Aeneas' narrative, working expressively as it does, went into the receptive mind, and helped to produce the wonderful interaction of assonance in 'the Barge . . . like a burnisht Throne Burnt on the water . . .'. The short discussion between Dido and Anna sounds the note of Cleopatra and Charmian, where Charmian, like Anna, has been championing another man.

> *Dido.* Yet must I heare that lothsome name againe?　　(712)

> *Cleopatra.* . . . if thou with *Cæsar* Paragon againe
> My man of men.　　(I. 5)

Dido's internal conflict too has some of Cleopatra's quick turnings.

> *Dido.* I loue thee not,
> And yet I hate thee not . . .;   (805)

> *Cleopatra.* Let him for euer go, let him not.   (II. 5)

The quickly changing moods of Dido's scene with Iarbas might be sketches for Cleopatra's infinite variety.[1] And the final connection between the plays is their treatment of love. 'Eternity was in our Lippes, and Eyes' says Cleopatra, and Marlowe's Dido: 'In his lookes I see eternitie'. The knowledge of lovers' infiniteness is present in both plays. So is the knowledge of a world elsewhere, and in both, the tragedy results from a tension between the two.

In his edition of *Dido*, Tucker Brooke wrote: 'There are lines in this play at which Shakespeare may well have smiled.' He, at least, could afford to; but the likelihood is that he smiled with pleasure rather than condescending amusement. The Marlowe of Chapman's tribute to one 'vp to the chin in the Pyerean flood' is there on every page, and his lines are still able to haunt the memory as they probably did Shakespeare's.

---

[1] Note also:

> A Burgonet of steele . . . fits Æneas.   (1248)

> That I may tice a Dolphin to the shoare,
> And ride vpon his backe vnto my loue.   (1657–8)

3

'TAMBURLAINE'

'TAMBURLAINE' is the most solid and unflawed of Marlowe's plays: more consistent in quality than *Dido* or *Faustus*, more whole and substantial than *The Jew of Malta*, and more vigorous in imagination and sustaining power than *Edward II*. The two parts together make an impressive achievement; the work, one would say, of a man writing with full confidence in his powers, and with assurance, poise and singleness of mind.

The apparent singleness of mind also informs the work with an apparent singleness of moral purpose which, judged by Christian or humanitarian or liberal standards, is an evil one: to find it anything else involves either misjudgment of the plays or dissociation from those standards. But the singlenesses referred to *are* only apparent. In the moral purpose the diabolonian predominates, and in the whole mind it has a prominent place, though in neither is it exclusive. There is, in fact, beneath the ringing speeches and triumphantly sensational episodes, a basic instability: a to-and-fro movement in which the feelings alternately support and recoil from the protagonist, and which gives the plays something of the character of an unevenly matched debate.

Nothing is extenuated in Tamburlaine's non-Christian character and career—the cruelty, bloodshed, suffering, violence, ruthlessness, pride, fanaticism. Yet the essential working of the drama impels admiration for the super-humanity of one who by Christian values is detestable as subhuman. This I think is true for an Elizabethan audience as for a modern reader. Tamburlaine is the hero of his tragedy: of Part 2 as well as Part 1. It seems reasonable to doubt this at one point only. This is (II. 5. 1) where Tamburlaine orders his men to burn the Mohammedan books, daring Mahomet out of his heaven and turning from him in disgust. But the god proves not so sleepy, for less than twenty lines later Tamburlaine feels himself 'distempered sudainly' with the fever which is to kill him. 'Sicknes or death can neuer conquer me' is his boast, and the irony tells savagely against him even while his strength and authority still command respect. But from this point on, in spite of the continued irony of death's growing power over the man whose servant death has been, his heroic status is maintained and even increased. As Tamburlaine is dying Marlowe offers no morality comparable with Cambises' 'a just reward for my misdeeds my death doth plaine declare'. The last speech in the play does not say 'Cut is the branch that might have grown full straight': it contains nothing about a 'hellish fall', a death which might warn the wicked and encourage the devout. On the contrary, it laments the passing of one whose worth will never be equalled: the death is felt as tragic principally because it is a deprivation. Hubris is forgotten in admiration—admiration, that is, for a man whose 'worth' is entirely anti-Christian.

Even so, much in the play weighs against this assessment or virtual apotheosis of Tamburlaine. The verdict is in his favour but he has at least been put on trial. It is worth following the play (taking for the present the two parts as one) with this trial or debate form in mind. For the first seven scenes, counting for much in determining an audience's attitude, the judgment is completely in his favour. One becomes aware of a scale of manhood in which the individuals have their place, Mycetes at the bottom,

Tamburlaine at the top. He is established qualitatively: the superior of Cosroe, Theridamas and the others, themselves worthy men. But his duplicity in dealing with Cosroe introduces the debate's opposition. Cosroe's speech strikes the note:

> What means this diuelish shepheard to aspire
> With such a Giantly presumption,
> To cast vp hils against the face of heauen:
> And dare the force of angrie *Iupiter*. (812–15)

We are made to feel an ambiguity in the success and character we have admired. Ortygius expresses it in the next speech, and this is, in fact, the question to be debated or dramatised throughout the play:

> What God or Feend, or spirit of the earth,
> Or Monster turned to a manly shape,
> Or of what mould or mettel he be made,
> What star or state soeuer gouerne him . . .
> Whether from earth, or hell, or heauen he grow.
>
> (826–34)

Tamburlaine counters in the same scene with his own creed:

> Nature that fram'd vs of foure Elements . . .
> Doth teach vs all to haue aspyring minds. (869–71)

With this speech feeling turns in his favour, not because of the doctrine he voices but because such is the compulsion of the drama. His words and actions are stronger than his enemies', more noble even. Yet the doctrine virtually asserts might as right; the survival of the fittest is seen as natural law; aspiration is the natural and admirable thing. There is no opposition from Cosroe probing the morality of ends or means, merely an observation that Tamburlaine's people are 'the strangest men that euer nature made'. The bewilderment hints that rather than disciples of nature and representatives of her truth, they are products of un-nature, monstrous and uncanny. But Cosroe is dying, Tamburlaine succeeding; and the scene ends in enthusiasm for him.

Opposition now devolves upon Bajazeth, whose greater power acts as a measure of Tamburlaine's growth, and whose pomposity and decadence give him no respectable dramatic standing. More effective in denunciation is Agidas (III. 2), though Zenocrate's praise of Tamburlaine counts for more, and Agidas anyway is found out and dies. Ultimately even this death contributes to Tamburlaine's honour, because his henchmen are gentlemanly and generous about it. In the next scene he gains in prestige by mighty speech and advocacy of the Christians, and when the debate is continued by the women, support goes to Zenocrate; that is, at one remove, to Tamburlaine. At the defeat of Bajazeth, pride in Tamburlaine is very high, far outweighing in its dramatic strength any misgivings roused by the unscrupulousness of his dealings with Cosroe and the ruthlessness of his treatment of Agidas.

The Soldan (IV. 1) does the opposition little credit since his indignation is so impotent and arises so largely out of sheer envy. The scorn with which he stamps Tamburlaine as a 'pesant ignorant' only intensifies admiration for the man who without advantage of birth has achieved so much. With the tormenting of Bajazeth, however, a more serious opposing movement makes itself felt from somewhere deeply within the play. On the whole I think the scenes vaunt sadistically the conqueror's rights and pleasures; just as, when at the end of the scene Tamburlaine will not yield to Zenocrate's plea for mercy to her people, we are meant to see his inhumanity primarily as a strength. But the further taunting of Bajazeth and Zabina tests loyalty to Tamburlaine much more strenuously. The caged Emperor and his wife are now allowed dignity and pathos, and the slaughter at Damascus, with the massacre of the virgins, is presented as savage and tragic. The feeling against Tamburlaine and all that he stands for is voiced movingly and with serious dramatic status accorded it in Zenocrate's speech:

> Ah myghty *Ioue* and holy *Mahomet*,
> Pardon my Loue, oh pardon his contempt,
> Of earthly fortune, and respect of pitie,
> And let not conquest ruthlesly pursewde
> Be equally against his life incenst,
> In this great Turk and haplesse Emperesse.
> And pardon me that was not moou'd with ruthe,
> To see them liue so long in misery.   (2146–52)

In the episodes which culminate in this speech the opposition has full scope, and if the dominant feeling of the play were behind it Tamburlaine could not be allowed to reinstate himself with all the glory and glamour invested in him hitherto. Yet that is what happens. All ends triumphantly and, in intention, he emerges as indisputable hero. He is victorious in battle, merciful to the Soldan, gracious to Zenocrate, secure and dignified in the majesty of his rhetoric, commanding allegiance everywhere. The dramatic effect is to compel a justification of bloodshed and tyranny in the name of genius, magnificence and power. The suffering and all other things for which the dramatised opposition can cry out against Tamburlaine are not softened or lessened; they seem often to be gloried in. But in this first play Tamburlaine is tried and ultimately accepted with undiminished enthusiasm on his own terms.

In Part 2 the opposition speaks first. The Mohammedan Orcanes forms an alliance with the Christian Sigismond. When Sigismond betrays his ally, Christianity loses face and Christians forfeit the right to be morally smug about Tamburlaine. A more creditable force for the opposition is Callapine, Bajazeth's son. He is allowed a good deal of Tamburlaine-like speech and a measure of success. But Tamburlaine's entrance, held back to good dramatic effect till the fourth scene, eclipses any heroic impression made by others. Zenocrate, speaking sensibly against militarism, tells against the Tamburlaine-world; but her scruples are 'womanish' in contrast with the 'manly' bloodthirstiness of her husband and sons. Then, as Theridamas and Techelles offer up their crowns which Tamburlaine graciously restores, we have a ritual representative of the fruits of triumph— homage and fellowship, banquets and a rest for the soldiers, and so forth.

The second act opens with Baldwine's persuading Sigismond to break faith. This is moral debate and with the rest of the episode shows a mind unmistakably thinking in moral-religious terms. When Orcanes learns of the treachery he prays to Christ-Mahomet, a sort of universal spirit. He wins respect partly by success (which counts for much in the play's values) and partly by a certain breadth and nobility:

> Yet in my thoughts shall Christ be honoured,
> Not dooing *Mahomet* an iniurie,
> Whose power had share in this our victory. (2954–6)

This episode affects the general debate in two ways. It undermines Christian assumptions of superiority, for here you have heathens acting more admirably (by Christian standards) than Christians themselves; and it again works pyramidally, establishing a scale of manhood, in which Sigismond is placed appreciably lower than Orcanes who in turn becomes as nothing when brought face to face with Tamburlaine.

The death of Zenocrate, however, strengthens the opposition considerably. Her quiet dignity contrasts favourably with Tamburlaine's ranting and she also 'places' his world:

> *Tamb.* Tell me, how fares my faire *Zenocrate*?
> *Zen.* I fare my Lord, as other Emperesses,
>   That when this fraile and transitory flesh
>   Hath suckt the measure of that vitall aire
>   That feeds the body with his dated health,
>   Wanes with enforst and necessary change. (3009–14)

Her death comes as a defeat for Tamburlaine, particularly in that he has made such a personal issue out of it:

> Proud furie and intollorable fit,
> That dares torment the body of my Loue. (3046–7)

On the other hand, the burning of the town, which might have been given some dramatic condemnation as crazy destruction, is presented with dignified ceremonial as a fitting marvel. Moreover, new life and hope exist in the sons: Tamburlaine's governing his grief and turning his energies to the future register essentially as an admirable stoicism (which is the note struck throughout, to the endurance of pain in lancing the arm).

The next episode presents victims of Tamburlaine's violence, and this time with no sadistic pleasure in their discomfiture but with dignity and recognition of suffering and heroism. Admiration and sympathy go to the Captain, valiantly opposing Theridamas, and pity and wonder to Olympia, whose misery and fortitude tell strongly against Tamburlaine—he is responsible for the one and cannot outshine the other. Even so, the effect is not so straightforward, for her strength of character and purpose stands to be ranked highly by the mind which also places Tamburlaine highest in the scale of manhood. That is: Olympia's virtues are to some extent a reflection of Tamburlaine's own; the strong-minded killing of her son compares with Tamburlaine's killing of Calyphas (to most of us the actions are poles apart, but both episodes appear to be offered as demonstrations of abnormally strong character). There is even a feeling that the tragedy of Olympia shows that kind of heroism which only war will produce: she is at once one of the victims and glories of warfare. The ambivalence of the episode, then, lies in this: (*a*) it evokes pity and admiration for the sufferer and therefore opposition to the cause of the suffering; (*b*) it exalts a world of violence and strong will, which is also the world of the conqueror.

For the rest of the play there is less and less to like in Tamburlaine. His actions are marked by a growing extremism and an obsessive megalomaniac destructiveness. The trouble is that there is so little evidence of the author's dissociating himself from it. The enemies of Tamburlaine never oppose him in principle, but only in strength and pride. Callapine, for instance, is quite happy to 'sacrifice Mountaines of breathlesse men': there is no question of humanitarian opposing military dictator. Moreover, the mere presence of Tamburlaine is enough to deprive Callapine of authority. His protégé Almeda asks of Tamburlaine permission to take the crown Callapine offers him. The opposition is reduced to an almost farcical absurdity here. Again, it is significant that the only thorough-going nonconformist to the conventions of Tamburlaine's world is the utterly despicable Calyphas. He could well have been an effective spokesman for the opposition, but his hatred for all his father stands for has no status whatsoever: it is given as the self-indulgent evasions of a pathetic, ludicrous decadent whose cowardice serves also to flatter his brothers' manliness. His lines,

> I know sir, what it is to kil a man,
> It works remorse of conscience in me, (3700–01)

are there to be laughed at. The whole concept of conscience is ridiculed in Calyphas' advocacy.

When he is killed by Tamburlaine, one recognises a sort of rough justice. On the other hand, the act undoubtedly shocks, and Orcanes represents the opposition with his comment,

> Thou shewest the difference twixt our selues and thee
> In this thy barbarous damned tyranny.　　　　(3812–13)

And in Jerusalem's 'Thy victories are growne so violent' there is a sense, naïve enough, that the line must be drawn somewhere. Yet the last of Tamburlaine's triumphs, the capture of Babylon and the 'pampered Iades of *Asia*', are presented as *tours de force* rather than excesses. Everything is done to satisfy a sadistic taste. The opposition of the Governor of Babylon is not seen as heroism but foolhardiness, and Tamburlaine's massacre of the population does not seem to be condemned dramatically. After this orgy of destructiveness, however, follows Tamburlaine's own piece of foolhardiness. His 'daring' of Mahomet brings the crisis in which dramatic condemnation does seem to have been made. But the debate continues. The new hopeful alliance between Callapine and Almeda could have been triumphant and the play could have ended in Tamburlaine's overthrow. If Marlowe were intent upon a nemesis this would be the point. But the last scenes increase Tamburlaine's status, steadily preparing for the death of a tragic hero. He triumphs in his last military exchange: feverishly absurd in form but an impressive and final proof of superiority in what it symbolises. His words about the future of his empire cut both ways, and even here occurs this opposition of ideas or ambiguity of intention which I have called debate: on the one hand he can die with comfort, 'my flesh deuided in your precious shapes'; on the other a shadow is cast by the warning that

> The nature of thy chariot wil not beare
> A guide of baser temper than my selfe.   (4635–6)

In his death he evokes much admiration. The words to his sons are wise and moderate; the fortitude and dignity of his deathbed utterly irreproachable. Ultimately death does not come as a defeat, for he has every confident expectation of eternal life:

> Now eies, inioy your latest benefite,
> And when my soule hath vertue of your sight,
> Pierce through the coffin and the sheet of gold,
> And glut your longings with a heauen of ioy.   (4616–20)

The epitaph spoken by Amyras ends the play in grief for a dead hero:

> Meet heauen & earth, & here let al things end,
> For earth hath spent the pride of all her fruit,
> And heauen consum'd his choisest liuing fire.
> Let earth and heauen his timelesse death deplore,
> For both their woorths wil equall him no more.   (4642–6)

The last line defines the motion debated, and there is little doubt that it has been carried. The dominant emotion dramatically compelled is something like Cleopatra's as 'the crown o'the earth doth melt':

> The oddes is gone,
> And there is nothing left remarkeable
> Beneath the visiting Moone.
>   (*Antony and Cleopatra*, IV. 13)

*   *   *

The most interesting study of *Tamburlaine* is that by Professor Roy Battenhouse, who devotes his whole book to the play and its place in Renaissance moral philosophy.[1]

---

[1] R. W. Battenhouse: *Marlowe's Tamburlaine: a Study in Renaissance Moral Philosophy* (Nashville, 1941).

Often mentioned in essays and bibliographies, the book is rarely found in this country on the shelves of bookshops or public libraries, so a short account of its argument may be useful.

In his introduction, the author dissociates himself from what is called romantic criticism as represented, for instance, by Una Ellis-Fermor, whose 'criticism fails, because she has studied the drama not with the eyes of an Elizabethan to whom ambition was sin, but with the eyes of a modern, to whom upward striving is noble'. The play should be seen as an Elizabethan audience would see it, and they would observe that 'the parts and the whole of *Tamburlaine* have pattern demonstrably in accord with certain formulas and chief doctrines of Elizabethan Humanism'. It is a didactic play in conformity with a conventional morality, and the career of the protagonist demonstrates that 'the tragic fall is both a consequence and a punishment of sin'. In this the play may be compared with, for example, *The Mirror for Magistrates*. Marlowe himself has usually been seen as a rebel against religion yet he is supposed to have associated with Raleigh and Chapman, both devout men even if not entirely orthodox. Like them, Marlowe wrote with the assumption that poetry had a moral function and his method in *Tamburlaine* is within the tradition, letting 'wickedness grow until it destroys itself by its own excess'. Marlowe's sources condemn Tamburlaine (Thevet, for instance, engagingly calls him 'le plus grand brigand & detestable vilain') and so far from presenting him more favourably, Marlowe if anything shows him in a worse light. Whereas the historical Tamburlaine 'ended his days amongst his children, as a peaceable governor of innumerable countries', Marlowe's dies in fevered madness, justly punished for his sins. The evils of Tamburlaine are like those of Seneca's Hercules and Spenser's Orgoglio and are to be judged in the same way: verbal parallels show that Marlowe had these prototypes in mind. 'The tragic flaw in Tamburlaine's nature goes deep. As judged by sixteenth century standards, his passions have fallen victim to three ills: immoderation, misdirection, and delusion. Or, to put the matter another way, his tragedy is explainable in terms of the degenerate source of his inspiration, the mistaken goal of his aspiration, and the intemperate course of his desire.' Of the play, Battenhouse concludes: 'certainly these ten acts of *Tamburlaine* offer one of the most grandly moral spectacles in the whole realm of English drama'; and of its author: 'Marlowe differs from his Protestant contemporaries . . . not in his moral outlook, but only in his ability as an artist.'

This interpretation differs spectacularly from previous readings, but over the last fifteen years or so it has gained support. It infects, for example, Miss Mahood's essay in *Poetry and Humanism*: she also sees the play as a study of misdirected aspiration. And this essay is one of the best things written on Marlowe.

One of the basic flaws of Battenhouse's argument can be seen in his stricture on the criticism of Ellis-Fermor. We must look at the play 'with the eyes of an Elizabethan'. This seems reasonable until you ask what sort of Elizabethan, for this 'an' with all its innocent singularity is wonderfully inclusive. The answer comes, 'an Elizabethan to whom ambition was sin'; so this attribute of 'most' Elizabethans is, by the deftly inclusive 'an', transferred to all. The assumption is that Marlowe wishes you to watch the play with a conventional mind because he is giving something which will fortify you in your conventionality. That such an assumption is at odds with the excitement and thrust of the poetry does not appear to bother or even to occur to the writer, who is involved in a kind of scholarly detection and litigation and not directly concerned with poetry. But the fault seen here in miniature is writ large in the whole work. Having marshalled majority Elizabethan opinion, the author concludes that he has Marlowe. Amongst Renaissance moralists, for instance, La Primaudaye is frequently quoted. He spoke of 'the full and whole fruition of the essence of God', a phrase sharply opposed to Tamburlaine's 'sweet fruition of an earthly crowne'. But one cannot therefore infer, as Battenhouse does, that Marlowe is intentionally illustrating a blasphemy and a sin. Or if he is, it is more likely that the line, coming as it does as the climax of one of the finest utterances in the play, is intended to challenge normal values and assert opposing ones.

Fulke Greville also is called into the box to witness for Marlowe. He praises 'mediocrity, that reciprocall paradise of mutuall humane duties' and remarks that 'in man's muddy soule the meane doth not content . . . This makes some soare and burn' (*Alaham*). This is certainly a remark relevant to Marlovian drama, but the cool observation of a fact is something far unlike the heated aspirations, passions and, later, the humiliations of Marlowe's heroes. That is not to identify Marlowe with his protagonists, but it is to say that the works show a passionate involvement with the substance of that quotation so that its dispassionate tone carries a meaning different from any that could be attributed to Marlowe. Greville cannot speak for Marlowe here. Nor can he in the remark about his purpose and method in writing *Alaham*: 'to trace out the high waies of ambitious governours, and to show in the practice of life that the more audacity, advantage, and good successe such soveraignes have, the more they hasten to their own desolation and ruin'. Battenhouse quotes this as part of his study of a tradition with which he wants to draw

Marlowe into line. What he does not mention is that Fulke Greville is at pains in this passage to dissociate himself from the purposes of modern dramatists (and he must have thought of Marlowe among them). He regarded himself as doing something specifically outside any tradition. So it seems probable that he himself, at any rate, did not see *Tamburlaine* in this light at all.

The main arguments and procedures of the book beg the most important questions with apparent ingenuousness. Because Tamburlaine would be generally condemned, it is assumed that Marlowe condemns him; because he resembles Seneca's Hercules and Spenser's Orgoglio, it is assumed that Marlowe has the same attitude towards his creation that Seneca and Spenser had to theirs. 'Such parallels', Battenhouse writes, 'if we are to accept their evidence,[1] obviously presume an interpretation of Marlowe's characters in accord with morality tradition.' But this does not follow at all. If these 'Vice' characteristics from earlier poetry and drama are attracted into Marlowe's portraiture, it is likely to be for his own purposes and these need not be the traditional ones. When Tamburlaine is described by Theridamas as

> . . . so imbellished
> With Natures pride, and richest furniture,
> His looks do menace heauen and dare the Gods,
>
> (350–52)

Marlowe is expressing the wonder and fascination which Theridamas is beginning to feel and which is to be

---

[1] But not all the 'evidence' is acceptable. A parallel is drawn between Orgoglio ('this monstrous masse of earthly slyme') and Tamburlaine ('grosse and like the massie earth'). But Marlowe's text has been misconstrued. The construction is:

> For he is grosse and like the massie earth,
> That mooues not vpwards, nor by princely deeds
> Doth meane to soare aboue the highest sort. (882–4)

Theridamas is giving his reasons for joining with Tamburlaine. In his view it is the others who are 'grosse'; Tamburlaine is the opposite.

maintained to the end. Perhaps the figure of Orgoglio *is* somewhere at the back of this:

> An hideous Geant horrible and hye,
> That with his talnesse seemed to threat the skye.
>
> (*F.Q.* I. 7. 8)

But its emergence in this context suggests, if anything, that in his reading of Spenser Marlowe had felt at these lines a fascination not unlike that of Theridamas for Tamburlaine. It is in fact this incorporating of 'Vice' characteristics into the hero-figure that constitutes the whole challenge:

> View but his picture in this tragicke glasse,
> And then applaude his fortunes as you please.   (7–8)

The challenge is to accept the verdict of the debate: that in spite of all things Tamburlaine is still the pride of earth's fruit and the choicest living fire of heaven:

> Let earth and heauen his timelesse death deplore,
> For both their woorths wil equall him no more. (4646–7)

Those lines are spoken by one of Tamburlaine's sons, but placed as they are as the last words in the tragedy they have the weight and authority accorded (in *Faustus* for instance) to the chorus.

In a footnote, Professor Battenhouse makes a concession: 'it is altogether conceivable', he thinks, 'that Marlowe was in some very subtle sense—as Blake claims of Milton—of the devil's party without knowing it'. From this I would infer (for the point is not expanded) that the attractive side of Tamburlaine, his heroism perhaps or the fine lines he is given to speak, did, after all, 'get out of hand', and so threatens the basic morality. Battenhouse goes on to defend Marlowe against any charge of hypocrisy, but the admission is more damaging than he seems to realise. He has been presenting *Tamburlaine* as essentially a moral or didactic drama. If the fulfilment of its moral intention is undermined from within in this way, then the artistic success of such a drama must also be in jeopardy. Its author has committed himself to a task for which he has no real capacity. He is inwardly given over to an evil, the vitality of which overwhelms everything else on the stage, for goodness or opposition to the evil has indisputably far less life. The vigour, the real creative sympathy, goes into the protagonist and the presentation of the world he stands for. This state of affairs has been thought to affect the success of *Paradise Lost*. But, supposing this to be true about *Paradise Lost*, it remains only a (serious) 'particular fault'. If it is true of *Tamburlaine* the whole substance takes corruption from it, for in such a play the failure to create the protagonist according to the moral intention would be fatal. For the century (or centuries) of what Battenhouse would call misreading, the author, and not merely the readers' ill-informed romanticism, would then have to take responsibility.

Not merely the weighing of men, however, but also the relative dramatic status accorded to their views of life, goes to define the moral attitude of the play. Nature is seen predominantly as a disruptive force. Cosroe and his men stand as traditionalists with a feeling that they are supported by a basically stable and beneficent nature:

> . . . we all haue suckt one wholsome aire
> And with the same proportion of Elements . . . (836-7)

This stability and wholeness contrast with the ambiguity and disruptiveness of their opponents. But those qualities are the very ones which Tamburlaine proclaims as philosophically natural. He takes up the term 'Elements' in the famous lines:

> Nature that fram'd vs of foure Elements,
> Warring within our breasts for regiment,
> Doth teach vs all to haue aspiring minds. (869-71)

Where Cosroe had assumed a harmonious nature with the elements in just proportion, Tamburlaine sees as reality a disruptive nature, making the elements war within the breast. To him, strife is the law of a nature which works by competition, the weak succumbing, the strong surviving, as the 'doting father' had to give way in mythological evolution to Jove. 'The restles Spheares' are of this Nature, and this same Nature made man's mind to follow the same laws. The claim here, then, is that Tamburlaine is in accord with nature, itself warring, restless and amoral. Moreover, the claim is placed as an answer to the traditional conception, voiced by Cosroe, of a good and ordered nature: and to this answer no counter argument is ever offered.

Similarly, the nature of God is a recurrent subject. The Christian God of mercy, love and self-sacrifice is never posited: no effective divinity competes with the only one Tamburlaine himself will acknowledge:

> There is a God full of reuenging wrath,
> From whom the thunder and the lightning breaks,
> Whose Scourge I am, and him will I obey.   (4294–6)

This is the God who made the disruptive Nature of which Tamburlaine is a triumphant part. Moral apologists for Marlowe stress the role of Tamburlaine, important to Elizabethans, as God's scourge; but it is a terrible Old Testament Yahweh and no Christian God who punishes the earth in this way, a God whose spirit and ethics differ little from those of the tyrant his worshippers are supposed to find so satanic. And when the Scourge is himself punished in the last act, it is again by a God 'full of reuenging wrath': Tamburlaine's theology and natural philosophy only receive confirmation. 'The God that sits in heauen, if any God' (4312) is moved, not by the cries of suffering humanity (the cause of the suffering has indeed had his sanction), but by the indignity of having one thumb his nose and burn the holy books.

With a warring, amoral Nature and a jealous God of power and blood, Tamburlaine's aspirations emerge as a harmonious part in the order of the universe, transcending in their vitality every other thing:

> . . . shall we wish for ought
> The world affoords in greatest noueltie,
> And rest attemplesse faint and destitute? (777-9)

The rhetorical question accepts the challenge to manhood thrown down by a world rich in potentiality. If a man can 'ride in triumph through *Persepolis*' and does not, he is so much less the man. Power and success will make him so much more the man: for with power, 'looks breed love . . . Such power attractiue shines in princes eies'. The enthusiasm of the maxim 'A God is not so glorious as a King' is reiterated in the climax to the speech 'Nature that fram'd vs of foure Elements', where the essential creed is stated:

> . . . the ripest fruit of all,
> That perfect blisse and sole felicitie,
> The sweet fruition of an earthly crowne (878-80)

This last line has sometimes been seen as bathetic, revealing either Marlowe's critical detachment from Tamburlaine or the failure of his vision to achieve a fitting climax to a noble speech. But the crown was a more imposing symbol in Tudor times than it is today, and to Tamburlaine it is the symbol of absolute power, the reward of aspiration, the climb after knowledge. Aspiration and knowledge are no use without power, and the crown represents it, the greatest a man can obtain. Within Tamburlaine's philosophy (and I have argued that this is still the dominant spirit of the play) the crown is the essential symbol: the means to all desirable ends.

That Tamburlaine's philosophy and the dominant spirit of the play are one is further borne out when one considers how scornfully opposing ideas and forces are so often treated. As Tamburlaine glorifies war, and as his Nature and God are both militarist forces, so any Christian sentiment in favour of peace is presented in such a way as to incur its destruction in derision. I suppose that in this militarist play the lines most likely, by their sentiments, to appeal to us today are these:

> Accurst be he that first inuented war,
> They knew not, ah, they knew not simple men,
> How those were hit by pelting Cannon shot,
> Stand staggering like a quiuering Aspen leafe,
> Fearing the force of *Boreas* boistrous blasts. (664–8)

The lines are spoken by the fool Mycetes. He is trying to hide his crown, and if the audience is not laughing at the mere sight of him (as in the earlier scenes they have been trained to), they laugh immediately after this passage at his remark:

> In what a lamentable case were I,
> If Nature had not giuen me wisedomes lore? (669–70)

The moral, humanitarian feelings are discredited as weak, effeminate, cowardly and foolish. The vividness of his picture of those hit, staggering in the last moments of their life, is weakened by the 'poetic' simile; but it is sufficiently realistic to make the levity of its context a callous outrage to any decent feeling. But it is none the less within 'the dominant spirit of the play' for that.

Mycetes' lines about warfare are echoed in Part 2:

> I know sir, what it is to kil a man,
> It works remorse of conscience in me,
> I take no pleasure to be murtherous,
> Nor care for blood when wine wil quench my thirst. (3700–3)

This passage too might command moral support and tell against Tamburlaine and his world of 'revenge, war, death and cruelty'. But in Part 2 as in Part 1, the most potentially just and effective comment on his world is given to the most despicable character. It is spoken by the wretched Calyphas and carries no weight whatsoever. Or rather, as with Mycetes, the effect is positively to discredit the Christian, peaceloving, conscientious values which it seems to be upholding. And, of course, it does only 'seem', for Calyphas himself is an immoralist, given to cards and lechery, perfectly prepared to 'kil a man' as long as the conditions are auspicious:

> If any man will hold him, I will strike,
> And cleaue him to the channell with my sword.
>
> (2671–2)

He is admittedly given a tongue smart enough to score against his hearty brothers:

> Away ye fools, my father needs not me,
> Nor you in faith, but that you wil be thought
> More childish valorous than manly wise. (3688–90)

The acid satirist is there also in his dismissal of these two conformists:

> Goe, goe tall stripling, fight you for vs both,
> And take my other toward brother here,
> For person like to prooue a second *Mars*,
> Twill please my mind as wel to heare both you
> Haue won a heape of honor in the field,
> And left your slender carkasses behind,
> As if I lay with you for company.
> *Amyras.* You wil not goe then?
> *Calyphas.* You say true. (3706–14)

But this laugh in his favour stands alone; for the rest he is presented as a dishonour to manhood. Moreover, the sophisticated irony of these speeches defines the tone for the lines about 'remorse of conscience', though the humorously opportunist turn given with 'Nor care for blood when wine wil quench my thirst' makes it clear enough in any case. The point is worth making at this length because the passage has, I think, been misinterpreted. Paul Kocher writes of Calyphas in Act IV: 'He even repeats some of the ideas which made him ridiculous before. But the trouble is that now they are given much too lengthy, vivid and unanswered expression. To the attentive spectator it must sound like a satire on all the basic themes of the play.' And he concludes: 'In the Calyphas scene his [i.e. Marlowe's] outraged sense of proportion took its revenge through mockery.' The satirist is himself, however, the object of most of the satire. His pacifism is only weakness: in his mouth the saying 'it works remorse of conscience in me' is ludicrous and hypocritical. His brothers 'goe into the field', and as for him—'Ile to cardes' and thoughts of 'a naked Lady in a net of golde'. Vengeance falls terribly upon this witty degenerate, and he is buried by harlots as befits his effeminate lechery. So much for 'remorse of conscience'.

The only character who at all effectively opposes Tamburlaine's morality is Zenocrate. Her pity for Bajazeth and Zabina, her pleading with Tamburlaine to show mercy to her people, her wish when she is seen in Part 2 with her family that he should leave 'the dangerous chances of wrathfull war', the humility and religious calm of her death, are all admirable and appeal to a nature and a view of life very unlike Tamburlaine's. But, although she is given far more dramatic status than any other representative of the opposition, the emphasis is still upon her womanliness. And this is all part of the Fascist outlook: 'conscience and tendre herte' are endearing and suitable in women but a dishonour to manliness. Tamburlaine's sons 'looke on their mothers face' and, he fears, their looks are

> ... amorous,
> Not martiall as the sons of *Tamburlaine*.   (2590–91)

Calyphas, the coward, is essentially the mother's boy:

> But while my brothers follow armes my lord
> Let me accompany my gratious mother.   (2634–5)

In these ways, the peaceableness and tenderness of Zenocrate are 'placed': and the placing involves a cynical belittlement of women, found also in *Hero*, *Edward* and *Dido*—it is a Marlovian characteristic.

A contempt for peace as effeminate is expressed by Tamburlaine in this same scene, and what he says receives no answer in the play. He fears that his sons may be milksops,

> ...too dainty for the wars.
> Their fingers made to quauer on a Lute,
> Their armes to hang about a Ladies necke:
> Their legs to dance and caper in the aire.   (2597–2600)

This is the tone of Shakespeare's Gloucester, disdainful of 'this weake piping time of Peace'. The difference is that Gloucester is 'determined to proue a Villaine', and Tamburlaine is not: there is no doubt that, for all his vitality, Richard III is seen as evil, whereas, for the most part, in *Tamburlaine* evil has become, dramatically, good. Tamburlaine's concept of peace as decadent is never challenged, whereas the whole force of Shakespeare's histories is to make us see war as an evil, involving, for its success, at best a Henry V or more probably a Coriolanus.

The Fascist spirit extends beyond this mere upholding of martial manliness as against peaceloving effeminacy. The graces of peace and civilisation are despised, held as poor things by comparison with the excitements of fighting and barbarism. After the defeat of Bajazeth, for instance, the

captive king and queen are brought in to entertain the
victors (I. 4. 4) 'Dooth not the Turke and his wife make a
goodly showe at a banquet?' asks Tamburlaine. Zenocrate
replies 'Yes, my Lord', and Theridamas adds 'Me thinks,
tis a great deale better than a consort of musicke'. Now it is
possible that the lame affirmative and the flagrant reversal
of civilised values implied by Theridamas' speech are
Marlowe's way of criticising Tamburlaine; and, whatever
the intention, they may be said to have that effect in the
debate. For what we have seen is extremely brutal and the
exact reverse of the harmony and sweetness of 'a consort
of musicke'. There has been baiting, cursing, stamping,
flinging food to the ground. The violence and distasteful-
ness of the scene are the more marked in that they take
place at a banquet where orderly ceremony should prevail:
this is a violation of everything civilised. The appeal is an
appalling one. Nevertheless, it is an appeal: to those forces
which make us bully, attract us towards the infliction of
pain and discomfort upon others, make us want to kick
over the traces and break things—in fact, to the evil and
disruptive within our nature which civilisation can normally
discipline or refine; and, in Marlowe's presentation it is this
appeal which is uppermost. The last part of the scene
shows Tamburlaine with dignity unimpaired, speaking
nobly and looking forward to still further good fortune:
the fun of Bajazeth-baiting seems to be placed as amongst
the fruits of success.

If that is so, it may be as well to recall just how sadistic
this baiting is. The savage excitement rises as Tamburlaine
offers Bajazeth food from his sword: 'here, eat sir, take it
from my swords point, or Ile thrust it to thy heart'.
Bajazeth does take it but stamps on it.

Tamb. Take it vp Villaine, and eat it, or I will make thee slice
the brawnes of thy armes into carbonadoes, and eat them.

Usumcasane. Nay, twere better he kild his wife, & then she shall
be sure not to be staru'd, & he be prouided for a moneths
victuall before hand.

Tamb. Here is my dagger, dispatch her while she is fat, for if she
liue but a while longer, shee will fall into a consumption with
freatting, & then she will not be woorth the eating.

(1681-90)

The expert cruelty of these lines is very recognisably one
with so much more in Marlowe. With the brutality of
detail, for instance, in Aeneas' tale of Troy: the Pyrrhus
who raises up Priam and Hecuba at his falchion's point,
strikes off the old man's hands, while the soldiers swing the
Queen by her heels howling. It comes from the same mind
which shows us Edward II forcibly shaved, washed in
puddle water, thrown his meat like a dog and killed with
obscene and ingenious brutality; or which, less violently
but still unpleasantly, presents with amusement the spectacle of Hero wriggling like a fish on a hook, caught by a
love which is 'deaffe and cruel, where he meanes to pray'.
Elizabethan drama is full of violence and cruelty, but these
are examples of an individual and particularly nasty kind.
It is clear that, whether in pleasure or repulsion, Marlowe
was attracted to cruelty; and here in *Tamburlaine*, although
the mind is divided, the division is unequal and the larger
part seems to rate violence and cruelty as among the
enviable excitements of life.

This same attraction is felt in the scene where Tamburlaine rejects the pleas of the virgins of Damascus. The
First Virgin speaks eloquently and Tamburlaine replies
with a wonderfully vivid image and fine dramatic effect:

Behold my sword, what see you at the point?
Virgin. Nothing but feare and fatall steele my Lord.
Tamb. Your fearfull minds are thicke and mistie then,
For there sits Death, there sits imperious Death,
Keeping his circuit by the slicing edge.

But I am pleasde you shall not see him there,
He now is seated on my horsmens speares:
And on their points his fleshlesse bodie feedes.
Techelles, straight goe charge a few of them
To chardge these Dames, and shew my seruant death,
Sitting in scarlet on their armed speares.
Omnes. O pitie vs.
Tamb. Away with them I say and shew them death.

(1889–1901)

The personification makes a grim joke. So does the ordering of the manner of their killing: 'charge a few of them to chardge these Dames'; and there is something almost obscene in the reiterated 'shew them death'. Later, Zenocrate describes the slaughter with pity and horror:

Thy streetes strowed with disseuered iointes of men,
And wounded bodies gasping yet for life.
. . . the Sun-bright troope
Of heauenly vyrgins . . .
On horsmens Lances to be hoisted vp.   (2104–10)

Very typically Marlovian is the humiliating, undignified brand of violence in the 'hoisted vp'. Yet it is this scene that contains the most tender and beautiful of Tamburlaine's speeches to Zenocrate, including the famous passage 'What is beauty saith my sufferings then?' with its conclusion: 'That Vertue solely is the sum of glorie'. It begins with him 'all in blacke, and verie melancholy', the reluctant murderer:

What, are the Turtles fraide out of their neastes?
Alas poore fooles, must you be first . . .   (1845–6)

He parades a sort of righteous sorrow, marvellously shifting the moral responsibility for the massacre from himself to the Governor who should have surrendered the town on the first day, when 'sweet mercie' shone through the milk-white flag. This refined sensibility together with firmness of purpose are presumably supposed to constitute the 'Vertue' of which he speaks. But 'sweet mercie' is a touching phrase to come from the man who with harsh humour sends the women off to their death and who, before being in his melancholy mood, had relished the dreadful anti-cipations of the Damascans ('While they walke quiuering on their citie walles, Halfe dead for feare before they feele my wrath'). And there is no evidence that Marlowe sees it with any critical sense; he is simply augmenting Tamburlaine's heroic prestige, loading him with the best from all worlds. He is allowed a similarly endearing absurdity in the last lines of the scene (which is also the last in the play). The bodies of Bajazeth and Zabina are still on the stage and Tamburlaine promises honourable burial to 'this great Turke and his faire Emperesse'. That he should honour the bodies of those whom he persecuted and humiliated so cruelly in life is no doubt better than dishonouring them but is still grossly sentimental and sanctimonious (for there is no question of repentance or pity). But this is the climax of Tamburlaine's fortunes in Part 1 and he is at the height of his glory. He gives scarlet robes and. 'royall places of estate' to his followers, spares the Soldan's life, marries Zenocrate and 'takes truce with al the world'. He has taught a lesson to those who 'presume to manage armes with him'. Again there is an utter disregard of any possible moral criticism—a typical trick of words or crookedness of thought throws any possible blame on to the others. The magnanimity, magnificence and magniloquence are dazzling, and the assumption of righteousness can appear less monstrous than it is only because of the stardust in the eyes of author and audience alike.

So far, this discussion of *Tamburlaine* has treated the play as 'an object of interest', with its moral attitude as the centre of inquiry. But the essential dramatic and poetic effect is not covered by an adjective like 'interesting', and modern criticism has tended to proceed as if it were. The verse is more imaginative, even subtle, and the dramatic technique more varied and masterly than has commonly been allowed. Acts I and II are constructed to form something like a symphonic first movement, and with these scenes I shall try to illustrate in more detail the play's quality.

Most readers find the Prologue memorable and there are many good reasons why this should be so:

> From iygging vaines of riming mother wits,
> And such conceits as clownage keepes in pay,
> Weele lead you to the stately tent of War,
> Where you shall heare the Scythian *Tamburlaine*
> Threatning the world with high astounding tearms
> And scourging kingdoms with his conquering sword.
> View but his picture in this tragicke glasse,
> And then applaud his fortunes as you please.   (1–8)

These tones chase one another through the eight lines: contempt, brag, pride, nobility, enthusiasm sweeping and then checked, measured solemnity, pugnacious and defiant courtliness. Statement becomes direct address through the imperative. The lines contain aggressive dramatic criticism and the promise of a new programme; also statement of theme, introduction to story and directions to audience. It is restless, energetic verse, with pride as the unifying factor (there is none of the charm of the *Henry V* Prologue, where there would be every excuse for a similar flourish). It is like a drum roll, growing and having its climax in the sweep and run-on of lines four, five and six. The fine contemptuous force in the mincing vowels of 'jigging . . . wits' contrasts with the open strength and finality of 'War' which is the goal, or the pole furthest from this despised 'clownage'. The brag is emphasised by an accent on 'weele'; and the final phrase, 'as you please', comes with an unlooked-for, defiant, aggressively cavalier swirl of the actor's cloak.

The first scene shows Mycetes, the ludicrously weak King of Persia, with his much more capable brother Cosroe. The realm is threatened by Turks and Tartars, who are taking advantage of the king's weakness, and by a 'sturdie Scythian thiefe' called Tamburlaine. Mycetes' first speech is, I take it, an early throw-up of Marlovian farce:

> Brother *Cosroe*, I find my selfe agreeu'd,
> Yet insufficient to expresse the same:
> For it requires a great and thundring speech:
> Good brother tell the cause vnto my Lords,
> I know you haue a better wit then I. (9–13)

He is made to speak in the first person lines which are more conceivable as a savage mimic's satire. His 'insufficiency' is the antithesis of Tamburlaine's fullness. By presenting him first, Marlowe defines the base of a pyramid of which Tamburlaine will be the apex. Mycetes is treated with contempt and is a shame to mankind: in him the species is humiliated by the un-Tamburlainian within it. Human nobility or promise rises from Mycetes through Meander, Cosroe, Ortigius and Theridamas, to Tamburlaine. The move from Mycetes to Tamburlaine involves a typical Marlovian extreme: it is the move, sketched in the Prologue, from Clownage to the Stately Tent of War.

The scene presents a decadence which Tamburlaine comes to redeem:

> The warlike Souldiers, & the Gentlemen . . .
> Now liuing idle in the walled townes,
> Wanting both pay and martiall discipline,
> Begin in troopes to threaten ciuill warre. (148–56)

They will be given plenty to do under Tamburlaine's military dictatorship. Uppermost in the scene is the sense of indignity. The Persian crown is scorned, and to Cosroe the position is intolerable (as, with less dignity, the younger Mortimer passionately resents the slights put upon the nobility by Edward and Gaveston):

> But this it is that doth excruciate
> The verie substance of my vexed soule:
> To see our neighbours that were woont to quake
> And tremble at the Persean Monarkes name,
> Now sits and laughs our regiment to scorne. (121–5)

There is a movement afoot to dispossess Mycetes and later in the scene Cosroe is offered the crown. One of the effects of all this is to show Tamburlaine as superman coming to supply the realised need for some power that can sweep away petulant weakness, political intrigue and politic double-talk; all pettiness gives way before his nobility, and through him men can realise what lies within them (Theridamas shall have 'the leading of . . . an host'). There is a sure dramatic instinct in Marlowe's making these points by contrast, and in his initial presentation of Tamburlaine commanding admiration not through battle, but through a double wooing: of woman and man. He wooes Zenocrate and Theridamas and wins them, and through them, us.

His first appearance brings a sense of sureness, power and grace which is new to the play. Yet the power is also felt as a disturbing thing, at one with a turbulent Nature:

> . . . these that seeme but silly country Swaines,
> May haue the leading of so great an host
> As with their waight shall make the mountains quake,
> Euen as when windy exhalations,
> Fighting for passage, tilt within the earth. (243–7)

There is a sense of pent-up force working underground, something as yet unrecognised disturbing the sure and firm-set earth: an energy latent in nature, now to break out, reflected in a social upheaval and embodied in an individual. The immediate dramatic effect is to sweep Zenocrate off her feet, as he supports with 'great and thundring speech' the hypnotic 'must' of:

> . . . this faire face and heauenly hew
> Must grace his bed that conquers *Asia*:
> And meanes to be a terrour to the world.   (232–4)

Techelles and Usumcasane act as a chorus backing Tamburlaine's speeches. Agydas, a Lord attendant on Zenocrate, tries to treat with him:

> Returne our Mules and emptie Camels backe,
> That we may traueile into *Siria*.   (272–3)

But this is dealing in petty matters and Tamburlaine ignores him, addressing himself only to Zenocrate, talking in terms of 'all the Gold in *Indias* welthy armes' and giving a splendid exhibition of the 'high astounding tearm' throughout.

Marlowe establishes Tamburlaine partly by building up a sort of human pyramid, partly by his own speeches and behaviour, and partly by the often-noted geographical references in the verse. In the opening of the play we have Persea, Affrike, Europe, Persepolis, Asia, Scythia, Easterne India and a comprehensive catalogue in the speech where Ortygius offers the crown to Cosroe. The references are also racial: Turkes and Tartars, Babylonians, Affrike captaines, and so forth. Also cosmic: the Sun, Cynthia, Saturne, meteors, Plantes, the Moon. That is the backcloth, but it is also the whole stuff of creation and Tamburlaine is to command it. His superiority to it, fully recognised by himself, is there in his wooing of Zenocrate. The speech

contains vast promises of worldly magnificence and cul-
minates in a dedication:

> Shall all we offer to *Zenocrate*,
> And then my selfe to faire *Zenocrate*.   (300–301)

The great man comes last and first, as nature's masterpiece.

Act Two begins with a eulogy of Tamburlaine by
Menaphon, one of Cosroe's lords. The effect is again choric:
it helps to shape the audience's attitude, and though
Professor Battenhouse argues that the mention of pallor and
fiery eyes would signify to Elizabethans the most dangerous
form of choleric humour, the impact of the speech is overwhelmingly to increase enthusiasm. These eyes, 'fiery
cyrcles', have also 'a heauen of heauenly bodies in their
Spheares'. This is typical, in that the whole portrait is
larger than life and is within this proud humanistic tradition
where man is the crown of all things: the head 'a pearle
more worth, then all the world'. There is also the usual
pleasure in male beauty:

> . . . a knot of Amber heire,
> Wrapped in curles, as fierce *Achilles* was,
> On which the breath of heauen delights to play,
> Making it daunce with wanton maiestie.   (477–80)

The climax of the speech points to the future. The being
described is

> In euery part proportioned like the man,
> Should make the world subdued to *Tamburlaine*. (483–4)

To point forward in this way is the other main function
of the scene. Cosroe sums up what Menaphon has said
(and what Marlowe has, in any case, shown):

> Wel hast thou pourtraid in thy tearms of life,
> The face and personage of a woondrous man:
> Nature doth striue with Fortune and his stars
> To make him famous in accomplisht woorth.   (485–8)

Tamburlaine's worth is not yet 'accomplisht' in the sense that it is not yet expressed, revealed through action. It is still in effect a potential. The play is to show the 'accomplishing' of the worth: that worth which is made by Nature and furthered by Fortune—in other words, backed by a world-spirit (for Nature and Fortune add up to that). Now the shock of the play is to find that this creature in whom the 'world-spirit' so defined is incarnate, 'accomplishes' his worth in action based on anti-Christian principles. It comes as a deadly shock, later in the play, to the speakers themselves: there is an obvious irony in the prey praising its own killer—that side of Nature 'red in tooth and claw' is fully represented in this 'woondrous man' made famous by Nature. But Cosroe's lines are the summary of what we and Menaphon have seen. In fact, the build-up which these scenes make for Tamburlaine is so powerful and deliberate that however the worth manifests itself, we shall be dramatically impelled to accept it. Only the most open kind of choric denunciation could cancel the status and authority invested in Tamburlaine in these early scenes. If, at the end of the play, our attitude to him is like what Antony says of Cleopatra, 'Would I had neuer seene [him]', the play also compels acceptance of Enobarbus' retort: 'O sir, you had then left vnseene a wonderfull peece of worke . . .'

Cosroe and his lords decide to form an alliance with Tamburlaine to overcome Mycetes; and in their self-congratulations there is a certain cruel irony. Ceneus wonders what the man who has already achieved so much will do now that he has the support of a king; and, of course, the situation is full of hidden menace to themselves. It is notable that Ceneus imputes a motive of righteousness to Tamburlaine:

> He that with Shepheards and a litle spoile,
> Durst in disdaine of wrong and tyrannie,
> Defend his freedome gainst a Monarchie . . . (508–10)

This may be another example of Marlowe's allowing Tamburlaine not merely his own strength but also, in words if nothing else, the virtues which his career for the most part negates. On the other hand, it may be offered with irony as the sentimentalist's version of Tamburlaine's rise: the speakers themselves will suffer from his own 'wrong and tyrannie'—and, the spirit of it is, the more fools they.

In the remaining scenes, the human pyramid is reviewed. From him that hath not is taken that which he hath, and to Tamburlaine more is added. Mycetes, *in extremis*, naïvely expresses self-pity and impotent, farcical resolution. 'Would it not grieue a King to be so abusde', he asks, the weak word 'grieue' being pathetically insufficient. His later lines ('by heauens I sweare, *Aurora* shall not peepe out of her doores . . .') are a parody of kingly utterance: the poor best that he can manage by way of 'great and thundring speech'. Later Meander speaks for him to his soldiers and the worthy effect of his oratory is thrown away by Mycetes' absurd enthusiasm and petulant patronage. Much higher in the scale of manhood is Cosroe, but his inferiority to Tamburlaine is again betrayed in the contrast between his verbal competence and Tamburlaine's brilliance. Tamburlaine's speech is full of colour, majesty and confidence, coming to its climax in the fine lines:

> And with our Sun-bright armour as we march,
> Weel chase the Stars from heauen, and dim their eies
> That stand and muse at our admyred armes.   (620–22)

A messenger announces the approach of Mycetes' army and the excitement of the moment is caught up in Cosroe's hyperbole:

> Come, *Tamburlain*, now whet thy winged sword
> And lift thy lofty arme into the cloudes.   (649–50)

Tamburlaine's reply sustains the martial exultation:

> See where it is . . .
> These are the wings shall make it flie as swift,
> As dooth the lightening . . .   (654–6)

The war which men are shown as welcoming is now cursed by the wretched Mycetes, who has an alarming personal encounter with Tamburlaine in Scene 4. Extremes meet and there occurs a brief excursion into comedy with Tamburlaine himself involved: the worlds of this and *Edward II*, antithetical plays, come into ludicrous and momentary contact. But Mycetes is not seen again. Cosroe longs, as he says, to sit upon his brother's throne 'and ride in triumph through *Persepolis*'. He leaves Tamburlaine behind to collect the troops, and his last lines contain an ominous ambiguity:

> . . . till thou ouertake me *Tamburlaine* . . .
> Farewell Lord Regent.   (749–51)

Though Cosroe has appointed him to high office, Tamburlaine has established himself beyond question as the greater man:

> Thinke thee inuested now as royally,
> Euen by the mighty hand of *Tamburlaine*.   (708–9)

Cosroe does not enjoy his triumph for long, and it is here that so many of the crucial attitudes already discussed are first voiced. Theridamas' doctrine 'A God is not so glorious as a King' (762) catches again the excitement of the moment; as the words 'ride in triumph through *Persepolis*' echo in Tamburlaine's speech, all these soldiers have their eyes on the future. With Tamburlaine, the greatest of them, to want is to attempt, and not to attempt is weakness. Moreover, the whole adventure will be 'a pretie iest'. It is fun to play cat and mouse with 'this triumphing King', for '[we] only made him King to make vs sport'. It is also treachery, and at this point the debate really begins, the motion being stated by Ortygius:

> What God or Feend . . .
> Whether from earth, or hell, or heauen he grow.
>
> (826–34)

Conventional morality sees the betrayal as infamous and unnatural, nature being benevolent and harmonious. The challenge of both propositions is met in Tamburlaine's first speech in this scene. The conception of nature, as discussed earlier in the present chapter, is countered by another nature, restless and disruptive, and for the remainder the word 'aspire' is taken up to become the cornerstone of this natural morality: the greater the 'presumption', the better nature's lesson has been learnt. Meander's speech, stating what I have called the 'debate-motion', does 'objectify' Tamburlaine: that is, make you look at him from the outside, question, judge and so forth. But it is notable that even those who have most reason to hate him still feel uncertain whether it is not in fact a godlike superhumanity that they have to encounter. Even Cosroe, who speaks fatalistically of 'the lothsome Circle of my dated life', unwittingly imputes to Tamburlaine something which the weight of the play enforces as heroism: he is one

> That thus opposeth him against the Gods,
> And scornes the Powers that gouerne *Persea*. (850–51)

Cosroe is allowed dignity and eloquence in his death, though he dies with a curse which had no effect in Part 1 and is forgotten by Part 2. Tamburlaine in the meantime has ennobled himself by a statement of the philosophy he represents. Instead of flights of angels or any kind word over him, Cosroe is forgotten and there goes up a universal shout of acclamation: 'Tamburlaine, Tamburlaine'. He has the prize which nature gives to the superior; and his

superiority is felt at this point to be one of quality as well
as strength:

> Our soules, whose faculties can comprehend
> The wondrous Architecture of the world:
> And measure euery wandring plannets course,
> Stil climbing after knowledge infinite,
> And alwaies moouing as the restles Spheares,
> Wils vs to weare our selues and neuer rest . . . (872–7)

This is one of the great passages in the play, and when it is
given Tamburlaine at a point where conventional morality
condemns him its effect must be to afford a protection
against the hostility of that morality. He certainly needs no
other kind of protection, for the end of this first movement
brings him the crown, 'the sweet fruition', and he stands
supremely successful, caring nothing for curses, scruples or
conventions, proud and spirited, with a boast that ought
to look like the pride which precedes the fall but is in fact
only the prelude to more success:

> So, now it is more surer on my head,
> Than if the Gods had held a Parliament:
> And all pronounst me king of Persea.   (916–18)

In these scenes, then, a good deal is happening. The construction is deliberate and effective, determined rigorously
by the particular purposes of the drama. Everything tells,
much of the effect being achieved by implicit methods such
as contrast and juxtaposition. Memory is often unjust: one
recalls a string of sensational episodes and concludes that
there is no more 'construction' than that. Similarly, the
rest of the characters are eclipsed by the hero, and the
verse resolves itself into a perpetual martial clang. Obviously, these impressions have their origin, but inattentive
reading and the predigested formulas of not-very-interested
critics have probably contributed. In the two acts reviewed

here, there is considerable depth of interest, pointedness of
construction and suppleness of mood and expression. These
qualities are sustained throughout the plays.

There are, of course, many weaknesses and limitations.
There is still some validity, for instance, in the common
complaint about a lack of form, the episodes, it is said,
being of the same kind and in more or less arbitrary
sequence. However good the construction of individual
sections (as illustrated by these first two acts), there may
still be a lack of overall form. In the two parts of *Henry IV*
many different threads are worked together to make a rich,
varied pattern, each developing its own individuality yet
all interrelating. There is nothing like this in the *Tamburlaine* plays. Episodes such as the Sigismond-Orcanes or
Olympia stories might have been sub-plots but remain
episodes. Is there any reason, one wonders, why the one
should precede or follow the other? And is the taking of
Damascus in Part 1 or Part 2? Or is one thinking of the
taking of Babylon? And does it matter? Surely in a well-
constructed drama it should.

Three aspects of the plays' construction do something to
decrease the weight of these criticisms. One is that a basic
function of this drama is the manipulation of sympathies
for or against the hero, and the form is determined by that.
The climax of Part 1, for instance, occurs when Tamburlaine
is able to emerge triumphant from the hostilities steadily
built up by the tragedies of Bajazeth and Zabina and by
Zenocrate's sorrow and misgivings. At this point the conflict about the assessment of Tamburlaine ('whether from
earth, or hell, or heauen he grow') becomes most intense.
The query which has been posed in the play's first movement is reiterated through the Bajazeth scenes, the scale
magnified. The effect is that the climax in the end is felt
not as a mere success in battle, but as a victory in human

status—the fears, scruples and compassions of Christianity are forgotten, outshone by the power and glory of the man who denies them. This is only to say, perhaps, that the form responds to the particular demands upon it. The episodes play their part in the manipulation of sympathies, and the single plot meets the needs of the drama much as in *Coriolanus*.

The second consideration which should mitigate the charge of formlessness is that the plot effectively exposes development. As the demonstrations magical in the middle part of *Faustus* become more silly and limited and so show progressively the depressing limitations of the world Faustus has entered, so the episodes here show progressively the heights or depths (according to the point of view) of Tamburlaine's career. The victory over Bajazeth is more spectacular than that over Cosroe, just as that is a greater triumph than the defeat of Mycetes. But the most impressive and ruthless of these is less in scope than the victory which harnesses four kings to Tamburlaine's chariot, the grief which burns a whole city to consume it, or the power which drowns the entire population of Babylon in Asphaltis lake. And all these are less than the final *tour de force* in which the mere appearance of Tamburlaine is sufficient to deter a whole army. These scenes, then, show not merely the nature of power and mightiness of concept but also the expansion of them stage by stage and, with or without the author's conscious intention, the hero's progressive abandonment of Christian principles.

A third and minor point is the existence of details which link the two parts or which help to tie up the play into a unity by reference backwards or forwards. Zenocrate's death, for example, recalls her earlier reflections on the deaths of Bajazeth and Zabina. Bajazeth says that if he is victorious he will make Tamburlaine's captains draw

Zabina's chariot, so suggesting Tamburlaine's ultimate extravaganza. This recurs in a later scene (I. 4. 2) where he refers to

> . . . the back of *Baiazeth*
> That should be horsed on fower mightie kings. (1521-2)

At other points Tamburlaine does implicitly recognise that 'the scourge of God must die' and so prepares for the last episodes. Such details will strengthen a play, though they need to be more numerous and noteworthy than they are here.

Another fault, probably affecting the dramatic success more seriously than weaknesses of construction, is Marlowe's failure to render convincingly emotions of grief and despair. One recognises this first at the death of Cosroe:

> An vncouthe paine torments my grieued soule,
> And death arrests the organe of my voice.
> Who entring at the breach thy sword hath made,
> Sackes euery vaine and artier of my heart. (858-61)

These are good lines: the image (the 'fell Sergeant') carries the force of the play's militarist world and there is considerable dignity in spite of the overt pathos. But it is in this overtness that the failure lies.[1] Cosroe states too explicitly what he feels, and it registers as information rather than experience. This is more marked in the soliloquy of Agidas who has realised that Tamburlaine has overheard his disparagements:

> Surpriz'd with feare of hideous reuenge,
> I stand agast. (1053-4)

With his mind's eye, the dramatist has observed his man and has stated the facts to himself: Agidas' condition is that

---

[1] It is perhaps asking too much of Marlowe that at this stage in the development of Elizabethan drama he should be able to avoid such 'overtness'. Clemen's *English Tragedy before Shakespeare* reminds us how deeply conventions were intrenched. But 'historical perspective' does not eliminate the weakness.

he is surprised at being discovered and fearful of revenge. This is then written in the first person instead of the third and there the dramatisation ends. What follows is far too eloquent to be true: a nine-line Dantesque simile in an oddly Miltonic passage with all the time in the world for literary elegance and classical allusion. The speech has effect as an involuntary tribute to the impressiveness of the hero and again reflects Marlowe's real interest. But one is never within Agidas; one never experiences his terrors but is merely told about them by him. 'He who can say exactly how he burns is in no great fire,' says an Italian proverb, and the explicitness of statement does in fact belie its own truth.

In Part 2 the death speech of the Captain is another attempt to make explicit the pains which no one suffering them will describe. The lines themselves are good, as are those of Olympia's complaint, a fine passage but for the basic falsehood of its being there at all. Similarly Tamburlaine's grief over the dying Zenocrate attains limited pathos simply because the lament is so articulate. Given that, the speech is magnificent, with its passionate sense of beauty and the mournful ritual of the refrain; far more moving than the rant following Zenocrate's death. There the fault is part of the same general failure to dramatise grief. The verse strives for still more and more astounding conceits where one would be moved far more by restraint.

> . . . *Techelles*, draw thy sword,
> And wound the earth . . .
> Batter the shining pallace of the Sun,
> And shiuer all the starry firmament.
>
> (3064–5, 3073–4)

Tamburlaine's reaction is understandable, seeking in violent activity an outlet for the impotency of his suffering. The straining of language is probably inevitable where great

events are to call forth mighty speech. But Marlowe seems
to feel that 'the breaking of so great a thing should make
a greater crack', and there is this attempt to feel a grief in
a way that people think they should but in fact most
often do not. Perhaps Marlowe is more objective in his
characterisation here than these criticisms imply. Certainly
the division, or debate element, comes into play with the
sensible words of Theridamas:

> Ah good my Lord, be patient, she is dead,
> And all this raging cannot make her liue . . .
> Nothing preuailes, for she is dead my lord.
> *Tamb.* For she is dead? thy words doo pierce my soule.
>
> (3087–8, 3091–2)

Theridamas also finds the right word:

> . . . our murthered harts haue straind forth blood. (3091)

It is the straining that one is so much aware of: the will to
achieve an emotion not truly experienced. Whether one
sees this as a failure in Marlowe or in Tamburlaine depends
on many of the more general problems already discussed.
On the one hand, it is true that the ranting destructiveness
contrasts very unfavourably with the self-possession and
dignity of Zenocrate and with the moderation of Theridamas. On the other, the eloquence, the high resolve, and
the immensity of devotion as measured by its monument in
the burnt town, all seem meant to tell for Tamburlaine.
And the instances elsewhere in these plays of failure to
dramatise grief and despair only point to the limitations
being Marlowe's own and not those of an objectively drawn
character.

This account of the plays' failures and limitations is not
yet complete. Sometimes Marlowe writes in an alien style
borrowed for the occasion from English Seneca. So that in
Bajazeth's curses (I. 5. 2) the ingredients include ghosts,
howling groans, ugly Ferryman, Stygian snakes, and so

forth. It is notable how the quality improves in his last speech (the prayer beginning 'O highest Lamp of everliuing *Ioue*') which is made of the characteristic stuff of the play, with its images of sun, earth, night and thunder. Zabina's discovery and mad-scene follow and neither can be called successful. The prose allows freedom and there are some imaginative touches. The nightmare world of Tamburlaine's tyranny is evoked in 'Streamers white, Red, blacke, here . . .', but the potential horror of distortion in a mad vision is never realised, and the scene affects one as being chiefly and rather cheaply sensational. So is much else: the shooting of the Governor of Babylon, the king-drawn chariot, the caged Bajazeth. These scenes do something to enact the hyperbole which is the basic figure of speech, but there are many occasions where the spoken or enacted hyperbole comes so near to farce that a normal sense of humour would have restrained it.

The charge most commonly levelled against *Tamburlaine* however, is that it is monotonous in its language. The lines by Sir William Watson represent the feeling well enough:

> Your Marlowe's page I close, my Shakespeare's ope:
> How welcome, after gong and cymbals' din,
> The continuity, the long slow slope
> And vast curves of the gradual violin.

The poet was closing his Marlowe after reading in *Tamburlaine*, and there the 'din' is certainly loudest. He might be thinking of Part 1 at the point where the Soldan enters trumpeting at 'three or four Lords':

> Awake ye men of *Memphis*, heare the clange
> Of Scythian trumpets, heare the Basiliskes,
> That roaring, shake *Damascus* turrets downe. (1372–4)

Or of Part 2 where Orcanes, Trebisond and the rest number their forces with twenty proper names resounding through as many lines. In both plays the immensity and hyperbole have by this time begun to cloy. The astounding term has become the expected mode, defeating its own purpose. The reasonable tone of Zenocrate's speeches, the plea of the Damascan virgins, the more tender utterances of Tamburlaine himself, are distinct relief.

Nevertheless the relief comes, and there is far more flexibility and variety than is usually acknowledged. 'Gong and cymbals' din', in any case, implies only half the truth. The proper names and violent tone do make for a percussive style, but the ample blank-verse line, the sentence often rolling on over five or six lines, the sustained eloquence often aria-like, all counteract this. 'Continuity' and 'long slow slope' are in fact terms which might well grace a poetic eulogy of the plays. But it is easy enough in reading to miss points which the actor's voice or producer's hand can bring to life. The heroic tone of aggressive, high-pitched declamation is what memory retains as the norm, but there are many deviations from it. Sometimes it is a matter of short, incidental remarks which break the lyrical or heroic flow; sometimes a colloquial tone lightening the weight of overmuch 'mighty line'. An example of this occurs in the second scene, where Tamburlaine's aria to Zenocrate is followed by an off-hand, jocular comment from his follower Techelles: 'What now? In loue?' This is after the superb climax, 'And then my selfe to fair *Zenocrate*'. In unimaginative reading or inept production it is likely to register simply as an anti-climax, an example of Marlowe's dramatic immaturity. Then critical heads can shake, as they do in *Dido* over 'Gentle *Achates*, reach the Tinder boxe', and give themselves to thinking up a bright way of talking about the sublime and the ridiculous. But this flexibility, even the suddenness with which the tone changes, is one of the exciting things about

Marlowe, and what in fact we have here is a welcome step from the pedestal to the ground, from set-piece oratory (deserved by the occasion) to colloquial pleasantry. On the stage it could be performed so as to have this effect. At the end of Tamburlaine's speech, Zenocrate's silence must be held as Tamburlaine steps back towards his followers. He is amongst his men and the joke is a natural one. As is the reply:

> Techelles, women must be flatered.
> But this is she with whom I am in loue. (303–4)

Even there the suppleness is notable. The first line answers Techelles in his own tone, but knowingly, man to man, with a light implication of male superiority. The second line is sincere and dignified, wards off cynicism and returns the scene gracefully to its serious level.

At several points, a rough colloquial touch keeps the play, for all its romance and extremism, close to reality. In the banquet scene (I. 4. 4), after the ceremonial drinking to 'the God of war' and the fierce taunting of the caged king, Tamburlaine calls out with a sort of grim heartiness,

> Wel Zenocrate
> Techelles, and the rest, fall to your victuals. (1652–3)

This in turn is succeeded by the sustained Thersites-like imprecations of Bajazeth, and throughout the scene there is a play-off between unpoetic, colloquial roughness and lofty and intense rhetoric.

One final example, again on a small scale. Theridamas challenges Olympia's husband, the Captain.

> *Captain.* What requier you my maisters?
> *Therid.* Captaine, that thou yeeld vp thy hold to vs.
> *Captain.* To you? Why, do you thinke me weary of it?
> *Therid.* Nay Captain, thou art weary of thy life,
>   If thou withstand the friends of *Tamburlain*. (3363–7)

This is the kind of give and take in dialogue which is to be developed in *Edward II*. Here it is quite incidental, but it and its kind do much to free *Tamburlaine* from what might otherwise be a sort of Cornelian operatic staginess.

Incidental comedy[1] relieves the dramatic seriousness rather as the colloquial tone relieves the thundering and mighty speech. The play begins with laughter. This is directed against the political clownage of Mycetes: laughter in Marlowe is always a savage thing, always at somebody's expense. P. H. Kocher[2] says about Marlowe's humour: 'It is saturated with pride of power, pride of intellect. In varying degrees it is hostile, stinging, or callous, but it always revolves in the orbit of scorn. It is never gay, never kind.' The first scene illustrates this well; even the first lines.

> *Mycetes.* Brother *Cosroe*, I find my selfe agreeu'd,
>   Yet insufficient to expresse the same.   (9–10)

The expression and its placing are like the music hall comedian's blank-faced announcement, 'I'm not well': except that Mr Muddlecombe provoked a kind of derisive sympathy, and this, spoken from the throne, provokes only scorn. Mycetes' essays in kingly speech are given with this characteristic pleasure in ludicrous spectacle:

> Yet liue, yea, liue, *Mycetes* wils it so.   (35)

The regal verb, absurd in that line, does of course suit Tamburlaine, who uses it with exuberant confidence:

> Wel said *Theridamas*, speake in that mood,
>   For Wil and Shall best fitteth *Tamburlain*.   (1138–9)

---

[1] The original version probably contained more comedy. Robert Jones, the printer, writes in his introduction (1590): 'I haue (purposely) omitted and left out some fond and friuolous Iestures, digressing (and in my poore opinion) far vnmeet for the matter, which I thought, might seeme more tedious vnto the wise, than any way els to be regarded, though (happily) they haue bene of some vaine conceited fondlings greatly gaped at, what times they were shewed vpon the stage in their graced deformities, neuertheles now, to be mixtured in print with such matter of worth, it wuld prooue a great disgrace to so honorable & stately a historie'.

[2] *Op. cit.*, p. 277.

But the wretched Mycetes, with all the uneasy vanity of weakness, looking around for a little support, must ask 'Is it not a kingly resolution?' He receives the answer, ironic and scornful, 'It cannot chose, because it comes from you' (63–5). Later when Cosroe censures him openly, Mycetes acts like an outraged Dogberry:

> Vnlesse they haue a wiser king than you?
> These are his words, *Meander* set them downe. (101–2)

Cosroe adds more unwelcome truths and as Mycetes' indignation increases so does the comic relish for the absurdity of his discomfiture:

> *Mycetes.* Well here I sweare by this my royal seat——
> *Cosroe.* You may doe well to kisse it then.
> *Mycetes.* . . . Monster of Nature, shame vnto thy stocke
> That dar'st presume thy Soueraigne for to mocke.
> *Meander* come, I am abus'd *Meander*. (105–14)

The last line offers the actor a tone somewhere between pouting child and outraged dowager. The preceding couplet is in the despised vein of rhyming mother wits. Mycetes often speaks in rhyme: perhaps this is characterisation and dramatic criticism in one—Mycetes and the rhymsters being a well-matched association.

The next opportunity for the humour of discomfiture is provided by Bajazeth. He appears in great pomp (I. 3) and speaks with the ludicrous boastfulness of the Duke of Austria in Shakespeare's *King John*. He is, he says, 'the high and highest Monarke of the world'. The pomposity of speech conditions one to relish his downfall, which is all the funnier and baser because of this brag and pride. His world of gross flattery and complacency is another decadence which Tamburlaine comes like a clean wind to sweep away:

> *Argier.* . . . all flesh quakes at your magnificence.
> *Bajazeth.* True (*Argier*) and tremble at my lookes. (966–7)

He is complacent too about his other enemies, the Greeks. At the end of Scene 2 he plans to have them nicely bottled up:

> Batter the walles, and we will enter in:
> And then the Grecians shall be conquered.   (984–5)

The neatness of the lines matches the confidence and power of his war-machine. But this fat yet formidable complacency is heading for a fall, and when Tamburlaine mocks the captive Emperor we have already been trained in spirit to do so too.

In Part 2 humour comes more kindly with the introduction of Almeda, Callapine's gaoler. The dialogue in his first scene (2, I. 3) unfreezes the officialdom of speech so far. Almeda is presumably a comedian's part: he sometimes speaks in prose, has a recognisable character and may well have been one of the clowns in the scenes 'omitted and left out' by Jones. Even here the comedy has its hard side, for Almeda is tempted to release Callapine by visions of Tamburlaine-like power which his prisoner puts before him. The effect of this appeal is not to cheapen the Tamburlaine-ideal, but to see Almeda as ludicrous for taking such a grandiose vision as a possibility (similarly, in *Faustus*, the servant Wagner apes his master's performances as magician —again exposing the comic inadequacy of the little man). The absurdity is realised in III. 5. where, in front of Tamburlaine, Callapine honours his promise to the ex-gaoler and offers him the crown. Tamburlaine has already, with a suitable collective noun and ironical comparison, poked fun at the gathering:

> See a knot of kings
> Sitting as if they were a telling riddles.   (3560–61)

The situation becomes farcical when Almeda, petrified by Tamburlaine's presence, asks his permission to accept the crown. Callapine's exasperation is well caught in the rough colloquial tone: 'Doost thou aske him leaue? Here, take it'. This too is the characteristic Marlovian comedy of humiliation and weakness in the presence of strength.

The other source of laughter in Part 2 is Calyphas, whose scenes have already been discussed.

But the humorous and colloquial are exceptional: there is a well-recognised norm and success depends on the quality of that. Memory again plays tricks. As in some operas, one tends to recall a few fine passages in a few set pieces, and to remember these as surrounded by much insignificant sound and fury. In fact, the writing is remarkably even throughout both parts: in only a very few places has the imagination gone dead. Often there is an exhilaration rare in poetry, carried by the span of the images, thrust of verbs, boldness of hyperbole and the confident balance and long stride of the rhetoric. A brief example:

> Besiege a fort, to vndermine a towne,
> And make whole cyties caper in the aire. (3250–51)

It is the verb 'caper' which stamps these lines as Marlovian. Not simply vigorous hyperbole, the word is a microcosmic sample of the prevailing spirit: make them caper; prod them with your aggressive vitality; blow them sky-high and they can dance to your tune up there. This same aggressive energy sometimes turns in upon itself, as it is to do in real earnest later in Marlowe's career. Agidas, trying to dissuade Zenocrate from Tamburlaine, asks how she can 'fancie one that lookes so fierce':

> Who when he shall embrace you in his armes,
> Will tell you how many thousand men he slew,
> And when you looke for amorous discourse,
> Will rattle foorth his facts of war and blood. (1025–30)

These lines make fun of Tamburlaine in a manner like that which Prince Hal employs to satirise Hotspur. Again the strength of expression lies in the verb ,'rattle foorth', with its comic belittlement of the high astounding term, the mighty and thundering speech which is to this play as blood to the body. But generally the thrust of the verse is one with the aspirations of the hero. As his imagination and will-to-power stretch over the world and into the whole of creation, so the poetry owes its energy and character largely to this attraction towards the immense, spacious and universal which by the attraction are lit up with the brightness of air and fire:

> The golden balle of heauens eternal fire,
> That danc'd with glorie on the siluer waues. (2970–71)

> Batter the shining pallace of the Sun,
> And shiuer all the starry firmament. (3073–4)

> Making the Meteors, that like armed men
> Are seene to march vpon the towers of heauen,
> Run tilting round about the firmament,
> And breake their burning Lances in the aire. (3876–9)

> So will I ride through *Samarcanda* streets,
> Vntil my soule disseuered from this flesh,
> Shall mount the milk-white way and meet him there.
> To *Babylon* my Lords, to *Babylon*. (4109–12)

> Ile ride in golden armour like the Sun. (4094)

> Come let vs march against the powers of heauen,
> And set blacke streamers in the firmament. (4440–41)

These lines are all spoken by Tamburlaine and are expressions of his mind. But they also represent the essential mind of the play, for it is into this that the creative vitality goes; it is by the glamour of this universe there for the aspiring man to enjoy that the dramatist is clearly most moved. Hence the double wrongness of a formulation like Battenhouse's: 'Marlowe differs from his Protestant contemporaries . . . not in his moral outlook, but only in his ability as an artist'. This artistic ability involves imagination and technical skill. But the superior technical skill created the stately blank verse, the mighty line, as the mode of expression most fitted to the subject; and the imagination worked to create both a character

> . . . proportioned like the man,
> Should make the world subdued

and poetry like that quoted which should express his soul. The artistic ability proceeds from the mind in which attitudes are moral: ultimately the individuality of the one reflects that of the other. This, obviously, is not to identify dramatist and dramatis personae, but it does presume that the total weights and balances of the play will be 'an allegory of the mind at the time of creation'. By 'weights and balances' I mean the pointers to judgments and sympathies, and, more important, places where the presentation is merely nominal or where the imagination is genuinely caught up and creative. It is in these places that the author's real intentions, conscious or not, are to be found. In *Tamburlaine* the poetry is alight with the aspiring and aggressive spirit which the protagonist embodies, and for all the presence of debate there is no answering vitality, rendered by the 'artistic ability', to counter the vitality owned by this markedly different 'moral outlook'.

So aesthetic criticism leads back to the moral inquiry with which we began. We have noted a conflict within the play and concluded that one side in the conflict emerges, in apparent intention, as superior. The superiority asserted involves much that we see as evil: pushing the self careless of cost to others, vaunting war, taking the humiliation of others as an emblem or measure of the power enjoyed, relegating conscience, mercy and peacefulness as unmanly and even contemptible attributes. It also involves abnormal vitality of action, imagination and speech. So the mind of the author, as we see it in his play, is divided. A particular combination of evils is justified and even gloried in, though opposed fitfully by the misgivings, revulsions or positive assertions of normal moral judgment.

But the division in the mind is further complicated by the fact that evil in Tamburlaine coexists with a good which is beyond the wonderful but amoral vitality already described. The massive indifference to human suffering and death is part of the mind which also places the human being above everything on earth, and so reveres above all things what it considers to be human worth.

> Disdaines *Zenocrate* to liue with me?
> Or you my Lordes to be my followers?
> Thinke you I way this treasure more than you?
> Not all the Gold in *Indias* welthy armes,
> Shall buy the meanest souldier in my traine. (278–82)

This is not merely an impressive gesture but a part of the essential thought: it emerges logically from the humanist pride which in the same speech makes Tamburlaine, without conceit, offer himself last to Zenocrate as a man and nature's ultimate treasure. The same note is heard in these lines:

> If all the christall gates of *Ioues* high court
> Were opened wide, and I might enter in
> To see the state and maiesty of heauen,
> It could not more delight me than your sight. (2722–5)

This is a magnificent compliment to his followers on the part of a man who would otherwise rate such a triumphal entry higher than anything else. His magnificence is most potently and reasonably felt in the warm appreciation he has of his friends. Again the valuation has its place within a philosophy of which the whole play is an expression: pride in man as lord of the earth and as potential superman. The world is the magnificent setting made for the complete man, who is its jewel. When Tamburlaine wounds himself to edify his sons, he exults in terms which assert at once the worth of this world and man's superiority to it:

> Blood is the God of Wars rich liuery.
> Now look I like a souldier, and this wound
> As great a grace and maiesty to me,
> As if a chaire of gold enamiled,
> Enchac'd with Diamondes, Saphyres, Rubies
> And fairest pearle of welthie *India*
> Were mounted here vnder a Canapie.   (3306–12)

In that speech, with its Volumnian advocacy of war as manhood's proof and glory, one sees how the good and the evil come to connect.

Another good is the sensitivity to beauty 'with whose instinct the soule of man is toucht' (1960). The reverence for beauty human and cosmic is felt in the lines to Zenocrate:

> Eies when that *Ebena* steps to heauen,
> In silence of thy solemn Euenings walk,
> Making the mantle of the richest night,
> The Moone, the Planets, and the Meteors light.
> There Angels in their cristal armours fight . . . (1928–32)

Here the passage develops beyond the artifice of its beginning to evoke a solemnity that is almost religious. The feeling is sustained in the fourteen lines on beauty and the

> immortall flowers of Poesy,
> Wherein as in myrrour we perceiue
> The highest reaches of a humaine wit.   (1947–9)

This speech combines three articles of Tamburlaine's creed: reverence for beauty, pride in man, and aspiration seen as an essential part of natural living. These are held with a remarkable intensity. Our souls 'still climing after knowledge infinite' are 'alwaies moouing as the restles Spheares' (875). Nature teaches this thirst and restlessness and

> Wils vs to weare our selues and neuer rest
> Vntill we reach the ripest fruit of all.   (877–8)

This is a religion more than a philosophy; and, when all has been said, *Tamburlaine* must be recognised as in its extraordinary way fundamentally and deeply a religious work.

God is the great unseen actor, felt increasingly as a force, and as of a nature undefined by any single religion that the world knows. Throughout, Tamburlaine is his scourge and there is no sense that his purpose and morality differ from those of his instrument. He is the God of war but also of beauty:

> . . . in this sweet and currious harmony,
> The God that tunes this musicke to our soules:
> Holds out his hand in highest maiesty
> To entertaine diuine *Zenocrate*.   (2998-3001)

In his palace is a spiritual purity and loveliness which have their places in the creed of the man who is also the crudely brutal tormentor of Bajazeth:

> The christall springs whose taste illuminates
> Refined eies with an eternall sight,
> Like tried siluer runs through Paradice
> To entertaine diuine *Zenocrate*.   (2990-3)

The reverence for beauty is not, as we say, 'a religion in itself' but is part of the conception of Eternity and its God, whose existence is never dramatically in doubt. Tamburlaine dares Mahomet out of his heaven when he burns the sacred books and speaks of 'the God that sits in heauen, if any God' (4312). Of the 'if' phrase, P. H. Kocher writes: 'The agnosticism it entailed was treated in Elizabethan times as one of the characteristic and dangerous forms of atheism', and he regards it as a piece of sly Marlovian sniping against religion. I think it does again reflect the divided mind, but the most obvious thing about it is that it brings retribution.[1] God also seems to participate in human affairs when Orcanes invokes Christ's aid against the Christians who have broken faith (2,II.2). On both occasions when supernatural power is challenged the challenge is met. Mahomet answers one, the Christian God the other, and the effect of this and much else in the play is to resolve the world's gods into a single deity. Pagan and Christian symbols mingle, Christ is honoured by a Mahomedan 'not doing Mahomet an iniurie', and Tamburlaine himself worships only an unnamed God of power and beauty, most fully acknowledged in a speech of Orcanes':

> . . . he that sits on high and neuer sleeps,
> Nor in one place is circumscriptible,
> But euery where fils euery Continent,
> With strange infusion of his sacred vigor. (2906–9)

The universal spirit has power and dignity which extend beyond local allegiances, nomenclatures, rites and myths, and his essential attribute is energy. This God, immanent in his creation, is known by vigour rather than (in any Christian sense) virtue. He is a dynamic rather than a moral force. His nature reflects human ideals, and the mind which postulates this divine vigour also places at the head of humanity the man with most vitality. It is that quality which above all is saluted in Tamburlaine. In his superabundance of energy he comes near to the essential being of this God, for energy is an infusion and he who has most of it has most of the God within him.

Tamburlaine becomes a religious symbol. It is the fact

---

[1] To Kocher this is not obvious at all, but he is surely disingenuous: 'Tamburlaine merely announces "But stay; I feel myself distempered suddenly", and it never occurs to him or to anyone else that there is any connection between his burning of the Koran and his illness . . . Marlowe made the illness follow close upon the abjuration because he considered that the time had arrived for ending the play, and wished to compress the remaining events'. But if any placing can be assumed to be pointed and deliberate, this can. Within thirty lines of daring Mahomet to 'Come downe . . . and worke a myracle' he is struck by the fever which is to kill him.

that what he embodies touches religious depths in Marlowe that gives these plays that poise, confidence, stamina and solidity which is theirs in notable contrast to his other works. The division, or debate, within the apparent unity proceeds from another quality also deep in his character: an aggressively critical spirit making for an uneasy scepticism. Marlowe was at that time in his mid-twenties. When such characteristics coexist in such a man at such an age it should not be surprising if developments are rapid, extreme and perhaps painful.

4

'DOCTOR FAUSTUS'

Approach . . . and destroy your sight
With a new Gorgon.[1]

JUST SUCH a monster, flourishing its three heads and involving the eyesight in a formidable commitment, guards the scholarly approaches to the play we comfortably and familiarly call 'Marlowe's *Faustus*'. That harmless-looking term is really no more than a sort of shorthand, and it begs a number of important questions. There are three main problems: date, authorship and text. It may indeed be unwise to raise them without going into considerable detail. The present discussion will be brief, however, and has the purposes of drawing attention to what others have written and clarifying the assumptions which underlie the present study.

The essential document is Sir Walter Greg's edition of the play in parallel texts. This contains an examination of the variants in minute detail, and all evidence available at the time (1950) is marshalled with a scholarship and perceptiveness that are beyond praise. It is, however, worth turning up the review by Dr Harold Jenkins (*Modern Language Review*, no. XLVI), where some qualifications are suggested.

On the problem of date, Greg decided in favour of 1592 or after. In this he agreed with other scholars, Tucker

---

[1] *Macbeth*, II. 3.

Brooke[1] and Dr Boas amongst them, who had been un-convinced by the traditional placing of *Faustus* in 1588 or 1589 immediately after *Tamburlaine* and had argued for a later date. The issue is complicated, but the verdict depends partly on the date when Marlowe's source, the English *Faustbook* was published. Greg argues this to be about 1592 when a court case arose about the publishing rights. Dr Jenkins claims that the assumption is unwarrantable: 'At least', he concludes, 'there is stronger evidence for dating it not later than 1590 than for dating it not earlier than 1592'. This being so, the date of Marlowe's play remains an open question, and other evidence needs to be considered more thoroughly. A strong case for the earlier date is made out on stylistic and other grounds by P. H. Kocher in *Modern Language Notes* LV (pp. 95–101) and LVIII (pp. 539–42). Of stylistic 'evidence' Greg says little, but finds it astonishing that critics should be willing to place 'anything so spiritually mature' as '*Faustus*' so shortly after 'the rant and youthful crudity of *Tamburlaine*'.[2] That last phrase involves, I think, a misrepresentation of *Tam-burlaine*, and the sentence implies a corresponding limitation in the powers of development credited to a writer of genius, particularly at that age and of that restless disposi-tion. The development from *Tamburlaine* to *Faustus* is certainly remarkable (in the way that Marlowe *is* remark-able), but the alternatives strain credulity still more severely. *The Jew of Malta* (which would then come next in the canon) is far more remote from the heroic dignity of *Tamburlaine* than *Faustus* is. *Faustus*, on the other hand, does much to explain the bitter deflating mood of *The Jew*, *Edward II* and

---

[1] In the introduction to his edition (Oxford, 1910) Tucker Brooke assigned the play to the winter of 1588–9, but by 1922 he had changed his mind, and in 'The Marlowe Canon' (*Publications of the Modern Language Research Association of America*, no. XXVII) suggests a later date.

[2] W. W. Greg, *Doctor Faustus, 1604–1616: Parallel Texts* (Oxford, 1950), p. 10.

(in its different way) *Hero and Leander*. To go from the flat verse of *Edward* to the Tamburlaine-like relish of Faustus' early speeches looks very like going backwards. Nor has the sophisticated wit, sympathy and savagery of *Hero and Leander* much in common with the tone of *Faustus*. Affinities of style and thought, it is true, provide very unsure ground for dating, but if a choice is to be made I would support the contention of Miss Mahood, who writes: 'in the absence of conclusive evidence for a late date of *Doctor Faustus*, this natural kinship of the two states of mind suggests that the play was successor to *Tamburlaine*'.[1] There is some amplification of this in my final chapter where the practical importance of the question, such as it is, really belongs.

The play is rarely, if ever, claimed for Marlowe in its entirety. In one sense, Sir Walter Greg comes nearest to doing so. He sees 'no reason to doubt that it was he who planned the whole', and that collaborators 'carried out his plan substantially according to his instructions'. On the other hand, he cuts down Marlowe's share in the writing to not more than about 825 lines. This attributes to others not merely the comic scenes and the demonstrations magical but also, for instance, some of the Old Man's speeches and the soliloquy 'Now Faustus must thou needs be damn'd'. His reasons are often subjective, and sometimes based on the assumption that Marlowe could not write loosely. For example, the Old Man in the 1604 Quarto speaks of 'the gole That shall conduct thee to celestial rest' (1275–6). Greg comments: 'a goal cannot conduct to an end'; and of the whole speech, he says it 'has a turgid extravagance that recalls the worst of "English Seneca" rather than Marlowe'.[2] Whether Greg has in mind

---

[1] M. M. Mahood, *Poetry and Humanism* (London, 1950), p. 66.
[2] *Op. cit.*, p. 384.

here the brag and bounce of Kyd and Heywood or the
'thwacking thumps' of the translations, it seems an odd
thing for this measured, biblical verse to recall. The loose-
nesses too, although acutely observed, are not quite as
criminal as the prosecution insists. The way of life leads to
the goal of holy dying, which is both an end in itself
(a goal) and something which 'conducts' to heaven; and
when he says of the same passage that mercy (1282–3)
cannot expel but can only forgive, he seems to be putting
language and mercy into the same strait-jacket. In any case,
even if the criticisms are granted it does not follow that
Marlowe did not write the lines. Nor is the weakness of
the middle scenes in itself proof that Marlowe is not their
author. It is quite clear that he was not very interested in
them: no poet of genius could write so thinly of anything
that really concerned him. On the other hand, genius is
unlikely to manifest itself if it is writing up as hackwork
tedious episodes from the source-book. There is no
evidence that this is what did happen, but it does not seem
as impossible as is usually assumed.

It is most likely, however, that others, or another, beside
Marlowe wrote considerable portions even of the shorter
1604 version. P. H. Kocher[1] argues that many of the non-
Marlovian scenes are by Nashe. He points out phrases and
expressions in *Faustus* which occur outside that play only
in the work of Nashe. Greg deals briskly with Kocher's
study, dismissing it in a footnote: he does not think that
Kocher establishes 'much of a case'.[2] It certainly contains
a very remarkable collection of finger-prints, and Kocher
even finds what he sees as Nashe's signature. In *Strange
Newes* (1592) Nashe wrote: 'A perse can do it; tempt not
his clemencie too much. A perse a? Passion of God,

---

1 'Nashe's Authorship of the Prose Scenes in *Faustus*', *Modern Language Quarterly*,
III (1942). 2 *Op. cit.*, p. 136.

how came I by that name? my godfather Gabriell gaue it mee, and I must not refuse it.' Gabriel Harvey had presumably conferred the nickname upon Nashe as the author of *Pierce Penniless*. Kocher quotes Robin in the 1616 version (799) and comments: 'Since "per se" means "Pierce" and "Pierce" is Nashe's pen name, Nashe has in effect here written his signature to his share in the play'. But although this is ingenious and much of the rest is impressive, an essential quality of Nashe, the 'mighty lashing gentleman' as Harvey called him, is missing: if the scenes were his, as Greg says, 'we should expect them to possess rather more savour than is to be found'. It is not that these scenes are too poor to be Nashe's work, but it is exactly that: they haven't the savour. The scene of Wagner with the students, for instance, is one which does a good job in the play, but it hasn't Nashe's kind of verbal energy. And when Kocher attributes the Seven Deadly Sins to Nashe with the comment 'Marlowe's loss must be Nashe's gain', one feels that the loss and gain are minimal either way.

But whoever wrote what, the play remains. Criticism in this chapter will not be affected much by considerations of authorship. Whether or not there is one single conscious planner behind it, certain effects remain to be observed: certain details have good effect and others (arguably) do not. Where the uncertainty of authorship does enjoin one to caution is when one comes to attribute qualities to Marlowe on the basis of details in the play. To my mind, for instance, the verse interpolation in the Horse-courser scene (1604) has a particularly fine effect and I would like to credit it to Marlowe. The lines strike Greg, however, as being un-Marlovian, and Percy Simpson writes them off as the work of 'the botcher'—moreover 'the botcher was more than usually clumsy'.[1] If it was indeed the botcher,

---

1 'The 1604 Text of Marlowe's *Doctor Faustus*', *Essays and Studies*, VII (1921).

it seems to me that, as on other occasions, he botched to good effect. The dangers of this sort of speculation on authorship are clear: one gives what one happens to like to the author one likes, and the interpolator or the botcher takes the rest. My own judgment is briefly as follows. About the material which is in the 1616 version but not in the 1604 I see nothing Marlovian. In either version, if Marlowe or Nashe is responsible for the magical and comic scenes, he is working at extremely low pressure. The two Wagner scenes (1604) are exceptions to this. They are so well integrated in the play as to suggest either a remarkably sensitive collaborator or Marlowe's own authorship. Similarly, the balance and effectiveness of the 1604 text suggest a single controlling intelligence. A single control might, of course, be behind the 1616 version, but 'intelligence' would then be a term less suitably used.

This introduces the textual problem, which is probably the most important. For a long time the 1604 Quarto was regarded as the best, and the 'additions' in the 1616 Quarto were explained as the work of William Birde and Samuel Rowley who in 1602 were paid £4 by Henslowe for their 'adicyones in doctor fostes'.[1] That second belief is now untenable, and the first is severely undermined. Percy Simpson's essay referred to above was one of the first to claim superiority for the 1616 text. Not all of his arguments are textual, however, and some are very questionable. He observes, for example, that the 1616 version shows more of Faustus' attainments, his conjuring tricks being poor little affairs in the 1604. He quotes Faustus' speech starting 'Had I as many soules as there be starres' (338–50) and remarks: 'This passage echoes the imperial note of *Tamburlaine*, but what is done to maintain it in the play?' The

---

[1] *Henslowe's Diary*, ed. Greg, I, 172.

argument seems to run: the 1616 Quarto maintains it better than the 1604; therefore it is to that extent preferable. This supposes that it was Marlowe's intention to maintain the Tamburlaine note; which would imply a strangely limited understanding of the play.

But what is 'the play'? The A text (1604) differs very considerably from the B text (1616). B is held by Greg, Boas and Kirschbaum (for example) to be the better, but it is not as simple as that. Greg maintains convincingly that some parts of B are based on A and that A is locally superior. He therefore offers a reconstruction (published separately), which presents the student with a C text. This conflation has, as Dr Jenkins notes, 'a subjective element'; there are, in fact, places where Greg 'prefers his own conjecture to the reading of either text'. So there is probably a call for a D text.

When the scholars speak of the superiority of the B text it is as well to understand what they mean. The text is 'good' in the sense that it is believed to be working from manuscript antedating the 'bad' version. The latter is seen as a shortened edition, probably as acted by a touring company and dictated by an actor. Greg writes about the play: 'I do not believe that as originally written it differed to any material extent from what we are able to reconstruct from a comparison of the two versions in which it has come down to us'.[1] This means that 'as originally written' it had about twice as much magical demonstration, which is almost certainly non-Marlovian. It also contained material which is, I think, generally considered regrettable: a re-entrance of the scholars after Faustus' death, and a scene before the clock strikes eleven, in which Mephastophilis gloats, the Throne descends, the Good Angel shakes its head, Hell is discovered and the Bad Angel gives a vivid but conventional

[1] W. W. Greg, 'The Damnation of Faustus', *Modern Language Review*, XLI (1946).

commentary.[1] These are in the 'good' Quarto, not the 'bad', and as Dr Jenkins says, this involves important consequences for literary criticism: 'future criticism of the play must, I think, accommodate itself to an acceptance of B's fifth act'.

This is not the first time that scholarship has cheerfully directed the student into the wilderness. Greg admits the A text to be preferable in many important passages where Marlowe's hand is indisputably present. The B text mainly presents one with several more scenes from which his hand is more or less indisputably absent. Perhaps to prefer the A text is 'to suspend historical judgment', but to prefer the B text is to suspend every other form of judgment. The 1604 version is a great play in spite of the aridities and the occasional disappointments at climax. But the 1616 version is weaker in the fine passages and longer and more tedious in the weak ones. 'Historical judgment' may tell us that these magical-demonstration episodes were not tedious to Elizabethan audiences (there was the thrill of playing with fire), but if it tells us to spend our time with them it does us a disservice, for their merit is negligible.

And, of course, the play is weakened. The lack of austerity works against the morality's power even in the A text, but the B text is so full of knockabout, silliness and cheap spectacle that it all but kills it. Much more

---

[1] J. P. Brockbank writes of this scene as having a powerful and fine effect, and holds that without Mephastophilis' speech 'the exploration of the mystery of evil would not be complete' (*Marlowe*, 'Dr. Faustus', p. 55). This speech contains the devil's statement that it was he who turned the leaves of the Bible and directed Faustus' eye, so damming up his passage to heaven. Dr Brockbank points out that the devil *symbolises* the wilful pride and also represents the adversary to whom man is a prey. But both of these ideas have been present in the play, and this explicit statement is not needed to complete anything. It is, admittedly, vivid and memorable, possibly even 'terrifying' as Dr Brockbank says. The intensity is all lost, however, in the conventional speeches that follow—and of *all* this there is no need for the really terrifying thing is the state of Faustus himself. This needs nothing to enhance it and it already implies the power of sin and the devil over man. What is unnecessarily explicit is bound to weaken.

recognisably than the A text, it carries the seeds of the ultimate degeneration into what Pepys saw ('We were sick of it': 26 May 1662) and Pope wrote about:

> See now, what Dulness and her sons admire . . .
> . . . a sable Sorc'rer rise,
> Swift to whose hand a winged volume flies:
> All sudden, Gorgons hiss, and Dragons glare,
> And ten-horn'd fiends and Giants rush to war.
> Hell rises, Heav'n descends, and dance on Earth . . .
>
> (*Dunciad*, III. 228, 233–7)

(The last line, incidentally, refers not to *Faustus* but, according to Pope's notes, Tibbald's *Rape of Proserpine*: however, he obviously associated the 'monstrous absurdity' of the one with the other. 'Doctor Faustus', he writes, was 'the subject of a set of farces'.)

The B text in all its emphasis leads away from what is valuable in the play, and destroys what in A is an acceptable balance of fineness and triviality. Greg argues that the Roman scene is given a more serious touch and the scene with the Emperor 'at least developed into some dramatic coherence'. 'This', he says, 'only brings out more pointedly the progressive fatuity of Faustus's career, which in the clownage and conjuring tricks at Anhalt sinks to the depths of buffoonery'.[1] The 'progressive fatuity', however, is made quite clear in the A version; in making it clearer, the B text simply becomes progressively more fatuous. The Roman scene is not more serious in any relevant sense, and no additional dramatic coherence in the Emperor scene could make it less boring in our sight unless it were to shorten it (in fact it is three times as long).

In this essay, then, I am using the 1604 *Faustus*. This may be subjective and unhistorical. But the only historical gain in the 1616 version is a certain light on Elizabethan

[1] *Modern Language Review*, XLI.

popular taste. In the meantime a great play is spoilt, and one is no nearer to anything significant in Marlowe. This carries for many small points in the text as well as whole scenes. Few readers would regret the loss of much peculiar to the B text yet there is little that could be spared from the A, for even the weaknesses play their part, while the strengths are greater than perhaps commonly believed.

*   *   *

The first lines of the play are curiously out of key. The Chorus swaggers forward to 'the swelling bombast of a bragging blank verse', evoking for a moment the music of *Tamburlaine*. But the effect is to define by contrast. As the Prologue to *Tamburlaine* offered to 'lead you to the stately tent of War', so the Chorus here leads away from that world ('not marching now'). It evokes 'the pompe of prowd audacious deedes' only to dismiss it, and a cooler and more moderate tone is heard in the next lines:

> Onely this (Gentlemen) we must performe,
> The forme of *Faustus* fortunes good or bad.
> To patient Iudgements we appeale our plaude.   (7–9)

A new note has been struck in this gracious appeal to 'patient Iudgements', very unlike the cavalier, almost aggressive hand-out of the *Tamburlaine* Prologue:

> View but his picture in this tragicke glasse,
> And then applaud his fortunes as you please.   (7–8)

As the Chorus tells of new subject matter, so the old rhetoric disappears from his speech. The quiet narrative does without rhetorical flourish, and a rare sweetness and serenity is attained in 'The fruitfull plot of Scholerisme grac't'.[1] The gentle flow of the line works with the image

[1] The line is not included in the 1616 text. Greg conjectures that its slight obscurity may have led to the omission.

of order and fertility to give a vivid sense of the good and natural world which Faustus abandons. The repeated 'grac't' is something better than a Polonian play on words, as it has been called: it expresses the mutual blessing between the scholar and the study. The measured quietness is violated by the swelling movement of the Icarus lines, as the natural order is by Faustus' unlawful aspirations. The construction (main clause arrived at only after subordinate phrases) involves the reader in a crescendo coming to a climax at 'mount above' and dropping back again in the next line. So the movement sensitively mirrors the rise and fall, enacting in brief the image which the play is to enact in full. In still more violent contrast to the serenity of 'the fruitfull plot' which Faustus has renounced is the harshness of the 'exercise' he has turned to:

> He surffets vpon cursed Negromancy.
> Nothing so sweete as magicke is to him
> Which he preferres before his chiefest blisse. (25-7)

The sibilants hiss like hell-fire, made more effective by the sound-organisation of the previous line:

> And glutted now with learnings golden gifts. (24)

That is the glib and oily way to the everlasting bonfire. The whole weight of the speech now lies behind the last line:

> And this the man that in his study sits. (28)

'This the man' has already meaning and intensity, and the Chorus can gracefully yet ominously point to the protagonist and take his leave.

'The man' is caught at that decisive moment in his life when he is to choose and 'be committed':

> Settle thy studies *Faustus*, and beginne
> To sound the deapth of that thou wilt professe. (29-30)

'Settle', 'beginne' and 'sound the deapth': they are the terms of a man impatient to decide, make a fresh start, come to that kind of maturity involved in a profound commitment. This and what follows is representative and symbolical, a technique for telescoping, derived from mediæval convention, and neater and more dramatic than most examples of the more sophisticated explanatory opening conversation. But the character is there too, flesh and blood and individual. His vigour, his impatience and extremism are already felt. As each field of study is dismissed and a phase of his life represented, the pride and scorn and something like an undergraduate quality of enthusiasm are made real and living in the manner of speech:

> Sweete *Analutikes* tis thou hast rauisht me.   (34)

Soon we are to hear:

> Tis Magicke, Magicke that hath rauisht mee.   (138)

Both betoken the extreme enthusiasm of a youthful 'craze': the modish metaphor, the eagerness and conviction, and, in their incautious heady ebullience, an equally youthful superficiality. From the facts of his career, Faustus should be well on in life; but psychologically he is the young graduate.

It is a characteristic irony that the man whose superficiality is one of his damning qualities should be first seen expressing his genuine will to profundity. He wishes to 'leuell at the end of euery Art'. The 'end' here seems to mean the ultimate purpose, and the whole line I take to mean 'try to hit or ascertain what it is that all arts attempt to do'. This has been related to a passage in the Nicomachean Ethics: 'Every art and every study, likewise every action and moral decision, seem to aim at some good. Therefore they have rightly called that the good, at which everything aims.' Faustus is explicitly concerned here with 'ends' or 'aims' ('finis logices', 'Logickes chiefest end'), and, being also explicitly concerned with '*Aristotles workes*', is inquiring into the 'good' which should be 'the end of euery Art'. But no 'good' commensurate with his conception of it is offered. The depressing force of limitations is already being felt, and that essentially is what the play is dramatising: the limitations imposed by the world, heaven and hell, the limits within which humanity must be content to breathe. If it aspires too proudly it may soon be wriggling pathetically as it is stifled in a strait-jacket of conformity to the absolutism of at least one of these forces.

The limitations are felt most keenly in this review of studies when it comes to Divinity, traditionally the pinnacle of scholastic achievement and endeavour. What Faustus thinks he has exposed is not one of those 'contrarieties out of the Scriptures' mentioned in the Baines note, but a cramping and unacceptable fatalism. The short line 'Why then belike' may be an accidental irregularity,[1] but it plays usefully into the actor's hands. He must give pause as the force of this determinism is realised, slowing down delivery as the realisation grows. The increased pace, responsive to the growing intensity, gains impetus from the slow movement:

> Why then belike
> We must sinne, and so consequently die:
> I, we must die an euerlasting death:
> What doctrine call you this, *Che sera, sera,*
> What wil be, shall be? Diuinitie, adieu.   (72–6)

Scorn and impatience bite harder into the soul as the denunciation derives added force from the alliterative *d* throughout; and possibly there is an added, almost jaunty irreverence in the literal sense of 'Diuinitie, adieu', meaning 'let God have it, I'll none of it'.

[1] It is printed as a single line by Tucker Brooke, but not by Greg.

It is because of the freedom and scope they offer to the 'studious Artizan' that 'Negromantike bookes are heauenly'. A comparison with Divinity is implicit, giving extra point to the irony and paradox in 'heauenly'. A kind of hand-rubbing miserly gloating straightens itself out into a Tamburlaine-like vision of possibilities to be realised on an immense geographical scale: 'a world of profit and delight'; 'all things that mooue betweene the quiet poles'. And there is still, Tamburlaine-like, a proud Renaissance humanism involved in:

> But his dominion that exceedes in this,
> Stretcheth as farre as doth the minde of man. (88–9)

The mind of man is creation's masterpiece. The irony of this part of the speech is seen retrospectively (and is not therefore invalid). These lines do in fact sketch the middle episodes:

> . . . Emperours and kings
> Are but obeyd in their seuerall prouinces. (85–6)

Faustus thinks to be greater, but as we see him in their courts he is only a superior and honoured entertainer. The bitterness of this tragedy lies not only in the nature and wages of sin, but in the triviality of the profit and delight the world offers, grace not being present in the soul.

Faustus chooses and acts: he sends for Valdes and Cornelius. The wheels have been set in motion, and it is right that this moment should be marked by the first appearance of the Good and Evil Angels (at once, as James Smith[1] pointed out, beings from a real supernatural world and externalisations of the conscience). The Evil Angel has the last word, representing the relative weight of these forces in Faustus' mind. Faustus echoes the Chorus's word 'glutted'; but he is at his most engaging here, for the

[1] 'Marlowe's *Doctor Faustus*', *Scrutiny*, VIII, 1 (1939).

ambitions have a sort of boyish freshness and eagerness. The boyishness is emphasised by his reference to the 'sage conference' of Valdes and Cornelius. Similarly the youthful extremism is seen not only in the enthusiasms but in the hatred: Divinity which once was 'best' is now 'basest of the three'.[1] And going with this is an extraordinary energy, often located in the verb and placed forcefully at the beginning of the line:

> . . . with concise sylogismes
> Graueld the Pastors of the Germaine Church,
> And made the flowring pride of *Wertenberge*
> Swarme to my Problemes. (140–43)

The same vigour and violence are felt in the more famous lines:

> Ile haue them flye to *India* for gold,
> Ransacke the Ocean for orient pearle. (110–11)

What one actually has in Faustus (whatever Marlowe's intention) is not so much intelligence as energy.

Valdes' reply evokes a glamour which recalls the word's former magical significance. The '*Almaine* Rutters' and 'Lapland Gyants' have an exotic wonder, the latter 'trotting by our sides' as in some marvellous fairy tale. But more strange, and strangely beautiful, is the image of the spirits

> like women or vnwedded maides,
> Shadowing more beautie in their ayrie browes,
> Than has the white breasts of the queene of Loue. (156–8)

The fine, spiritlike delicacy and insubstantiality plays off its own odd warmth against the somewhat cold convention, sculptural in association, of the white breasts of Venus. There is something perverse in the sexual evocations: normality is challenged and not, I think, for the mere bravado of hyperbole. It is a haunted elder world that these

---

[1] Omitted 1616: presumably censored.

131

lines enter, but the remoter glamour is blown away with the breezy topical reference to 'olde *Philips* treasury' with its assurance of a lively reception in the pit. Cornelius continues in optimistic vein and they all feel the excitement and confidence of comradeship:

> Then tell me *Faustus*, what shal we three want? (177)

The answer comes pat: 'Nothing *Cornelius*.' And the rest of the line, 'O this cheares my soule', echoes the irony of 'Make me blest' and is in fact complementary to it.

Faustus presses forward ('Come' is a recurrent demand). His hopes are extreme. Disappointed optimism and a cramped forward urge are both part of the tragedy, but here for the moment the world seems to open before him, and the first section of the play is over. The man has 'settled' and chosen:

> This night Ile coniure though I die therefore. (195)

The second half of the sentence foreshadows ironically the consequences of his choice.

The First Scholar's words come as a testimony from the outside world. The fervent admiration which Faustus commanded as he 'graueld the Pastors' with his logic and learning is conveyed vividly in the verb: 'that was wont to make our schooles ring with *sic probo*' (there one has the probing, 'protesting' Wittenberg scholar). The dramatic point is that it provides a brief reminder of '*Apolloes* Laurel bough That sometime grew within this learned man', and the students' concern reinforces this as they learn of his 'hellish fall' ('falne into that damned art').

A rather sinister irony darkens the comic business:

> 1. *Sch.* How now sirra, wheres thy maister?
> *Wag.* God in heauen knowes. (199–200)

God indeed knows, and so does the devil. There is irony

too in 'is not he *corpus naturale*': which is just what Faustus is in the process of un-becoming. 'It were not for you to come within fortie foote of the place of execution' contains a humorous but pointed warning to keep clear. Wagner has scored off the students by parodying their own business; he ends with a parody of holiness. The 'precisian' or Puritan had his cant phrases and zealous manner, and Wagner catches them accurately: 'truly my deare brethren ... and so the Lord blesse you, preserue you, and keepe you my deare brethren, my deare brethren'. This parodied benediction is obviously 'organic' (like most of this scene) in a play of damnation. The humour has its overt seriousness as Wagner sees the students' faces fall when he names Faustus' associates: Wagner knows what 'they two are infamous' for, and he knows that the scholars know.

Then comes the first of several sudden drops into seriousness. The scholars left alone look at each other in dismay. The second scholar says 'Were he a stranger, and not alied to me, yet should I grieue for him'. He represents the Christian norm: the charity and altruism of the Christian in a state of grace. The Rector, with his 'graue counsaile', is similarly a norm or a positive, a part of 'the fruitfull plot' which Faustus has rejected. Even the last two lines of the scene are 'organic', recalling the see-saw movement of Faustus' own irresolution and the Good and Bad Angels' externalising of it.

We realise the fears of the first scholar to be well-judged as Faustus begins to conjure. The night sky is evoked in strong Marlovian verse:

> ... the gloomy shadow of the earth,
> Longing to view *Orions* drisling looke,
> Leapes from th'antartike world vnto the skie. (235–7)

The leap and longing are projections of Faustus' own

aspirations and the universe is seen characteristically in terms of man's desire. It was presumably at the climax of the Latin invocation, with its proper names fearfully intelligible through the mumbo-jumbo, that the audience would become most alarmed.[1] But it is remarkable that the tension so skilfully created should immediately be lost in laughter: 'that holy shape becomes a diuell best' is a sure Reformation laugh-line. It illustrates a sort of instability which is a flaw in the play as it is in Faustus himself. There is point in the speech, of course: man, proud and successful, commands the situation, and the joke helps to put the audience with him. Here for the present is Faustus enjoying his power. The Magician is never to be such a 'mightie god' again.

He asserts an utterly unfettered will in his speech to Mephastophilis and assumes complete power to enforce it. His will may extend to world-destruction, to make 'the Ocean to ouerwhelme the world'. But with Mephastophilis' reply things already begin to close in; already limitations are stated. The devil, always so quietly, soberly unmelodramatic after the first appearance, states the truth, cold and damp after Faustus' eager expectancy. He brings the drama to a new level, as he 'places' the hocus-pocus of the conjuring and gives a realistic, adult account of the state of sin. In the famous lines on the fall of Lucifer we are made to realise that Faustus' sin ('aspiring pride and insolence') is the same as that original sin in which, theologically, all fallen nature has its origin. But the deepest note in the play so far is struck by Mephastophilis in his line:

> Why this is hel, nor am I out of it.   (312)

---

[1] *The Black Book*, by T. M. (1604), refers to 'a head of hair like one of my devils in Doctor Faustus, when the old theatre cracked & frighted the audience'. Bullen's *Middleton*, VIII. 13. (See ch. I, p. 14.)

The firmness, unexpectedness and passion impress deeply and throw into relief Faustus' eager, inexperienced buoyancy. Faustus now opposes this deep personal statement with text-book Stoicism:

> Learne thou of *Faustus* manly fortitude,
> And scorne those ioyes thou neuer shalt possesse. (321–2)

In a way this is admirable: the man stands on his own feet, proud and even heroic in his nonconformity. But truth lies with the devil, servile, tormented and drab as he is.[1]

The next scene holds up the last in a comic distorting mirror: it too is 'organic'. The chat has not gone far before the theme is heard, made to frisk strangely but still recognisable: 'I know he would giue his soule to the Diuel for a shoulder of mutton, though it were blood rawe.' But the Clown is wiser than the wise man: 'How, my soule to the Diuel for a shoulder of mutton though twere blood rawe? not so good friend, burladie I had neede haue it wel roasted, and good sawce to it, if I pay so deere' (362–5). He estimates the price with more wisdom than Faustus, and he preserves a more wholesome sense of it when he realises what he must pay for the guilders Wagner has given him:

> *Wag.* Why now sirra thou art at an houres warning whensoeuer or wheresoeuer the diuell shall fetch thee.
> *Clo.* No, no, here take your gridirons againe. (391–3)

The scene runs to farce (not the 'terribly serious' kind), but for a moment the agonies of Faustus' compact have been held up to the mirror and grin back distorted and grotesque. There are other moments: 'Ile turne al the lice about thee into familiars, and they shal teare thee in peeces' (cf. 'If thou repent diuels shall teare thee in peeces'; 'Reuolt or Ile in

---

[1] There are some good comments on this scene by J. C. Maxwell in *The Pelican Guide to English Literature*, vol. II, pp. 170–73.

peecemeale teare thy flesh'; 'the diuell threatned to teare mee in peeces, if I namde God, to fetch both body and soule'); 'How? A Christian fellow to a dogge or a catte, a mouse or a ratte?' (cf. '. . . and I be changde Vnto some brutish beast: al beasts are happy . . .').

As the Clown, impressed and cheerful, commits himself as disciple to the little Faust, Faustus himself with the first burst of depression recognises the price that he is paying. This speech ('Now *Faustus* must thou needes be damnd'[1] (432–46)) introduces that agony of irresolution which *Faustus* dramatises as wonderfully as *Macbeth*. There are in fact many points of comparison, but for the present one calls to mind L. C. Knights's description of the 'sickening see-saw rhythm' of 'cannot be ill; cannot be good'. Possibly another metaphor may be helpful in reading the speech. A child bathing within his depth in a rough sea is knocked off his balance; he feels himself drawn back by the pull of the water, then pushed forward on a powerful wave so that he can again stand and grasp with his hands to pull himself out, but again the process is repeated; and so on. Faustus is knocked off balance, flounders but comes in confidently with 'Despaire in God, and trust in Belsabub'. Immediately the sickening pull is felt:

> Now go not backeward; no Faustus, be resolute,
> Why wauerest thou? (438)

Again the roll forward and the temporary firmness: 'I and Faustus wil turne to God againe'. And once more the pull backward: 'To God?'. Inevitably he grasps at the 'fixt . . . loue of Belsabub', forcing it into the exaggerated villainy of 'offer luke warme blood of new borne babes' (this *is*

---

[1] Critics seem to be scandalised by the irregularity of the verse and are convinced that the speech is not by Marlowe. Simpson: 'The wretched verse of the fifth and sixth lines . . . shows how the manager went to work'. Greg credits Marlowe with the eighth and ninth lines (ninth omitted 1616), but says that the last two 'read more like parody'.

perhaps felt as farcical, and serious: compare the Jew of Malta's 'kill sick people groaning under walls And sometimes go about and poison wells'). The forcing of spirit brings in the Good Angel, giving additional point to its 'leaue that execrable art'[1]; and the see-saw motion of the Angels' antiphony continues the miserable irresolution within Faustus.

Macbeth again comes to mind when irresolution is coupled with 'sights' and omens: 'What should the staying of my bloud portend' (cf. 'Wherefore could not I pronounce Amen'), and:

> My sences are deceiu'd, here's nothing writ.
> I see it plaine . . . (511–12)
> (cf. 'I see thee still . . . There's no such thing.')

The scene lurches into these uncertainties after the bargain has been conducted with almost an odd merriment:

> Then stabbe thine arme couragiously,
> And binde thy soule. . . .
> Loe *Mephastophilus, for loue of thee,*
> I cut mine arme . . . (481–2, 485–6)

Mephastophilis trots off for coals and returns with the gloating melodramatic aside: 'O what will not I do to obtaine his soule?'. The excited adolescent (for so he sometimes seems) and the wily, sophisticated devil playing up to him present a curious spectacle. There are moments, however, when the excitements of devil-ritual and blasphemy (*Consummatum est*) give way to a sickened realisation of the truth. The writing, *Homo fuge*, like the Good and Bad Angels, is both 'real' and subjective. Seeing it, Faustus knows for the first time the terror of imprisonment:

> . . . Whither should I flie?
> If vnto God hee'le throwe thee downe to hell. (509–10)

---

[1] A point lost in the 1616 version where the editor seems to have added a line copied, as Greg points out, from A 106.

The divine who in his study 'overlooked' the continuation
of his text ('But if we confess our sins He is faithful and
just to forgive us our sins') is not likely to remember it in
his present panic-stricken condition: there seems to be no
escape. This panic recurs, and is always near: Faustus is
experiencing the hell which Mephastophilis has told him is
personal and perpetual. To make the personal hell tolerable,
a man must 'take his mind off it', 'have a good time',
'make the most out of life', and this is Mephastophilis'
present remedy—'Ile fetch him somewhat to delight his
minde'. Later it is Lucifer's remedy also: and, with the
millionaire's world-tour that he undertakes, Faustus seems
to have learnt the lesson.

The tension is now relaxed. The deed of gift provokes a
shudder by its businesslike explicitness and by the awful
image of 'Lucifer prince of the East'. There are grim
moments: 'I, thinke so still, till experience change thy
minde'. But generally the scene continues with a well-
judged lowering of temperature. Faustus is seen again as
rather engagingly naïve and decent in his wantonness.
Mephastophilis appears as the amused, sophisticated roué:

> How, a wife? I prithee *Faustus* talke not of a wife. (575)

Corruption advances as Faustus is initiated into the chic
world of the freethinker's emancipated aphorisms:

> Marriage is but a ceremoniall toy. (583)

For Faustus's higher education there is the Devil's 'Enquire
Within' which he receives with wide-eyed incredulity—as
well he might, for it is not in his nature to take to the idea
of all knowledge being bound, confined and expressed
within a single volume.

In the beginning of the next scene complete seriousness
is reaffirmed. Here are Faustus' last efforts to break free,

the second attempt being so strong that it needs Lucifer himself to crush it. These moments of agony, panic and surrender form the climax of this first movement of the play. Everything in the scene leads to that climax. Ironically, the instrument in this attempted repentance is the Devil's book. As Faustus studies the heavens, he thinks of God and curses Mephastophilis for having deprived him of heavenly joys. He is beginning to experience the hell of deprivation which Mephastophilis has described. Mephastophilis answers the objections with a ready piece of flattering humanist sophistry which only confirms Faustus in his rebellion. There follows a serious effort to repent:

> I wil renounce this magicke, and repent. (622)

The Good Angel has a place to enter the soul, and the see-saw motion begins again. Faustus' state is not unlike that of Claudius in *Hamlet*:

> Try what Repentance can. What can it not?
> Yet what can it, when one cannot repent?
> Oh wretched state! Oh bosome, blacke as death! (III. 3)

Within Faustus is a strong element of morbid fatalism, perhaps one of the reasons why the overt fatalism of *Che sera, sera* is so abhorrent to him. He believes he must be damned, and the belief is memorably expressed:

> But feareful ecchoes thunders in mine eares,
> Faustus, thou art damn'd. (631-2)

The religious awe of thunder couples with the nightmare clangour of echoes; the suicidal 'deepe dispaire' is vividly understandable.

It is warded off, of course, by pleasures that are indeed, as he says, sweet. His character still has a refinement, and to the end there are what one would normally call redeeming features. His pleasure now has been to make 'blinde *Homer* sing'. A further pleasure, as that thought cheers him up, is to seek for more understanding of the universe. Again the Devil is disappointing: he answers all the 'fresh mens suppositions', but there is one door to which he provides no key and he is stubborn-chaste against all suit. As Faustus' insistence and irritation grow,[1] so Mephastophilis becomes more formidable. He is loyal to his party and the deviationist must be bullied into submission:

> Thinke thou on hell *Faustus*, for thou art damnd. (685)

But the reply comes as though by reflex in pattern with the characteristic antiphony:

> Thinke *Faustus* vpon God that made the world. (686)

It is a bold rebellion, explicitly 'against our kingdome', daring to name what Mephastophilis will not. Its power is recognised by the devil, who leaves menacingly, and Faustus turns the intensity of his will towards repentance. 'Ist not too late?' he calls, and the fearful echo of the Evil Angel thunders in his ears. This too re-echoes as the Good Angel counters it, but the Evil Angel can invoke the fear of unknown physical torment. The intensity of Faustus' will to repentance is so great, however, that the Good Angel, for the only time, has the last word. The short, uneloquent, essential and agonised prayer emerges from the struggle which has been taking place in and around Faustus throughout these scenes:

> Ah Christ my Sauior,
> Seeke to saue distressed *Faustus* soule. (695–6)

In this prayer and its renunciation is the climax of the play thus far. It is unmistakably 'placed' as such by the necessitated intervention of Lucifer himself. If so, is not

---

[1] In this the 1616 text is better than the 1604:
> *Meph.* Vnder the heavens.
> *Faustus.* I, so are all things else; but whereabouts?

the climax, we may ask, sketched and willed rather than achieved? The script is thin; there is no intensity of language to match the intensity of situation. If Lucifer is terrible it must be because of the fearfulness, real or symbolical, of his appearance, for he is not poetically terrible. Furthermore, the tension is allowed to dissipate itself in the thin naïveté of the Deadly Sins. Marlowe is in fact disappointing. But the absence of a poetic intensity which we might have hoped for should not blind us to the nature of the reality which is captured. In these two simple lines the suffering has been created by the poet, not imported by the actor or reader. The five hammered beats of the second line after the irregularity of the first render the force of will, intensified by the insistence of alliteration. The prayer is 'short and uneloquent', but it is the essential prayer of the penitent and expresses a greater agony there in its unadorned form than it would convey if mixed with the less essential or permitted a hint of rhetorical fluency. The only possible expansion or development would seem to involve an anticipation of the final speech. Moreover, the dramatic movement here is extraordinarily powerful. Lucifer's sudden interruption, with the brisk common-sense finality of his 'Christ cannot saue thy soule', takes Faustus utterly unawares. He has no reaction to what Lucifer says, but is paralysed with the sudden horror of what he sees: 'O who art thou that lookst so terrible?' The reply is the most fearful yet dimly foreseen one, and Faustus, panic-stricken, shrinks from the devils and talks as in a nightmare to himself:

O Faustus, they are come to fetch away thy soule. (702)

This is the dreaded, yet almost impossible, appearance of the party bosses in a totalitarian state before one guilty of thought-crime, battered into submission without the need of open threat, knowing the terrors of party machinery: the Evil Angel's threat still echoes in the ears—'If thou repent diuels shall teare thee in peeces'. As Faustus shrinks and chatters out his plea for forgiveness, Lucifer can afford to be suave and moderate. Faustus, still in panic, but with the hysteria of relief, is extravagant in his promises: 'make my spirites pull his churches downe' (a desperation like Macbeth's 'though you vntye the Windes, and let them fight Against the Churches'). But Lucifer is a perfect gentleman ('Do so, and we will highly gratifie thee'), and Faustus is himself again.

Lucifer offers Faustus the classic remedy: 'some pastime' to take his mind off his troubles. There is a poignancy in the reply:

> That sight will be as pleasing vnto me,
> As paradise was to *Adam*, the first day
> Of his creation.　　　　　　　　　　　(716–18)

The perversity of this reference to the state of innocence reflects the power of evil over Faustus, and his pliant degeneration into talking its language. He has, however, not spoken very tactfully to this gentlemanly impresario, for paradise and creation are touchy subjects. Strict censorship is reinforced:

> Talke not of paradise, nor creation, but marke this shew: talke
> of the diuel, and nothing else: come away.　　　(719–20)

The Seven Deadly Sins are a disappointing lot, but Faustus makes a receptive audience: 'O this feedes my soule'. The irony is characteristic, as it is in his enthusiastic acceptance of Lucifer's book: 'This wil I keepe as chary as my life'. Perhaps the scene is morally appropriate in that these sins are so many humorous caricatures: a 'show' devised by Lucifer, beguiling Faustus into a sense of detachment from them (he recoils from them all). It gives dramatic perspective to the true evil, this picture-book evil which cannot be taken very seriously, but on the whole the scene is regrettable. It is in this sort of thing, mere diversion, that the integrity of the play is compromised.

'Mere diversion' is both the subject and the function of the middle section, the series of episodes taken from the *Faustbook*.

The introductory speech (792–802) has the true Marlovian touch in its excitement: the 'mounting' image, the 'burning bright', and the glamour of 'yoky dragons neckes'. Similarly, Faustus' first speech, though not distinguished, is of a piece with the play. The Temple that 'threats the starres with her aspiring toppe' sounds the Icarus motif, and there is the familiar spirited extremism in the 'ayrie mountaine tops, With walls of flint, and deepe intrenched lakes'. For the rest, the proper names dazzle and the verse has a certain sonority. The same is true of Mephastophilis' rather elementary travel-talk. An interesting change in Mephastophilis' 'persona' is that he becomes, as a travelling companion, very much the good chap, almost the 'regular guy' who knows the ropes, can get you in anywhere and has a good trick or two up his sleeve. When he says that he has taken 'his holinesse priuy chamber' for their use the audience brighten with anticipation, and as he brushes aside Faustus' uncertainty with his man-of-the-world's 'weele be bold with his goode cheare', they positively warm to him: the text illustrates persuasively evil's insidious good-chap guise. Meanwhile Faustus' reply ('Now by the kingdomes of infernall rule'), fervent rhetoric rather than good poetry, still comes as expressing the enthusiastic impatient character of the first scenes. There is good fun in the Vatican (the scene still plays well, particularly the burlesque Commination) and Faustus' excitement is a little like Hamlet's high-pitched elation at the success of the play. He rhymes excitedly and the couplet has its own irony:

> How? bell, booke and candle, candle, booke and bell,
> Forward and backward, to curse *Faustus* to hell.   (887–8)

The excited student has become the naughty schoolboy: 'Come on Mephastophilis, what shall we do?' This fresh, boyish merriment is not to be heard again.

The Chorus speech is plain and functional, but it does a little more than merely connect episodes. We feel an orderly, measured normality in these lines where the natural order of things is again evoked:

> Hee stayde his course, and so returned home,
> Where such as beare his absence, but with griefe,
> I meane his friends and nearest companions,
> Did gratulate his safetie with kinde words.   (907–10)

This links forwards and backwards with the two scenes with the scholars. 'And in their conference' speaks of that dignified, profitable world, 'the fruitfull plot of Scholerisme', of which Faustus, by taste and reputation, is still a part. The Scholars' admiration of his 'learned skill' enforces the sense of tragedy in the cut branch. Faustus is, of course, betraying their trust. Later, his confession to the scholars, 'Ah Gentlemen! I gaue them my soule for my cunning' (1393), shows him in the predicament of the brilliant schoolboy who has come top of his form by the use of cribs and now has to own up.

Robin, Rafe and the Vintner provide amusement which might be acceptable even in this context but for the involving of Mephastophilis. He has come all the way from Constantinople and his sense of outrage is comical. The audience laugh with Robin's terrified comment, 'you haue had a great iourney'. There is an odd dramatic indecorum and irresponsibility: the attitude seems to be 'it makes good fun so never mind how it fits'. Here is the penalty of what Sidney called 'to thrust in the Clowne by head and shoulders to play a part in maiesticall matters'. On the other hand, Robin and Rafe do a neat double-act and the comedians are given a good script. Robin is the lively one and Rafe the lugubrious, gawping foil. The first sentence promises well for broad comedy. There is a good pun in 'search some circles for my owne vse'; and Robin's agitation as Rafe comes in fidgeting about commonplace things is all very vivid: 'Keepe out, keep out, or else you are blowne vp, you are dismembred *Rafe*: keepe out, for I am about a roaring peece of work' (933-5). A nice bit of teamwork is involved in the dealings with the Vintner. Robin rubs his hands gleefully: 'Hush, Ile gul him supernaturally' (the scene is in its essentials another burlesque of the serious supernatural dealings). As Robin finds the place in the book, keeps off the Vintner, and painfully spells out the words, he has a corner of his mouth for his confederate: 'looke to the goblet *Rafe*'. At its Marx-brotherly level, the comedy is good.

Little can be said for the humour at the expense of the Emperor's knight. The joke is crude and tiresome, and the rest of the scene, for all its courtliness and dignity, almost as tedious. In these exploits Faustus is, of course, the hero, and in some ways captures admiration justly. His courtesy and modesty are marked, and he manages to sublimate his personal vexation with the sceptical knight so that punitive measures are undertaken for the general good of scholars: 'and sir knight, hereafter speake well of Scholers'. He is indeed a very superior conjurer, if not exactly a 'mighty god'. Meanwhile, he is aware that 'time doth runne with calme and silent foote' (1107). For the 'payment of [his] latest yeares' he will return to Wittenberg. The approach of the play's last movement is sounded here, dimly, for the first time in this section.

It sounds more insistently in the Horse-Courser scene. This is also for the most part silly, unworthy stuff, but it has its distinction. Mephastophilis is again humorously on the side of the good chaps: 'I pray you let him haue him, he is an honest felow, and he has a great charge, neither wife nor childe' (1125–6). The cynical eyebrow comes into play with the paradox. A good, rather poetic line occurs in the Horse-Courser's prose as he admires the horse: 'Hee has a buttocke as slicke as an Ele'. There is a memorable moment in the midst of all this foolery. Faustus, keeping up the high spirits of the farce, shouts after the Horse-Courser: 'Away you villaine, what doost thinke I am a horsedoctor?' The mirth cools and there is nothing between the man and his self-knowledge. His last words echo in the mind and he can do nothing but face reality: 'What art thou *Faustus* but a man condemned to die?' The line makes another sudden and poignant lurch into seriousness, now preparing for the last section of the play. When he is left alone, the bottom drops out of his world, and there is a return to the swimming uncertainty of mind experienced in the earlier scenes:

> Dispaire doth driue distrust vnto my thoughts. (1145)

But with the weak hope of last-minute reprieve and the possibility of enchanted sleep, he can rest 'quiet in conceit'. These few lines are highlighted by their context of crude buffoonery, which now returns (with the Horse-Courser's leg-pull) to round off the scene.

The weakest of all the scenes follows. But memory tends to expand these stretches: this particular scene, concerning the Duchess of Vanholt's grapes, is only forty lines long.

'I thinke my maister meanes to die shortly' (1237): Wagner's first line announces the last movement. He is perplexed by the belly-cheer though really it is very much in character. His words cast a sadness on Faustus' last 'glorious deed'. There is over this scene a certain beauty and dignity: the magic of Helen's reputation, the associations evoked by the lines, the hush ('Be silent then, for danger is in words'), and the music as she 'passeth ouer the Stage'. The decorum and 'curtesie' which have done something to redeem the scene of the grapes, are again marked here. The happiness of the episode, with the students' good wishes ('Happy and blest be Faustus euermore'), has a bitterly ironical tinct, overcast as it is by the shadowy figure of the Old Man, a living *memento mori* chilling the after-supper warmth.

The Old Man is a positive, whose measured language with its biblical tone ('guide thy steps vnto the way of life') recalls the serenity and poise of 'the fruitfull plot of Scholerisme grac't'. He brings hope: Faustus may still gain 'celestial rest'. But the way to it is by a reverse of that enchanted 'quiet sleepe' with which he shrugged off thoughts of his 'finall ende':

> Breake heart, drop bloud, and mingle it with teares,
> Teares falling from repentant heauinesse.   (1277–8)

He speaks forcefully and Faustus is moved to acknowledge what he already knows. The Old Man's comfortable words soothe with the oil of grace where the 'roaring voyce' of Hell has burned into the soul; and again characteristically Faustus is moved to despair and an attempted suicide.

There follows the first climax of this last 'movement'. It parallels but intensifies the panic and degeneration suffered in the Lucifer scene. The see-saw motion returns: 'I do repent, and yet I do dispaire' (1301). The line 'Hell striues with grace for conquest in my breast' shows the agony of self-division recognised by the introspective man. Faustus can look over his own shoulder and know himself, yet he is powerless to solve his spiritual problem because of his bondage to self. His condition is like that of the Ancient Mariner:

> I look'd to Heaven, and Try'd to pray;
> But or ever a prayer had gusht,
> A wicked whisper came and made
> My heart as dry as dust.

The Mariner has the same ingrowing self-concern, and he too has to learn the technique of repentance. He is luckier than Faustus, whose misery leads him not to bless but to curse.

Mephastophilis breaks suddenly into the soliloquy as Lucifer did. This corresponds to a memorable passage in chapter 48 of the *Faustbook*:

sodainly his Spirit appeared vnto him clapping him vpon the head, and wrung it as though he would haue pulled the head from the shoulders, saying vnto him, Thou knowest FAUSTUS, that thou hast giuen thy selfe body and soule vnto my Lord LUCIFER, and hast vowed thy selfe an enemy vnto God and vnto all men . . . write another writing with thine owne blood, if not then I will teare thee all to peeces.

Mephastophilis is no longer the pliant Pandar but the Gauleiter with all the unknowable terrors and powers of the party behind him:

> Thou traitor *Faustus*, I arrest thy soule
> For disobedience to my soueraigne Lord,
> Reuolt, or Ile in peece-meale teare thy flesh.   (1304-6)

'Peece-meale' is hissed through the teeth, and 'teare thy flesh' opens out violently with its sudden wide vowels. This is the threat to consummate the worst thing in the world. It is the fearful echo that has thundered down from the Evil Angel's 'If thou repent diuels shall teare thee in peeces': that moment of most intense suffering in the play ('Ah Christ my Sauiour', the cry that brings in Lucifer) until the present. In this Faustus is again broken and panic-stricken. He crawls: 'Sweete *Mephastophilis*, intreate thy Lord'. The verse moves expressively; the growing panicky speed of Faustus' plea is enforced by the short words, quick syllables and run-on lines. Like a schoolmaster whose wrath is not lightly to be appeased, Mephastophilis maintains his sternness. The threat contained in 'with vnfained heart' suggests perhaps a more apt description already hinted. The inescapable telescreen of religious authority is the omniscience of the supernatural powers: they know the secret chambers of the heart and from them nothing is hid. In his panic Faustus commits the ultimate betrayal of his humanity. The Old Man, formerly his 'sweetc friend' (Mephastophilis is now that) has become 'that base and crooked age', and Faustus wills his own torments upon him. Let them do it to *him*: Winston Smith's cry as the fear of 'the worst thing in the world' drives the last trace of redeemable humanity (love or, here, charity) from him. The devil grumblingly acquiesces, but the tension has relaxed and Faustus, knowing the technique of forgetfulness by this time, asks for something to take his mind off it. It is perhaps the best of his pleasures, the most damnable, and the last. Mephastophilis becomes again the smiling Admirable Crichton, and everything runs like clock-work.

The first two lines of the address to Helen are so famous that some of the wonder is lost. They strike exactly the right note, achieving in two vivid miniatures a swift and powerful evocation of the tremendous past. Faustus has still the Tamburlaine-like feeling that the individual super-human is the crown of all things. The immensity of the

historical events is felt as no more than proportionate to
the magnificence of the individual who caused them; and as
her lips 'suckes forth' his soul, this world and the next
seem well lost. Faustus goes on to rant with pitiful heroism.
But his subsequent raptures are indeed 'all air and fire':

> O thou art fairer than the euening aire,
> Clad in the beauty of a thousand starres,
> Brighter art thou then flaming *Iupiter* . . .   (1341–3)

The glamour of earth and sky links with the glamour of
the proper names, but it is all to make essentially (though
not in Donne's sense) 'some lovely glorious nothing'.[1]

Again the bright enchanted scene is overshadowed by the
Old Man. Faustus goes away with Helen in the happiness
of his enchantment, but the observer knowing the truth
sees him as a 'miserable man'. Conversely, in real physical
torment the Old Man is blest. His pains are vividly
expressed:

> Sathan begins to sift me with his pride:
> As in this torment God shal try my faith.   (1351–2)

Here is a tormented but righteous end, to be contrasted
with Faustus' internal agony and 'hellish fall'. The strength
of will and goodness is vigorously felt in the strong monosyllables, and the actor can put all his force into them:

> Hence hel, for hence I flie vnto my God.   (1356)

The vitality which righteousness promotes even in
suffering old age contrasts with the once energetic Faustus,
who now languishes in weakness and despondency. He
sighs to his friends: 'Ah Gentlemen . . . Ah my sweete
chamber-fellow'. But the mood is jerked into sudden

---

[1] There is an interesting and detailed discussion of the speech in Greg's essay
'The Damnation of Faustus' (*M.L.R.*, XLI, April 1946). Cf. also the substantial
'bed-fellow and Concubine' of the *Faustbook*.

tension with his panic-stricken cry: 'looke, comes he not?
comes he not?' In his terror at these 'sights' he does not
hear the scholar's question. The actor is still to cower in
the horror of his vision, as the Scholars observe him and
talk among themselves. Their comfort and piety are well
rendered: they offer that benevolence and rightness of
advice which still never quite meet an unhappy man's
condition. Faustus, always unstable, has moved from his
'Tush, Christ did call the thiefe vpon the Crosse' to complete certainty that he is damned. Very moving is the
personal note of his love for the University: 'Though my
heart pants and quiuers to remember that I haue beene a
student here these thirty yeeres, O would I had neuer seene
Wertenberge, neuer read booke'. The eloquence of the rest,
in style and intensity like a scriptural lament, brings the
panting, quivering heart pitifully before us. The anguished
'must remain in hel for euer, hel, ah hel for euer', with its
sad echo as Faustus controls himself and remembers his
friends—'sweete friends, what shall become of Faustus,
being in hel for euer'—has an expressiveness rarely found
outside the mature Shakespeare.

That the devil haunts and obsesses his mind is clear in the
unnamed 'he' and 'they' ('Comes he not?' 'O he stayes
my tong, I would lift vp my hands, but see, they hold them,
they hold them'). The chill of the scholars' question 'Who
Faustus?' and the unforced dismay and piety of their
response, 'God forbid', are both impressive in their simple
rightness. Faustus seems to be more in control for having
made the plain statement: 'I gaue them my soule for my
cunning'. He can utter the facts, for at this moment the
scholars' horror is greater than his: he has lived with it.
When he says 'the date is expired', the audience has its
first certain knowledge that this is his 'play's last scene',
and this talk of the past and what might have been is the

more poignant in consequence. It gives an insight into the
long period of misery:

1. Schol. Why did not *Faustus* tel vs of this before, that Diuines
might haue prayed for thee?
Faustus. Oft haue I thought to haue done so, but the diuell
threatned to teare mee in peeces, if I namde God, to fetch
both body and soule, if I once gaue eare to diuinitie: and now
tis too late.

(1400–5)

Very fine too is the short passage following. Faustus gains
sympathy again by taking thought for his students, who are
themselves very human and representative in their differences (the impetuous loyalist and the other, who makes
piety and discretion come to terms). Faustus' 'what noyse
soeuer you heare' is fearfully suggestive in its vagueness, and
an impressive self-control is exercised in the soberly factual
statement of the morrow's alternatives: perhaps after all it
won't happen, this is a bad dream; 'if not, *Faustus* is gone
to hel'.

Left alone, he faces that last line as expressing a predicament which has no real alternative. The statement of it,
factual and controlled, as the clock strikes, shows the man's
need to make himself realise the horror of the moment—
that this dreaded future which he has been living in sight
of for these years has now come to be the present: that inevitable thing which one feels nevertheless cannot happen.
The powerful 'Stand stil' (monosyllables to be uttered with
the actor's strength) is an effort to push this crushing inevitability from him.

Faustus is wonderfully and dramatically placed in the
speech as against a great cosmic background: 'you euer
mouing spheres of heauen . . . Natures eie, rise . . . the
starres move stil . . . streames in the firmament . . . you
starres . . . now draw vp Faustus like a foggy mist, Into the

intrailes of yon labring cloudes . . . my soule may but ascend to heauen'. The individual is painted against this black night sky, dominated as in some Byzantine church by a God who 'stretcheth out his arme, and bends his irefull browes'. Beneath the night sky with its outline of mountains and hills is the blackness of the earth. The man who stood proudly in the 'lustie groue' conjuring against just such a sky, is now pitifully alone: powerless, hunted and terrified. He batters himself blindly to and fro: 'Then wil I headlong runne into the earth'. He visualises and wills ('Earth gape') but is frustrated and again jerks his head upwards to the stars.

The speech is so intensely realised that everything is done for the actor. The line movement is wonderfully expressive:

> Ah, halfe the houre is past:
> Twil all be past anone:
> Oh God,
> If thou wilt not haue mercy . . .   (1450–52)

Here the tension is such that one feels the agony even more acutely than in those lines where it finds vent in a torrent of concentrated language. The lines also provide a point of quietness from which the last climax can rise. The end of this man, once proud and confident in his Renaissance humanism, is a wish to forfeit his humanity altogether: to descend to the status of 'some brutish beast'. The proud scholar has already recanted his intellectual pride: 'would I had neuer seene *Wertenberge*, neuer read booke'. The last utter humiliation of his manhood comes when we hear the aspiring individualist wishing for anonymity, the forward wit praying for a place at the lowest point in the Chain of Being, the point where existence is virtually non-being; and worse remains to be endured.

The chastened, awestruck Epilogue is spoken by the Chorus who had foreseen all, and who some hours back had swaggered forward so boldly with the sonorous rhetoric of his first lines.

If *Faustus* is a great work, it is also a flawed one. It is not merely a matter of two poor scenes and two which degenerate into nonsense, a sequence of trivial episodes and two occasions where the climax is disappointingly followed up. There is also, more seriously, a lack of sustained concentrated writing in places where one might have hoped for it, and often, by Shakespearean standards at any rate, a poverty of poetic texture. Sometimes, as one is thinking how to describe something in the play, a Shakespearean phrase comes to mind: Faustus, for instance, might be described as

destil'd
Almost to *Ielly* with the Act of feare.

(*Hamlet*, I. 2)

It is a very unremarkable phrase in the richness of its context but would represent a remarkable enrichment of vocabulary in a Marlovian context. How far Marlowe is *responsible* for these shortcomings is an irrelevant query when one is concerned, as I have been, with the text as the object or fact which exists for us.

This 'fact' has rarely been the critics' prime apparent interest in the play. Perhaps an exception is Mr James Smith, whose essay in *Scrutiny*[1] was limited to certain aspects of *Faustus* as a work of art. But the prime concern seems to have been with *Faustus* as a significant phenomenon rather than a work of art. Mr Levin's close study, for instance, appears to have as its prime concern an act of relating or connecting; that is, it seems for the most part to be interested in the text when it can be related to something outside itself, a whole body of European culture, adduced with breadth and knowledge, but involving the

---

[1] 'Marlowe's *Doctor Faustus*', *Scrutiny*, VIII, 1 (1939).

play more as a portent, a significance, than a work of art. This is true also of Miss Mahood's penetrating remarks in *Poetry and Humanism*. The effect of this kind of interest has been both to shrug off too lightly the flaws in the play (its 'significance' remains) *and* to insulate the reader from the full force of the work (as opposed to recognition of the 'phenomenon').

It is true that some of these flaws are not beyond defence. The middle section, writes Harry Levin, 'is unquestionably weak. The structural weakness, however, corresponds to the anti-climax of the parable; it lays bare the gap between promise and fruition, between the bright hopes of the initial scene and the abysmal consequences of the last.' There are other points of correspondence. I understand Mr Levin to mean that these middle scenes act, in their weakness, as a gap between the first and last sections, throwing them and the contrast between them into relief. He seems, then, to be referring to the *ultimate* fruition. But the disappointment of the immediate fruition is enforced also. The 'world of profit and delight' turns out, as dramatised, to be sadly trivial, even progressively trivial, and ever-less vital. There is a certain wonder in Faustus' European travel, as described by himself and the Chorus; also a certain zest about the doings in the Vatican. Both the wonder and the fun degenerate in the scene with the Emperor. The fun is at its lowest with the Horse-Courser, and wonder is practically extinguished in the Vanholt scene. So that this middle section does not exactly 'lay bare' the gap between the promise of the first scene and the fruition of the last, but shows the stages between them. The scenes illustrate the growing emptiness of the way of life Faustus has chosen. That is (and must have been then to the sensitive part of the audience) the moral effect; though there is some relevance in the objection that there are better ways of presenting boredom than by being boring, or triviality than by being trivial.

It is not likely that Goethe had this sort of discussion in mind when he made that famous remark, 'How greatly is it all planned'. Yet these are the points that need facing in order to say it and mean anything very much by it. This dictum, like the middle section of the play, has something to be said for it, not so much by virtue of its doubtful intentions, but because, in itself and as it stands, it has point. (The intended meaning seems not to be what the modern critic would like to make it, for the adjective *gross* suggests something more like 'on a large scale', great in the sense of large, rather than a qualitative judgment; and, although in English the emphasis of the sentence comes meaningfully on 'planned', in German the emphasis probably falls on *gross* rather than *angelegt*, which anyway suggests 'laid out' as of a park or garden, which is not really very appropriate to *Faustus*.)

The great planning, however, is plentifully in evidence. Miss Mahood justifies the term by reference to the 'philosophical structure'; and one might add the creation and development of character, the working of dramatic climax, and the linking backwards and forwards, by means open to the dramatic poet (and Marlowe is primarily that, not a philosopher), of lines and phrases which thus gain in intensity and relevance.

Other kinds of planning it clearly has not. Any complex interplay of plots and characters, for example. It has the structural bareness of the fifteenth-century *Everyman* which in several ways it resembles. The grave dignity of that play is absent (in its mirth and knockabout mixed with serious matter, *Faustus* is more like the normal Morality than *Everyman* is). Moreover, Marlowe has, characteristically, reversed much in the traditional Morality pattern. *Everyman* and *Mankind*, for instance, dramatise Holy Dying and Holy Living respectively: *Faustus* is about evil living and consequently desperate dying. Mankind and Everyman crawl up to their God; Faustus even in his last hour still aspires to leap, and it can't be done. The earlier pair, in a pilgrim's progress, climb the steep ascent of Heaven, and flights of angels sing Everyman to his rest; Faustus, the Devil's disciple, goes the primrose way and Hell calls with a roaring voice. But the admonitions of *Everyman* are those of *Faustus*:

> The story sayth: man, in the begynnynge
> Loke well and take good heed to the endynge,
> Be you never so gay.

And in both plays, a man's soul is the stage; the forces from without correspond to forces within, and Heaven and Hell play for the victory.

The people of the mediæval psychomachia have the representative characters of their names. That is, they are not distinctive characters at all, however convincingly human in their reaction to the given situation. Faustus is an individual in spite of the tendency the morality element has to categorise him among the 'forward wits'. He is inevitably one of a class or type—the young extremist, eager and buoyant, with a brilliantly energetic, inquiring mind, intoxicated by his enthusiasms, heady in his dislikes, and fundamentally superficial in both. But the character develops. After the Vatican scene, the boyish quality disappears and there is a sense of ageing. The keynote of the weak Vanholt scene is its courtesy, and in that and the two later scenes with the scholars it is a quieter and more mature Faustus who is admired. As in the beginning he was placed in a relationship of youth with age by the 'sage conference' of Valdes and Cornelius, so in the last act he is felt to be a senior man in company with the scholars. His sheer energy has declined. 'Confound these passions with a quiet sleepe'; later the scenes with Helen have almost the quiet dignity of an Indian summer; and his sighs in the last scene with the scholars are those of a man whose vitality is weakened. But in all these things he is still, partly, representative. In other respects he is a very unusual man indeed.

He is a chaos of will and impotence. His humanism, proud and aspiring, is expressed in the lines:

> All things that mooue betweene the quiet poles
> Shalbe at my commaund, Emperours and Kings
> Are but obeyd in their seuerall prouinces;
> Nor can they raise the winde, or rend the cloudes,
> But his dominion that exceedes in this,
> Stretcheth as farre as doth the minde of man. (84–9)

'The mind of man' is the nearest thing in creation to infinity; it is creation's crown. But it is checked by nature: the winds and clouds are nothing in the scale of being, yet they remain as symbols of intractable matter. Man is limited (this is the feeling) not by his own nature, but by the nature of the world that encloses him. Miss Mahood says, 'Pride in man's potentialities is swiftly reversed to despair at his limitations':

> Yet art thou still but *Faustus*, and a man. (51)

She also writes of the 'extreme swings of the pendulum' in Faustus: 'contemptuous pride and incredulous despair'. What sets the pendulum in motion concerns the will; here there is a fundamental instability. Faustus sees the will as the ultimate power within man, but it is a will which at the same time he morbidly suspects to be illusory and governed by something outside itself.

He dismisses Divinity because it seems to involve a hateful determinism which denies the real freedom to 'settle', 'begin' and 'be'. Faustus is intent, as the essential means to any worth-while end, on asserting his will. His first speech is that of a man determined not to run on wheels; he is to make the existentialist choice and start living. His will may, as he implies to Mephastophilis, be boundless and crazy. He may assert it in something like Gide's *acte gratuit*:

> Be it to make the Moone drop from her spheare,
> Or the Ocean to ouerwhelme the world. (273–4)

He might in fact will to act out Ulysses' Order speech, 'and make a soppe of all this solid Globe': 'Then euery thing includes it selfe in . . . Will'.

But the rejected biblical texts also proclaimed (in their truncated form) a necessary, fated damnation. It is no accident that precisely those texts are chosen, or that Faustus should have overlooked or have deliberately and proudly set his face against that text which follows the quotation from St John: 'But if we confess our sins, he is faithful and just to forgive us our sins, and cleanse us from all unrighteousness'. That is the Christian doctrine of grace, and Faustus has no conception of it. Clearly, then, in his mind, he must be damned if there is any truth in Divinity. He has made a gesture of dismissal towards Divinity and acted on the assumption that he has done more than that. But he has not in fact dismissed it from his mind at all. This lurking sense of damnation *precedes* the invocation to Mephastophilis, and the conviction of it precedes the formal deed with Lucifer:

> Now *Faustus* must thou needes be damnd,
> And canst thou not be saued? . . .
> To God? he loues thee not,
> The god thou seruest is thine owne appetite.
> (433–4, 442–3)

In this speech is expressed not only the certainty of damnation but a deep sense of sinfulness: he does not deserve God's love for he has served his appetite ('Will into Appetite'). Again, the sinfulness is not just the result of his dealings with the devil but also the cause of them: it was not his 'coniuring speeches' that raised Mephastophilis, but his spiritual condition. The conviction of worthlessness and inevitable damnation grows:

> If vnto God hee'l throwe thee downe to hell.   (510)

The words of the Evil Angel strengthen it:

> Thou art a spirite, God cannot pitty thee.   (624)

And the fearful echo of Faustus' own thought: 'Too late'. Scepticism, hope and attempted repentance all challenge this conviction in Faustus, but it is deeply embedded in his thought and emerges ultimately in the last speech:

> You starres that raignd at my natiuitie,
> Whose influence hath alotted death and hel . . . (1443–4)

The free-thinking Renaissance humanist only hides a traditionalism which is basically mediæval: the conservatism of Lear's Gloucester as against the bright scepticism of the 'new man' Edmund.

The forces represented in this tension within the individual are deep in European civilisation, and that explains why commentators have been so much concerned with *Faustus* as a 'significance'. Strangely, the man whose story comes to mind as being most Faust-like in this way lived neither in the Renaissance nor the Middle Ages, but in the 'Age of Reason'. Cowper's biography contains a terrible latter-day psychomachia: 'His bedroom was every night the battle-ground of a struggle between good and evil spirits, and . . . in the end the evil always vanquished the good, and then "Bring him out!" they would cry, "bring him out!"'. Cowper was convinced of his damnation: 'On the night of 24 February he had a dream. What it precisely was no one knows; but in it amid circumstances of unspeakable horror, he heard from the lips of God himself the certain and irrevocable sentence of his damnation . . . Within the centre of his consciousness remained unaltered the conviction that he was damned, that every day he passed brought him a day nearer to an eternity of torment; and he had fixed his eyes exclusively on such things as could still give him pleasure, had laboriously derived from them the whole elaborate scheme of occupation and habit and amusement which was his mode of life, in order to distract himself from the frightful fate that awaited him.'[1] This is from what another writer has described as 'the saddest and sweetest life in English literature'![2] Here are two of Cowper's own utterances, the first from an early poem (*Hatred and Vengeance*):

> Damned below Judas; more abhorred than he was,
> Who for a few pence sold his holy Master!
> Twice betrayed, Jesus me, the last delinquent,
> Deems the profanest.

And the second from his diary:

Friday, Nov. 16th . . . Dreamt that in a state of the most insupportable misery, I looked through the window of a strange room, being all alone, and saw preparations being made for my execution. That it was about four days distant and that then I was destined to suffer everlasting martyrdom in the fire, my body being prepared for the purpose and my dissolution made a thing impossible. Rose overwhelmed with infinite despair, and came down into the study, execrating the day I was born with inexpressible bitterness.

This 'sweet, sad life' is, in this, not unlike what Marlowe presents us with in *Faustus*. Conscious of the Romantic

---

[1] Lord David Cecil, *The Stricken Deer* (London, 1961). [2] G. Sampson, *The Concise Cambridge History of English Literature* (Cambridge, 1941), p. 577.

heresy, one wonders whether it has anything in common with Marlowe's own.

The involvement of the author in his work is, of course, much debated. John Bakeless 'feels an autobiographical touch, feels it keenly too'. Miss Josephine Preston Peabody, quoted by Bakeless, had no doubt about it. She makes the Marlowe of her play cry: 'I am the man, the devil and the soul'. Others imply it in their judgments. Michel Poirier writes: 'That more or less conscious distortion of the Christian doctrine is rather to be ascribed to the author's nature, to his narrow logic, to his incapacity to understand the grandeur and beauty of the message of the Gospel.' That is to make Marlowe 'the man' at least, and virtually 'the devil' as well. Critics in the opposing camp include Miss Mahood, James Smith and Roy Battenhouse.

A decision here depends partly on the attitude one already has to questions of this kind, and partly on the amount of weight one allows such biographical evidence as the Baines note. With P. H. Kocher, I take the note seriously. As Faustus had used 'such meanes whereby he [was] in danger to be damnd', so (the evidence suggests) had Marlowe. It does not follow that Marlowe is making a personal recantation as some have thought, or that he had no more idea of grace than Faustus had (as Poirier implies), or that the play is essentially a sermon on the explicit 'moral' of the Epilogue. But when Miss Mahood says that 'In his tragic heroes he has embodied the spiritual adventures of his own generation, as he observed them', one has to add that as he was himself 'of his own generation' he probably, like his introspective Faustus, observed his own spiritual adventures with particular closeness. He does in fact seem to me to be 'giving of his own substance', as Professor Waldock says of Milton[1]; and this does not open him to Dr Leavis's

[1] *Paradise Lost and Its Critics* (Cambridge, 1947).

charge which he makes—justly, I think—against Milton, of failing to depersonalise 'the relevant interests and impulses of his private life'.

For if 'his own substance' is there, and if the biographical evidence for supposing this is true, then Marlowe achieved a rare degree of detachment. The Marlowe of the Baines note and the tales is treated with little respect. The knight in the Emperor's court, for instance, is in some ways an enlightened freethinker. He will not accept Faustus on authority: 'Ifaith he lookes much like a coniurer'. That, according to the Baines note, was very much Marlowe's attitude to the reputation of Moses. The knight is contemptuous of the conjuring, and smart in the style of his commenting. In his promise to the Emperor, Faustus has allowed himself a fairly generous logical loop-hole. The knight observes it and says 'Ifaith thats iust nothing at all'. One might suppose this sceptical intelligence to be congenial to Marlowe, but in fact the knight is humiliated. This scene may not be Marlowe's own, but the same is true of Faustus himself in a scene which is certainly authentic. He too is a freethinker with advanced notions: 'Come, I thinke hell's a fable'. And later:

> Thinkst thou that *Faustus* is so fond, to imagine,
> That after this life there is any paine?
> Tush, these are trifles and meere olde wiues tales. (565–7)

And:

> This word damnation terrifies not him,
> For he confounds hell in *Elizium*.
> His ghost be with the olde Philosophers.[1] (294–6)

These are all in spirit like the Marlowe of the Baines note, willing men 'not to be afeard of bugbeares and hobgoblins'

[1] J. C. Maxwell (*Notes and Queries*, cxciv) has noted the identity of the last line with a saying attributed to the Arabic philosopher Averroes, expressing his hostility to Christianity.

and persuading them 'to Atheism'. This boastfully independent freethinking always carries with it a dramatic
irony in the play, and provokes the bitterly ironical comment of Mephastophilis: 'I, thinke so still, till experience
change thy minde'.

Perhaps it would seem that Marlowe could not have the
views attributed to him by the Baines note and at the same
time hold them up to irony and humiliation in the play.
But it surely is possible, understandable and moving. It
would only argue in Marlowe a division and uncertainty
like that he dramatises with this characteristic see-saw or
wave motion in Faustus. Indeed if there is any truth in his
reputation as it has come down to us, some such division
is surely inevitable. However firmly a man believed with
his reason that traditional religion is essentially superstition,
he must also, in his soul, have felt that traditional wisdom
affirming the religion could not be so utterly mistaken.
The Baines note shows a nonconformist, confident in his
attack and almost heroic in his boldness. But the weight of
ages cannot be shaken off, and if the ages are not wrong
then the freethinker must be. If he is wrong, they are right;
and if they are right there is pain after this life; and for
those who abjure the Scriptures, exercising their pitiful
intelligence where a blind understanding is required, the
ten thousand doors of hell wait ajar. The Marlowe who wrote
Faustus need not have renounced publicly or privately the
nonconformity of the Baines note, but he must have known
doubts and fears of an agonising kind. Such a tension
would involve a very Faust-like instability.

Instability is fundamental in the play, as a theme and a
characteristic. *Faustus* is a play of violent contrasts within
a rigorous structural unity. Hilarity and agony, seriousness
and irresponsibility: even on the most cautious theories of
authorship, Marlowe is responsible at times for all these

extremes. This artistic instability matches the instability of the hero. The extremes of optimism and depression, enthusiasm and hatred, commitment to Hell and aspiration to Heaven, pride and shame: these are the swings of the pendulum in Faustus' world, and they are reflected by the sickening to-and-fro motion of the verse—an ambivalence first felt in the Prologue's 'forme of *Faustus* fortunes good or bad'. But this to-and-fro of extremes is not the only movement in the play. The other movement (and this seems to me fundamental in Marlowe's career as a writer, as it is in this play) is one of *shrinkage.* Faustus stands on his own two feet, a proud thing in creation, as he conjures in his lusty grove; but in the end, he cowers and hides, wishing his manhood to be shrunk to the stature of a brutish beast and finally to that of the lowest, least individual thing in the creation he once thought to dominate. He is bent and shrunk not merely by his contact with evil, but because in the first place he would not bend and shrink submissively to the will of the powers that shape the world. Man has to crawl between heaven and hell. In *Tamburlaine* that space seemed so ample that he could strut wonderfully and challenge the other worlds to match his splendour. In *Faustus* this world (and Faustus like a millionaire tourist has 'done it all') yields less. In the other plays it is to yield less still.[1]

[1] See also Appendix II: '*Doctor Faustus*: the Diabolonian Interpretation'.

5

'THE JEW OF MALTA'

THERE is a general feeling that this is a play of distinctive character, and an equally widespread difference of opinion as to what that character exactly is. Few plays have been given more names: tragedy, comedy, melodrama, farce, tragical-comical, farcical-satirical, 'terribly serious' or 'tediously trivial'; 'terrifying', it seems, cannot be too heavy a term, nor 'absurd' too light. There is no real need, of course, to tidy it away into any particular dramatic category; some of these descriptions are more helpful than others, but probably none is definitive. It is best to regard the play as *sui generis*, and ask what is distinctive about it.

What, for a start, is *not* to be found in it? In the play of *Dido*, a man leaves a country he loves, and comes to a country where he is loved. When he leaves this it is to call into being a new world which will begin to compensate for the loss of the old. These situations involve some warmth, some looking outward from the self: the conflict is the classic one between love and duty, and as usual there is a lot to be said for both. In *Tamburlaine*, we have a hero who draws all men to him; who is brave, eloquent, passionate, alive to the beauty around him and the vast inheritance which is his if he will stir his body and stretch his spirit to attain it. In *Faustus*, grace strives with hell within a man of great ability and energy, who has also a feeling and relish for the beauty and variety of creation. The three plays contain much evil, but these virtues are present as forces strongly felt, widening man's character to match the wonder of the earth he seeks to dominate.

In *The Jew of Malta* one has to search hard to find any comparable virtues in the world dramatised. Love for another person does indeed survive as a never-very-robust, ever-more-sickly element, until it meets a violent end half-way through the play. With its decease goes also that of the only character whose nature knows any compunctious visitings at all (as Mr Levin notes: 'Abigail, the single disinterested character in the play, . . . is characterized by the first four words she speaks: "Not for my selfe"').[1] Mercy, selflessness, affection, loyalty, beauty, warmth have no place in this world. But then the world itself has become a comparatively poor thing. It is large (the opening contains a procession of countries, seas and cities which reminds us of *Tamburlaine* and *Faustus*); but its size is no longer significant, exciting or even very real. Slaves rip up the bowels of the earth, ships sail from one country to another, like pieces of mechanism which can stir the blood only because power is involved in pulling the strings which control them. But this power robs space of its majesty and remoteness of its magic. By their fruits are they known and to Barabas the fruits are 'fiery *Opals* . . . hard *Topas* . . . sparkling *Diamonds*' which when gathered remain as fiery, hard and sparkling as in their own land. He knows and possesses the fruits, and the significance and value of the world lie here, a concentrated reality: 'infinite riches in a little roome'.

The little, congested room of Malta is in fact presided over by Riches, the dumb god who creates men after his own image, hard, sparkling and fiery like the jewels they possess or are possessed by.[2] The world of 'Volpone' is

---

[1] *The Overreacher*, p. 90.
[2] Cf. 'Riches, the dumbe god, that giu'st all men tongues, That canst doe nought, and yet mak'st men doe all things' (*Volpone* I. i. 22) and 'These possesse wealth, as sick men possesse *Feuers*, which, trulyer, may be said to possesse them' (ibid. V. 12. 157).

very close, as Eliot pointed out, and in more ways than one. 'Haile the worlds soule, and mine': matins before the shrine of Volpone's gold opens with this *Ave Divitiae*, and the line trumpets the brazen theme which dominates the play. In a harsher tone of abrupt, business-like realism it is heard as a theme in *The Jew* also:

> Governor. Welcome, great *Bashaws*, how fares *Callymath*,
> What wind drives you thus into *Malta* rhode?
> Bashaw. The wind that bloweth all the world besides,
> Desire of gold. (1420–23)

All comings and goings in Malta are similarly motivated: the Turks come for tribute money, the Spaniards for trade in slaves. It is gold that determines peace or war:

> This truce we haue is but in hope of gold,
> And with that summe he craues might we wage warre.
> (731–2)

Barabas is the most successful representative of a materialist society which also victimises and condemns him: a society where those in power are hypocrites and where low life, nasty, brutish, and shorter than usual, thrives on blackmail, prostitution and theft.

We have a more comprehensive survey than Jonson gives in *Volpone*, going into high and low places and taken even into foreign and economic politics. Here the dumb god's interests are served by 'that smooth-fac'd Gentleman, tickling Commoditie'. The ethos is something like that of Shakespeare's *King John* (or its first three acts), where kings come to the field as 'Gods owne souldier' and yet 'breake faith vpon commoditie', or where the *seeming* is of majesty or holiness and the *being* is a counterfeit resembling it. Expediency is all. So here, the Governor's smooth-faced act of piety and courtesy (in his relationship with Jew, Spaniard and Turk alike) is belied, according to the circumstances, by his ruthless activity or the practical necessity of his passiveness. Right and wrong, sin and honour, Fate and Heaven; the noble terms glide from his tongue, and it is all part of 'the policie', the Machiavellism which he and his like, the respectable, are supposed to abhor. The Establishment does eventually triumph over the Outsider in this play; but only because they can outdo the unscrupulousness for which they condemn him.

With wealth their end and opportunism their means, the people of the play cannot be other than hard and ruthless. The prevailing morality is that of Al Capone's Chicago, and so, very often, is the language:

Ithamore. That's braue, M^r. but think you it wil not be known?
Barabas. How can it if we two be secret.
Ith. For my part feare you not.
Bar. I'de cut thy throat if I did.   (1516–19)

The tough, wise-cracking idiom manages also to convey that careless menace of the shrewd moron as American films have made it familiar to us. I mean, in such a passage as this, where Pilia-Borza turns from comic lout into blackmailer:

Pil. Iew, I must ha more gold.
Bar. Why wantst thou any of thy tale?
Pil. No; but 300 will not serue his turne.
Bar. Not serue his turne, Sir?
Pil. No Sir; and therefore I must haue 500 more.
Bar. I'le rather——
Pil. Oh good words, Sir, and send it you were best; see, there's his letter.
Bar. Might he not as well come as send; pray bid him come and fetch it: what hee writes for you, ye shall haue streight.
Pil. I, and the rest too, or else——   (1870–81)

At another point, a hard negative slices savagely through the suave, sweet-reasonableness with which the Governor has been bringing it home to Barabas that, for reasons of state, he and the other Maltese Jews are to be robbed. He begins by 'requesting their aid'. Barabas pretends not to understand:

> *Bar.* Alas, my Lord, we are no souldiers:
>   And what's our aid against so great a Prince?
> *1 Knight.* Tut, Iew, we know thou art no souldier;
>   Thou art a Merchant, and a monied man,
>   And 'tis thy mony, *Barabas*, we seeke.
> *Bar.* How, my Lord, my mony?
> *Gov.* Thine and the rest.
>   For, to be short, amongst you 'tmust be had.
> *Iew.* Alas, my Lord, the most of vs are poore!
> *Gov.* Then let the rich increase your portions.
> *Bar.* Are strangers with your tribute to be tax'd?
> *2 Knight.* Haue strangers leaue with vs to get their wealth?
>   Then let them with vs contribute.
> *Bar.* How, equally?
> *Gov.* No, Iew, like infidels.   (280–94)

Of course, the Governor never *was* 'requesting aid', and he now cuts the smooth-faced seeming down to the hard bones of real business. It is sudden and savage like the line in *Edward II* where Lightborne, impatient with the cat-and-mouse game he has been playing with the King, answers Edward's fearful question 'And therefore tell me, wherefore art thou come?' with his abrupt and terrible

> To rid thee of thy life.   (2555)

This aggressive, harsh dialogue is a foretaste of the manner of speech most characteristic in *Edward II*. In the world of that play too the dominant elements are 'voyd of . . . compassion, loue' or any tenderness or altruism. They too are hard as Barabas' Topas. In anger they may be fiery like the opals. But they certainly do not sparkle like the diamonds, for theirs is a grey world, a little room full of wilful, snapping people and destitute of riches in any form. This leads to another observation: that *The Jew of Malta*, for all its inhumanity, is not a depressing play, whereas *Edward II*, for all its comparative warmth of feeling, is.

Edward's England speaks and acts out its conflict of petty wills against a dull, drab background (Gaveston's first speeches stand out in retrospect, like a butterfly hovering near the blind cave of night); the Malta of Barabas does however, by comparison, sparkle. He himself is a comic villain but a brilliant one, the man whose personality dominates all around him and who (until the last throw) can beat them all in resourcefulness and enterprise. He is also the man who makes you laugh; and, in a lively and imaginative reading, *The Jew of Malta* is a very funny play. There are several levels of humour, and for the moment I am not referring to the 'serious' kind which has received some critical notice, but to the sort of thing at which a good actor can make his audience laugh outright as (say) Guinness or Sellers can in films, or as an Olivier or Marius Goring can when playing Richard III. This aspect of the play is often passed by (because its readers are busy hunting for thematic unity, significant thought and other important matters). But it is an essential factor, contributing to the play's character, helping to shape our attitude to the people in it, and so affecting the serious content by theatrical workings which a study-reading is liable to overlook.

The actor who is comically one-down is usually the man we take to our hearts. The little fellow who nervously bows himself out of a queenly presence and backs into a window which he topples out of is profoundly discomfited, and then rewarded by our laughter. And it *is* a reward, because we feel more warmly towards him, perhaps with our less official, more indignity-prone selves, and look forward with fearful joy to his next mishap, with the confidence that fortune will be good to him in the end. This is basically a kindly humour, and there is very little of it in Marlowe. But there is also the actor who is comically one-up: he appeals to our heads—except that the head's approval is usually communicated to the heart, and so we find he has some emotional allegiance too. This is so with Barabas. There is a Marlovian complication here, however, in that what one quick-witted part of the head conspires with the heart to support is exactly what another morally-directed part tells the feelings to condemn. Laughter will by-pass that countering reason and carry our inner allegiances into places where we have no sober intention of their going: hence its importance.

We laugh a good deal *with*, and hardly ever *at*, Richard III. When we see him, earnest in the service of his God, the good book in hand, a bishop ('Two Props of Vertue, for a Christian Prince') on either side, we are witnessing a fraud practised on simple, bewildered folk, and the consequences of its success are to be dire. We are also seeing the devil hoodwink God's people, playing games with the apparatus of religion, relishing every caper he cuts in the guise of mild-mannered piety. But we laugh, and an essential part of us is with him. 'It is this unholy jocularity, the readiness of sarcastic, sardonic, profane and sometimes blasphemous wit, the demonic gusto of it all, which not only wins the audience over to accepting the Devil as hero, but also points us towards the central paradox of the play.' The quotation is from A. P. Rossiter's study of *Richard III*,[1] which also seems to me to offer the best critical light on *The Jew of Malta*. Marlowe's play is mentioned only once, but there is much that is wonderfully apposite. It is, however, a point that needs some discussion: how far is it true that an audience is won over to accept, in Barabas,

[1] *Angel with Horns* (London, 1961), p. 19.

'the devil as hero', or to 'write "good angel" on the Devil's horns'? The answer involves us in (at least) a brief survey of the play. Machiavel's Prologue itself sets the pattern of dramatic doublethink. It is a cunningly devised speech, the subversive matter clearly and memorably expressed, sandwiched between conventional hiss-the-villain mouthings of a stock stage figure. The gloating tone of the opening ('you thought Old Nick was dead and buried, didn't you: but here we are, you see') evokes a popular response of the kind that has greeted a long line of melodramatic villains— through to Sweeney Todd, whom Barabas also fitfully resembles. Similarly the last lines of the speech imply, perhaps, an invitation to throw things:

> . . . let him not be entertain'd the worse,
> Because he fauors me.   (34–5)

this and a suave withdrawal can hardly have been received with enthusiastic or respectful consideration. But the 'lecture' he reads in between is a different matter. The attitude, contemptuous and proud, is one we associate closely with Marlowe[1]:

> And let them know that I am *Machevill*,
> And weigh not men, and therefore not mens words. (7–8)

He speaks with the egoism of Elizabethan villains, and also with the dignity of their heroes, risen from the dead to the Senecan and Renaissance tune of '*Medea superest*' and 'I am

---

[1] The 'lecture' itself might be said to be within a convention. Michel Poirier particularly has claimed a marked 'crystallising' influence in Gabriel Harvey's *Epigram* of 1578. Here Machiavelli speaks an eloquent and dignified oration which has some points of similarity. But the contrast is more interesting than the comparison, for the earlier speech reads as a rhetorical exercise: the writer reverses normal values but his cold statements have no persuasive power and are not intended to have. With Marlowe, there is an urgency and feeling which, being expressed in the most characteristic manner of the writer, show a quite different kind of involvement.

Duchesse of *Malfy* still'.[1] This is followed by lines which are 'mighty' in the firmness of statement and the exact fit of idea and iambic pentameter:

> Admir'd I am of those that hate me most . . .
> I count Religion but a childish Toy,
> And hold there is no sinne but Ignorance. (9, 14–15)

The energy, firmness and balance are admirable. In thought, there is a link with the Marlowe who was said to have exhorted men not to fear 'bugbeares and hobgoblins' (religion being superstitious and superstition being childish). If religion is childish, as the idea of fairies, or bogeys in the dark place under the stairs, there is a corollary which St Paul teaches: 'when I became a man I put away childish things'. Superstition (so runs the line of thought) was useful in man's infancy,[2] but the enemy now is ignorance. The Reformation, the ambitions of Science, the inquiries of Raleigh's 'school', all link forward with the new-man, whose philosopher is Hobbes,[3] and who says with Shakespeare's Edmund or with Marlowe's Machiavel:

> Birds of the Aire will tell of murders past;
> I am asham'd to heare such fooleries. (16–17)

Here, in Machiavel, is another angel with horns. The arguable (and argued) right on his side is this: power is in fact frequently gained by great men without legitimate claim, otherwise the greatness of a Caesar might have been wasted; cunning and ruthlessness have in fact been needed to maintain this power; even professedly moral governors go on these principles and are hypocrites when they denounce Machiavelli who is their real master—a man who

---

[1] Cf. Eliot, *Selected Essays*, p. 132.
[2] Cf. 'That the first beginning of Religioun was only to keep men in awe' (Baines note).
[3] Cf. J. F. Danby, *Shakespeare's Doctrine of Nature* (London, 1949).

has made a bid for human freedom, freedom to make progress in the pursuit of knowledge, freedom from old restraints imposed in a dark age and kept alive by a dead-handed tradition. Against him seem ranged the hypocrites, simpletons and fuddy-duddies. He makes a bid, too, for Protestant approval by his reference to unscrupulous Popes. And there is some humour (in Marlowe's Lucan's vein) in Phaleris bellowing in the brazen bull.[1] In Shakespeare we are constantly aware of the vitality in evil (Richard, Iago, Edmund, Antonio), and often it reminds us of the amiable and humorous independence of Faulconbridge or Falstaff. In Machiavel the vitality is felt not principally through humour, but through pride. The paradox of the 'good devil' remains: he is the man you love to hate and hate to love—though with the other side of your mind you do that too. He is the Goldstein of the Two Minutes Hate:

Goldstein was delivering his usual venomous attack upon the doctrines of the Party—an attack so exaggerated and perverse that a child should have been able to see through it, and yet just plausible enough to fill one with an alarmed feeling that other people, less level-headed than oneself, might be taken in by it. He was abusing Big Brother, he was denouncing the dictatorship of the Party, he was demanding the immediate conclusion of peace with Eurasia, he was advocating freedom of speech, freedom of the Press, freedom of assembly, freedom of thought, he was crying hysterically that the revolution had been betrayed . . . And yet . . . at one moment Winston's hatred was

[1] On this line and its possible bearing on the interpretation of the Prologue and the play see 'Marlowe's Prologue to *The Jew of Malta*' by Antonio D'Andrea (*Mediæval and Renaissance Studies* v, 1960). The essay is complicated, but one of its conclusions is that the Prologue is 'a reasoned and polemical manifesto of the fierce and immoderate realism which Marlowe brings to the stage'. In the Phaleris image he is aiming at men of letters, and the speech strikes a personal blow with its Poetomachia-like allusions. I find the argument hard to take in even when unravelled in prose. Its compression and obscurity in verse (even if Mr d'Andrea has interpreted it aright) would seem to be self-defeating and I doubt whether it caused Greene, Nashe and the rest any great distress. On the other hand, the essay contains a most interesting study of the origin of the reference to Phaleris—interesting principally as an illustration of the nature and extent of Marlowe's reading.

not turned against Goldstein at all, but, on the contrary, against Big Brother, the Party, and the Thought Police; and at such moments his heart went out to the lonely, derided heretic on the screen, sole guardian of truth and sanity in a world of lies. And yet the very next instant he was at one with the people about him and all that was said of Goldstein seemed to him to be true.[1]

I do not suggest that Machiavel's speech constituted a Two or Three Minutes Hate, or that the stage Machiavelli evoked a feeling as intense as that aroused by the tele-screened Goldstein. Or that more than a few would experience anything like Winston's instability of feeling; though I think it very Marlovian. But the effect of the speech is worth considering not only for itself but because it presents in little the basic paradox of the whole play. 'He fauours me', says Machiavel of Barabas (meaning, probably, 'resembles'), and the presentation and response will be similar in the two cases—except that laughter also is going to weight the scales as the play develops.

The resemblance becomes immediately clear in the first scene: pride again is the keynote. 'Goe tell 'em the Iew of *Malta* sent thee, man' says Barabas with the same proud tone as in 'let them know that I am *Macheuill*'. In 'Who hateth me but for my happinesse?' (150) we have the same scornful diagnosis of perverse hostility as in Machiavel's 'Admir'd I am of those that hate me most'. It is interesting to compare Barabas' first speech with the opening of *Volpone*: what seemed, in *The Jew*, a similar hymn in praise of gold is seen as above all a *scornful* utterance. When an enthusiastic, rhapsodic tone does develop it is with an energy derived from belittlement. Volpone accepts the fact of riches very simply and in a sense impersonally; his character is a harmonious one and his liking is for the thing

[1] Orwell, *1984*, Penguin ed., pp. 13–15.

itself. But Barabas is egoistically involved in it—his wealth is a personal adjunct that establishes superiority. He, the member of a race treated as inferior, can beat the Christians at their own business, and is, at least, not a hypocrite about it. If gold is his god, so is it theirs. Money's rant is on, and 'who is honour'd now but for his wealth?'. He looks at the Christians and can see

> no fruits in all their faith,
> But malice, falshood, and excessiue pride,
> Which me thinkes fits not their profession. (154-6)

That is a nice dry way of putting it: the horns begin to glitter dangerously here with a little of the light of ironic truth. Occasionally, he goes on, you may meet an unlucky fellow with a conscience, and he (Christian society being what it is) 'for his conscience liues in beggery'. 'I wouldn't have your conscience, not for all your income', says the poor man to the millionaire. 'I wouldn't have your income, not for all your conscience', replies Undershaft, a latter-day Machiavellian devil with wings. Again the comparison becomes a contrast. With both Undershaft and Barabas money is a religion; but whereas for Shaw's character it is a social and moral religion (money saves the soul from the Seven Deadly Sins—which he enumerates), for Marlowe's it is a personal and amoral force (it guarantees power and status, gratifies the ego, and further rights and wrongs are irrelevant). His justification is simply the negative and cynical one that everybody else is just as bad morally and not as good practically. The meanness of spirit is quite characteristic of Marlowe's world in this play and the next.

The meanness is inner; outwardly there is much lavishness and grandeur. The two soliloquies are separated by a brief episode which shows us, as in a flashback or a marginal illustration, 'a typical moment in the life of a financial wizard'. The modern jargon comes to mind because the scene itself is curiously modern. We see Barabas' extraordinary busy-ness, the network of merchants and enterprises which he controls from Malta. One merchant enters as another leaves, and to both Barabas gives the snap-decisions of the master-mind—it is all very like the Wall Street tycoon answering several phones at once, sending his breezy, brassy commands to the uttermost ends of the earth. He is, in a sense, god-like: he says to his servant 'Do this . . . and he doeth it'. But it is an ugly god, whose own caricature grimaces from behind the swivel-chair grinning in fat complacency as the obedient Merchant trips off with his spirit-like 'I goe'.

The soliloquies, with this episode between them, are a kind of second prologue; the action of the play begins when some Jews enter and tell Barabas that they fear trouble. Here we admire Barabas' public bonhomie: he is the big man among them, a father-figure. It is a part he is acting, and the real self is there only in a brief Richard III-like aside:

> If any thing shall there concerne our state
> Assure your selues I'le looke vnto my selfe. *Aside.*
>
> (211–12)

I take it that the lines are spoken with the grand, reassuring manner of the elder statesman except that the last two words emerge from the corner of the mouth in a different voice altogether. It's morally indefensible, but we laugh with him. When the Jews have gone he speaks in a different tone again: this is the Machiavel in his thinking-cap ('search this secret out') and the reassuring performance we have just seen has to be reappraised as a piece of controlled dissimulation. On the other hand, villainy is before us: 'Why let 'em enter, let 'em take the Towne', he says of the Turks (whose arrival has alarmed the other Jews).

The Jew as non-national and a possible collaborator in invasion cannot have been an endearing concept.

But the fears of Zaareth and Temainte were justified, for the Turks demand payment from Malta and the Governor hands on their demands to the Jews. The shifts of attitude here are very rapid. At first Barabas is heroic, exhorting his people to firm resistance. Then he collapses with almost comic desperation. Then finally he regains support as against the Christians' sanctimonious harshness. He has been unjustly stripped of all he possesses, and the religious overtones of the affair are strong and subtle. Barabas challenges the action on its consistency with the Christian faith:

> Is theft the ground of your Religion? (328)

The Governor justifies the 'theft' by iterating a fine principle of expediency ('the plea of Caiaphas', Dr Boas notes):

> Better one want for a common good,
> Then many perish for a priuate man. (331-2)

One man bears the sins of his world and is judiciously crucified, despised and rejected of men ('make thee poore and scornd of all the world')—the pharisaical Christians confer an almost Christlike status on the Jew. The argument goes further. The Governor disclaims responsibility for Barabas' misfortune, referring it to 'thy inherent sinne'. Barabas' reply is strong and carries a weight of feeling against hollow piety:

> What? bring you Scripture to confirm your wrongs?
> Preach me not out of my possessions. (343-4)

He weakens this with a piece of straight-and-crooked thinking:

> Some Iewes are wicked, as all Christians are. (345)

and then strengthens his position again by strong argument against original sin (his protest 'shall I be tryed by their transgression' can extend that far). He too can 'bring scripture' and quotes 'The man that dealeth righteously shall liue'. But he profits still more from the speeches of his enemies, for the Governor is at his most unctuous in patronising the man he has wronged:

> Be patient and thy riches will increase,
> Excesse of wealth is cause of covetousnesse:
> And couetousnesse, oh 'tis a monstrous sinne. (355–7)

With Richard III, Undershaft or the later Barabas, this would have been a piece of humorous mock-piety; but here it is simple self- (and others-) deception. As such it is repeated in:

> No, *Barabas*, to staine our hands with blood
> Is farre from vs and our profession. (377–8)

A dignified and fit reply further enhances Barabas' status:

> You haue my wealth, the labour of my life,
> And comfort of mine age, my childrens hope,
> And therefore ne're distinguish of the wrong. (382–4)

A long line of social critics is represented in the other sentence of this speech:

> Why I esteeme the iniury farre lesse,
> To take the liues of miserable men,
> Then be the causers of their misery. (379–81)

Fielding in *Jonathan Wild* put it thus: 'Is it not more generous, nay more good-natured, to send a man to his rest, than, after having plundered him of all he hath, or from malice or malevolence deprived him of his character, to punish him with a languishing death, or, what is worse, a languishing life?' (Chaplin's *Monsieur Verdoux* was a modern variation on the same theme.) Barabas closes the exchange with a line which carries the weight of the scene:

> Your extreme right does me exceeding wrong. (386)

and another which with its mean, realistic stoicism is closer
to the general tone:

> But take it to you i' th deuils name.   (387)

The exceeding wrong done to Barabas is more serious
than he knows (or perhaps than Marlowe knew, for it is
hard to discern conscious moral purpose in this). He has
experienced injustice and disaster and his character changes.
He is represented as being in Job's position: the comparison
is explicitly made by one of the two feeble Jews who are
with him, and implicitly by the irritating correctness of
their Job's-comforting as well as by lines which are close
to Job's own lament:

> For onely I haue toyl'd to inherit here
> The months of vanity and losse of time,
> And painefull nights haue bin appointed me.[1] (429–31)

Barabas himself thinks that his position is far worse than
that of his Biblical prototype. Job had no sorrow like unto

[1] Wolfgang Clemen's book called *English Tragedy before Shakespeare* (a misleading
title since the author is concerned with one limited aspect—the set speech) catalogues
various kinds of speech in Renaissance drama, one of them based on the formula
'Can there be a sorrow more hard to bear than mine?' (see p. 230). He does not
instance this speech, but it would have served; and many speeches in *The Jew*, and
of course in Marlowe generally, fall into the categories he has analysed. When
this 'typing' of speech is emphasised or isolated for study, we tend to see plays
more and more as exercises in certain literary conventions; and the more conventional
(in this sense), the less significant. At this point in *The Jew of Malta*, for example,
one might apply a mind fresh from Clemen and say 'Ah yes, the situation concerns
suffering, so the author writes a "Can-there-be-a-sorrow" type of speech. The
convention was there for him to use, and here he is trying his hand at it'. But while
the classical tradition behind Renaissance drama may prompt such an approach, the
Morality tradition directs towards thought and significance. So, as a reader of
The Jew, one could at this point make the marginal note: 'Lines in convention *x*:
cf. Herc. Furens, Phoenissae, Locrine, Selimus'. And one could note that Barabas
in Job's situation reacts in a manner which is the opposite of Job's. One would
then ask what *attitude* seems to be invited: condemnation, as in the traditional
Morality, or a something of admiration which would in turn redound on Job as
servile, spiritless and less than a man? The first note may afford a useful caution
or corrective, but it has this danger: that, having 'placed' such a passage within a
convention, you think you have done with it, whereas the essential thing about it is
that it is not really conventional at all but highly particular and characteristic—and
so engages the interests in the ways in which literature (as opposed to literary
detection) can.

his sorrow, for neither had he wealth like unto his wealth. Barabas calculates tragedy by bulk—he is twice as wealthy and so twice as wretched. But as soon as the Jews leave him, he drops this, snaps out of his self-pitying inactivity, and we see that this is the point where some new form of life is going to emerge from the cocoon of misery in which he has been wrapped. What it turns out to be is not the man who patiently rebuilds, or the Job who submits and still blesses, but a vindictive and still more self-centred schemer. This is the natural development. We recognise the change but also the essential continuity in a short soliloquy where the old pride and scorn reassert themselves:

A reaching thought will search his deepest wits.   (455)

Barabas is speaking the language of Tamburlaine with the unbroken spirit of Satan (and, lest we should be sentimental, or think that we have here a hero, with the bottle-nose of the stage Jew). It is a short step from this to the man-monster, 'determined to prove a villain'. The common complaint that the change is sudden and unnatural has no justification.

The change is not effected by a single spasm of the will, and the struggle continues in Barabas' first dialogue with Abigail. Abigail is seen as a loving daughter; the monster-farce does not extend to her, and her love ennobles Barabas dramatically, as Zenocrate's did Tamburlaine. With her, Barabas appears at his most amiable and human, speaking with unusual moderation and normality:

No, *Abigail*, things past recouery
Are hardly cur'd with exclamations.
Be silent, Daughter, sufferance breeds ease,
And time may yeeld vs an occasion
Which on the sudden cannot serue the turne.   (470–4)

This too recalls Milton: the Satanic predicament and the arguments of the Infernal Debate. Abigail brings news of a further disaster, however. Barabas' house is in enemy hands and so he has no access to his secret nest-egg. The robbed miser's abyss is partly comic, and some of the ensuing speech is fustian. But again the reaction divides. His desperation leads him first to a Faust-like wish for extinction:

> That I may vanish ore the earth in ayre,
> And leaue no memory that e're I was. (499–500)

But then he performs one of these impulsive Marlovian about-turns:

> No, I will liue; nor loath I this my life:
> And since you leaue me in the Ocean thus
> To sinke or swim, and put me to my shifts,
> I'le rouse my senses, and awake my selfe. (502–6)

This is surely admirable; Faustus as he might have been— whole-hearted in evil—[1] and by implication Job as he should have been—defiant and active instead of tame and submissive. It is another bridge-passage leading to the emergence of the monster, convincingly motivated and ending with the Machiavellian key-word:

> Be rul'd by me, for in extremitie
> We ought to make barre of no policie. (507–8)

The couplet both links with what has gone before and prepares for what is to come.

Another transition is prepared in this scene as religious criticism develops, through satire, into farce-comedy. Barabas wants to reclaim the gold hidden in his house, which has become an establishment for convertites. Abigail is to persuade the Friars of her contrition. They will take

---

[1] Cf. Nicholas Brooke on 'Dr Faustus' (*The Cambridge Journal*, v, 11, 1952) and comments in Appendix II, p. 365.

her in, she can find and deliver the gold, and escape. 'Religion Hides many mischiefes from suspition', says Barabas, meaning that there is many a nun as fraudulent in her holiness as Abigail will be. When the Friars enter, the cant and clichés of their talk are well caught ('No doubt, brother, but this procedeth of the spirit . . . She has mortified her selfe'), and satirical amusement broadens during the rather hectic comedy in which Barabas' *sotto voce* instructions to Abigail alternate with hypocritical high grief for the benefit of the Friars. Barabas here is The Entertainer. He is a man of many voices and poses, with the mobile actor's face which can suddenly drop the mask for an aside and return (to our increased delight) to the part he has had the effrontery, wit and resourcefulness to assume. He will continue in this character throughout; and to a large extent he will have us with him.

But nothing is static in Marlowe, and at the next appearance of Barabas he too becomes a victim to the deflationary tricks of the play. Not without dignity in adversity, he is ludicrous in rejoicing. Abigail flings down the gold and Barabas hugs his money-bags, passionately absurd as any conventional comic figure in rapture:

<blockquote>Oh girle, oh gold, oh beauty, oh my blisse.   (695)</blockquote>

Shylock is caricatured in just the same way by Salanio, though the effect is more subtle, for grief is involved: Marlowe's laughter is characteristically harsher.

Barabas has already moved into the realm of caricature, and it is not surprising that when we see him next he has progressed a stage further towards the monster-man. Time has passed and he has become as wealthy as he was. He is also, as is natural, much more vindictive, eccentric and extreme as worked on by his hatred. He mouths malevolently ('In spite of these swine-eating Christians . . .')

and rejoices in the extreme forms of his 'Machiavellian' tactics:

> I learn'd in *Florence* how to kisse my hand,
> Heave vp my shoulders when they call me dogge,
> And ducke as low as any bare-foot Fryar.   (784–6)

But the human being has not disappeared, and it is in this same scene that he reminds us most, not of the ludicrous or villainous in Shylock, but of Shylock as a man with a valid grievance. Lodowick, the Governor's son, comes to him with an eye to his daughter—'canst help me to a Diamond'—just as Antonio comes to Shylock and 'would have moneys'. Barabas answers him with some of Shylock's scorching irony:

> Good Sir,
> Your father has deseru'd it at my hands,
> Who of mcere charity and Christian ruth,
> To bring me to religious purity,
> And as it were in Catechising sort,
> To make me mindfull of my mortall sinnes,
> Against my will, and whether I would or no,
> Seiz'd all I had, and thrust me out a doores,
> And made my house a place for Nuns most chast.
>   (832–40)

Lodowick is evidently a chip off the old block, for the pious reply comes pat: 'No doubt your soule shall reape the fruit of it'. This leads to more jokes about nuns and more play with the cant and jargon of religion. But through all this, and for all the melodrama and absurdity surrounding him, we are still made to feel the strength of personality in Barabas as against anyone on the stage with him. It is not sufficient to say that Marlowe could not create minor characters and that this is simply a limitation of his art. These other characters are as real as they need to be (and sometimes very vivid); but it is the character or purpose of his art still to exhibit a dominant central figure.

The interesting thing is that after Tamburlaine and (probably) Faustus, the dominant figure should be of this sort.

The masterful personality and the lively wit (Volpone and Mosca in one) are again exhibited as Barabas plays off one suitor (Lodowick) against another (Mathias), bamboozling Mathias with earnest assurances and at the same time impersonating a book-lender to hoodwink his watchful mother. We see him also in the slave-market, a firm, powerful man in his dealings. The slave he buys is Ithamore, with whose entrance, says Dr Boas, 'there is a subtle change in the atmosphere of the play'. It is true that we have now seen all we are going to see of Barabas as 'a figure of wellnigh tragic stature'. But the lowering of tone which Dr Boas observes at Ithamore's line 'I worship your nose for this' (938) has been insidiously in progress from the start: the movement, that is, towards farcical action, melodramatic, roughly colloquial speech, and caricatured *personae*. What follows, the manner which establishes itself in this scene and now remains dominant throughout the play, is a culmination. I would say that it has been in sight from the first. The ambivalent figure of Machiavel as Prologue (rather than the heroic swagger of the Prologue to *Tamburlaine* or the eloquent dignity of the Chorus to *Faustus*), even this prepares the tone; and the figure of the stage Jew who speaks the blank verse of soldier and scholar itself marks a further move towards burlesque. The essential unity of the play seems plain, and the point is laboured here only because it has been so often denied.

This culmination, a duet for two misanthropes, presents Barabas as a man-made-monster (made by Christians) in the popular image of Machiavelli:

> Hast thou no Trade? then listen to my words,
> And I will teach that shall sticke by thee:

First be thou voyd of these affections,
Compassion, loue, vaine hope and hartlesse feare . . .

(932–5)

If this were all, a dispassionate lecture in the tone of Gabriel Harvey's *Epigram*, there would indeed be a disunity. In a sense, unity is *preserved* rather than violated by Ithamore's 'Oh braue, Master, I worship your nose for this', which follows at this point. For it expresses and encourages that kind of glee which our serious mind will hardly acknowledge but which accompanies the appearances of Barabas throughout. Barabas' next speech then is heard not in solemn disapproval but with amusement:

As for my selfe, I walke abroad a nights
And kill sicke people groaning vnder walls . . . (939–40)

It is clearly made for laughter. There follows a nice play-off between the colloquial-matter-of-fact and the grotesque-macabre: the off-hand way in which Barabas tells how he has made 'now and then one hang himselfe for griefe', or, when his own catalogue of crime is over, the absurdly urbane conversational lead offered to Ithamore—

But tell me now, how hast thou spent thy time? (966)

Ithamore's prompt answer ('Faith, Master, In setting Christian villages on fire') introduces his verse in the duet:

Once at *Ierusalem*, where the pilgrims kneel'd,
I strowed powder on the Marble stones,
And therewithall their knees would ranckle, so
That I haue laugh'd agood to see the cripples
Goe limping home to Christendome on stilts. (973–7)

The whole episode is conceived with the exotic relish and cruel humour of Nashe's Executioner towards the end of *The Unfortunate Traveller*. It is extravagant comic stage-villainy and everybody knows it is: Barabas is still The Entertainer, and a highly successful one.

We next see him plot the downfall of his daughter's

Christian suitors. Again the resourceful villain commands admiration, making up a vivid, satirical love-fantasy to deceive Mathias and deftly inciting Lodowick to anger at the same time. Nor is it true that the more human manner of the earlier scenes has entirely disappeared. A rare note of reason and warmth is struck in Abigail's words to her father:

> I cannot take my leaue of him for teares:
> Father, why haue you thus incenst them both?
> *Bar.* What's that to thee?
> *Ab.* I'le make 'em friends againe. (1120–23)

But she is 'put in' by Barabas and Ithamore who relish their villainy in further half-comic dialogue.

Barabas is still effective in satire and irony. When planning the downfall of the young men, he justifies himself with the argument:

> It's no sinne to deceiue a Christian;
> For they themselues hold it a principle,
> Faith is not to be held with Heretickes. (1074–6)

This too links back, with the earlier criticisms of Christians. Then, when the suitors fight, Barabas provides a superbly ironical commentary:

> *Bar.* Oh brauely fought, and yet they thrust not home.
> Now *Lodowicke*, now *Mathias*, so;
> So now they haue shew'd themselues to be tall fellowes.
> *Within.* Part 'em, part 'em.
> *Bar.* I, part 'em now they are dead: Farewell, farewell.
> (1186–90)

The family griefs which this double death occasions are presented in a very perfunctory and conventional way: the parents' discoveries seem to us in fact ludicrous, but whether this is dramatic immaturity, a bad text, a lack of interest or a deliberate befarcing of the situation, it is hard to say. The scene merely seals Barabas' triumph, and his glee is still in the air when it is over.

THE JEW OF MALTA

Ithamore now develops into a useful comic as his master develops monstrosity to its extreme point. Barabas has learned that Abigail, deserting her father and her faith, is entering a convent. His fury craves vengeance, so he determines to poison her and the whole nunnery besides. Stirring the poisoned pot he mouths his curses:

> The iouyce of *Hebon*, and *Cocitus* breath,
> And all the poysons of the Stygian poole
> Breake from the fiery kingdome; and in this
> Vomit your venome, and inuenome her
> That like a fiend hath left her father thus. (1404–8)

But this is still comedy, and Ithamore picks up the laughter invited by the whole episode: 'What a blessing has he giv'nt? was euer pot of Rice porredge so sauc't? what shall I doe with it?' We laugh *at* Barabas here, as the perpetually shifting manner of the play is. We laugh *with* Ithamore, who shares in the villainy (as we laugh also with the pickpocket Pilia-Borza). And meanwhile in the next scenes, the respectable world—the Establishment in Church and State —itself grows monstrous. 'Desire of gold' is seen as 'the wind that bloweth all the world', while honour and other fine statesmanly ideals accommodate themselves accordingly. Similarly, the holy men of the Christian Church are seen as lecherous and greedy, prevented from having much success only by their timidity and silliness. Barabas is monstrous in a comic or melodramatic context; the Establishment's monstrosity has a context much closer to reality. Moreover, Barabas has the wit to amuse us; the Establishment has not.

In the last acts, Barabas performs a variety of roles: convert to Christianity, handman to Justice Incorruptible, the Turk's best friend, the Governor's industrious deliverer, and a French musician with preposterous accent and conveniently out-of-tune lute. His conversion is a ruse to quieten the feeble Friars who have heard, through Abigail's

confession, of Barabas' complicity in the deaths of Lodowick and Mathias. The burlesque of mediæval penitence
must have been written much as Fitzgerald tells us of
St Simeon Stylites that 'A.T.' read it laughing.[1] Barabas
promises:

> To fast, to pray, and weare a shirt of haire,
> And on my knees creepe to *Ierusalem.*   (1570–71)

Boas says Barabas is 'in terror', but he surely has them on
a string all along. He piles up the bribe promised to 'some
religious house', and the comic fable enacts itself promptly.

> *1 Fryar.* Oh good *Barabas*, come to our house.
> *2 Fryar.* Oh no, good *Barabas*, come to our house.
>   And *Barabas* you know——
> *Bar.*   I know that I haue highly sinn'd,
>   You shall conuert me, you shall haue all my wealth.
>   (1586–90)

Radix malorum est cupiditas, as *The Pardoner's Tale* demonstrates. The Friars are now in competition, and divided
they fall. Again we laugh *with* Barabas and *at* his enemies,
especially as he affects their speech idiom when at Ithamore's
pious request he parts them: 'This is mere frailty, brethren,
be content' (cf. Gloucester's 'Oh do not sweare, my Lord
of Buckingham'). Then one of the Friars is murdered with
a grim joke ('Blame not vs but the prouerb, Confes & be
hang'd. Pull hard'); and the guilt is neatly pinned on
the other. Barabas' pose of scandalised virtue is a good
one:

> *Iocoma.* Villaines, I am a sacred person, touch me not.
> *Bar.*   The Law shall touch you, we'll but lead you, we:
>   'Las, I could weepe at your calamity.
>   Take in the staffe too, for that must be showne.
>   Law wils that each particular be knowne.   (1711–15)

---

[1] Quoted in Hallam Tennyson's *Alfred, Lord Tennyson, A Memoir.*

Giving a further turn of the screw, Barabas and Ithamore say they are so shocked to find such villainy in Christians that they cannot any longer see their way to conversion.

The same high-spirits (over 'low-toned' comedy maybe) persist in the last act. Barabas is denounced to the Governor and seems to be done for. Thrown out of the city, he is left as dead but, to our delight, rises ... like Falstaff, though his 'What, all alone?' is not quite up to 'Imbowell'd?'. For revenge, he helps the Turks to enter the city. They reward him with power, and his old enemy, the Governor, is haled off to jail. At this, of course, he should have rested content: 'This is our master-peece: We cannot thinke, to goe beyond this', says Mosca at the corresponding point in *Volpone*. But Barabas wants to regain the Governor's favour too and undertakes to deliver the Turks into his power. He over-reaches sadly, and here begins the nominal 'tragedy' of the rich Jew of Malta which the title-page has promised. He patronises the Governor:

> Gouernor, I enlarge thee, liue with me,
> Goe walke about the City, see thy friends:
> Tush, send not letters to 'em, goe thy selfe,
> And let me see what mony thou canst make. (2192–5)

Left alone, he restates his 'policy', the Machiavellism with which we started, ending with the jibe which is repeated throughout:

> Thus louing neither, will I liue with both,
> Making a profit of my policie;
> And he from whom my most aduantage comes,
> Shall be my friend.
> This is the life we Iewes are vs'd to lead;
> And reason too, for Christians doe the like. (2213–18)

The soliloquy looks confidently to a future, but he has only his last scene to play. The Turks have been invited to a banquet where Barabas will deliver them to the Governor of Malta, so gaining recognition and security as the island's saviour. A false gallery has been constructed for the Turks, who at the cutting of a cable will fall into a boiling cauldron below. But the Governor, his enemies now well in his power, cuts the cable himself and it is Barabas who boils. The scene is so famous as a theatrical *tour de force* that subtlety of achievement is rarely accredited. The action is crude, but the reaction should not be for the play's characteristic doubleness is clearly focused here. If one at first sees a crude moral exemplum, good defeating evil, a second look finds the 'good' nowhere to be seen; and if 'crude theatrical knockabout' was a first diagnosis, elements of genuine tragedy mixed with some farce and much irony soon press forward to modify it drastically.

Of course Barabas cuts a partly comic figure. *Enter Barabas with a Hammar aboue, very busie*: the bottle-nosed master-of-ceremonies, fixing his murderous mechanism and bustling to and fro, is absurd enough. The ludicrous sight of him bellowing in the pot, the engineer hoist, induces no more pity or tragic feeling than the appearance of the baked witch in *Hansel and Gretel* (and it may well seem to modern audiences about as obnoxious). His speech—'Dye life, flye soule, tongue curse thy fill and dye'—cannot have passed, even around 1590, as tragic utterance intended to impress a straight-faced audience. True it does not read as a parody, comparable with Bottom's Pyramus. But situation, character and diction all combine to produce farce. T. S. Eliot's word is surely the right one, and *almost* as right, I believe, are the other terms of his much-disputed judgment: 'it is the farce of the old English humour, the terribly serious, even savage comic humour'.[1]

For what is serious and savage is that we can laugh as the stage-monster (who was once a man) stews in his own juice;

1 'The Blank Verse of Marlowe' (1919); in *Selected Essays* (London, 1932), p. 123.

but the respectable survivors (normal men in a world of affairs) are just as mercenary in practice and murderous at heart, are hypocrites into the bargain, and have no compensating genius to match that of the famous Jew. Barabas is in fact allowed some little tragic dignity before his death. His share of hubris gives to his last boasts some shadow of classic status:

> . . . why, is not this
> A kingly kinde of trade to purchase Townes
> By treachery, and sell 'em by deceit?
> Now tell me, worldlings, vnderneath the sunne,
> If greater falshood euer has bin done. (2329–33)

His waxen wings are mounting, taking the unheroic body some little way above the ordinary view of men. He even seems to have a certain pride in honour, refusing the Governor's money till he has completed his undertaking:

> . . . nay, keepe it still,
> For if I keepe not promise, trust not me. (2305–6)

And his death, for all his absurdity, has at least a faint smatch of honour:

> . . . in the fury of thy torments, striue
> To end thy life with resolution. (2363–4)

But just as in life the sense of Barabas' speeches spoke for him less eloquently than the hypocrisy of his enemies', so in death his status is enhanced most by the repulsiveness of Respectability. The Governor performs a fine service of hand-washing and finger-wagging:

> Now *Selim* note the vnhallowed deeds of Iewes. (2376)

He himself has betrayed a trust just as Barabas did, and has in fact happily acquiesced in the greater wrong—the massacre of Turkish soldiers which has happened in another place according to Barabas' plan. He calls it 'a Iewes curtesie' and contentedly points out how favourably to himself it has worked. With classic unction, he speaks the play's last lines:

> So march away, and let due praise be giuen
> Neither to Fate nor Fortune, but to Heauen.[1]

It is impossible to be certain that this was written tongue-in-cheek. It may be part of the convention which also sees Tamburlaine as the scourge of God and as therefore having a place in the divine scheme. Or it may be simply in the convention which says that this sort of play may end with this sort of remark. But the satire elsewhere and the placing of the lines after a piece of plain Machiavellism surely suggest a cynical purpose. 'And reason too', said Barabas in defence of his own *policy*, 'for Christians doe the like'. Exactly. This last speech is completely in key with the play's harsh and disenchanted mood. There is characteristic tough humour in the Governor's response to Calymath's naïve suggestion that he might be allowed to go: 'Content thee, *Calymath*, here thou must stay'. It is this *realpolitik* that has gained the victory, and the Governor now rallies his right-little tight-little islanders with the conventional rhetoric:

> As sooner shall they drinke the Ocean dry,
> Then conquer *Malta*, or endanger vs. (2407–8)

The lines make another connection with the commodity-driven world of *King John* ('Come the three corners of the world in Armes, And we shall shocke them': V. 7). Then finally we have the conventional pious flourish, offering the last irony as the whole foxy business is ascribed unto the Lord. But Machiavelli's is the kingdom, the power and the true glory; and in the play's end is its beginning.

---

[1] Cf. 'Heauen, and not wee haue safely fought to day'—Prince John of Lancaster's piety after a similarly Machiavellian success. (*Henry IV*, III. 4.)

This survey has concerned itself principally with the attitude to Barabas, but it should do something also to demonstrate the *unity* of the play. This has been much in question. Tucker Brooke's remarks are representative: 'It is beyond question that the vigorous flow of tragic interest and character portrayal with which the play opens wastes away amid what, for the modern reader, is a wilderness of melodrama and farce. The change is so marked as to suggest grave doubt whether the tragedy as we have it can represent even remotely the conception of a single man'.[1] A textual issue is also involved. The play was written about 1590 and the earliest extant text is the edition of 1633. This has an introduction by Thomas Heywood, famous for his large output of original plays and for having had, as he said, 'a main hand' in a great many others. Tucker Brooke assumes that we have the text 'in a form sadly corrupted and altered from that in which it left the hands of Marlowe' and adds that Heywood may have altered the play for performance at court. H. S. Bennett, a later editor, notes that Heywood's 'well-known, unusual diction' is not much in evidence, and Dr Boas has pointed out that in his Epistle Dedicatory Heywood seems specifically to deny 'a hand' in the authorship. Recent critics, Harry Levin and J. C. Maxwell for instance, have been much more inclined to accept the play as essentially Marlowe's own, but Professor Wilson, writing in 1951, denies this with (for him) unusual vehemence: 'To suppose that the same man who wrote the first two acts was wholly responsible for the last three is revolting to sense and sensibility, for these belong to a different world of art, if indeed they can be said to belong to the world of art at all'.[2] Most writers agree with H. S. Bennett that 'the play as a whole fails lamentably to live out its

---

[1] C. F. Tucker Brooke, *Works of Christopher Marlowe* (Oxford, 1950), p. 232.
[2] F. P. Wilson, *Marlowe and the Early Shakespeare* (Oxford, 1953), p. 65.

early promise'. Again, Professor Wilson puts the case most strongly: 'So the first two acts, and they are the work of genius. In the last three, genius has almost disappeared and except for a few passages here and there so too has the talent. There is little in the first two acts that could have been written by any other man: in the last three there is very little that could not have come from the pen of another writer—and a small writer at that'.[1]

Certainly there are points of contrast. Barabas begins as a credible human being and ends as a prodigious stage 'character'. The early scenes develop the character in the round; there is a psychological interest and with it some sympathy. There are also longer and better speeches; later the soliloquies are few, the emphasis is on the quick give-and-take of essentially unpoetic dialogue, and so much happens that there is little time for the action to stand still while speeches are made. This in itself strikes me as suggesting Marlowe's authorship rather than calling it in question, for it bridges the way to *Edward II*. It was in this direction that his interests as a dramatist were moving. Nor should the absence of fine images or lyrical movement be surprising; the tough nature of the plot makes no call for such writing and again its relative absence from *Edward II* suggests that at this period Marlowe's spirit and art alike were antipathetic to any sort of lyricism or 'poesy'. He seems in fact to have an impulse to defile. Ten lines of charming Arcadian delicacy do find their way into the script (1806–16), but the Passionate Shepherd here is Ithamore, Love's Queen is a grasping prostitute, and the context a ludicrous passage of high-class love-making during which Pilia-Borza is off blackmailing Barabas. Of course, it is possible that Marlowe had a few lines of poetry he wanted to find a place for, and in they went. It

---

[1] *Op. cit.*, p. 63.

may be simply a set-speech, character and situation forgotten. But the subtler effect of incongruity is over the whole scene, and I have no doubt that it is intentional: a laugh at poetic prettiness, a harsh, rather savage comedy (in keeping with the rest) where the high-falutin' idyll is grotesquely cheapened by a setting which cheapens itself further in the process. This is a play of debasement. The interests and language of the first scenes are not those of the play as a whole, and they could not have been maintained. One may regret this, but there is much in J. C. Maxwell's remark that 'objections to the play as we have it are largely the result of building up a picture of the sort of play critics would like Marlowe to have written'.[1] The objections seem to me to be mistaken in all respects.

A marked change in quality and character is said to take place with the beginning of Act III. But there is no sudden change at all. Farce, caricature, sardonic humour, a tough cut-and-thrust dialogue, a quick-moving plot—all these are characteristics of Act II as of Act III. The transition from the manner of the opening has been effected smoothly and rather subtly in the second act, and there are any number of places where the second half of the play takes up themes introduced in the first. There is, then, no abrupt change in the character of the play. But what of its quality?

F. P. Wilson finds the deterioration so pronounced that Marlowe cannot be responsible. To Michel Poirier the first two acts are vastly superior and Marlowe 'seems to have shuffled through the rest of the play'. Again I think there is a little truth and a great untruth. No author 'shuffles' with such liveliness. The middle episodes in *Dr. Faustus*, especially those not published in the 1604 text, are a different matter. There the general flatness of language along with the silliness of the situations do deserve just

[1] *Pelican Guide to English Literature*, vol. II, p. 166.

these criticisms. But there is much more vigour and point in even the worst scenes of *The Jew of Malta*—and there are admittedly some bad ones.

The opening of Act V is particularly absurd. In this the Governor prepares for Calymath; the Courtesan and Pilia-Borza denounce Barabas; the Governor believes them, but Barabas' poison works on them and they die; Barabas pretends to be dead too; the Governor orders his body to be thrown over the walls; Barabas, left alone, presents himself to the Turks and promises valuable assistance. All this happens in a hundred lines. The scene could not be produced today without laughter. Could it in Marlowe's own time, one wonders? The laughter of another age (or even of another country in one's own age) is notoriously difficult to gauge. Did the Elizabethans, for instance, laugh at *Alphonsus*, the play once attributed, incredibly enough, to Chapman?[1] Or were they able to take it seriously? Or was laughter in fact intended, and is it possibly intended in this scene of *The Jew* also? Was Barabas' Machiavellian villainy ('I hope the poyson'd flowers will worke anon') a parody of itself even then? Perhaps the answer is that it was in the process of becoming one and that this explains the off-hand half-melodramatic, half-comic tone of the text. Otherwise it is simply a choice between the author's bad writing and the actor's bad memory.

There are other weaknesses. The scene which follows this moves at a less hectic pace, but is quite unremarkable

---

[1] *Alphonsus* begins with a Machiavellian lecture and continues as a play of revenge and intrigue. The situations and dialogue are often very funny and sometimes clearly meant to be. It is full of lines like 'What wretched dame is this with blubberd cheeks . . . What, my Imperial Aunt? Then break my heart'. Or as two kings wonder whether they have been poisoned:

> *Bohemia.* For my part I feel no distemperature.
> How do you feel yourself?
> *Alph.*   I cannot tell,
> Not ill, and yet methinks I am not well.   (III. 1. 187)

in quality. Nor is the previous scene, where Barabas impersonates a foreign musician, at all 'significant'. It is nevertheless amusing and up to standard as fast, racy comedy of caricature. So are the other episodes which make up what Harry Levin calls the subplot (meaning that it has a 'low' social setting, as opposed to the 'overplot' where we are concerned with high matters, national and international.)[1] The 'low' comedy of the Courtesan, Pilia-Borza and Ithamore is usually written off as worthless. But these characters come within competing distance of Doll Tearsheet, Bardolph and Pistol (in the comic hierarchy, the play's Falstaff, largely absent from Eastcheap, is Barabas himself). They have nothing in common with the fooleries peculiar to the 1616 *Faustus*, and they are integral, not mere random make-weights. Their world of snatch-as-snatch-can is the Governor's too: 'top', or overplot, people stripped of expensive clothes and ways of speech, as at the Judgment, look like this—except that subplot people are often much more lively and less hypocritical. Marlowe, like Jonson, seems to have known his Bartholemew birds, and his comic trio is lifelike and vigorous.

Pilia-Borza, for example, is described by both Ithamore and Barabas with some wonderfully deft caricaturist's strokes. 'A fellow met me', says Ithamore, 'with a muscha-toes like a Rauens wing, and a Dagger with a hilt like a warming-pan, and he gaue me a letter from one Madam *Bellamira*, saluting me in such sort as if he meant to make cleane my Boots with his lips' (1744–8). Barabas' portrait is equally vivid and imaginative:

> . . . a shaggy totter'd staring slave,
> That when he speakes, drawes out his grisly beard,
> And winds it twice or thrice about his eare;

---

[1] *The Overreacher*, p. 88.

> Whose face has bin a grind-stone for mens swords,
> His hands are hackt, some fingers cut quite off;
> Who when he speakes, grunts like a hog . . .   (1858–63)

Writers do not often 'shuffle through' with this Dickensian energy. Nor do they often shuffle off the kind of comic scene in which the Courtesan plays Titania to Ithamore's Bottom:

> Now, gentle *Ithimore*, lye in my lap.
> Where are my Maids? prouide a running Banquet . . .
>   (1800–1)

This grandiose, shabby-genteel romantic fantasy is another Dickensian touch (there are no maids and there will be no banquet).

> *Curt.* Send to the Merchant, bid him bring me silkes,
>   Shall *Ithimore* my loue goe in such rags?
> *Ith.*   And bid the Ieweller com hither too.   (1802–4)

The ten lines of pretty idyllic lyricism follow and then Pilia-Borza returns with the gold which blackmail has extorted from Barabas. In a magnificent parody of the grand manner, Bellamira spurns the gold:

> 'Tis not thy mony, but thy selfe I weigh:
> Thus *Bellamira* esteemes of gold;   *Throws it aside*
> But thus of thee——   *Kisse him*
> *Ith.*   That kisse againe.   (1843–5)

Self-parody sharpens the tone: Tamburlaine wooed both Zenocrate and his followers with an expansion of the Courtesan's lines, and 'that kisse againe' anticipates the swooning Orsino, but also recalls Faustus with Helen. As the preposterous pair, stately as Dido and Aeneas, go off to 'sleepe together', Ithamore sighs forth his soul in Ovidian commonplace:

> Oh that ten thousand nights were put in one,
> That wee might sleepe seuen yeares together
> Afore we wake.   (1849–50)

The Courtesan's rejoinder—'Come Amorous wag, first banquet and then sleep'—draws a coy curtain over the farce and yet preserves the ludicrous air of regal propriety. The 'wilderness' of these last acts, then, is less disorderly and arid than it is said to be. These scenes are usually thought of as the worst of a bad lot, yet the characters are vivid, the lines lively, and the humour works often on the relatively subtle plane of parody and mock-heroic. Not that the character of the humour in its context is adequately suggested by those terms, and it is here that one returns to the idea of 'serious farce' as thrown out in T. S. Eliot's essay.[1]

What does it mean? Eliot himself is characteristically 'economicál', and his allusion to 'the enfeebled humour of our times' seems to suggest that we would not understand anyway. In 1919, when the essay was published, we might have had some excuse, for *Sweeney among the Nightingales* did not appear until 1920, but thereafter 'terribly serious, even

---

[1] The term has not, on the whole, found favour with the scholars. H. S. Bennett does most to explain why: 'This view seems to postulate considerable powers of detachment from contemporary taste and practice on the part of Marlowe. Around him he saw the work of such writers as Kyd, whose *Spanish Tragedy* set the fashion which long outlasted Marlowe—a fashion which gave to the Elizabethan stage tragedies of blood as innumerable as they were successful. Marlowe himself in *Tamburlaine* had made considerable play with this love of rant and bloodshed, and other works of his are not free from it. What is there to make us believe that suddenly he saw the folly of all this and turned to make it material for caricature? Even if we do so believe, there still remains unexplained the differences between different parts of the play. Suppose we swallow the theory of farce (as here defined) for the last acts, in what spirit are we to believe Marlowe conceived the first two acts?' (Introduction, *op. cit.*, p. 17). To take the last point first, Acts I and II have many of the ingredients which make 'farce' in the last three. Also the differences, the existence of deeper and more serious parts, are here conditions of 'serious farce'. Although Mr Bennett speaks of farce 'as here defined', neither he nor Eliot himself really defined it: certainly it is not *defined* by reference to caricature. I do not know that anybody claims that Marlowe 'suddenly saw the folly' of the manner in which he wrote *Tamburlaine*. The earlier works have much debate, oscillation and chafing within them and, leaving *The Jew* out of it, the change from *Tamburlaine* to *Edward II* or *Hero and Leander* is a remarkable one. *The Jew* as 'farce' is a very credible step between them. And surely the more we read of Marlowe the more 'considerable powers of detachment from contemporary taste and practice' have to be postulated as part of his character: it was, after all, a remarkable force that struck out in so many ways in so few years.

savage comic humour' was found again in the land and enjoyed no small success. The close relationship between Eliot's poetry and his criticism makes it often possible to illuminate a dark critical utterance by reference to his poetic practice at the time; and in fact the justice and insight of his tiresomely brief commentary on *The Jew* seem to me best grasped along with a recognition of a kinship between the play and the Sweeney poems.

In *Sweeney among the Nightingales* a cheap, flashily well-to-do world is overshadowed by an uncertain menace. The murdered Agamemnon's cry from his bath rings out against the crude laughter of a debased mankind. A shrunken present is measured by the poetry of the past, paraded only to be punctured and vulgarised in its new associations. The 'shrunken seas', the 'murderous paws', the 'stiff dishonoured shroud' stained by 'liquid siftings', the belly-laugh, and the farce, seem to me, with so much of the rest, to be ingredients basic to both works and to come from similarly disturbed minds.

> The person in the Spanish cape
> Tries to sit on Sweeney's knees
>
> Slips and pulls the table cloth
> Overturns a coffee cup,
> Reorganised upon the floor
> She yawns and draws a stocking up.

On their own, the lines are absurd and insignificant as Barabas slipping into his pot or Bellamira vamping Ithamore. Put in their context, they are all of the things Eliot says of *The Jew*, and 'terribly serious'. I do not quite see an urgency which can justify that 'terribly' in its application to *The Jew of Malta*: Eliot was sensing a doom hanging over modern society and there is nothing corresponding to that in Marlowe. But Marlowe too is parading a debased humanity, shrunk in stature from his own earlier world of heroes and lovers; living, too, in a shrunken, cheapened world of showy wealth; hollow men, among whom Barabas guards the hornèd gate, or at his death Machiavelli. Greed, hypocrisy and littleness provide a setting against which we follow the fortunes of the devil-as-hero. In the first scenes we have predominantly realistic drama and the ambitions, fears and sufferings of a human being. Gradually the man becomes monster and, with the established monstrosity of the man and the society around him, the strokes of portraiture thicken to caricature. Amongst the desolation of a murderous, hollow and little world, the dignity involved in tragedy gives way before the absurdity involved in farce. This is the 'savage comic humour' of which Eliot wrote, and if it is not '*terribly* serious' in the urgency or concentration of its tone, it is at least a kind of writing not lightly arrived at by a man whose work began with such a very different vision of the world and the men it was made for.

D. M. Bevington (*From Mankind to Marlowe* (Harvard, 1962)) offers a theory of composition which might explain the 'uneasy juxtaposition of moral structure and secular content'. Briefly it is that there is a 'conflict between the intricacy of character portrayal and inherited moral structure'. Marlowe was interested in Barabas as a character and therefore had to give some reason for his villainy, namely his harsh treatment by the Christians. But also Marlowe was writing in the tradition of the homiletic drama, where Barabas is a Vice, and the Christians would normally be the Virtues. So 'the difficulty is that in rationalizing Barabas' original plight, Marlowe has created villains out of those very persons who must later become the agents of retribution'. This is not capable of proof or disproof, of course, though it is surely a good and ingenious theory. 'But look you how poor a thing you make of me', Marlowe might have complained. 'My Barabas is the Stage Vice (even his humour and resourcefulness are explained by the convention that that Vice was traditionally an 'artist in evil'); my Christians are Morality Virtues but have got out of hand because my material doesn't really suit my purposes. I am allowed an interest in 'the intricate causality of human behaviour' (though it comes to little more than 'Those to whom evil are done do evil in return'), and reference is made to my play's 'greatness'. Yet the critic shows my work as having a fundamental artistic flaw; and basically he makes my work non-significant.'

(Additional Note, 1970)

6

'EDWARD II'

THE NATURE of both the achievement and the material makes *Edward II* as unhappy a play as any in the period, yet criticism usually gives a cheerful enough account of it. Marlowe is seen as developing towards true maturity, even normality, and doing at last a good workmanlike job requiring skill rather than brilliance: he is 'settling down'.

The 'job' certainly involved skilful construction. Twenty-three years are compressed so that the events seem to pass credibly in something like twelve months. The handling of the chronicle is bold and effective: in historical fact, for example, Gaveston's execution took place ten years before the war against the barons, but in the play it serves convincingly as the stimulus to provoke Edward to battle, and so the one event neatly becomes the cause of the other. This compression is sometimes criticised as excessive, and the editors Charlton and Waller put the point well: 'The dramatist sometimes seems like a man trying to tie up a parcel in a piece of paper too small for it'.[1] This has enough truth to be discussable, and in fact discussion of the structure has usually ended there. But the parcel-and-paper controversy does not lead to what is distinctive about the unusual design of this play. A dramatist's selection and arrangement take place behind the scenes, and here they have attracted investigators who rarely come forward to look at the scene itself.

A remarkable feature of the construction is its symmetry. At a performance one has the impression that there are really

[1] *Edward II*, ed. H. B. Charlton and R. D. Waller: Introduction, p. 35.

two plays: in the first half the subject is the homosexual king and his favourite; in the second it is the rise of Mortimer and the fall of Edward. The impression is not quite accurate, however, partly because the interval has cut across the middle. Actually the construction includes an important middle section marked out from the rest by the fact that in it the king is for a short time strong, determined and victorious. This point of equilibrium holds the balance between the two main blocs, in both of which Edward, succumbing as his power is challenged, suffers loss and humiliation. These two blocs contain also the tragedies of two other men, Gaveston and Mortimer. The Gaveston story is the longer, but dramatically they divide evenly either side of the middle section, both having four major climaxes. The climaxes within the first bloc are these: Gaveston returns from exile; Edward agrees to banish him; the nobles revolt at Tynemouth; Gaveston is killed. And within the second half: Edward's capture; Mortimer's triumph and the death of Kent; the death of Edward; the fall of Mortimer. These two blocs, then, with their own tragedies of ambitious men, both show the humiliation of the king, and weigh equally around the pivot of his temporary triumph.

This is what used to be called aesthetically satisfying, but I think it is unlikely that the form (partially imposed, of course, by the facts of the chronicle) was determined 'in an artist's humour'. This does not prevent its having an expressive function beyond the 'aesthetic', and in fact it does work to define the peculiar nature of the tragedy. Chaucer's Monk provides a reminder of the classic idea of tragedy:

> Tragedie is to seyn a certeyn storie,
> As olde bokes maken us memorie,
> Of him that stood in greet prosperitee

> And is y-fallen out of heigh degree
> Into miserie, and endeth wrecchedly.

Superficially, *Edward II* tells such a story; Leicester's tag—
Quem dies vidit veniens superbum, Hunc dies vidit fugiens iacentem
—illustrates it. But the initial prosperity and high-degree
of the tragic hero are normally real and habitual: the high
ground is also firm ground except in that place where is
the tragic circumstance. Oedipus treads the solid, reliable
ground of his kingdom until it dissolves beneath him
revealing the abyss into which he must fall. Greatness,
power and security have been there in the beginning, and
the ending accomplishes a reversal. In *Edward* the secondary
tragedies of Gaveston and Mortimer follow this pattern;
but the final tragedy of the king himself is only a worsening
of the situation in which he was found at the beginning of
the play. Instead of greatness, power and security, we were
presented from the start with pettiness, impotence and confusion. These are the norms of the play. It is a mean, petty
world that is exhibited, and when Edward 'endeth
wrecchedly', his death is all of a piece with his miserable
life. Nevertheless, he does fall from the height of his
momentary triumph: '*Edward* this day hath crownd him
king a new'. At that central point in the drama, he stood
'in greet prosperitee' on a peak of success and confidence
which is, however, isolated in a context of frustration and
dread. Man is seen as a pathetic creature, bickering or
suffering; and he is still more pathetic for having been
dressed in a little brief authority.

Dr M. C. Bradbrook has written very justly: '*Edward II*
is generally acclaimed as Marlowe's greatest dramatic
success; but this is only possible by ignoring Elizabethan
standards and judging purely on "construction". As
poetic drama, the last speech of Edward is far inferior to
the last speech of Faustus or even to the earlier soliloquies

of the Jew of Malta, and how it is possible to fail as poetry
and succeed as drama is not easy to understand'.[1]

The verse is indeed normally thin and drab. Gaveston's
first speech is fine, but generally it is a matter of only lines
and phrases here and there having any considerable poetic
merit. Among them are the famous lines

> But what are kings, when regiment is gone,
> But perfect shadowes in a sun-shine day? (2012–13)

And Edward's earlier lament:

> My heart is as an anuill vnto sorrow,
> Which beates vpon it like the Cyclops hammers,
> And with the noise turnes vp my giddie braine.
> (609–11)

I like the violent, almost surrealist image in the lines:

> This Ile shall fleete vpon the Ocean,
> And wander to the vnfrequented Inde. (344–5)

There is a finely evocative rhetorical ring in:

> Gallop a pace bright *Phoebus* through the skie,
> And duskie night, in rustie iron carre. (1738–9)

These last lines are virtually Marlovian-routine, but with
their vividness and colour one is grateful for them. Similarly with the characteristic violence, particularly of the
verb, in 'rip vp this panting brest of mine' (1933), and

> Weel steele it on their crest, and powle their tops ... (1333)

> And marche to fire them from their starting holes. (1436)

Sometimes Marlowe achieves a classical eloquence which
avoids artificiality:

> And to the gates of hell conuay me hence,
> Let *Plutos* bels ring out my fatall knell,
> And hags howle for my death at *Charons* shore.
> (1955–7)

---

[1] *Themes and Conventions of Elizabethan Tragedy* (Cambridge, 1935), p. 160.

An eloquence movingly reminiscent of Faustus' last speech is present in Spencer's grief for the king:

> Rent sphere of heauen, and fier forsake thy orbe,
> Earth melt to ayre, gone is my soueraigne.   (1969–70)

The Spenser of *The Shepheardes Calender* is heard in the queen's lines:

> Whose pining heart her inward sighes haue blasted,
> And body with continuall moorning wasted,   (1121–2)

and in Gaveston's

> The sheepeherd nipt with biting winters rage
> Frolicks not more to see the paynted springe.   (864–5)

But already, in the attempt to harvest a few fragments in the general aridity, we have come to the second-rate, and have to observe that such poetic distinction as there is *is* fragmentary—there is little sustaining power.

Nor, with a single exception, does the imagery work together purposefully as in *Tamburlaine*, *Faustus*, and *Dido*. The exception is the sun-image, which runs through the play and has a rudimentary symbolical force. As in *Richard II*, where the symbolism is much more clear and effective, the sun represents the crown. The 'glorious planet Sol' in the Elizabethan world picture is habitually 'in noble eminence enthroned'. In this play the sun symbolises the majesty and also, rather ironically, the happiness of kingship. Edward apostrophises the crown thus:

> Continue euer thou celestiall sunne,
> Let neuer silent night possesse this clime.   (2050–51)

Gaveston rejoices in the king's love and in his independence of lesser lights:

> What neede the artick people loue star-light,
> To whom the sunne shines both by day and night?
> Farewell base stooping to the lordly peeres.   (16–18)

When Edward is taken, Baldock exclaims:

> We are depriude the sun-shine of our life.   (1973)

'What are kings when regiment is gone, But perfect shadowes in a sun-shine day?'; these lines, memorable in themselves, become doubly powerful by their relation with the whole series of images.[1] The complementary use of night and darkness in association with the evils suffered by the deposed king is still less developed, but it too can be observed. The scenes of Edward's tragedy take place in the dark or dusk. In the Welsh scene, for example, 'the day growes old'. Mortimer gives directions: 'Remooue him still from place to place by night'. Later: 'Come, come, away, now put the torches out, Weele enter in by darkenes to Killingworth'. Inside the castle, Gurney remarks: 'Yesternight I opened but the doore . . . and was almost stifeled with the sauor'. The murderer (ironically named) is given 'a light to go into the dungeon', where Edward cries out of the darkness 'Whose there, what light is that?' This is not imagery in a Shakespearean sense, and the script rarely explores the poetic and dramatic possibilities of symbolism, realised most fully in *Macbeth*. But the possibilities are hinted; the Shakespearean working is there in embryo, represented in miniature by Edward's lines to the crown quoted above:

> Continue euer thou celestiall sunne,
> Let neuer silent night possesse this clime.   (2050–51)

But everything mentioned up to now registers as no more than a number of incidental felicities. The observation that the verse is generally very arid remains true. Moreover, much of the speech is high-sounding but rather conventional rhetoric. Sometimes the artifice of the verse may be

---

[1] Line references for the sun images are as follows: 16–17; 311–12; 638–9; 1357–8; 1384–6; 1473–4; 1969; 1973; 2013–14; 2029–30; 2050–51; 2055.

taken to express the superficiality or weakness of the speaker: in the queen's lament, for instance, or Edward's anti-papal rant, or Gaveston's 'policy' speech (he is speaking of the artifice of distraction which Edward likes to put round himself). Many of Edward's later speeches, such as the surrender of the crown, betray a sort of sentimentality which in its artificiality is reflected by the verse. But one would be more convinced that this was intentional and to Marlowe's credit had he given us the measure of this artifice in some more genuine speech.

That does not occur, however, save in very different circumstances, and it is only then that a real distinction of language is to be found. Its peculiar character is derived from a movement away from the heroic stylisations which might seem to be imposed by verse, towards a tougher, more colloquial naturalness. This is found after Edward's heroic-poetic-artificial speech to the nobles, for instance, in Gaveston's aside: 'Well doone, Ned' (98). Or after Kent's impassioned speech ending:

> . . . and let these their heads,
> Preach vpon poles for trespasse of their tongues.
> *Warwicke.* O our heads.
> *Edward.*   I yours, and therefore . . .   (118–20)

Or as Mortimer cuts into Gaveston's sentence:

> *Gav.* Were I a king——
> *Mort.* Thou villaine, wherefore talkes thou of a king,
>   That hardly art a gentleman by birth?   (322–4)

Or in Mortimer's breezy, colloquial reply to the queen:

> *Queen.* Ah *Mortimer*! now breaks the kings hate forth
>   And he confesseth that he loues me not.
> *Mort.* Crie quittance Madam then, & loue not him.
>   (490–92)

There is often a hard, tough give-and-take of dialogue:

Lancaster. Weele haile him by the eares vnto the block.
Edward. Looke to your owne heads, his is sure enough.
War. Looke to your owne crowne, if you back him thus.
Edm. *Warwicke*, these words do ill beseeme thy years.

(893–6)

The exchange between Edward and Warwick is an example of what Dr Bradbrook analyses as 'a new pattern' of speech which she calls 'the retort repetitive'. Another instance is provided by the queen and Gaveston:

Qu. Villaine, tis thou that robst me of my lord.
Gav. Madam, tis you that rob me of my lord. (456–7)

Gaveston's impudent perversity deepens into Hamlet's passionate ruthlessness:

Gertrude. Hamlet, thou hast thy Father much offended.
Hamlet. Mother, you haue my Father much offended.

(III. 4)

But in *Edward II* as in *Hamlet* the 'pattern' is not felt as a convention, but as part of the natural expression: here it is the natural expression of these people who snap and bite at each other like a pack of angry dogs. Similarly in the hard-hitting, quick-moving lines where the nobles are taunting Edward:

Lan. What forraine prince sends thee embassadors?
Mort. Who loues thee? but a sort of flatterers. (972–3)

Or in the tough offhandedness of the bishop:

Lei. My lord, the king is willing to resigne.
Bish. If he be not, let him choose. (2080–81)

Mortimer uses an oddly modern phrase, which sounds like an Americanism:

And you shall ransome him, or else.[1] (947)

[1] Cf. *The Jew of Malta*, 1881 ('I, and the rest too, or else—').

The dialogue between Mortimer and Lightborne has the same character:

> *Light.*   Relent, ha, ha, I vse much to relent.
> *Mort. iu.* Well, do it brauely, and be secret . . . .
>   . . . and neuer see me more.
> *Light.*   No?
> *Mort.*   No, vnlesse thou bring me newes of *Edwards* death.
>   (2359–77)

This hard, colloquial realism is the distinctive 'music' of the play. It is later caught in the talk of Iago and Edmund, or more amiably in the backchat of Eastcheap and the tough humour of Faulconbridge and Hotspur; but this is its first striking appearance. The only contemporary rival in natural speech outside comedy seems to me to be *Arden of Feversham*, the naturalness of which is probably superior because not confined to dialogue of a particular kind: one realises in making the comparison how markedly *Edward II* speaks with a voice of its own. Not that the merit of the writing is confined to the quick give-and-take of dialogue. Several longer incidental speeches (as opposed to the official royal utterances or the big set-pieces) move flexibly and catch successfully natural colloquial inflections. Rice ap Howell's prose would illustrate this, or the Prince's advice to his mother:

> Madam, returne to England,
> And please my father well, and then a Fig
> For all my vnckles frienship here in Fraunce.
> I warrant you, ile winne his highnes quicklie,
> A loues me better than a thousand *Spencers*.   (1613–17)

The verse of *Edward II*, then, has no real distinction in the Shakespearean way of metaphor, concentration and imaginative imagery. It is thin, unsustained and virtually unpoetical. But it is often remarkably natural. Those parts of the play where this naturalness is achieved must have helped to free dramatic poetry from the too rigid pentameter and from poetic convention. In this respect they take a big stride in the Shakespearean direction. The remarkable thing is that this should be the achievement of the author of *Tamburlaine*. A fast-moving, unelaborated prosaic manner has evolved from a stately blank-verse measure almost as remote from colloquial speech (and as deliberately so) as the diction of *Paradise Lost*. This is less surprising when the corresponding revolutions in subject-matter and attitude are considered. The changed style expresses the changed mind: a mind which seems to be expressing itself most creatively in the snapping backbiting noises of resentful pettiness.

The people of the play are on the whole most unlikeable. The historian Stubbs, quoted by Charlton and Waller, writes of the actual reign words which could well have been written of the play: 'outside of the dramatic crises it may be described as exceedingly dreary. There is a miserable level of political selfishness, which marks without exception every public man; there is an absence of sincere feeling except in the shape of hatred and revenge . . . and there is no great triumph of good or evil to add a moral or inspire a sympathy'.[1]

The only character to combine humanity with strength is the prince. He is not a full-grown character and is not really of the same world. He merely provides a hint of better things to come and a marked contrast with this presentation of an essentially decadent age. A few lords, Leicester and Pembroke for example, occasionally voice moderate good sense and decent feeling, but it is Kent who makes the only major exception to the historian's generalisation quoted above. And even he is not as complete an exception as is usually assumed.

His function has been described by Mr Levin: 'Amid these bewildering shifts of moral winds, Kent is a sort of

[1] *Chronicles of the Reigns of Edward I and Edward II*, ed. Stubbs.

weathervane whose turnings veer with the rectitude of the situation, not unlike his namesake in *King Lear*'.[1] Kent certainly talks more wholesome sense than the others. He is usually loyal and straightforward, and his eventual defection from Edward shows the extent to which the king is to be condemned. He advises Edward to renounce Gaveston when he sees that the favourite will be the ruin of the king and the realm: in this he is wise and disinterested. Later, in conference with Mortimer, he stands (though not very strongly) for moderation. He recognises the evil of the rebellion and in support of the 'lawful king' is the mouthpiece of some fundamental Tudordoxy as he invokes the God

> ... to whom in iustice it belongs
> To punish this vnnaturall reuolt.　　(1794–5)

He retains his moral sense when all around him are losing theirs, and his clear-sightedness tells him that Isabel and Mortimer 'do dissemble'. He exercises a good influence over the prince and makes an attempt to save Edward.

He is, then, to some extent a choric weather-cock. But he has not in fact the authority to fulfil the office. His counsels of moderation are timidly and ineffectually proffered, and when Mortimer is talking war Kent merely observes sadly that it would be better if 'all were well and *Edward* well reclaimd'. He is still more timid when he sounds the queen:

> Madame, without offence if I may aske,
> How will you deale with *Edward* in his fall?
>
> 　　　　(1816–17)

The prince implies a reproach in his subsequent query and Kent admits 'I dare not call him king'. In this timidity and ineffectiveness he is, of course, most *un*like his namesake in

---

[1] *The Overreacher*, p. 121.

King Lear. So is he when he abandons Edward. Lear's Kent also was banished, but his way was very different; so were his motives. This Kent joins the rebels because he resents the way the king has treated him: 'doost thou banish me thy presence? But ile to Fraunce' (1596–7). Lear's Kent had far better grounds for complaint, but Edward's shares in the general littleness. His right-mindedness does not always stand the test, and he has not sufficient energy and courage to command much respect.

Mortimer, on the other hand, is energetic and courageous, but wrong-headed. He forfeits respect partly because he knows 'tis treason to be vp against the king' yet up he is; and partly because the motivation is extremely petty. He explains the real cause of his fury when he is talking with his uncle. The personal and not the official self speaks here and it is moved by no moral or patriotic considerations but merely by petty annoyance:

> . . . the king and he
> From out a window laugh at such as we,
> And floute our traine, and iest at our attire:
> Vnckle, tis this that makes me impatient.   (713–16)

Impatience is the excuse for treason. Elizabethans may have more sympathy with the cause (though certainly not with the crime), and it is true that elsewhere Mortimer appeals more legitimately to a sense of outraged honour. But callow resentment cannot at any time have passed amongst people of discernment as honourable anger.

In the beginning of the play, he is the angry young man, impudent to his king ('And vnderneath thy banners march who will, For *Mortimer* will hand his armor vp'), fiercely impetuous, the outspoken spokesman for his elders. He is the most scornful of them and the quickest to rebel:

> Let vs leaue the brainsick king,
> And henceforth parle with our naked swords.   (125–6)

The others see his anger swell and urge him to bridle it, but he will not:

> I cannot, nor I will not, I must speake. (122)

What speaks, however, is selfish pride and an exaggerated class-consciousness. To him Gaveston is a peasant, 'a night growne mushrump', 'swolne with venome of ambitious pride', the last accusation being strictly an affair of pot and kettle.

Mortimer, like Edward, gains in prestige towards the middle of the play. His irritation with Gaveston, although no excuse for his rebellion, is understandable enough. So is his fury with Edward for 'playing soldiers' (984–9) and with Gaveston as a 'shame and dishonour to a souldiers name'. He tries to recall the king to a sense of duty:

> You haue matters of more waight to thinke vpon,
> The King of Fraunce sets foote in Normandie. (810–11)

And he has a genuine grievance when his uncle is captured in the king's wars. Edward himself gives Mortimer an unintended testimonial in saying 'the people love him well', and the glamour of the past is evoked to substantiate the leadership which is his by nature:

> This tottered ensigne of my auncesters,
> Which swept the desart shore of that dead sea,
> Whereof we got the name of *Mortimer*. (1090–92)

But power corrupts and the unprincipled ambitious youth becomes the unscrupulous power-politician of the later scenes. He becomes greedy, scheming and cruel; and his cruelty is as petty as his original grievances against the king ('speake curstlie to him . . . if he chaunce to weepe But amplifie his greefe with bitter wordes'). Like Macbeth and Richard III he knows what his situation is: 'Feard am I more then lou'd; let me be feard'. Power makes a Machiavel of him and his soliloquy (2379–403) smacks soundly of the policy. His hubris clearly precedes a fall:

> As for my selfe, I stand as *Ioues* huge tree,
> And others are but shrubs compard to me.
>
> (2579–80)

Yet he makes a good end, in which there is no self-pity, but some pride of a more admirable kind. His last speech is the only one in the play which is truly heroic:

> . . . weepe not for *Mortimer*,
> That scornes the world, and as a traueller,
> Goes to discouer countries yet vnknowne. (2632–4)

He is a minor Tamburlaine in a shrunken setting.

Gaveston, the other ambitious failure in the play, also bears some pathetic relationship to the Scourge of God. Tamburlaine had relished 'the sweet fruition of an earthly crowne'. In Tudor England the middle-class man could not aspire to that, but the career of Wolsey had given both a fearful warning and an encouraging example. For his own goal, Gaveston sets out with a practicable modification of Tamburlaine's programme:

> What greater blisse can hap to *Gaueston*,
> Then liue and be the fauorit of a king? (4–5)

Occasionally he aspires also to Tamburlaine's language, but his pride is merely pert and his bravado peevish and unimpressive:

> Whose mounting thoughts did neuer creepe so low
> As to bestow a looke on such as you. (879–80)

This 'dapper jack' is to Tamburlaine what the Pantomime's principal boy is to man—an effeminate parody. He has little dignity *vis-à-vis* the lords, and snaps pettishly and poisonously at the queen. His influence would make of the Court a couch for pampered luxury or a *Yellow Book* paradise. In part a Machiavellian self-seeker, he intends to manipulate 'the pliant king' as he chooses.[1] Nevertheless, although this self-seeking deprives him of respect or heroic status, it does not kill all sympathy. In the first place, the nobles are no better than he is. They speak of his upstart pride, but he, with the voice of the disruptive outsider, can give a fair retort:

> Base leaden Earles, that glorie in your birth.   (876)

In the skirmish with the bishop of Coventry he probably gains as much sympathy as he loses. On the one hand, he is sacrilegious in his violence and 'God himselfe is vp in armes' when the Holy Church is outraged. On the other, 'Holy Church' is only the Roman Catholic Church, and Reformation principles are brought to the defence:

> What should a priest do with so faire a house.   (206)

'Heele complaine vnto the sea of Rome' no doubt, but Reformation independence finds this quite as outrageous as the act itself.

---

[1] In this he resembles the villain of Greene's *James IV*. This is Ateukin, a sinister corrupter of the king and realm, whose ambition is expressed in soliloquy:

> Why so, Ateukin, this becomes thee best:
> Wealth, honour, ease and angelles in thy chest . . .
> Vnto this high promotion doth belong,
> Meanes to be talkt of in the thickest throng.
> And first, to fit the humors of my lord,
> Sweete layes and lynes of loue I must record;
> And such sweet lynes and louelayes Ile endite
> As men may wish for, and my leech [liege] delight:
> And next, a traine of gallants at my heeles,
> That men may say the world doth run on wheeles;
> For men of art that rise by indirection
> To honour and the fauour of their king,
> Must vse all meanes to saue what they haue got,
> And win their fauours whom he neuer knew.   (I. 2)

The nobles resent him. Douglas's complaint is representative:

> If we but enter presence of his Grace,
> Our payment is a frowne, a scoffe, a frumpe;
> Whilst flattering Gnato prancks it by his side,
> Soothing the carelesse king in his misdeeds.   (II. 2)

More seriously, in spite of the scheming parasitical self presented in the second main speech, Gaveston is shown as having real affection for the king. In the first soliloquy he says he values London because

> ... it harbors him I hold so deare,
> The king, vpon whose bosome let me die. (13–14)

And in his last (1168–74) he speaks of the hope to 'see his royall soueraigne once again'. It seems to be a sincere regard. To the lords he is 'a monster of men', but not to Marlowe. Gaveston would normally have been portrayed dramatically like Ateukin, a caterpillar of the kingdom not merely in function but in remoteness from recognisable humanity. But as Marlowe's play has no hero, so is it (amongst major characters) without villains. Gaveston is merely part of a struggling, thwarting, humiliating world. The middle-class careerist is shunted hither and thither at the will of the powers-that-be. He had seemed to be secure and the realisation that he must again submit is pathetic:

> My lord, I heare it whisperd euery where,
> That I am banishd and must flie the land. (402–3)

In the end he suffers the further indignity of Mortimer's jibes, Pembroke's coldness and Warwick's treachery. He is finally hustled off the stage to the accompaniment of Warwick's harsh joke in the play's characteristic manner:

> *Gav.* Treacherous earle, shall I not see the king?
> *War.* The king of heauen perhaps, no other king.
> (1302–3)

But Gaveston's humiliations and sufferings are far less than Edward's. Indignity here makes its masterpiece. Forcibly shaved, washed in puddle water, confined in darkness and filth, maddened by a beating drum, thrown his food like a dog, denied human contact except with the gaolers who taunt and insult him, this king is the very embodiment of humiliated mankind. The murderer Lightborne plays at pity, grotesquely mimicking the compassion which is Edward's right:

> O speake no more my lorde, this breakes my heart,
>
> (2519)

and earlier in the scene he exclaims 'O villaines!'—at which the insensitive part of the audience will probably have laughed. The overwatched king lies down to sleep and dramatic tension increases with the quietness. Edward's fearfulness spoils Lightborne's plan, and the assassin, tired of playing and waiting, tells the truth with terrible suddenness:

> *Ed.*   And therefore tell me, wherefore art thou come?
> *Light.* To rid thee of thy life. *Matreuis* come.   (2554–5)

The drum stops and the obscene murder is committed.

This terrible death matches a humiliating life (Empson sees more specific correspondences[1]). Throughout the play, except in the brief middle section, Edward is insecure at best and at worst quite impotent in the face of force and insolence. His first line ('Will you not graunt me this') presents the pathetic spectacle of a king pleading. Shortly he adds to this the further indignity of impotent rage. To Kent, who speaks moderately, he uses language which would have been better bestowed on the rebellious nobles:

> Cease brother for I cannot brooke these words.   (160)

His pride has in fact to brook a great deal more than that. He is weakly self-pitying:

> Was euer king thus ouerruld as I?   (333)

He rages powerlessly against the power of Rome. The antipapal speech, demagogic and Balelike, is undermined partly

---

[1] *Nation* CLXIII (1946), no. 16, pp. 444–5.

by its own hysterical excess, and partly by the subsequent abject capitulation:

> It bootes me not to threat, I must speake faire,
> The Legate of the Pope will be obayd.   (358-9)

Excitedly violent when he has a chance to vent his frustrated resentment, he puts upon the bishop a humiliation which foreshadows his own:

> Throwe of his golden miter, rend his stole,
> And in the channell christen him anew.   (187-8)

As a king he is effete and irresponsible. The 'pleasing showes' which Gaveston hopes to devise for him appear to be a mixture of sex and sadism: the 'louelie boye ... By yelping hounds puld downe, and seeme to die'. When told of the French invasion of Normandy he dismisses it as a trifle, and he has in fact no interest in his kingdom. With all these weak qualities he is despised, taunted and crossed. Nor does he achieve dignity in the abdication scene. Mr Levin describes him as 'a king with the soul of an actor', and the histrionic element detracts (as I think with Richard II) from the respect to which his sufferings entitle him.

This is not a complete account however, for though his sufferings do not induce respect, they do inspire pity. His love for Gaveston is in its way wonderful and moving:

> *Mort.* Why should you loue him, whome the world hates so?
> *Edw.* Because he loues me more then all the world.   (371-2)

(Out of context the reply may sound petulant and selfish, but because of his wretchedness and need for love it is not so contemptible.) Later, as his strength grows, fired by Gaveston's death, his dramatic stature grows too, and with it a new kind of sympathy felt first in the brief time of repose at the Abbey. His subsequent miseries are terrible enough to ensure the response which the verse of itself is incapable of arousing. But there is nothing of the tragic hero in him. His situation recalls Arnold's distinction between the tragic and the painful where 'everything is to be endured and nothing done'.

This, then, is a play of restless wills, petty resentment and unheroic misery. At the outset I described it as unhappy, and it is so not only for what is there but for what is notably absent. A. P. Rossiter in the Preface to his edition of *Woodstock* uses the term 'Moral History' as a 'name for history-plays where the shadow-show of a greater drama of state plays continually behind the human characters, sometimes (as in Shakespeare) upon something as large as the cyclorama of the stars'. *Edward II* is narrowly personal: the people are small, and beyond them is nothing greater. England and the realm are sometimes mentioned, but they are not emotionally or dramatically involved. Mortimer calls Edward 'England's scourge', but this is merely a rhetorical weapon, or, even if a sincere considera- tion, is never made to be *felt* in the poetry or the drama. The sun symbolism, which might be pointed to as an objection to this, has effect much less as order-imagery than as a glamorous personal accessory. If political *sententiae* are voiced they are usually vested with an obviously personal interest:

> Thy court is naked, being bereft of those,
> That makes a king seeme glorious to the world. (976–7)

But the speaker is one of 'those'. Sanctimonious common- place sounds doubly hollow in the mouth of an Isabella:

> Succesfull battells giues the God of kings
> To them that fight in right and feare his wrath. (1805–6)

A glance outwards towards the wider canvas is allowed the queen as she leaves England: 'Vnnatural wars, where suiects braue their king' (1394). Very clearly, the material for 'Moral History' exists, and Marlowe can hardly avoid an occasional gesture in its direction, but he shows no interest in it as such. The weak king, the untended kingdom, the parasite, the discontented peers, are essential ingredients of the Elizabethan play of disorder. But Marlowe's people cast no shadows: the self is all there is. Marlowe is here, as in so many things, exceptional. Normally vestigial Morality characteristics are to be observed in the history plays. *Gorboduc*, acted before the queen in 1561, is essentially moral history, and works at three levels: the family tragedy, the national disorder which it occasions, and the wider allegory in which Ferrex and Porrex, the warring brothers, represent civil war while their mother Videna is the motherland or Respublica. At the second level, the misgoverned king, like Edward or Richard II, is the original cause of the disaster:

> Hereto it commes when kinges will not consent
> To graue aduise, but followe wilfull will.
> This is the end when in fonde princes hartes
> Flattery preuales, and sage rede hath no place.
>
> (V. 2. 234–7)

Gorboduc has violated the primogenitive and due of birth and it follows that

> When fathers cease to know that they should rule,
> The children cease to know they should obey.
>
> (I. 2. 207–8)

Action enforces these verbal generalisations. The domestic-tragedy figures embody and shadow forth the national woe. Videna, the mother, is torn in soul by her warring sons:

> Or should not this most hard and cruell soile,
> So oft where I haue prest my wretched steps,
> Sometime had ruthe of myne accursed life,
> To rende in twayne, and swallow me therin?
>
> (IV. 1. 11–14)

Mother earth, that is, should rend her in twain as she is rent by her sons. Later she charges Porrex with his unnatural aggression. None would

> Suffice to make a sacrifice to peaze[1]
> That deadly minde and murderous thought in thee,
> But he who in the selfesame wombe was wrapped
> Where thou in dismall hower receiuedst life? . . .
> No, traitour, no! I thee refuse for mine:
> Murderer, I thee renounce; thou are not mine.
>
> (IV. 1. 49–52 and 65–66)

So England disowns her unnatural sons as traitors: 'England . . . hath made a shameful conquest of itself'.

> Ciuill dissention is a viperous Worme,
> That gnawes the Bowels of the Common-wealth.
>
> (1 H. VI, III. 1)

The words are Shakespeare's, but they might well be the motto of *Gorboduc*. It illustrates a way of thought, altruistic and outward-looking, which Shakespeare inherits, and Marlowe in his real interests does not. It becomes one of the great enriching forces in Shakespeare; and its absence is part of Marlowe's ingrowing narrowness.

The pattern of *Gorboduc* has much in common with *Edward II* and *Henry VI*. In all three the 'guidelesse realme' is left 'an open pray To endlesse stormes and waste of ciuill warre', and the way is open to power, will and appetite. In *Gorboduc* the 'mounting spirit' is Fergus:

> If euer time to gaine a kingdome here
> Were offred man, now it is offred mee. (V. 1. 132–3)

In *Edward II* disorder permits the dictatorship of Mortimer, and in *Henry VI* it is Edward:

> . . . I am *Edward*,
> Your King and *Warwickes*, and must haue my will.
>
> (3 H. VI, IV. 1)

---

[1] Appease.

'Will' here carries both its modern sense ('What I want') and the Elizabethan sense of carnality ('the lustful Edward'). This 'will' which becomes appetite, loses for itself France, the support of Warwick and, for a time, of Clarence, and plays into the hands of Gloucester, 'an indigest deformed lumpe' like civil war, the ultimate symbol of England's afflictions and of the universal wolf:

> Like to a Chaos, or an vn-lick'd Beare-whelpe,
> That carryes no impression like the Damme.
>
> (*3 H. VI*, III. 2)

Henry's prophecy to Gloucester that all 'shall rue the houre that euer thou was't borne' foreshadows horrors to come; and the whole trilogy, with its references back to the reign of Richard II, dramatises the chain-effects of an original disruption of the married calm of states. The prophecy over Richmond, it is true, foretells the Tudor redemption. There is a similar dawn of better things suggested at the end of *Edward II* and in *Gorboduc* when it is said that 'wrong can never take deep root at last'. But here for the meantime nature's course is 'perverted in disordered wise'. The rude son strikes his father dead, a tragedy spoken of in *Gorboduc*:

> The father shall vnwitting slay the sonne;
> The sonne shall slay the sire and know it not.
>
> (V. 2. 213–14)

and represented in *3 Henry VI* (II. 5) where symbolical figures step out of the drama to lay the tragedy before us. As this happens, the mind turns outward beyond the individual (though never in Shakespeare—unlike *Gorboduc*— to its exclusion) to see the scene as representative:

> O pitteous spectacle! O bloody Times! ...
> O pitty God, this miserable Age!
> What Stratagems? how fell? how Butcherly?
> Erroneous, mutinous and vnnaturall. (*3 H. VI*, II. 5)

In this play, written before *Edward II*, the personal wills, honours and ambitions, like the individual violences and sufferings, all take their place in a larger setting. All life is involved, and the application of the then-and-there is extended as the scene is magnified beyond what it visibly presents.

But in Marlowe's play there is nothing of this. Life beyond the passionate yet petty play of personal will is barely glimpsed, and the realm seems to be only of nominal importance. The dominant attitude implied in the play is that the realm is a counter: one of the factors in the working of personal desires. To Edward it is a poor thing: let it float away, be divided up, let the nobles have the treasury: one nook in which to play with Gaveston would be worth more. Edward is not Marlowe, nor is Mortimer; but Marlowe despises, I think, *and* sympathises with both, and this not with a normal detachment, for he seems to know of nothing better. Obviously in a theoretical way he does: there is the prince and Kent. But no inner knowledge, dramatised or rendered in the poetry, nothing 'beyond' which comes from any depth or speaks with any passion makes itself felt in this play.[1] If it were there, 'moral

---

[1] It is for this reason that I am unconvinced by the kind of account Irving Ribner gives of the play (*The English History Play in the Age of Shakespeare*, 1957). He, like many other critics, finds a real political and moral interest there. Thus Mortimer's fall illustrates Marlowe's new recognition 'that to rule well in the secular absolutist state, the Machiavellian brand of virtù alone will not suffice. Combined with it must be a private humanity' (p. 131). An example of the political concern occurs at Edward's brief reconciliation with the barons where the queen 'directs an important bit of didacticism to the audience:

> Now is the king of England riche and strong,
> Hauing the loue of his renowned peeres.   (663–4)

This theme of a king's relation to his nobles is one of the chief political themes of *Edward II*' (p. 133). Of course, the relationship is an important feature of the story, but this does not make it a 'theme'. Similarly the fact of Mortimer's fall may very naturally give rise to the kind of moral reflection that Mr Ribner expresses, but it does not necessarily follow that such reflections interested Marlowe. Both ideas, of 'theme' and 'recognition', must I think be related to a sense of *quality*. A story can be told and the appropriate 'bits of didacticism' be put into a character's mouth with only the superficial engagement of the author; but when the imagination is working creatively and intensively there is 'meaning' at quite a different level. And in this play of Marlowe's I can see such intensity only in what is personal.

history' must have emerged: some positive, or some feeling for the values of stability and restraint. But Marlowe appears to see nothing beyond his men. To that extent there is a personal involvement as with Tamburlaine and Faustus. The aspiring mind, which may be a term ennobling the selfish go-getter, whether sated like Tamburlaine or thwarted like Faustus, has none of that altruistic interest and sympathy by which the mind grows. Fewer and fewer things outside the self really matter. But the selfishness does survive: the personal condition is the one thing that is important. And because Edward's self-love is reflected by Gaveston, he is the only thing in the world with real significance:

> *Mort.* Why should you loue him, whome the world hates so?
> *Edw.* Because he loues me more then all the world. (371-2)

There has always been in Marlowe the sense that the world is less than man (Tamburlaine offers himself to Zenocrate as the last and best gift; and Faustus' ambitions stretch 'as farre as doth the minde of man', creation's crown). The world is the setting for man: man is the stone in the ring. But the setting cheapens with the jewel. Tamburlaine is great (subjectively) and so is his world; Edward is a poor creature, and the world's worth has decreased proportionately.

It is interesting to note how, when a speech does 'apply' a particular event to a wider context, the words are placed so that their authority is belittled, and finally treated without any respect whatsoever. The queen addresses her supporters:

> sword and gleave
> In ciuill broiles makes kin and country men
> Slaughter themselues in others and their sides
> With their owne weapons gorde, but whats the helpe?
> Misgouerned kings are cause of all this wrack . . . (1752-6)

Isabella is not a Gloriana, but a pathetic, strained and un-loved woman, whose dramatic authority weighs light. For the moment she is in high buoyant spirits because by trea-son, foreign aid and the help of an ambitious rebel, her luck has turned. Nor is this one of those choric speeches where character is superseded by convention, for interest is now focused upon the speaker by Mortimer's interruption of the speech. With the queen's eloquence in full flight, another rolling sentence just begun, Mortimer stops her and takes the wind out of her sails with a satirical silencer:

> *Qu.* And *Edward* thou art one among them all,
> Whose loosnes hath betrayed thy land to spoyle,
> And made the channels ouerflow with blood.
> Of thine own people patron shouldst thou be,
> But thou——
> *Mort.*   Nay madam, if you be a warriar
> Ye must not grow so passionate in speeches. (1757–63)

If the audience found themselves recalling their own queen (and perhaps her Tilbury speech), the rude deflating joke must have made a still odder impression than it does today. Mortimer then takes charge with an air of getting down to the real business, and the queen is left with no more to say for herself. Marlowe's interest here is not in the fine words, the truth or otherwise of the statements, but in the play of wills and in the situation of belittlement. Heroical eloquence is allowed to blow itself up to a fine size and then pricked.

That represents the spirit of the play. Here, as in much of the snapping give-and-take of dialogue, it is semi-comic; in other places it is tragic. But the dominant spirit is one of belittlement, where dignity is undermined, nobility turned to pettiness, and man made abject, thwarted and humiliated. The scene is never transcended by poetic life or breadth of reference or positive values felt in any dramatic counterpoint. The nature of the achievement is depressing.

This is not to deny that considerable things have been achieved. Many common criticisms of *Edward II* are unjust. A frequent complaint, for instance, is that the characterisation is unsubtle and even incredible. It is the queen who has probably most failed to convince. Michel Poirier's criticisms are representative: 'She is one instance of that negligence or clumsiness we have already noted in Marlowe's delineation of minor characters . . . such a sudden volte-face has nothing in common with the usual workings of the human heart'. These accusations have not passed unchallenged: F. P. Wilson defends the characterisation effectively, admitting at the same time that it needs defending. The volte-face is, in fact, prepared for and is, I think, completely credible. One sees the process whereby the queen's fidelity is worn down, strained beyond endurance. Edward is peevish, unjustly suspicious, deceitful and insulting, where Mortimer is gallant and affectionate. Her weariness speaks in the words 'These hands are tir'd with haling of my lord From *Gaueston*', and it is clear when she says 'Yet once more Ile importune him with praiers' that this will be the last attempt. In France she concludes that nothing can be hoped for from her marriage: 'we iarre too farre'. Then for a time success brightens her life, though she needs to justify herself and has to be cheered up by Mortimer. She comes to depend on him and, with him, she degenerates. Weakness has become evil in her half-ashamed admission that she would welcome Edward's death: 'I would hee were [dead], so it were not by my meanes' (2188). In the end she will go to any shift to keep life ('Shall I not moorne for my beloued lord?') and her last words ('He hath forgotten me, stay, I am his mother') are an undignified, humiliating cry as she is forced off the stage. She is a poor, sad woman, having just about as much loyalty and feeling as most people have, yet required to bear more than a non-heroic nature can endure. The strain and the development are only sketched, but the sketching is realistic and done with insight.

Critics also complain that 'there is no central feeling or theme' (Bradbrook) or that Marlowe 'has not found a single unifying theme or a single appropriate tone' (Maxwell). But the petty, undignified and humiliated are everywhere and this does make a distinctive tone or feeling in the play. I hesitate to claim 'a theme' for the term may suggest something more rigidly conceptualised than is there: an idea or 'point' behind the play and running through it, such as that defined by Mr L. J. Mills in 'The Meaning of *Edward II*'.[1] He sees friendship as 'the central thing in the play' and says, 'It is possible that the dramatic effectiveness of *Edward II*, realised by all readers of the play, may be explained by the drama's use in the tragedy of the Elizabethan friendship ideas.' This is what comes from the search for 'a single theme', a sense that somewhere there exists 'the meaning' if only you can find the clues. Mr Mills mentions 'those who wish to regard the play as a study in kingship'; his objection is not that they are trying to force the play into a mould of their own making but that he prefers to fit it into his. It is a sort of crossword puzzle: 'Again the solution may be found in the background of friendship ideas'. A few comparable passages are seen as constituting a convention and it is thought that this can somehow explain the effectiveness we feel today. 'Friendship' is quite patently *not* 'the meaning' because it excludes so much: the whole story of Mortimer, for example, and the last third of the play in which the favourites have been

[1] *Modern Philology*, xxxii, 1934–5.

virtually forgotten. There is no theme or 'meaning' in this sense.

But the play speaks with its own harsh voice and has its own bitter flavour. Edward weakly protesting to his barons ('Was euer king thus overrulde as I?'), weakly, impotently raging or abjectly and wretchedly submitting. Gaveston's pathetic strutting before the lords who not only hate but despise him; learning of his banishment, frustrated of his last sight of the king. Mortimer's petty motivation: his resentful pride, laughed at by the dapper jack, nobility humbled by the upstart. The pricking of the bubble of Isabella's eloquence; the humiliating violence offered to the bishop of Coventry; the enforced removal of the protesting queen; and above all the king subject to every indignity, crownless and washed in puddle water. There is surely a unity of tone and feeling here.

Several criticisms, however, have still to be made. The aridity of the verse and the limitation of interests have been mentioned. Comparison enforces this recognition. There is more poetic life in the first scene of *1 Henry VI* than in the whole of *Edward*. There is, for example, what one might call the Marlovian attack of the opening:

> Hung be the heauens with black, yield day to night;
> Commets importing change of Times and States,
> Brandish your crystal Tresses in the Skie,
> And with them scourge the bad reuolting Stars,
> That haue consented vnto *Henries* death.

Very Marlovian lines, with the strong verb placed at the beginning of the line, and the Tamburlaine-like 'scourge the . . . Stars'. The bold conceit would stand out in *Tamburlaine*, yet it would be typical in kind. But in *Edward* there is nothing like it or compensating for its absence. John Bakeless praises Marlowe here for a fine restraint: 'Marlowe overcomes for the first time his tendency to be carried away by the splendour of mere words. He has learned to restrain his love for resounding but bombastic lines.' But if Marlowe were *restraining* the poetic force within him which had formerly expressed itself in a gorgeous rhetoric now inappropriate, it would have come out in some other way—in some appropriate way, its images moving in terms of the new subject and attitude. There is no sign of that, except in the colloquial toughness of some of the dialogue (I do not agree with Dr Bradbrook's remark that 'Edward's feelings give what life there is to the verse'; there are some moving sentences, but when the verse should be strongest, in the more extended passages, it seems to me often artificial and histrionic, and all too explicit). The development shows not fine restraint but impoverishment. Not even on its own ground, the feeling of humiliation, is there anything as vivid as 'thou antique Death, which laugh'st vs here to scorn' (*1 Henry VI*, IV. 7). Nor does the plainness of the verse amount to an impressive and deliberate austerity. The Epilogue of *Arden of Feversham* asks the audience's pardon for

> . . . this naked Tragedy,
> Wherin no filed points are foisted in
> To make it gratious to the eare or eye;
> For simple trueth is gratious enough:
> And needes no other points of glosing stuffe.

The naturalness and warmth of *Arden* are ample justification. Similarly there is a warmth and humanity about *2 Henry VI* and *Edward III* (that uneven but at times very fine play in which Tennyson and others have not injudiciously detected 'the master's hand'); as a work of the human spirit *Edward II* is much narrower and, I think, much nastier.

The attitude is perhaps akin to Shakespeare's in *Troilus*

and Cressida, and yet there is a world of difference. Miss Mahood sees in *Edward II* something constituting 'a denial . . . of life itself'. Probably this involves more intensity than is there, and yet in one way the 'denial' goes deeper than Miss Mahood's study suggests. She does not discuss the quality of the verse and this seems to affect her estimation of the quality of the attitude. The denial does in fact spread itself to the verse, flat, thin and poetically weak as it is. If Shakespeare comes near to this sort of denial of life, with a bitter sense of the ignoble and putrid, it is in *Troilus*. But here an extreme mental vigour is called into play, an extreme concentration of images showing within the creator a vitality which transcends the barrenness it portrays. In *Edward II* there is no sense of the author transcending, by his own vitality or vision or moral sense, the pettiness and flat misery which he depicts.[1]

Presumably the humiliation of a petty and limited world of men is what attracted Marlowe to this reign. It is, after all, an extraordinary and therefore hardly accidental thing that the author of *Tamburlaine* should have chosen this of all reigns for his chronicle play. Even so, some might claim

[1] I am unconvinced by Mr Bent Sunesen's arguments in 'Marlowe and the Dumb Show' (*English Studies*, xxxv) partly because I see no evidence of Marlowe at work elsewhere in this play with the subtlety Mr Sunesen attributes to him in Gaveston's second speech. This speech ('I must have wanton poets') is taken to be a verbal enactment of a prefiguring dumb show. Like Actaeon in these lines, Edward is hunted and the king 'seems' to die. 'On a deep level of the tragedy there is an overwhelming rightness in that "seem". For in the underlying sacrificial ritual the king as national symbol does not really die.' One would like to believe this, but the 'deep level' seems such a fiction in the absence of profound national feeling or linguistic subtlety elsewhere that the whole argument registers as wishful thinking. It is very true that the speech makes a remarkable effect and stands out in one's memory of the play. It has poetic vitality of a kind not found in the rest; the mind is very genuinely engaged. But when Mr Sunesen says that many readers have no doubt 'felt the essential significance of the play pressing upon them' through these images I think he is led by his theory into overstatement. One could probably make a similar case for an image in Machiauel's Prologue to *The Jew of Malta* ('*Phaleris* . . . had neuer bellowed in a brasen Bull Of the great ones enuy'— after all, Barabas comes to a similar end, boiling and bellowing in his cauldron, and this speech too is one which makes a strong impression). But this would only be 'a case'.

that he was not making 'significant choice' at all, and that
there is accordingly nothing 'significant' in the events of
the drama: having 'hit on' the idea of treating that reign
(attracted perhaps by sex and sadism) he could do no other
than present the meanness already there in the Chronicle,
and so on. But a feeling for it, going much deeper than
that, must be involved in the choice of a subject which gave
his former characteristic strengths so little scope. His mind
must have changed; those characteristic strengths (which if
they were still within him must, one would think, have
compelled exercise) are no longer his. Moreover, this
distinctive tone and feeling in the play, with the life in the
hard give-and-take of dialogue, are the marks of a mind
involved sufficiently to create a new manner in its art to
express the non-heroic pride, shame and violence which
the Chronicle had impressed upon him—impressed because
it answered to something already there.

The real depth of feeling, which is somewhere lurking,
a partly-sullen-partly-sympathetic view of puny mankind,
expresses itself in this presentation of the facts of a sordid
reign. But intellect and imagination, sparking off something
fine in the chosen medium of a great writer, it cannot boast.
It is not, for instance, that in his virtual ignoring of the
Elizabethan idea of order, he is in rebellion against it. So
far from chafing against the conservatism of this political
thought, his own political generalisations and implications
(where there are any) come largely into line with Elizabethan
orthodoxy. Nor is he vindicating the relationship between
Edward and Gaveston; for, though his treatment is sympathetic, and the 'reasonable' attitude of Mortimer senior
carries some weight, the thing is seen as a degenerating
force, and both men are very un-admirable. Narrowness is
everywhere: in the men and the vision. The mind is not
stirred by anything outside the personal spite and suffering.

Edward's dungeon perhaps symbolises a very great deal. There seems to me a mind smouldering somewhere or other with a passionate disillusionment, keeping up a fairly bright appearance with its rhetoric, keeping itself alive in the shaping of its material, but fusting unused in most of those places where one would wish to see development.

NOTE. For my revised views on *Edward II*, see p. 373 below.

A NOTE ON
'THE MASSACRE AT PARIS'

THIS is probably the last of Marlowe's plays, and in its extant form certainly the least. No film director hungry for sensation could reasonably complain about its ingredients: twelve occasions for murder on stage (seventeen victims), a lustful duchess, a hint of perversion, religion . . . And all in an action-crammed script not half the length of *Edward II*. The characters are simple and static; the language is easy and racy; the politics are rousing but safe. A great success in its time, the play brought in as much as £3 14*s*. for one performance. It seems to have been aimed expertly at the box-office, to have arrived on target in 1593, and to have lost most of its claim on anybody's attention ever since. If what we have is what Marlowe wrote, his dramatic career came to as sad an end as his life.

It is fairly certain, however, that our text is a shortened version, and that abridgement has cheapened the original. It is also probable that the kind of alteration and loss can be gauged, by reference to the so-called 'Collier leaf'. This is a fragment of the play which John Paine Collier said he found with a London bookseller.[1] The manuscript exists, has stimulated much scrutiny and argument, and appears to be genuine: no one can establish that it is written in Marlowe's hand, but at least it is not one of Collier's forgeries, and Dr Boas tentatively follows J. Quincy Adams's suggestion that it was one of the 'foul sheets' on which the author made his first draft. The passage contains Mugeroun's death, the soldier's comic speech before it, and the Guise's serious speech after (in the octavo text, lines

[1] Dodsley's *Old Plays*, vol. VIII, introduction to *The Jew of Malta*.

812–27). The whole of the manuscript leaf is given by Dr Boas,[1] but the important difference occurs after the murder, the Guise having a speech of fifteen lines, only three of which are in the normal text:

> Thus fall, imperfect exhalation,
> (Which our great sun of France could not effect),
> A fiery meteor in the firmament!
> *Lie there the King's delight, and Guise's scorn!*
> *Revenge it, Henry, if thou list, or dar'st.*
> *I did it only in despite of thee.*
> Fondly hast thou incens'd the Guise's soul,
> That of itself was hot enough to work
> Thy just digestion with extremest shame!
> The army I have gathered now shall aim
> More at thy end than exterpation;
> And when thou think'st I have forgotten this,
> And that thou most reposest on my faith,
> Then will I wake thee from thy foolish dream
> And let thee see thyself my prisoner.[2]

If the loss of twelve lines in a serious set-speech is typical, then the play was more substantial than we might think, not so scrappy, not so weighted with sensational action. In one sense it is true that our text contains 'the pith of the matter', as Dr Boas says, and that the Collier leaf supports his view of the published version as preserving 'the essential features of Marlowe's play'. On the other hand, the loss seems to have involved what may well have been to us the play's most interesting features. If its *action* remains more or less unaffected, then we must ask what made the 1263 extant lines up into a play of normal length. It may have been fooleries, as in *Faustus* but with the massacre as

[1] *Op. cit.*, 169–70.
[2] The text given here is that transcribed, in modernised spelling, in Dr Boas's book. The version included in Tucker Brooke's complete edition (pp. 483–4) was the best available at the time but is inaccurate in several respects. The lines in italics are those included (with very slight differences) in the octavo edition.

their excuse. Or it may have been passages of sustained writing; and 'the pith of the matter' may then be precisely what is lost to us. The great speech of Guise apart, there are vestigial signs of a mind at work in the play: the full mind, that is, as opposed to that part which can do a neat job with sources and exploit a sense of theatre. If the Collier leaf is in any way typical, it suggests that the places where attitudes might have been shaped and thought developed have been exactly the places cut.

Not that the additional twelve lines are of remarkable quality. Another 200 or 400 of this sort would still not raise *The Massacre* to the level of the other works. It is very much a poetry of statement, if anything more arid than the verse of *Edward II*; and while it illustrates character it does not explore or develop it. Dr Boas refers to a contrast in lines 10 and 11 'of the two motives that drive him in different ways', but there is no real conflict. The first long soliloquy has fixed the Guise's character from the beginning: what he does is for ambition and excitement. He has never had any religious motive, and all that is concerned now— whether to use the army against the Huguenots or the king—is a decision about means.

Even so, the speech has some interest. The cat-and-mouse nastiness of 'the policy' is Marlovian enough:

> And when thou think'st I have forgotten this,
> And that thou most reposest on my faith,
> Then will I wake thee from thy foolish dream
> And let thee see thyself my prisoner.

There is also the egoist's sense that only *he* lives a full, waking life; the others dream or shoot momentarily across the sky like Mugeroun, 'a fiery meteor in the firmament'. The Caesarian boast implied here, placed shortly before the fall, is not a mere expansion or ornament, to use Dr Boas's terms. The speech is in fact strong enough for the loss of it and more of its kind to be an impoverishment, and it suggests that, in its original form, the bulk of the play might possibly have fulfilled the promise of the opening. This contains one of Marlowe's great speeches. It starts with a characteristic sense of exciting possibilities opening out before the speaker and carrying a feeling that this is the moment when the uncertainties of the past are to be resolved and the time of preparation is to bear fruit:

> Now *Guise* begins those deepe ingendred thoughts
> To burst abroad . . .   (91-2)

The moment caught in Guise's life matches the place where Marlowe takes up Faustus' story:

> Settle thy studies *Faustus*, and beginne . . .   (29)

With both men the period of indecision and preparation is to end, and the time has come for choice and commitment. The Guise has settled his studies much more firmly than Faustus:

> Oft haue I leueld, and at last haue learnd,
> That perill is the cheefest way to happines,
> And resolution honors fairest aime.   (94-6)

Zest and wit, a Jonsonian delight in the cunning purchase rather than the glad possession, the sense of being alive which is quickened by challenging the destructive element— these lines of the Guise's speech state the credo of the aspiring mind as well as any in Marlowe:

> That like I best that flyes beyond my reach.
> Set me to scale the high Peramides,
> And thereon set the Diadem of Fraunce,
> Ile either rend it with my nayles to naught,
> Or mount the top with my aspiring winges,
> Although my downfall be the deepest hell.   (99-104)

This has the crucial and familiar ambivalence. By one valuation we see the will to more than heavenly power permits and feel the normal horror of bloodshed and evil. By the other, we see a heroic and exciting immersion in dangerous waters. 'I know myself a MAN': the bold and aspiring can say so, the comfortable and tame cannot. Imagination is stirred in this speech as nowhere else in the play. The violence of tearing the crown at the pyramid's summit with victory as the only alternative to destruction is almost Yeats's 'lonely impulse of delight'. This too drives to a 'tumult in the clouds', and then the aspiring wings may fail: death to the body and damnation to the soul. But the eternity to come seems a waste that can be risked 'in balance with this life, this death'. There is little doubt that throughout the rest of the play, as it stands, the judgments evoked are simple and conventional; but at this particular point they are neither.

What follows is more rhetorical: the excitement which has been engendered by idea and image in the opening lines finds its vent in sound. Eight lines out of the next sixteen begin 'For this . . .'; and the second of two crescendos has its climax in 'Religion, *O Diabole*', so that the scornful dismissal carries the weight of the whole speech:

> Fye, I am ashamde, how euer that I seeme,
> To think a word of such a simple sound
> Of so great matter should be made the ground.   (124–6)

The Guise is making a realistic historical appraisal. A great undertaking will be justified by a religious excuse: what a poor thing humanity is (he being 'ashamed' because he is part of it) that this 'childish toy' should have such power over men that it becomes an indispensable tool in the policy.

The next eighteen lines sum up the situation: there is a weak, lecherous king (an Edward IV to Guise's Gloucester), the queen mother at work on his own behalf, a Church fat with resources—all this 'to bring the will of our desires to end'. The final section begins with lines recalling the speech to its sense of the future as an open region to be charted by individual will:

> . . . Then *Guise*,
> Since thou hast all the Cardes within thy hands
> To shuffle or cut, take this as surest thing:
> That right or wrong, thou deale thy selfe a King. (145-8)

He steels himself to become an immovable and terrible colossus, a Caesar amongst men:

> Giue me a look, that when I bend the browes,
> Pale death may walke in furrowes of my face. (158-9)

A look, a hand, an ear, these are to be the means: and the end, 'A royall seate, a scepter and a crowne'. All is set, the game is afoot, and the last lines appropriately balance the first:

> The plot is laide, and things shall come to passe,
> Where resolution striues for victory. (165-6)

After this speech, the most one can say of the play is that it does not dodder: there is nothing flabby about it, but on the contrary a certain hard, simple energy. This often takes sadistic forms, notably where death goes with a joke:

> *Admiral.* O let me pray before I dye.
> *Gonzago.* Then pray vnto our Ladye, kisse this crosse.
> *Stab him* (305-6)
> *Loreine.* I am a preacher of the word of God,
> And thou a traitor to thy soule and him.
> *Guise.* Dearly beloued brother, thus tis written.
> *He stabs him* (345-7)
> *Anjoy.* Stay my Lord, let me begin the psalme.
> *Guise.* Come dragge him away and throw him in a ditch. (345-9)
>
> *Seroune.* O let me pray vnto my God.
> *Mountsorrell.* Then take this with you.
> *Stab him* . . . (363-4)

Anjoy. Who haue you there?
Retes. Tis *Ramus,* the Kings professor of Logick.
Guise. Stab him. (385–7)

Guise [to the Schoolmasters]: Come sirs, Ile whip you to death
  with my puniards point.
                                      He kills them (446)
Cardinal. What will you fyle your handes with Churchmens
  bloud?
2 Murderer. Shed your bloud, O Lord no: for we entend to
  strangle you . . . *Now they strangle him* (1105–6)

1 Murd. So, pluck amaine,
  He is hard hearted, therefore pull with violence.
                                      (1116–17)

Sometimes the melodrama is amusing ('thou shalt have the
stab' is to this play what 'Off with his head' is to Alice's
Red Queen, or 'I shall have to polish him off' to Sweeney
Todd). Sometimes it is fairly sickening, as when Mugeroun
'cuts of the Cutpurse eare, for cutting of the golde buttons
off his cloake':

Cutpurse. O Lord, mine eare.
Mugeroun. Come sir, giue me my buttons and heers your eare.[1]
                                      (624–5)

This sadism—for there is always a comic twist that gives
the inevitable violence a sadistic turn—is one check to any
idea that the play marks another stage in some supposedly
happy development of Marlowe's outlook. P. H. Kocher
also warns against overestimating 'his progress towards
normalcy', for although the play contains conventional
political and religious sentiments, 'all this is obvious concession to prejudice at the lowest popular level'. But I am

---

[1] In his edition of the play, H. S. Bennett (pp. 217–18) quotes a probable source.
This is a story written up in *Merry Passages and Jests* collected by Sir Nicholas
Lestrange (*d.* 1655). The humour is not peculiar to Marlowe, but it is typical that
he should have used a 'jest' of just this kind.

not so sure of this. It is admittedly unsatisfactory to talk about what *may* have been, but there is enough in the opening and at odd points throughout the play to make one wonder whether the original did not, after all, have recognisable themes, and whether these were not as normal in the attitudes implied as, say, those of *Macbeth*.

Behind the formal religious war, for instance, there is a true religious sense of God at work and triumphing through Navarre. The association is made poetically—as in *Macbeth* ('the Powres aboue Put on their Instruments'; 'with him aboue To ratifie the Worke' etc.). The lines occur at scattered points (42, 56, 191, 580, 589, 714, 734, 795, 804, 934), but it is at the beginning that one can see most clearly, in embryo, the sort of thematic working that Shakespeare was to develop. Like *Macbeth*, this is a play of disorder: disruption nourishes evil and evil in turn promotes chaos. It begins with a picture of order and amity, symbolised by the marriage between Navarre and the daughter of the queen mother. The king, Charles IX, has the first speech, in which the key expressions are: honourable, good, union, religious league, knit, joined, nuptial rites, princely love. The discord that lurks to poison this harmony is heard in the queen's reference to religion, and the king's hasty, tactful 'Well, Madam, let that rest'. But concord returns and again the talk is of rites, holy Mass, honour, solemnity—this time to be cut clean through as the last line is given to the queen: 'Which Ile desolve with bloud and crueltie' (26). Navarre and his supporters are left on stage and their political talk has religious bearings which seem to be dramatised without cynicism, if anything with some dignity:

> *Na.* But he that sits and rules aboue the clowdes,
> Doth heare and see the praiers of the iust. . . . (42–3)

> Come my Lords lets go to the Church and pray,
> That God may still defend the right of France:
> And make his Gospel flourish in this land.   (55–7)

As they leave, the Guise enters and the grumbling discords
beneath the harmony now emerge as theme. In his eight-
line speech the images work together, the key expressions
here being: lowered, dusky lights, bloody clouds, terror,
ugly night, hue of hell, fatal night, fury. These are opposed,
in the speech, to: marriage rites, altars, sun, heaven, day;
so that the Guise is established as one who in his own person
reverses the normal values. Again, as in *Macbeth*, moral
order is overturned along with political authority. The
king, gentle and mild in his office, is to be worked as a
puppet; bloodshed and terror are to produce a situation
where 'everything includes itself in power'; and the world
will be left for the Guise to bustle in.

The Order of the opening, then, is really false, a sort of
political idyll where good-will and tact are to smooth over
the realities of power-politics and religious hatred that are
inescapable factors in the situation. But the end of the
play is very different. We are not left with a fairy-tale world,
where all is as it was in the beginning: order re-established
and everything happy ever after. What triumphs is a 'good'
(as opposed to Machiavellian) political realism, and it is a
hard and not idyllic re-establishment of order. Revenge,
death, curse and *rule* are the tone-definers in Navarre's last
speech (where religious league, princely love, hearts etc.,
were the relatively comfortable terms qualifying the initial
'order'). Whereas the weak benevolence of Charles IX has
exposed the country to its Machiavel, the 'good' Navarre's
realistic assessment is likely to ensure satisfactory government. Ending with the succession of Navarre rather than
with the death of Guise emphasises the political development as a main theme. The Guise is not so much the centre

of the play as one might think. He is, after all, a completely static character, while the political changes do mark a real development and one that was close to Elizabethan interest. Charles IX, weak but well-intentioned, corresponds in the general pattern to England's Henry VI; the debauched, extravagant Henry III is France's Edward IV, with the Guise as his Gloucester; and Navarre comes as a Richmond to bring in strong rule and better times.

So much is, I think, solidly 'there' in the play as it stands, and may have been developed in the original. There remains one further point which affects our idea of Marlowe's judgment and intention. That is, that although Navarre is a godly person (and a 'correct' one, saying the right things about religion and the queen of England), neither he nor any of the opponents of the Guise can be called Christian. They all talk of vengeance and promise that it shall take fearful forms. The last words of the play are hard and vindictive:

> And then I vow for to reuenge his death.
> As Rome and all those popish Prelates there,
> Shall curse the time that ere *Nauarre* was King,
> And rulde in France by *Henries* fatall death. (1260–63)

The king's dying speech has taken the same turn: Navarre is to whet his sword and 'keenly slice the Catholicks'. The God of these 'good' men is a jealous one, and the law is a stab for a stab and a massacre for a massacre. This law has in fact been enacted in the play, which divides neatly down the middle so that in one half the slaughtering is done by the Guise and his supporters and in the other half mostly by his opponents. In both cases it is brutal and pitiless, and in both cases it is done in the name of the true religion.

One would like to think that Marlowe was intending, or at least sensing, an irony; that with all the noise and savagery, a satire existed safe in the knowledge that a knavish speech sleeps in a foolish ear. But I doubt it, and we are left with what, when all is said, is an unfeeling and rather tasteless play, cashing in on still recent suffering which it never really enters. Marlowe read in De Serre's Commentary a dignified account of atrocities which might have moved him as we are moved to read of Jewish sufferings in our own time. When the modern popular stage has turned to these horrors it has been to stir that kind of pity and fear that *The Diary of Anne Frank* could command. But Marlowe's tastes and interests—and no doubt those of his audience—lay in other directions.

Part III

THE POEMS

7

THE FIRST BOOK OF LUCAN

LUCAN'S *De Bello Civili* or *Pharsalia* is an historical poem
of epic length describing the wars between Caesar and
Pompey. At his death in A.D. 65 Lucan had written nine
books and some 500 lines of the tenth, taking his narrative
beyond Pompey's death to Pothinus' plot against Caesar
in Egypt. It is generally supposed that twelve books were
planned, probably to include (as Robert Graves[1] conjectures) the suicide of Cato in 46 B.C. and to end with the
assassination of Caesar in 44. Marlowe translated the first
book only, giving a line-for-line version in blank verse.
In this, Caesar crosses the Alps and the Rubicon, takes
Ariminum, and causes panic in Rome. But Lucan is less
concerned here with furthering events than with preparing
feelings about the protagonists and the magnitude of the
struggle to come. The state of civil war is lamented and the
book ends with a vision of destruction and horror.

This translation is probably the least read of Marlowe's
works and is in fact, in a practical sense, the least readable.
Many editions of Marlowe do not include the translations
at all. Professor Tucker Brooke's edition reproduces the
1600 text, but with its misleading punctuation: the text is
often obscured quite seriously. L. C. Martin, the editor
of the poems in the six-volume *Works and Life*, gives a clear
text, but it has been out of print for years and is not often
found.

Commentators have kept at a more or less respectful

---

[1] All prose translations of Lucan quoted in this essay are taken from Robert
Graves's version (Penguin Classics).

distance. Most have allowed the work merit, and in writing
it off as 'rather dull' John Bakeless seems to be alone.
'Marlowe rendered the Latin, which is not particularly
inspired,' he says, 'line-for-line, and the result is quite as
bad as could be expected'.[1] He wastes no time examining
the badness, but then neither do its admirers discuss the
merits. It 'might be forgotten', Bakeless says, 'without
any detriment to his memory and without any great loss to
literature'. The facts of publication have done their best
to enforce the 'forgetting' and this chapter will be an
attempt to assess the 'loss and detriment' involved.

We have no idea whether Marlowe intended to write a
complete translation of the *Pharsalia*: there is much in it
which may have attracted him personally, and peculiarly
amongst his contemporaries. But to many Elizabethans the
first book would have stood by itself as significant and
moving in a way that it is unlikely to have done in later
times. In translating this first book Marlowe appears for
once to look at the centre of the Elizabethan world picture
without eccentricity of judgment or tone. The emphasis
is social and political, rather than personal: it is upon civil
war as an evil and a disorder against nature which, once
started, creates incalculable troubles and horrors for the
future. This concern, central to Elizabethan political
thought as to Shakespeare's histories, is just what is notably
absent as anything vital or developed in *Edward II*. In
thought and attitude the poem is far closer to Shakespeare
than the play is. It describes a civil disruption and its consequences in a way very like Ulysses' 'degree' speech in
Troilus and Cressida (I. 3). The importance of that speech
has become a commonplace of criticism: it is obviously
deep in the chronicle plays; less obviously, but no less

---

[1] *Christopher Marlowe*, pp. 262, 288.

deeply, in *Macbeth*; and represents much outside Shakespeare but deep in the age. In Lucan the Elizabethan preoccupation with the evils of civil war had its chief classical authority, and in Marlowe's translation of the first book it found as powerful an expression as any it ever had. The Latin has been assimilated and the work recreated in Elizabethan terms with a poetic intensity which only a very close and genuine involvement can make possible.

The poem begins with the phrase 'Wars worse then ciuill' and its first section ends with the line:

> These plagues arise from wreake of ciuill power. (32)

The Latin here reads *alta sedent civilis vulnera dextrae*, literally 'wounds caused by hands raised in civil conflict are deep and permanent' (or in Graves's free translation, 'only when brothers fall out is the sword driven home'). This is different from Marlowe's 'wreake of ciuill power', which is something very Elizabethan and akin to Ulysses' 'order': a picture of what happens 'when Degree is shak'd'. One consequence as seen by Ulysses is the breakdown of law: right and wrong lose their names, 'and so should Iustice too'. Lucan's second line (*iusque datum sceleri*) similarly stresses the violation of morality ('right given to crimes', i.e. the right to commit them); and in Marlowe this becomes 'outrage strangling law', the translation implying the process Ulysses outlines, whereby individual licence under a loosened morality undermines and eventually overturns civil law. Ulysses speaks of a condition which will

> rend and deracinate
> The Vnity, and married calme of States
> Quite from their fixure

and in Marlowe we have:

> Armies alied, the kingdoms league vprooted,
> Th'affrighted worlds force bent on publique spoile. (4–5)

In Ulysses' speech this disorder on earth mirrors a state in the heavens where 'the Planets In euill mixture to disorder wander', and so it is in the visionary's speech towards the end of Lucan's first book:

> why doe the Planets
> Alter their course and vainly dim their vertue?
> Sword-girt *Orions* side glisters too bright.
> Wars radge draws neare; & to the swords strong hand
> Let all Lawes yeeld, sinne beare the name of vertue . . .
>
> (662–6)

The breakdown of law is implied again, but as the wilful policy of power, in Caesar's:

> here, here (saith he)
> An end of peace; here end polluted lawes;
> Hence leagues, and couenants; Fortune thee I follow,
> Warre and the destinies shall trie my cause.   (226–9)

Caesar speaks for will and appetite in a situation where, in Ulysses' terms, 'every thing includes it selfe in Power': '*Mars* onely rules the heauen'. 'Force', says Ulysses, 'should be right'; or in Marlowe's Lucan:

> Force mastered right, the strongest gouern'd all.
> Hence came it that th'edicts were ouerrul'd,
> That lawes were broake, *Tribunes* with *Consuls* stroue,
> Sale made of offices, and peoples voices
> Bought by themselues & solde, and euery yeare
> Frauds and corruption in the field of *Mars*;
> Hence interest and deuouring vsury sprang,
> Faiths breach, & hence came war to most men welcom.
>
> (177–84)

In these circumstances Ulysses tells how 'the rude Sonne should strike his Father dead', and there is plenty of that throughout Lucan (in Book II, for instance: 'sons, bespattered by their father's blood, might quarrel for the privilege of beheading him'; or in Book VII: 'everyone had the same guilty desire, to drive their weapon through

a father's throat or a brother's breast'). In Book I it is
represented by lines 290-91,

> the sonne decrees
> To expel the father

and by the Centurion's professions to Caesar:

> . . . shouldst thou bid me
> Intombe my sword within my brothers bowels;
> Or fathers throate; or womens groning wombe;
> This hand (albeit vnwilling) should performe it;
> Or rob the gods; or sacred temples fire:
> These troupes should soone pull down the church of *Ioue*.
>
> (376-81)

Vandalism and sacrilege are not included in Ulysses'
catalogue of evils, but the lines ring Elizabethan bells;
Macbeth, the violator of order within Scotland and his own
'state of man', will, like Faustus, fight against the churches
and if need be plunge the world into chaos. This is the
conclusion of the process traced by Ulysses: the 'vniuersall
prey' at the mercy of 'an vniuersall Wolfe' brought to
power by the disruption of civil order. In Marlowe's
Lucan, the vision of a whole world in confusion provokes
some of the most deeply-felt writing and completes the
parallel with the *Troilus* speech (Shakespeare may well have
read the 1600 edition in the very year he was writing that
play):

> So when this worlds compounded vnion breakes,
> Time ends and to old *Chaos* all things turne;
> Confused stars shal meete, celestiall fire
> Fleete on the flouds, the earth shoulder the sea,
> Affording it no shoare, and *Phœbe's* waine
> Chace *Phœbus* and inrag'd affect his place,
> And striue to shine by day, and ful of strife
> Disolue the engins of the broken world.   (73-80)

Throughout the poem the imagery keeps this picture
living before us: 'the walles of houses halfe rear'd totter',

'thunder which the wind teares from the cloudes', 'cracke of riuen ayre', 'al the world Ransackt for golde', 'lofty *Cæsar* in the thickest throng', 'souse downe the wals', 'Puls them aloft, and makes the surge kisse heauen', or perhaps most in that violent and bold hyperbole:

> The earth went off hir hinges; and the *Alpes*
> Shooke the old snow from off their trembling laps. (551–2)

Confusion is wrapt too in the equivocations of the priest:

> Thus in ambiguous tearmes,
>   Inuoluing all, did *Aruns* darkly sing. (636–7)

And the book ends in a woman's frenzied whirl of questionings and half-glimpses of future horrors:

> Whither turne I now? ...
> New factions rise; now through the world againe
> I goe; ô *Phœbus* show me *Neptunes* shore,
> And other Regions, I haue seene *Philippi*.
> This said, being tir'd with fury she sunke downe.
>   (682 and 691–4)

In all this, the matter is of central and common Elizabethan interest, but the voice is distinctively and forcefully Marlowe's. Individuality emerges in every passage and although he is translating one often feels more aware of the characteristic and vital Marlovian than in much of *The Jew of Malta* or *Edward II*. His own involvement with Lucan, however, probably derives from an attraction more personal and less representative of the age (so that Michel Poirier is at any rate half right when he says that Marlowe's choice of the *Pharsalia* 'reveals his own taste more than that of his day').

The two writers had much in common. Their violent and early deaths (Lucan committed suicide when he was twenty-five) relate to the manner of their lives. On a cautious reading of biographical information, it seems likely that they were men of bold, independent mind, given to strong antipathies and enthusiasms, with an irreverent and ironical streak which courted danger. Suetonius' Life of Lucan[1] tells of a precocious youth, with abilities rated highly by the authorities who matter most in these things—Nero and himself. But Nero's favour did not last[2] and, if we believe Suetonius, Lucan's was not a submissive or docile spirit, or, eventually, a very stable or principled one. In spirit (though not in detail) Lucan's reputation has come down to us as something not unlike Marlowe's. Compare, for instance, the boldness and independence in 'Into whatsoever company he cometh he persuadeth men to atheism, willing them not to be afraid of bugbears and hobgoblins', or the less heroic habit attributed of giving men 'sudden privy injuries', and the unprincipled 'intemperate and cruel heart'. These phrases are not everywhere acceptable as biographical evidence, but at least we can say that in as far as we have biographical information about the reputation of these men, it is of that character.

The works themselves, however, provide surer ground

---

[1] *De Viris Illustribus*, c. 113.

[2] 'Nero interrupted a reading of Lucan's poetry by suddenly summoning a meeting of the Senate, and going out himself, with the sole object of ruining the performance. The hostility that Lucan thereafter showed him, in word and deed, is still notorious. Once, after relieving himself explosively in a public convenience, he declaimed a half-line of Nero's:

. . . and it sounded like underground thunder—

which made a number of men who had been easing themselves beside him take to their heels and run. He also satirized Nero, and his own influential friends as well, in a most bitter and damaging poem. Finally he became so to speak, the standard-bearer of Piso's ill-fated conspiracy, ranting publicly about how glorious it was to murder a tyrant, and even offering to present his friends with Nero's head. When the conspiracy came to light, however, he lost his cocksureness and was easily compelled to make a confession; after which he resorted to the most abject pleas for pardon, going so far as to accuse his own innocent mother of being one of the conspirators. Apparently he thought that, since Nero was a matricide, he would appreciate this lack of decent devotion. Nero did indeed allow him to choose the manner of his death. Lucan took advantage of the respite by writing his father a letter which contained amendments to some of his verses; then ate a huge dinner, and told a physician to cut the arteries in his wrists.' (Suetonius, tr. Graves, p. 8.)

for comparison. The boldness of (some of) Lucan's reputed life has its literary counterpart. Few histories are more partisan than the *Pharsalia*. The first book concentrates on the tragedy of civil war, but the tragedy which holds the centre of attention throughout the narrative is that the right side lost. 'We may be sure that no account of that battle will ever fail to excite alternate hope and dread in men unborn; that all will read the tragic tale with deep emotion, as if it were something still due to happen, and not ancient history; and that all will consistently side with Pompey.'[1] Pompey and Cato defended the republic; Caesar was the founder of the imperial Rome which Nero inherited. Of the Egyptian plot against Caesar's life, Lucan writes: 'Luckily, however, the Fates prevented this blow from being struck by anyone except Brutus—because the example which he set us Romans of how to deal with tyrants would have been lost had the Egyptians taken the initiative.'[2] The Stoical party were an influential opposition group to the court, and Lucan's enthusiasm for Cato erects stoical virtues to an eminence where they contrast forcibly with Nero's way of life. In Book X Cleopatra, abominated as another Helen, is described as living in decadent splendour, and the comparison with Nero is made explicit: 'Her banqueting hall was as large as a temple, and more luxurious than even our present corrupt age could easily imitate.'[3] Nor is the denunciation of the King of Parthia likely to be innocent of topical reference.[4] He is accused of incestuous relations with his mother, and Nero was known to be on particularly odd terms with his. Cato's speech to the soldiers of the dead Pompey even goes so far as to see that hero as a national misfortune: 'I see the case clearly, men. You were fighting in the same spirit as the Caesarians: to

---

[1] Graves's translation, p. 156.
[2] Graves's translation, p. 33.
[3] Graves, p. 227.
[4] Book VIII, Graves, p. 184.

defend tyranny. By this I mean that you were Pompeians, rather than Romans. However, Pompey was defeated, which spared you the need of suffering in the cause of a tyrant. You are at last free to live or die, as you wish: able at last to fight your own battles, instead of being engaged to win world sovereignty for any single leader.'[1] If so great a man as Pompey is to be regretted as a liability to Rome, how much more regrettable (it must be implied) is the 'single leadership' of 'our present corrupt age'.

It is not possible to say, of course, whether Marlowe read Lucan with an eye to this implicit protest or with any recognition of the risks involved. The only indications could be his own tone in translating, the attitude to Lucan of Marlowe's age, and the view that he translated with a depth of feeling which suggests what Harry Eevin calls 'a temperamental kinship'. It is certain, at any rate, that something of the thrusting, aggressive manner of Lucan's writing must have been felt with unusual closeness by one whose own basic style can be so similarly described. The hyperbole which expresses so much of Marlowe's thrust and stretch of spirit is—not, I think, *learnt* from Lucan, because it was in the air in those decades and essentially his own, but—so much nearer to Lucan than to any other author that it does indeed betoken a kinship of a rare closeness.

Certain unorthodoxies in artistic and religious matters form another link. For example, the gods are notably absent from Book I, when by Virgilian tradition they should be introduced as baleful or beneficent influences. But Lucan is breaking with that tradition and reverting to an earlier and native Roman line in taking (as Ennius and Naevius had done) recent historical events as the subject of serious tone and epic length (we remember that in

[1] Book IX, Graves, p. 203.

The Massacre at Paris Marlowe was the first to make drama out of contemporary events).

In Book VII Lucan explicitly denies the existence of powerful gods in a world where so much goes wrong: 'It is most false to say that Gods rule this world, and that Iuppiter rules the Gods; nothing but blind chance makes the world go round.'[1] Local gods, for instance, are put to the test when Caesar cuts down a sacred grove: 'Every Gaul present shuddered at the sight, but the defenders of Marseilles were delighted; they could not believe that such an insult to the Gods would remain unpunished.'[2] The defenders stopped laughing at the point where Lucan's more sceptical readers might start, for the Gods ignored the event and the Romans went ahead. In Book IX the sceptic in Lucan speaks through Pompey's desperate wife, Cornelia: 'But soon I shall pursue him through empty space, and through the dark Underworld—if there is any such place.'[3] Lucan's *Per Tartara, si sunt ulla* recalls the Thyestes of Seneca: *si sunt tamen di*, which in turn brings to mind Tamburlaine's:

> The God that sits in heauen, if any God. (4312)

In Elizabethan times such a phrase was a fair indication of 'atheism' and so we find in the Cerne Abbas inquiry into the opinions of Raleigh and his circle the question put to each witness: 'Whom do you know or have heard, that have argued or spoken against, or as doubting the being of any God? . . . Or to swear by God, adding if there be a God, or such like?'

But the most striking affinity between Lucan and Marlowe is in the sadistic trait which they had in common. An attraction towards pain and particularly to the humiliation associated with it has been repeatedly illustrated in these

---

[1] Graves's translation, p. 163.   [3] Graves, p. 199.
[2] Book III, Graves, p. 78.

studies of Marlowe's work. It sometimes goes in company with pity or indignation, as in Lucan it is covered sometimes by a verbal protest ('I cannot bring myself to describe . . .') and generally by the overall feeling that what we are witnessing is tragic. But the sensational reporting or imagining of sufferings carries with it its relish, of a sort I do not recognise in a book like, say, Leon Wolfe's *In Flanders Fields*, where the horrors of war are brought home and individual suffering is made painfully and unremittingly clear. The relish is Roman: the ingenious, surprising, obscene, pitiful, ludicrous, horrific characteristics of the show in the arena, shared by a large audience, must develop in a people the general human capability of a perverted pleasure. So in Lucan: 'A soldier standing on the poop had boldly grasped the stern-ornament of a Greek vessel which was trying to back off, when two javelins flew simultaneously from front and rear and met in his body; a great rush of blood loosened them both and he died of a doubly mortal wound.'[1] Or the sailor named Lycidas: 'He would have been dragged overboard had his comrades not grabbed at his legs, as he was disappearing, and belayed them to the bulwarks; but the grappling-irons wrenched them off at the thigh and his blood burst out in a torrent rather than a trickle. This was the most spectacularly brutal death of all, because the upper half of his body fell into the sea and could be seen for a while struggling hard not to drown.'[2] Lucan likes intestines and is particularly good with snake bite: 'Nasidius, once a Marsian farmer, died in a very different manner: by expansion not liquefaction. When a fiery prester struck at him, his face turned red as a glowing coal and began to swell until the features could not be recognised. Then the virus spread and puffed him out to the gigantic proportions of a ship's canvas in a storm.

[1] Book III, Graves, p. 82. [2] Graves's translation, p. 83.

The manhim self was buried deep inside this bloated mass,
and the breastplate flew off like the lid of a fiercely steaming
cauldron. Soon . . .' and so on.[1]

'I have always been very fond of ludicrous deaths.' The
engaging candour of this admission is Lawrence Durrell's
(the sentence is from *Justine*). In Barabas' cauldron Marlowe
gave the Elizabethan stage its best thing in ludicrous deaths;
Edward's is the worst of royal deaths for horror, ingenuity
and humiliation; a Lucanian taste is also recognisable in
the sensational barbarities of Tamburlaine, and probably
most of all in the details of Aeneas' narrative of the fall of
Troy. The manner of that description comes to mind
frequently when reading the *Pharsalia*. In describing, for
example, the seizure of Rome by Marius: 'Pools of blood
stood in the temples, and everywhere the pavements grew
red and slippery. Nor did the victors even spare the aged,
but cut short their declining years at a stroke.'[2] Or by the
way in which extremity of grief veers towards the ludicrous:
'She [Cato's wife, Marcia] hurried back to him, pulling out
handfuls of her disordered hair as she went and repeatedly
beating her breasts. She was still dusty from the pyre, and
tears coursed freely down her cheeks, yet she knew that her
one hope of finding favour in his eyes lay in thus presenting
herself.'[3] 'Then Cornelia sprang out of bed in frantic
grief, intent on beginning her new life of anguish without
the least delay.'[4] 'Vulteius now bared his throat and cried:
"Is anyone here worthy to kill and be killed by me?" No
more was needed: several comrades stabbed him and
earned his dying praises; but he showed a deeper gratitude
to the first assassin by dispatching him in return.'[5] 'Farce',
in the sense of T. S. Eliot's application of it to Marlowe,
is not far off.

[1] Book IX, Graves, p. 217.
[2] Book III, Graves, p. 30.
[3] Graves, p. 56.
[4] Graves, p. 127.
[5] Book IV, Graves, p. 100.

In fact, the whole cast of mind seems remarkably similar: the translation is not a piece of hackwork, but as essentially Marlovian as anything he did.

The reasons given here for supposing an unusual closeness between the two writers come from reading *outside* the first book, and they strengthen one's sense that the translation is a 'significant' work in the Marlovian canon. But in fact its own quality is enough to establish this, and it is to the work itself that we must now turn.

Not that this 'temperamental kinship' shows itself everywhere in patient and accurate translation. Silver Latin and Elizabethan English have, in any case, little in common as literary tongues. Out of his violent and sensational material Lucan manufactured verse which is polished and sophisticated. Marlowe's 'mighty line' fits it more naturally than the accommodation of bouncing fourteeners which Heywood and Studley found for Seneca's neat and tidy horrors; but, even though there is in Marlowe from time to time a markedly Augustan flavour, the antithetical point and sharp concentration of Lucan's style are often lost. Sometimes Marlowe does achieve a fair neatness, as in:

> *Pompey* could bide no equall,
> Nor *Cæsar* no superior, (125–6)

though even here, Lucan's reverse order is more pointed:

> *Nec quenquam jam ferre potest, Caesarve priorem,*
> *Pompeiusque parem.*

Again, even though he attempts a classical balance, Marlowe fluffs the famous line:

> *Victrix causa deis placuit, sed victa Catoni*

> *Cæsars* cause
> The gods abetted; *Cato* likt the other. (128–9)

There is nothing here to represent the organisation of
victrix . . . victa. But this essentially Augustan polish was
not within the scope of Elizabethan literature. Other
qualities desirable in a translation of Lucan were.

There are few howlers but many mistakes. Some are due
to limited historical knowledge. For example, Caesar is
made to cry out:

> Thou thunderer that guardst
> Roomes mighty walles built on *Tarpeian* rock. (197–8)

The walls were not built on this rock, however; the rock is
the point from which Jupiter watches Rome. Later, Caesar
is said to be

> incenst as are *Eleius* steedes
> With clamors; who though lockt and chaind in stalls,
> Souse downe the wals, and make a passage forth. (294–6)

Very probably Marlowe did not know what Eleian horses
were. Graves's translation runs: 'He resembled a race-
horse at Olympia, straining at the closed wooden gates of
the barrier, and trying to work the bolts loose with his
head'. The horses are in the starting-pen, not in a stall,
and they attack, not the walls, but—sagacious animals as
they are—the gates. Vigour of image and language has
been gained at the expense of an exaggeration for which
Lucan gave no excuse. The Scholiast had understood the
passage, and no doubt Marlowe could have found out the
meaning of the reference had he tried. There are several
further mistakes concerning proper names: 'Nor capitall
adorn'd with sacred bayes' (288) should have 'Capitol';
conversely (531–3) 'lightning . . . Blasted the Capitoll'
should be the capital city of Latium, Alba Longa[1]; in 564–5
'*Sibils* priests' should read 'Cybele's'; '*Sicillian* Pirates'
(336) should refer to the Cilicians; and 'the church of *Ioue*'
(381) is in fact the temple of Juno. The confusion between

---

[1] These may be typographical errors and not mistranslations.

Cybele and the Sybil recurs in line 599 along with other misunderstandings:

> they . . . keepe, and read
> *Sybilla's* secret works, and washt their saint
> In *Almo's* floud.

The saint washed in the Almo is not the Sybil as Marlowe seems to think, but an image of Cybele. There are other places where ignorance or uncertainty about references must have hampered. But most of the mistakes are in fact due to misunderstandings not of references but of language.

Omissions are inevitable if the Latin is to be rendered line-for-line, but sometimes the loss is serious and should not have been incurred. Early in the book, for instance, the poet laments the misfortune which Rome has brought upon itself and adds, in Marlowe's version:

> All great things crush themselues, such end the gods
> Allot the height of honor; men so strong
> By land, and sea, no forreine force could ruine.   (81–3)

Lucan reads:

> *In se magna ruunt. laetis hunc numina rebus*
> *Crescendi posuere modum. nec gentibus ullis*
> *Commodat in populum, terrae, pelagique potentem,*
> *Invidiam Fortuna suam.*

The idea of an envious fortune which had got it in for Rome, wanting to have revenge herself, is nowhere present in the translation. Another loss (and a very Marlovian addition) occurs in lines 166–8:

> Pouerty (who hatcht
> Roomes greatest wittes) was loath'd and al the world
> Ransackt for golde, which breeds the world decay.

Lucan reads:

> *foecunda virorum*
> *Paupertas fugitur; totoque accersitur orbe,*
> *Que gens quaeque perit.*

Marlowe has not appreciated the distributive force of *quaeque* and has added the reference to gold. Graves translates: 'they rifled every foreign land of whatever product had most contributed to its downfall'. The tartness and sophistication of this are not represented in Marlowe's robust downrightness but blunter sense.

It may be worth looking at a specimen passage in some detail. The speech of the Centurion Laelius contains the following characteristically Marlovian lines:

> Well, leade vs then to *Syrtes* desart shoare;
> Or *Scythia*; or hot *Libiaes* thirsty sands.
> This hand, that all behind vs might be quail'd,
> Hath with thee passed the swelling Ocean,
> And swept the foming brest of *Articks Rhene*.
> Loue ouer-rules my will, I must obay thee,
> *Cæsar*; he whom I heare thy trumpets charge
> I hould no Romaine; by these ten blest ensignes
> And all thy seuerall triumphs, shouldst thou bid me
> Intombe my sword within my brothers bowels;
> Or fathers throate; or womens groning wombe;
> This hand (albeit vnwilling) should perform it;
> Or rob the gods; or sacred temples fire:
> These troupes should soone pull down the church of *Ioue*.
> (368–81)

There are mistakes of all kinds here. One involves historical or geographical knowledge: '*Syrtes* desart shore', for instance, is in Graves's better-informed version 'the inhospitable Gulf of Sirte'. Another involves a loss due to compression: 'that all behind vs might be quail'd' omits *orbem* with its sense of a great land-mass left behind as a consolidated gain. Marlowe is also at sea over the difficult grammatical structure. Lines 368 and 9 contain a supposition ('suppose you should ...'); 370–72 contain reasons for the coming boast, and 373 ('It must be that I am able, as well as willing, to obey you') is the statement that

Laelius could fulfil the possible demands of 368 and 9. This is Housman's explanation of the lines, and it is true that by the year of Oudendorp's edition (1728) nobody had understood them very well. On the other hand, it is difficult to defend the mistakes in line 378, where 'womens groning wombe' (*in viscera partu conjugis*) is wrong in number and sense: 'My wife's pregnant womb' being the obvious and stronger meaning. Then in line 381: 'These troupes should soon pull down the church of *Ioue*' there is both the mistaken reference, noted already, to Jove instead of Juno, and a basic departure from the Latin which means, in Graves's translation: 'I will gladly break up the sacred images and melt them into coin for your war-chest.'

I have used this passage because it illustrates the various kinds of mistake. Mistakes here come more than usually thick and fast; but most passages do in fact contain some distortion. Often the points involved are not terribly important, though they show Marlowe as an undependable latinist, sometimes opting for the wrong interpretation when the right one was understood by others. An example of this occurs in Marlowe's line 220, where the watery moon is 'three days old'. Graves has 'it was swollen by three nights and days of winter rain following a change of moon'. Both interpretations were current in Marlowe's time. Micryllius preferred the right one; Sulpitius the one taken by Marlowe and rebutted by Housman.

More disappointing are the special occasions when one would have expected the 'temperamental kinship' to be manifest in the translation, and yet even here something characteristic in Lucan is missed. Such a passage occurs within a few lines of the previous example:

> Like to a Lyon of scortcht desart *Affricke*,
> Who seeing hunters pauseth till fell wrath
> And kingly rage increase, then hauing whiskt

His tàile athwart his backe, and crest heau'd vp,
With iawes wide open ghastly roaring out;
(Albeit the *Moores* light Iauelin or his speare
Sticks in his side) yet runs vpon the hunter.   (208–14)

Several ideas are missing. The lion aggravates his own anger by lashing himself with his tail, and the movement of his attack on the hunter will drive the spear still further into his body. One might have assumed such details to be amongst the attractions that Lucan held for Marlowe (with Bajazet and Edward in mind, and the Hero who 'hauing swallow'd *Cupids* golden hooke, The more she striv'd, the deeper she was strooke'). Their absence in translation is no doubt a caution to over-confident literary speculation.

These faults of translation matter to us now because on account of them we do not have as good an English poem as we might have had. Omissions and inaccuracies make the poem less rich in sense and sound than it might be, and they are often the sign of a mind less than wholly, creatively and critically, occupied in its task. Even so, the work has its magnificence. It is this (rather than its being interesting to Elizabethan and Marlovian students) that makes it worth reading, and reading with the kind of attention that good poetry requires and rewards.

Comparisons make standards, and it often happens that we are not really alive to an excellence until we see it side by side with mediocrity. Two translations of Lucan, written not long after Marlowe's, come to hand usefully for this purpose. The three versions of the first nine lines are worth comparing:

(*a*) A more then civill warre I sing,
   That through th'Emathian fields did ring,
   Where reins let loose to head-strong pride,
   A potent people did misguide:

Whose conquering hand enrag'd rebounds
On his owne bowels with deepe wounds.
Where Hosts confronting neare alies,
All faith and Empire Lawes defies.
A world of force in faction meetes,
And common guilt like torrents fleets.
Where like infestuous ensignes wave, ⎫
The Ægle doth the Ægle brave,   ⎬
And Pyle against the Pyle doth rave. ⎭
   Dear Citizens, what brainsick charmes?
   What outrage of disordered armes?
   Leads you to feast your envious foes,
   To see you goar'd with your owne blowes?

(*b*) Warres more then ciuill on Æmathian plaines
We sing; rage licensd; where great Rome distaines
In her owne bowels her victorious swords;
Where kindred hoasts encounter, all accords
Of Empire broke: where arm'd to impious warre
The strength of all the shaken world from farre
Is met; knowne Ensignes Ensignes foe defie,
Piles against Piles, 'gainst Eagles Eagles fly.
What fury, Countrymen, what madnesse cou'd
Moove you to feast your fooes with Roman blood?

(*c*) Wars worse then ciuill on *Thessalian* playnes,
And outrage strangling law & people strong,
We sing; whose conquering swords their own breasts
   launcht,
Armies allied, the kingdom's league vprooted,
Th'affrighted worlds force bent on publique spoile,
Trumpets, and drums like deadly threatning other,
Eagles alike displaide, darts answering darts.
Romans, what madnes, what huge lust of warre
Hath made *Barbarians* drunke with *Latin* bloud?

The first version is by Sir Arthur Gorges, published in 1614; the second is by Thomas May, 1627; and the third is Marlowe's. Gorges's octosyllabics tinkle inappropriately and impress only by their date (in one of the Universities' dating papers they would be assigned pretty generally and confidently to the eighteenth century). They are sometimes neat and sometimes not: in the sixth line, for instance, 'his' and 'with' come naturally but senselessly as accented syllables. Compared with both May and Marlowe this man is doing an exercise in a new, cool, courtly manner, where the 'outrage' is distanced by an ordered, untroubled verse form and a complacently literary diction. Gorges is perhaps a non-starter; but May is a genuine competitor and the translation which won the enthusiasm of Ben Jonson and Henry Vaughan[1] merits at least our respect. His verse moves freely and with dignity. He does not commit himself to a line-for-line translation yet keeps the expression

[1] From a couplet by Vaughan we gather that he had not read Marlowe:

> 'Rome had been still my wonder: I had knowne
> Lucan in no expression but his own'.

The verses by Jonson (who probably did know the Marlowe—a passage in *Catiline* —V. 6—recalls Marlowe, lines 100–104) deserve reprinting. Jonson marvels at the combination of order and power: 'due proportion' in an engine strained to bursting point.

> When, *Rome*, I reade thee in thy mighty paire,
> And see both climbing vp the slippery staire
> Of Fortunes wheele by *Lucan* driu'n about,
> And the world in it, I begin to doubt,
> At euery line some pinn thereof should slacke
> At least, if not the generall Engine cracke.
> But when againe I view the parts to peiz'd,
> And those in number so, and measure rais'd,
> As neither *Pompey's* popularitie,
> *Cæsar's* ambition, *Cato's* libertie,
> Calme *Brutus* tenor start; but all along
> Keepe due proportion in the ample song,
> It makes me rauish'd with iust wonder, cry
> What Muse, or rather God of harmony
> Taught *Lucan* these true moodes! Replyes my sence
> What godds but those of arts, and eloquence?
> *Phœbus*, and *Hermes*? They whose tongue, or pen
> Are still th'interpreters twixt godds, and men!
> But who hath them interpreted, and brought
> *Lucans* whole frame vnto vs, and so wrought,
> As not the smallest ioint, or gentlest word
> In the great masse, or machine there is stirr'd?
> The selfe same *Genius*! so the work will say.
> The *Sunne* translated, or the Sonne of *May*.

compact and manages his rhyming with skill. But after that
we can only observe, in comparison with Marlowe, a
certain uncharacterful passivity which stamps the work a
translation rather than a real addition to English poetry.
'Wars more than civil' says May, translating *Bella* . . .
plus quam civilia, where Marlowe has 'Wars worse than
civil'. The difference is tiny but typical; magnify it over the
whole book and you have an essential difference of kind.
Perhaps 'wars worse' is a jingle and so a crudity: critics
from Dryden to Greg might well have thought so. Or
perhaps, on a tiny scale and in its context, it has the very
stuff of poetry: the likeness of sound draws the words
together so that they intensify each other (like 'heart heard
of, ghost guessed'); the strong monosyllables thus intensified beat insistently forcing the line into an irregularity,
and the monstrous action of 'outrage strangling law' has
been evoked by the passionate analogous movement.
'Strangling' is Marlowe's own metaphor (*iusque datum
sceleri*) and its strength and violence are utterly characteristic
of the English poem Marlowe has given us. Again sound
works to intensify the sense: 'outrage . . . strangling . . .
strong'. This is not merely a technical or Spenserian
felicity, but an expressive thing, where the vowels gain
energy from the thick barrage of consonants (an effect
probably learnt from Chaucer whose 'through the thickest
of the throng gan threst' Marlowe twice imitates). The
retention of the main clause ('We sing') till the third line is
suggested by the Latin. Marlowe places it, however, not in
the middle of the line (as in the Latin) but where in English
it is going to ring with some splendour—at the beginning.
With still more grandeur, Milton's 'Sing Heav'nly Muse'
works in the same manner. May placed the clause at the
beginning of the second line and the effect is pedestrian:
a dignified but prosaic statement. Marlowe's construction,

seconded throughout the passage by vigour of image, sound and movement, achieves a double attack. The theme rings out aggressively in the first words, and the verb comes triumphantly where it can boast a fit object.

Throughout the passage the aggressive manner seconds the violence of the matter, and Marlowe's own images are powerful reinforcements: the image of 'uprooting' (stronger than *rupto*-'broken') and of the world not merely 'shaken' but 'affrighted', the noise of 'trumpets and drums'. The energy of this massive first sentence accumulates then to burst open in the rhetorical question with its expressive emphasis:

> Romans, what madnes, what huge lust of warre
> Hath made *Barbarians* drunke with *Latin* bloud? (8–9)

Why is May ineffective by comparison? Obviously, the rhyme is awkward and the enjambement particularly unfortunate. 'Feast' is poor compared with 'drunk' (which is Marlowe's idea—Lucan has *praebere*); and 'what madness' does not exist beside 'what huge lust of war' (again loose but effective for *quae tanta licentia ferri*). But quite apart from this, May's two lines have lost the impetus of the opening because that first sentence has controlled its own energy, put on the brakes and stopped gracefully in its last lines:

> knowne Ensignes Ensignes foe defie,
> Piles against Piles, 'gainst Eagles Eagles fly.

May has attempted to copy Lucan's word-patterning, and so literary grace is achieved—and all else lost. We see just how much that is only by reading Marlowe; and we realise just what Marlowe accomplishes by looking at May. Marlowe's Lucan is in fact an English poem.

This makes it a rare thing among translations, and especially among translations from Latin. There are, of course, passages where, as in a painting, the Latin shows through: there is no need to be told that the writer has a Latin model. It is noticeable, for example, when Caesar is working his troops to indignation by evoking the plight of the veterans:

> Whether now shal these olde bloudles soules repaire?
> What seates for their deserts? what store of ground
> For seruitors to till? What *Colonies*
> To rest their bones? (343-6)

Marlowe's English construction follows Lucan's Latin (*quae sedes . . . quae rura*, etc.). But then compare the lines in Ridley's translation[1]:

> Where shall the weary soldier find his rest?
> What cottage home their joys, what fields their fruits
> Shall to our veterans yield?

The rarity of Marlowe's book among blank verse translations from Latin has this second feature: the Latin is 'Englished' and not Miltonised. Marlowe has incorporated Latin construction only as far as normal English can absorb it. The eloquence and dignity of the rhetorical questions are preserved in an English form which can naturally mould itself on the classical; but there are no inversions or contortions of basic idiom—English is kept up.

One unlatinic strength of English as a poet's tongue lies in its wealth of monosyllables. It is a strength only for certain kinds of poetry, but Marlowe's is pre-eminently among them. An example is the force of 'huge lust of war' in the lines just quoted; or of these lines describing the ruin of the Roman towns:

> That now the walles of houses halfe rear'd totter,
> That rampiers fallen down, huge heapes of stone . . .
> (24-5)

With alliteration to help, the monosyllables of 'huge heapes

[1] *The 'Pharsalia' of Lucan translated into blank verse by Edward Ridley* (Longmans Green, 1896).

of stone' and 'now the walles of houses half reard totter'
hammer insistently like the destructive movement they
record. Or again in the lines describing Julia:

> Snatcht hence by cruel fates with ominous howles,
> Bare downe to hell her sonne the pledge of peace. (112–13)

Marlowe invented the howls, but more characteristic are
the 'bare down to hell' and the verb 'snatcht': both violent
and made more so by the monosyllabic jab. Quite different
is the effect of monosyllables in the following passage.
Caesar has entered Ariminum. There are confused noises of
trumpets and the tumults of war; the citizens fearful,
fetching out 'olde swords With vgly teeth of blacke rust
foully scarr'd'; Caesar in the thickest throng: and after this
hurly-burly, the people lament their situation. The poet
comments:

> Thus sighing whispered they, and none durst speake
> And shew their feare, or griefe: but as the fields
> When birds are silent thorough winters rage;
> Or sea far from the land, so all were whist.
> Now light had quite dissolu'd the mysty night,
> And *Cæsar's* mind vnsetled musing stood.   (259–64)

Compare the Latin for those last three lines:

> *Noctis gelidas lux solverat umbras:*
> *Ecce faces belli, dubiaeque in proelia menti*
> *Urgentes addunt stimulos.*

In the Marlowe, thirty-nine words out of forty-nine are
monosyllables. The proportion is always high—a measure
of the unlikeness of the languages—but here it is exceptionally so. The effect is again subtly expressive: after the
clangour of battle the brooding silence is held for six lines,
the stillness made more vivid by the simplicity of diction
and construction. The 'mighty line' has shrunk: clamour
and amplitude are minimised:

> Or sea far from the land, so all were whist.

The effect is of a musical diminuendo or a subtle change in orchestration; it is just the sort of thing Marlowe is commonly supposed not to do.

English and Latin differ also in the relative frequency of the finite verb. Latin, even in poetry, runs much more to participle and absolute constructions, its long sentences often containing a single finite verb where English might analyse the constituents into clauses. Moreover, strength of verb is a notable feature of Elizabethan writing as compared with modern; and amongst Elizabethans none used verbs more vigorously than Marlowe. Modern writing tends, unless consciously checked, to rely very much on the verb 'to be', the least colourful and vigorous of verbs. I look over a page of Marlowe, however, and among fifty or so verbs find the verb 'to be' used only twice. It is above all the strength of the verbs that makes Elizabethan English such a powerful medium in the passage where Cacsar is compared with a thunder-storm:

> So thunder which the wind teares from the cloudes,
> With cracke of riuen ayre and hideous sound
> Filling the world, leapes out and throwes forth fire,
> Affrights poore fearefull men, and blasts their eyes
> With ouerthwarting flames, and raging shoots
> Alongst the ayre and nought resisting it
> Falls, and returnes, and shiuers where it lights.　　(152–8)

Ridley's translation goes:

> As parts the clouds a bolt by wind compelled
> With crack of riven air and crash of worlds,
> And veils the light of day, and on mankind,
> Blasting their vision with its flames oblique,
> Sheds deadly fright: then turning to its home,
> Nought but the air opposing, through its path
> Sheds havoc and collects its scattered fires.

The difference is partly between the men and partly between the ages. Marlowe is enjoying himself and Ridley is doing a job: 'teares from the clouds', 'leaps out . . . and raging shoots' are indeed '*echt* Marlowe'. But by the late nine-teenth century the strong colourful verb no longer marks the language as it did.

Marlowe's characteristic placing of the verb at the beginning of the line reinforces the percussive and aggressive effect. So, for instance, with the horses

> who though lockt and chaind in stalls,
> Souse downe the wals, and make a passage forth[1] (295–6)

Or with Laelius' plea to Caesar to let them get at the enemy

> euen nowe when youthfull bloud
> Pricks forth our liuely bodies . . . .   (363–4)

The verb is likely (in Marlowe) to carry a sense of sexual vigour, and contrasts well with Lucan's more pedestrian *movet* or Ridley's pale 'fills'. A little later in the same speech the soldier says he would

> Intombe my sword within my brothers bowels   (377)

Lucan's verb is *condere* (to hide or sink); 'intombe' intensifies.

Another source of linguistic vigour common in Elizabethan English and rare elsewhere is the combination of heroic and colloquial. Neo-classic decorum regards this as a blemish; hence *All for Love* as an improvement on *Antony and Cleopatra*. This idea of classic dignity makes Ridley in 1896 write:

> Thou wouldst believe that blazing to the torch
> Were men's abodes, or nodding to the fall.

---

[1] Among illustrations of the verb 'souse' in usage, *O.E.D.* gives these: 'Hoyse her, souse her, bounce her, trounce her, pull out her throte-bole' from *Gammer Gurton's Needle*; and from Mrs Piozzi's *Journal in France*, 'The people always take delight to souse an Englishman's hat upon his head'.

Marlowe, three hundred years earlier, wrote what we might say today:

> You would haue thought their houses had bin fierd
> Or dropping-ripe . . .   (490–91)

Throughout Marlowe, however violent and extreme, one feels aware that this is fundamentally 'language such as men doe use': this, the 'pre-dissociation' distinction, is infrequent enough in such heightened and heroic writing, and in classical verse translations it is a rarity indeed.

So in reading the lines about the priest Aruns, it is partly this naturalness of diction that makes one aware how remote from Marlowe is the comfortable, reliable decorum of the neo-classics:

> On the Altar
> He laies a ne're-yoakt Bull, and pours downe wine,
> Then crams salt leuin on his crooked knife;
> The beast long struggled, as being like to proue
> An aukward sacrifice, but by the hornes
> The quick priest pull'd him on his knees & slew him.
>   (607–12)

But it is also partly a peculiarity of tone. Marlowe has in fact mistranslated: 'like to proue An aukward sacrifice' is given more closely by Ridley as 'the victim's struggles prove the gods averse'. In Marlowe the quick priest performs a dramatic but improbably accelerated feat and is given a nice brisk business-like line to do it in. The effect is peculiar and partly humorous. 'Merely to us?' we ask; 'something alien imported from our twentieth century, or a subtlety of tone in a poet capable of often uncredited flexibility?'

The example is unimportant on its own, and even supported by similar instances would not vitally affect enjoyment of the translation: yet in Marlowe as a whole the question is fundamental. Does one see, for instance, a sceptic's flippancy in the description of the Figulus

> Whose like *Ægiptian Memphis* neuer had
> For skill in stars, and tuneful planeting.   (639–40)

Or when Marlowe describes the superstitious antics of the sacred Romans, whose priests 'went the round, in, and without the towne' followed by 'an inferiour troope in tuckt vp vestures' (595), are we right in judging that the tone invites one to a ringside view of a ripe farce? And that an amused tone, faint but there to be caught, is present in such a line as

> While these thus in and out had circled Roome,   (604)

and even in such a phrase as 'with murmurs dolorous' used of the Priest's mystical utterance? Or, to turn to another part of the poem, are we wrong if we think that the lines about French poets are not as innocent as they look:

> And you French *Bardi*, whose immortal pens
> Renowne the valiant soules slaine in your wars,
> Sit safe at home and chaunt sweet *Poesie*.   (443–6)

The 'immortal pens' are not under suspicion; but 'sit safe at home' has a familiar, cosy sound, to be played off against the romantic literary 'chaunt sweet Poesie', and the lines are, in any case, amusingly placed, picturing this secure pacific body in the procession of militants.[1]

The very frequency with which these questions occur makes the answer difficult to resist. This is in fact surely a subtly and flexibly toned poetry; and that conclusion ought not to be surprising. For the subtly expressive techniques of the verse have already been remarked on, and the flexibility of tone and mind only matches and goes along with the flexibility of technique. In this poem blank verse

---

[1] No discussion of the Nero passage is included here though I think there is satirical intention in both authors. The grounds for speculation about Lucan's attitude and Marlowe's attitude to it are extensive and complicated: 'a riddle wrapped in a mystery inside an enigma'; but the profit of speculation is not great.

has already, virtually before Shakespeare, become the Shakespearean instrument. So the storm passage quoted earlier moves forward, the line running on and broken up with the assurance of a mature poet (there are a hundred run-on lines in the first four hundred):

> So thunder which the wind teares from the cloudes,
> With cracke of riuen ayre and hideous sound
> Filling the world, leapes out and throwes forth fire,
> Affrights poore fearefull men, and blasts their eyes
> With ouerthwarting flames, and raging shoots
> Alongst the ayre and nought resisting it
> Falls, and returnes, and shiuers where it lights. (152–8)

The run-on can have other and more subtle effects, as in the lion simile (208–15):

> Like to a Lyon of scortcht desart *Affricke*,
> Who seeing hunters, pauseth till fell wrath
> And kingly rage increase, then hauing whiskt
> His taile athwart his backe, and crest heau'd vp
> With iawes wide open ghastly roaring out . . .

As the second line pushes forward into the third the passage goes crescendo (the technique of Keats in *Hyperion*: 'one solitary gust/Which comes upon the silence . . .') and in the division 'whiskt/ His taile' the verse makes a similarly vigorous gesture.

Mind and technique, then, are alike flexible and subtle, both engaged in the making of a poem rather than merely doing a job of translation in verse. And the poem, in spite of deficiencies as translation and in spite of uninspired patches, is worth the reading. It is a good, central Elizabethan document as well as being the product of two authors of marked individuality. The kinship between them provokes a passion and vigour rare in original works and rarer still in translations. What remains to be shown is that it is part of the main stream of Marlowe's mind and work, not some side-channel as is so often assumed.

I have suggested that the *Pharsalia* as a whole was likely to appeal to Marlowe because of a certain independence and scepticism he may have found in it and because of the particular brand of sadism in which it specialises. In Book I, however, the concurrence of general tastes and character is less noticeable than the more specific links between passages of this and Marlowe's other work. These links are sometimes directly with the early Marlowe. The desires and glamour of that early world are felt as the Jew thinks of his power 'ripping the bowels of the earth' for riches; and in a context of disillusionment they are recalled in the *Pharsalia*:

> al the world
> Ransackt for golde, which breeds the world decay.   (167-8)

The description of the young Caesar picks up echoes of the young Tamburlaine:

> he restles,
> Shaming to striue but where he did subdue,
> When yre, or hope prouokt, heady, and bould,
> At al times charging home, & making hauock;
> Vrging his fortune, trusting in the gods,
> Destroying what withstood his proud desires,
> And glad when bloud, & ruine made him way.
>
> (145-51)

This itself is a portrait of the Marlovian hero, even including Mortimer, the little Tamburlaine of his petty world. But the large vision that dazzles Faustus is there too:

> Ay me, O what a world of land and sea.   (13)

Compare Faustus' 'O what a world of profit and delight'. Also when Laelius tells Caesar 'Loue ouerrules my will, I must obay thee' (373), we think of *Hero and Leander*: 'It lies not in our power to loue, or hate, For will in vs is over-rul'd by fate.' Laelius' line is remote enough from the Latin (*Jussa sequi tam posse mihi, quam velle necesse est*) but very close to Marlowe's own thought, which is again remarkable in the context of its strange development.

These links (and there are several more) are not mere echoes of incidental lines and phrases such as it would be an editor's duty to collect irrespective of significance. They are key-references, Marlovian touchstones. The central preoccupations, images and values of the mind all find themselves involved in the translation. It is ultimately because of this that so much of the poem, however close to the Latin, qualifies in one's mind as part of the essential Marlowe, and why certain fine passages count for still more than they would if unlinked with the rest of his work:

> So when the worlds compounded vnion breakes,
> Time ends and to old *Chaos* all things turne;
> Confused stars shal meete, celestiall fire
> Fleete on the flouds, the earth shoulder the sea,
> Affording it no shoare, and *Phœbe's* waine
> Chace *Phœbus* and inrag'd affect his place,
> And striue to shine by day, and ful of strife
> Disolue the engins of the broken world.   (73–80)

The superb ring of these lines deepens in one's mind during what follows:

> All great things crush themselues; such end the gods
> Allot the height of honor.   (81–2)

The tag *in se magna ruunt laetis hunc numina rebus Crescendi posuere modum* is itself memorable. But in Marlowe it stands with peculiar poignancy as a comment on the aspiring mind, greatness doomed by something in the nature of things to bring disaster to itself, a reminder of the limits of that which 'heauenly power permits'. It might be the motto of *Doctor Faustus* and so in a sense, of Marlowe's whole work.[1]

---

[1] Perhaps one should quote another point of view. 'If it were ever reasonable to reject a contemporary ascription on purely internal evidence, I should be tempted to deny this work to Marlowe. It is of very great merit.' (C. S. Lewis, *English Literature in the Sixteenth Century*, p. 486.)

8

OVID'S ELEGIES

THE OVID TRANSLATIONS appear also to be underread
and underrated poems. Readers have probably dipped into
them more often than into Lucan, but critical opinion,
which has accorded the Lucan translation some respect,
finds little to be said for the Ovid.[1] It is described as
'characterized alike by boyish stiffness of expression, by
metrical inexperience, and defective scholarship'.[2] Such
merit as is allowed it, youthful enthusiasm for instance, has
never, as far as I know, been represented as anything we can
reasonably enjoy for its own sake, but only as an object of
interest to 'the student', who may consider how far the
translations contain promise of Marlowe's later achievement. Indeed, Tucker Brooke finds only a single example
of mature versification in the collection and this is by
Ben Jonson. The Fifteenth Elegy of Book I was translated
by Marlowe with the rest, but Jonson included it in *The
Poetaster*, first giving it the polish it apparently needed.
So the two versions exist to be compared, the one 'crude',
the other 'mature'.[3] The comparison might serve as a
preliminary probe into the worth of the poems and the
judgment which dismisses them.

Ovid here defends his profession of poetry. Envy
charges him with idleness: he ought to be a soldier or a
lawyer. He replies that he works for a fame which will

---

[1] An exception to this is F. S. Boas (pp. 29–42) who makes interesting comparisons, in Marlowe's favour, with earlier translations of Ovid by Golding,
Churchyard and Turberville.

[2] Tucker Brooke, *Works of Christopher Marlowe*, p. 554.

[3] The full texts are printed in Appendix III, p. 370.

endure and that poets are better able to achieve it than
kings and plutocrats. This posthumous honour, and the
further honour of being read and remembered by suffering
lovers, are beyond the power of envy to harm. So it is in
death that the poet most triumphs and most lives. Jonson's
version is close to Marlowe's—evidently he thought enough
of it to preserve it as the basis of his own translation.
More than two-thirds of the couplets use Marlowe's rhyme
and are generally similar. Many of the changes are certainly
improvements, either neater or more accurate or both.
Language is moving towards Dryden and the eighteenth
century: double negatives are cleared up, ambiguities are
resolved, and neat antithetical expression is achieved when
possible.

> *Homer* will liue, whil'st *Tenedos* stands, and *Ide*,
> Or to the sea, fleete *Simois* doth slide:
> And so shall *Hesiod* too, while vines doe beare,
> Or crooked sickles crop the ripened eare.   (9–12)

The last line, with its 'crop the ripened ear', uses language
which is to become the poet's tongue for the next century
and more. It withdraws from Marlowe's

> *Ascræus* liues, while grapes with new wine swell,
> Or men with crooked Sickles corne downe fell. (11–12)

as being non-literary, inelegant, perhaps insufficiently
generalised, perhaps offending the ear with its unrefined
monosyllables. Yet it is the 'crude' version which gives the
livelier picture: the grapes swell, the wine presses for
release, men cut and the corn falls like ranks in battle. The
more vigorous, less formularised expression may well in
fact be found preferable to the 'mature' product. And this
is the usual story. Jonson writes best when he gives free
rein to his Elizabethan tongue and invention—as in

> Then shall *Lucretius* loftie numbers die,
> When Earth and Seas in fire and flames shall frie. (23–4)

This is livelier than Marlowe's couplet, though freer with
its Ovid. But generally, for similar reasons, it is Marlowe
who has all the life. The last five couplets, forming the
climax of the poem, ring splendidly in Marlowe's version:

> To verse let Kings giue place, and Kingly showes,
> And bankes ore which gold-bearing *Tagus* flowes.
> Let base conceipted witts admire vilde things,
> Faire *Phœbus* lead me to the Muses springs.
> About my head be quiuering mirtle wound,
> And in sad louers heads let me be found.
> The liuing, not the dead can enuie bite,
> For after death all men receiue their right.
> Then though death rakes my bones in funerall fire,
> Ile liue, and as he puls me downe mount higher. (33–42)

Where Jonson alters to gain polish or accuracy he does not
make better poetry. There is a world of difference between
Marlowe's 'in sad louers heads let me be found' and
Jonson's neatly rhyming, accurate and unmoved:

> The frost-drad myrtle shall impale my head,
> And of sad louers Ile be often read. (37–8)

And, beside Marlowe's last lines, Jonson's hardly exist:

> *ergo etiam cum me supremus adederit ignis,*
> *vivam, parsque mei multa superstes erit.* (Ovid)

> Then when this body falls in funeral fire,
> My name shall liue, and my best part aspire. (Jonson)

> Then though death rakes my bones in funerall fire,
> Ile liue, and as he puls me downe mount higher. (Marlowe)

But, of course, this is what was found in the Lucan
translation: Marlowe enters his text with sufficient spirit
to make it part of his own poetic life. There is nowhere
anything more Marlovian than the last line (compare
Faustus' 'Ile leape vp to my God: who pulles me downe?'),
or than the contemptuous tone, a little above, in 'Let base
conceipted witts admire vilde things.' It is pleasant to fancy

that Ben Jonson had his predecessor in mind when he concluded his last line with the most Marlovian of verbs; but Marlowe's real *life*, rather than his imitable *manner*, is in his own lines, and Jonson's are dead by comparison.

This poem is a fair sample of Marlowe's work: neither better nor worse as a translation or as English verse than most poems in the book. It is not entirely representative of the collection, however. Though lines and passages haunt the mind, the piece is as a whole less vividly memorable than most. The *Amores*, or *Elegies*, are principally about the pleasures and pains of love, the strange capers that lovers run into, the devices and shifts to make meetings, the frustrations of a lover kicking his heels outside closed doors, the fury of seeing another man, perhaps a husband, in possession, and the recognition that this is all part of a game which without it would lack savour. Ovid defends his life of poetry and wantonness, and says he might turn to other things later, though for the present, as far as an unappreciative money-ridden society will let him, he will go his own ways, conscious that poetry has its dignity and love its rewards. One probably remembers most clearly the poems based on a particular situation: his mistress goes to the races (*tu cursus spectas, ego te*); or, with her husband, to a banquet where by agreed gestures she will have surreptitious communication with her lover; or he has to pacify the mistress he has just struck; or her life is in danger during an abortion she has undertaken. Memorable also are the elegy to a dead parrot, the speech written for a crafty, insinuating old bawd, the famous piece of 'wantonness' *cum ea coire non potuit*, and the Thirteenth Elegy, written as the sun rises: one of the finest of love poems.

There are, of course, all sorts of virtues that Ovid's book does not have. Its attitudes are not responsible, its thought is not deep and its inspiration is often literary. Its value lies in what many readers probably class as comparatively poor things: wit and humour not, however, in responsible service; a polished and assured technique; a sophisticated manner; a certain breezy frankness and defiance which might be found engaging; shrewdness which might amount to a worldly sort of wisdom. These characteristics do not recommend an author to readers in this century all that much more than they did in the last. The reasons are different: in the nineteenth century, apart from the levity and immorality, it was, as L. P. Wilkinson suggests, the lack of warmth and 'heart' that repelled; in this century it is the irresponsibility, the literary-ness, the lack of depth. Defining the attitudes we are to expect, Mr Wilkinson writes: 'Ovid is no more passionate, romantic or senti-mental than Chaucer. However much he may affect to be the victim of the erotic situations he depicts, we feel, and are surely meant to feel, that he is really, like the Horace of the Odes, a detached observer of the tragi-comedy of sex, a witty connoisseur, no doubt experienced himself, but steeped in the literature of his subject. As such he came upon the world in his first poems, the *Amores*, which are more often intended to entertain us by their art and wit than to move us as a record of personal experience'. This is from *Ovid Recalled*,[1] which many readers must have found a wonderfully helpful and enjoyable study. 'Entertainment by art and wit': to speak of the limitations of such an enterprise seems pompous—why not take what is offered and be thankful? Personally I assume the best of both worlds to be the desirable end, and, noting with some severity the limita-tions, pass on with some cheerfulness to the entertainment.

It is as entertainment of this kind that Marlowe's transla-tions deserve first to be read. Commentators have given such discouraging accounts (in the little that has been

[1] Cambridge, 1955.

written), that one would never guess that here is a set of poems written with and for delight. Charges of incompetence and immaturity have so crabbed the approach that one feels a frowning countenance to be expected of the discriminating reader throughout. For myself, I find it impossible to maintain beyond a few lines:

> I meane not to defend the scapes of any,
> Or iustifie my vices being many.
> For I confesse, if that might merite fauour,
> Heere I display my lewd and loose behauiour.
> I loathe, yet after that I loathe I runne,
> Oh how the burthen irkes, that we should shunne.
> I cannot rule my selfe, but where loue please
> Am driuen like a ship vpon rough seas.
> No one face likes me best, all faces moue,
> A hundred reasons make me euer loue.
> If any eye me with a modest looke,
> I burn, and by that blushfull glance am tooke.
> And she thats coy I like for being no clowne,
> Me thinkes she would be nimble when shees downe.
> Though her sowre lookes a Sabines browe resemble,
> I thinke sheele do, but deepely can dissemble.
> If she be learn'd, then for her skill I craue her,
> If not, because shees simple I would haue her.
> Before *Callimachus* one preferres me farre,
> Seeing she likes my bookes why should we iarre?
> An other railes at me and that I write
> Yet would I lie with her if that I might.
> Trips she, it likes me well; plods she, what than?
> Shee would be nimbler, lying with a man.
> And when one sweetely sings, then straight I long
> To quauer on her lips euen in her song.
> Or if one touch the Lute with art and cunning
> Who would not loue those hands for their swift running?
> And her I like that with a maiesty
> Folds vp her armes and makes lowe curtesy.
> To leaue my selfe, that am in loue with all,
> Some one of these might make the chastest fall.

If she be tall, shees like an *Amazon*,
And therefore filles the bed she lies vpon.
If short, she lies the rounder: to say troth
Both short and long please me, for I loue both.
I thinke what one vndeckt would be, being drest:
Is she attired, then show her graces best.
A white wench thralles me, so doth golden yellowe
And nut-browne girles in dooing haue no fellowe.
If her white necke be shadoed with blacke haire,
Why so was *Lædas*, yet was *Læda* faire.
Amber trest is she, then on the morne thinke I,
My loue alludes to euery history:
A yong wench pleaseth, and an old is good,
This for her lookes, that for her woman-hood.
Nay what is she that any *Roman* loues
But my ambitious ranging minde approues?

(Book II, Elegy 4)

For a sure lightness of touch and a keen relish fresh and
infectious, one might look a long time through the an-
thologies without bettering this—as for delicacy, wit and
beauty in company of free sensuality this Fifth Elegy of
Book I is not easily surpassed:

In summers heate and mid-time of the day
To rest my limbes vpon a bed I lay.
One window shut, the other open stood,
Which gaue such light as twinckles in a wood,
Like twilight glimps at setting of the Sunne
Or night being past, and yet not day begunne.
Such light to shamefast maidens must be showne,
Where they may sport, and seeme to bee vnknowne.
Then came *Corinna* in a long loose gowne,
Her white neck hid with tresses hanging downe:
Resembling fayre *Semiramis* going to bed
Or *Layis* of a thousand wooers sped.
I snacht her gowne, being thin, the harme was small,
Yet striu'd she to be couered there withall.
And striuing thus as one that would be cast,
Betray'd her selfe, and yelded at the last.

Starke naked as she stood before mine eye,
Not one wen in her body could I spie.
What armes and shoulders did I touch and see,
How apt her breasts were to be prest by me?
How smooth a belly vnder her wast saw I?
How large a legge, and what a lustie thigh?
To leaue the rest, all lik'd me passing well,
I cling'd her naked body, downe she fell.
Iudge you the rest: being tirde she bad me kisse,
Ioue send me more such after-noones as this.

It would be a crabby response to mutter, after reading these poems, 'metrical inexperience'; and it would surely also be unjust and unhistorical. For what we have here is not a youngster blunderingly if enthusiastically learning his trade, but rather the efforts of a major poet to create a form which should be capable of rendering the pointedness, balance and poise of his original. What he created was in fact nothing less than the English 'Augustan' heroic couplet. It is the form that Pope was to bring to perfection and it is the poetic form most far removed from the blank verse of Elizabethan drama—which (as a dramatic medium) Marlowe also created. One can neither be surprised that the author of *Tamburlaine* did not manage to write like Pope, nor fail to be surprised that he was probably the first to try.[1]

---

[1] I have been much tempted to retract this. 'What about Chaucer?' one may ask; and that fairly obvious name might be coupled with others of which I am ignorant or forgetful. It is rather a relief to know that the claim has been made for Marlowe before now. An article by J. S. P. Tatlock in *The Nation* (April 9, 1914) drew attention to Heywood's translation of part of the *Heroides* as being the earliest example of this style in English. In a comment on this, E. C. Knowlton (30 July, letter headed 'The Origin of the closed Couplet in English') suggests that Bishop Joseph Hall's *Satires* were written about the same time and that these refer to Marlowe whose use of the form preceded either. He concludes: 'To Marlowe and to Hall therefore, as well as to Heywood and Drayton, we should look for the first good examples in English of sustained classical heroic couplet as distinguished from the romantic heroic couplet.' Thus Tatlock states that Heywood 'clearly strove . . . for the terse effect given by the final pause and by parallelism and antithesis'. These are characteristics of the classical couplet, and in the sustained attempt to write in that form Marlowe seems to have preceded him. Chaucer's use of the heroic couplet (as in *The Legend of Good Women*) is very different.

There is, however, a remarkable degree of success. The poems quoted above are by no means clumsy. Antithesis is nicely brought off; the couplet becomes the unit of expression without spilling over and usually without contortion or padding:

> A yong wench pleaseth, and an old is good,
> This for her lookes, that for her womanhood.

The jaunty colloquial freedom perhaps works against a fine polish, but compensates in vigour and humour:

> Trips she, it likes me well: plods she, what than?
> She would be nimbler lying with a man.

He is also capable of a well-turned final couplet possessed of a freshness which 'urbanity' does not usually suggest:

> Iudge you the rest: being tirde she bad me kisse.
> Ioue send me more such after-noones as this.

In these translations Marlowe is in fact probably more concerned with, and sensitive to, problems of style than in the *Pharsalia*. He tries with some scrupulousness to retain Ovid's repetitions and other stylistic devices. So, for instance, in III. 2 (the beloved at the races) where Ovid balances his lines as follows:

> *Sunt dominae rata vota meae, mea vota supersunt.*
> *ille tenet palmam| palma petenda mea est.*

Marlowe preserves the syntactical pattern:

> My mistris hath her wish, my wish remaine:
> He holds the palme: my palme is yet to gaine. (81–2)

Or in III. 5 (number 6 in the original) where Ovid has

> *ter molita fugam ter ad altas restitit undas,*

Marlowe reproduces the balance and repetition:

> Thrice she prepar'd to flie, thrice she did stay. (69)

Or in III. 8 (on the death of Tibullus):

> *sic Nemesis longum, sic Delia nomen habebunt,*
> *altera cura recens, altera primus amor.*
>
> So *Nemesis*, so *Delia* famous are,
> The one his first loue, th'other his new care. (31–2)

The technical preoccupations here differ so markedly
from those familiar to a man writing Marlovian blank verse
that one must ask what force, what lines of taste, thought
and feeling, could cause the change (whichever way round
it was) from one to the other. 'Student-work for love and
ambition, or hackwork for pay' is the down-to-earth reply
to a cloudy question. But the question really directs us to
look again at the translations, wondering whether there is
not more poetry in them than we have yet seen, and
questioning how it is that a young man with the stuff of
poetry in him can expend over another man's work the
energy involved in the effective creation of a new form.

As in the Lucan translation, there is an unusual degree of
personal involvement. Marlowe makes the poems his own,
and there are few that an attentive reader of the other works
would not with some ease identify as his. The two poems
quoted in full provide well-known examples. In the first,
Ovid's final couplet runs:

> *Denique quas tota quisquam probet urbe puellas*
> *noster in has omnis ambitiosus amor.*

which Marlowe gives as a rhetorical question with a
characteristic ring to both the idea and the diction:

> Nay, what is she that any Roman loues
> But my ambitious ranging minde approoues?

The other (I. 5) ('In summers heate and mid-time of the
day') constantly calls *Hero and Leander* to mind:

> And striuing thus as one that would be cast,
> Betray'd her selfe, and yelded at the last. (15–16)

This is developed in *Hero and Leander*:

> She trembling stroue; this strife of hers (like that
> Which made the world) another world begat
> Of vnknowne ioy. Treason was in her thought,
> And cunningly to yeeld her selfe she sought.
> Seeming not woon, yet woon she was at length,
> In such warres women vse but halfe their strength.
>
> (Sestiad II, 291–6)

Marlowe has caught not merely the epigrammatic pointedness but the worldly, sophisticated knowingness; and, typically, what in Ovid is amused but on the whole appreciative becomes in Marlowe a cynical amusement with a destructive undertone. He does, incidentally, intensify and perhaps coarsen Ovid in his translation. Ovid's line is more accurately translated 'Yet strove she not as one intent to win' (L. P. Wilkinson); Marlowe imports much more directly a sexual desire for the fulfilment which, again, he adds to Ovid:

> I cling'd her naked body, downe she fell. (24)

Ovid has *et nudam pressi corpus ad usque meum* (which the Loeb translator, Mr Showerman, renders with unflinching decency, 'I clasped her undraped form to mine'). There is nothing about 'down she fell', which is, of course, what Marlowe likes. He has it again in *Hero* ('He on the suddaine cling'd her so about, That Meremaid-like vnto the floore she slid'), and many other details reappear (cf. 'Starke naked as she stood before mine eye', I. 5, l. 17, and 'Thus neere the bed she blushing stood vpright etc.,' *Hero and Leander* II, 317). One line echoes the melody and even the tone of another with remarkable clarity:

> Such light to shamefast maidens must be showne
>
> (*Elegy* l. 5)
>
> Such sights as this to tender maids are rare
>
> (*Hero and Leander*, II. 238)

There is, then, in these poems very considerable closeness to Marlowe's own original work, and the technical influence goes along with the closeness of thought and feeling.

'My ambitious ranging minde' recalls *Tamburlaine*, while the contempt of 'Let base conceipted witts admire vilde things' resembles most the scorn of Mortimer and Gaveston in *Edward II*. 'God is a name, no substance, feard in vaine' (III. 3. 23) might be spoken by Faustus, as is, of course, the '*lente, lente*' of I. 13. 40. II. 19 with its 'Wee skorne things lawfull, stolne sweetes we affect' (3) is in the spirit of the Guise's 'That like I best that flyes beyond my reach'. And the theme of II. 27 and II. 1, the life and art of love as opposed to those of war, is related to the 'ticing' motif in *Dido*. A relationship with the whole corpus of work, then, is notable. But above all these poems call to mind *Hero and Leander*. Many writers have pointed to comparable passages: Douglas Bush lists nine in 'Notes on *Hero and Leander*' and remarks that so many parallels 'may at least suggest a query whether the *Elegies* and *Hero and Leander* could have been somewhat nearer each other than the beginning and end of Marlowe's career'.[1]

The verbal parallels present us with the most obvious and really the least important connections. They matter only because they are readily verifiable proofs that a connection exists, and because the considerable number of them suggests an influence that extends beyond the mere picking up of a few expressions and ideas. The technical and creative originality involved in the mastery of so apparently alien a style also tells of an interest intense enough to have become part of the essential poetic being. Marlowe was learning the technique he needed for *Hero and Leander*; but more than this, he was working in a mood largely in harmony with that of his own poem.

[1] *M.L.A.* XLIV, 1929, xxxi.

The first elegy serves as an example here. The technical endeavour and its success are roughly indicated by this kind of couplet:

> When in this workes first verse I trode aloft,
> Loue slackt my Muse, and made my Numbers soft.
>
> (21–2)

The Augustan flavour, unity of the couplet, balance within the second line, all gain from the touch of mock-heroic in the strutting old-Marlovian 'trode aloft'. It is this which Marlowe develops as a basis of his art in *Hero and Leander*: the mock-heroic feeding like an acid on much of his own former manner, destructive also of heroic and romantic conventions, sometimes poking fun, sometimes belittling with humour of a much more aggressive and even sadistic kind. Very lightly, this tone plays through the elegies:

> O woe is mee, hee neuer shootes but hits;
> I burne; loue in my idle bosome sits.
>
> (29–30)

The caricature of the smitten lover involves a certain mocking sophistication. Here, in Marlowe as in Ovid, it is merely fun, or, quartered, it is but one-part earnest—the jaunty, energetic context makes this quite apparent:

> Thus I complain'd, but loue vnlockt his quiuer,
> Tooke out the shaft, ordain'de my heart to shiuer:
> And bent his sinewie bowe upon his knee,
> Saying, Poet heere's a work beseeming thee.
> Oh woe is mee . . .
>
> (25–8)

And so it often is in *Hero*:

> Thence flew Loues arrow with the golden head
> And thus *Leander* was enamoured.
>
> (I. 161–2)

Here we smile when the preposterous rhyme makes the couplet click as surely as a piece of mechanism—or as surely as the power of love reduces the proud independent will into conformity. But we do not always smile; at least not with such *kindly* sophistication. Unlike Leander, Hero struggles, and we watch her closely. The spectacle is partly funny, but Marlowe's individuality leads us into places sufficiently intimate to deserve a respect or tenderness that he bestows on them only occasionally. The poem is not *without* tenderness and respect for the human being caught in indignity and in the grip of a force beyond its control; this is present in the lines:

> Loue is not ful of pittie (as men say)
> But deaffe and cruell, where he meanes to prey.
> Euen as a bird, which in our hands we wring,
> Foorth plungeth, and oft flutters with her wing,
> She trembling stroue . . .   (II. 287–91)

But tenderness and respect are not present alone: their opposites come into play just as strongly. There is also scorn: for the 'men' who say such a silly thing and perhaps for the meekness and pallor of the 'love' they unrealistically posit. 'Deaffe and cruell' are, on one reading, bad attributes, because hurtful; but, on another, they are stated as conditions of the power which, exercised, yields us most happiness. Hero's struggles beget a new world 'of unknowne ioy' and she gives herself to the strengths of love and man. Until this submission the man holds her as he holds and 'wrings' a fluttering bird. The image ought to be, and partly is, repellent and pitiless; but it is also an image of power and firmness, while the cruelty of it soon melts in the poem into an exaltation of masculine power and sensual delight. When sensual and sadistic elements touch as closely as this there is at least a faint odour of pornography. And such an odour does cling to *Hero and Leander* in spite of the beauty: it is not the innocent sunshine poem critics have made of it. What clears the air is not so much the 'uninhibited pagan beauty of sensuality' as the tenderness and respect which are subtly present in company with their opposites.

The lines which follow in this passage from *Hero* are
those quoted already in the discussion of Elegy I. 5:

> Treason was in her thought,
> And cunningly to yeeld her selfe she sought.
> Seeming not woon, yet woon she was at length,
> In such warres women vse but halfe their strength.

(293–6)

This light, humorous masculine knowingness, so like
Ovid's, is what eases the way to the more cynical tone in
Hero, which in its preoccupation with 'shame' and the
struggle of loving turns the Ovidian entertainment into a
deeper thing altogether. But the Ovidian element in Marlowe is itself clearly deeper and more selective than can be
suggested by lists of verbal parallels or by such a general
phrase as 'the spirit of the Ovidian erotic poems'. Out of
the many things which Marlowe might have developed in
Ovid, what he has chosen above all as congenial is that
sophisticated psychological comedy of love in which
knowingness borders on cynicism, and which the heroic
couplet, with its stinging neatness, emerges as the English
poetic form most apt to express.

In the *Elegies*, tones and attitudes typical of Marlowe
(and especially reminiscent of *Hero*) are present in lines like
these:

> Yeelding or strugling do we giue him might,
> Lets yeeld, a burthen easly borne is light. (I. 2)

> And roughe Iades mouthes with stuborne bits are torne (I. 2)

> Faire women play, she's chast whom none will haue. (I. 8)

> With much ado my hands I scarsely staide
> But her bleare eyes, balde scalpes thin hoary flieces
> And riueld cheekes I would haue puld a pieces. (I. 8)

> Yet thinke no scorne to aske a wealthy churle,
> He wants no gifts into thy lap to hurle. (I. 10)

Note the scorn in 'a wealthy churl' and the violent verb 'hurle'.

> To giue I loue, but to be ask't disdayne,
> Leaue asking, and Ile giue what I refraine. (I. 10)

There it is the pride, and the scorn of being importuned.

> Poore wretches on the tree themselues did strangle,
> There sat the hang-man for mens neckes to angle. (I. 12)

> Angry, I pray that rotten age you wrackes. (I. 12)

> Who first depriu'd yong boyes of their best part,
> With selfe same woundes he gaue, he ought to smart. (II. 3)

(The 'best' is characteristically Marlowe's own idea.)

> No little ditched townes, no lowlie walles,
> But to my share a captiue damsell falles. (II. 12)

Note the contempt in the first line, going with the jaunty flippancy of 'When *Troy* by ten yeares battle tumbled downe'.

> While rashly her wombes burthen she casts out. (II. 13)

(Again the violence of the verb.)

> Why with hid irons are your bowels torne? (II. 14)

> Foole, if to keepe thy wife thou hast no neede (II. 19)

Note the added emphatic savageness of the opening: cf. *Si tibi non opus est, servate, stulte, puella.*

> Tis said the slippery streame held up her brest,
> And kindly gaue her, what she liked best. (III. 5)

(But the joke is Marlowe's own.)

> Against they selfe, mans nature, thou wert cunning,
> And to thine owne losse was thy wit swift running. (III. 7)

—which might be part of the Epilogue of *Faustus*.

The quotations exemplify a sort of transubstantiation in which Ovid's text becomes an element to hold Marlowe's own essential self. It lends itself readily. Marlowe liked the sensuality and added a touch here and there when he saw an opportunity. He also liked the richness of mythological reference: that is quite plain from the abundance of it in his own work. But beyond these clearly apparent affinities there is a whole area of contact, involving violence and scorn, independence and impudence, a sharp undeceived sophistication, shrewd amatory Machiavellism, hard brilliance and youthful energy.

The erotic Machiavel is seen, for instance, in I. 8, the speech written for an old bawd called Dipsas:

> Dissemble so, as lou'd he may be thought,
> And take heed least he gets that loue for nought:
> Deny him oft, feigne now thy head doth ake:
> And *Isis* now will shew what scuse to make.
> Receiue him soone, least patient vse he gaine,
> Or least his loue oft beaten backe should waine.
> To beggers shut, to bringers ope thy gate.
> Let him within heare bardout louers prate.
> And as first wrongd, the wronged some-times banish,
> Thy fault with his fault so repuls'd will vanish. (71–80)

But the lover also, with a fine irony of disenchantment, instructs the mistress how to deceive him. In III. 13 we have an example:

> Slip still, onely deny it, when 'tis done,
> And before folke immodest speeches shunne. . .
> From him that yeelds the palme is quickly got,
> Teach but your tongue to say, I did it not,
> And being iustifide by two words, thinke
> The cause acquits you not, but I that winke.
>
> (15–16; 47–50)

That may appear to say little more than 'where ignorance is bliss . . .'; but in fact there is no ignorance, only sufficient worldly sense to say 'tis folly not to dissimulate

wisdom'. This subtlety is obviously congenial to the highly
disingenuous creator of the naïve Leander, as the decadence
of this sophisticated and elegant sensuality is home ground
to the creator of Gaveston and Edward, or Faustus, or, for
instance, Calyphas.

The pursuit of love as opposed to war and stern duty is
also a Marlovian as it is an Ovidian theme. Calyphas, we
remember, finds war 'more childish valourous than manly
wise', and prefers 'a naked Lady in a net of golde'. The
play of *Dido* sets the ticements of love and a luxurious
civilisation against the call of war and adventure in the
wilds. And for Edward II, the honours of battle and
patriotism have no charms compared with those of a nook
for frolic with his favourite. I think Marlowe's own
attitude here is divided, as in so many things. But Ovid
has no two minds about it:

> Let souldiours chase their enemies amaine,
> And with their bloud eternall honour gaine . . .
> But when I dye, would I might droupe with doing,
> And in the midst thereof, set my soule going,
> That at my funeralls some may weeping crye,
> Euen as he led his life, so did he dye.   (II. 10)

So much for a life and death in arms of one kind or
another; and when he comes to compare professions,
the same judgment emerges with the same Falstaffian
irreverence:

> *Heroes*, O famous names
> Farewel, your fauour nought my minde inflames.
> Wenches apply your faire lookes to my verse
> Which golden loue doth vnto me rehearse.   (II. 1)

But this golden love, although the stuff of life when
obtained, is a thing without tenderness, a rough-and-tumble
dominated by a hard, predatory energy. As part of the

convention, Corinna when sure of her conquest is full of
'disdainefull pride' and he is her 'prey' (II. 17). Love
seems always to involve the subjugation of the other party:

> Wee skorne things lawfull, stolne sweetes we affect,
> Cruell is he that loues whom none protect . . .
> What euer haps, by suffrance harme is done,
> What flies, I followe, what followes me I shunne.
>
> (II. 19)[1]

This is the deaf and cruel 'preying' love of *Hero and Leander*,
where the subjugation is of the woman:

> Thus hauing swallow'd *Cupids* golden hooke,
> The more she striv'd, the deeper she was strooke.
>
> (I. 333–4)

The scorn for 'things lawfull' extends also to orthodox
religious belief. Ovid begins his poem boldly and Marlowe
his with a more colloquial sceptical impudence:

> What, are there Gods?   (III. 3)

Later Ovid develops his theme—which is a humorous one.
His mistress has lied and the gods have done nothing:

> *Aut sine re nomen Deus est, frustraque timetur;*
> *Et stulta populos credulitate movet,*
> *Aut si quis Deus est, teneras amat ille puellas;*
> *Et nimium solas omnia posse iubet.*

Marlowe's version is close, but gains an aggressive tone by
omitting the *aut* construction and letting the first couplet
stand on its own as an affirmative atheistic epigram:

> God is a name, no substance, feared in vaine,
> And doth the world in fond beliefe deteine.   (23–4)

---

[1] *Quod sequitur, fugio*: 'If loving without being loved in return may be ranked as
one of the most painful of experiences, being loved without loving is certainly one
of the most boring' (Huxley, *Those Barren Leaves*, ch. 7 of 'The Journey'). The
chapter is a good exposé of Ovid's dictum.

He continues with the familiar formula, used in *Tamburlaine* and Lucan:

> Or if there be a God, he loues fine wenches,
> And all things too much in their sole power drenches.
>
> (25–6)

(an awkward line, though the verb is strong). Another couplet links with the Marlowe of popular reputation and the Baines note:

> Who now will care the Altars to perfume?
> Tut, men should not their courage so consume.
>
> (33–4)

This is again close to the original:

> *Et quisquam pia tura foris imponere curet?*
> *Certe plus animi debet inesse viris.*

But we remember 'Into whatsoever company he cometh he persuadeth men to atheism, willing them not to be afeard of bugbears and hobgoblins'. Similarly in III. 8 the couplet:

> When bad fates take good men, I am forbod
> By secreat thoughts to thinke there is a god.   (35–6)

is close to Ovid's:

> *Cum rapiant mala fata bonos (ignoscite fasso*
> *Sollicitor nullos esse putare Deos.*

But if Marlowe felt a spiritual kinship with honest Ovid, as with Lucan, no doubt these lines helped to seal the bond.[1]

We are left, then, with a work as essentially Marlovian as any, and so, of course, of considerable interest to 'the student'—having an interest, moreover, which is self-sufficient and not dependent on the promise it shows of greater things to come. But this kind of observation is very remote from the *Elegies*, both Latin and Elizabethan; and we are equally remote if we occupy ourselves with them

---

[1] Cf. C. S. Lewis: 'The *Amores*, despite the sensuality which may have attracted him to them, are not really a work very congenial to Marlowe.' (*Op. cit.*, p. 485.)

for a 'significance' rather then for a pleasure. There is an awful vicious circle in much critical endeavour: the texts are examined because they are significant in the study of an author or period, and author and period are studied because they produced the texts. One thing throws light on another and that thing 'provides an invaluable background to an understanding of' a third which in turn is significant because it is an emanation of the first. Let us, therefore, not read the *Elegies* with 'interest' ('Students of Marlowe will find it of interest to consider how far the Ovid translations, taken as early works, contain any promise of his later achievements': L. C. Martin, Introduction, p. 16; 'But the work is interesting because we can here trace in little those varying effects of the Ovidian couplet upon English poetry which are writ large elsewhere': C. S. Lewis, *op. cit.* p. 485). What they were written for, and are capable of giving, is enjoyment. Where in this chapter we have traced the connection with Marlowe's other work and remarked on the technical novelty, it has been with the primary purpose of suggesting that Marlowe's essential being is to be found in the translations as in the other works and that his evolution of a new technique is the sign of a mind vitally engaged in its creative task. The enjoyment is of a light kind, but its freshness and subtlety, the lightness which is so often in resonance with much deeper tones, are nevertheless valuable things. An anthology of good light poetry would be a slender volume and the *Amores* should have a place in it. Marlowe's lines are not even in quality, it is true (as Ovid's are), but the stamp of the great poet is there unmistakably enough. The limitations both in the handling of the Latin and the versification need far fewer apologies than have been made for them:

> Now ore the sea from her old Loue comes she
> That drawes the day from heauens cold axletree.

Aurora, whither slidest thou? downe againe,
And birdes for *Memnon* yearely shal be slaine.
Now in her tender armes I sweetly bide,
If euer, now well lies she by my side.
The aire is cold, and sleepe is sweetest now
And birdes send forth shrill notes from euery bough:
Whither runst thou, that men, and women loue not?
Hold in thy rosy horses that they moue not.
Ere thou rise, starres teach sea-men where to sail,
But when thou commest they of their courses faile.
Poore trauailers though tierd, rise at thy sight,
And souldiours make them ready to the fight.
The painefull hinde by thee to field is sent,
Slowe Oxen early in the yoake are pent.
Thou cousenst boyes of sleepe, and doest betray them
To *Pedants* that with cruell lashes pay them.
Thou mak'st the surety to the Lawyer runne,
That with one word hath nigh himselfe vndone.
The Lawyer and the client hate thy view,
Both whom thou raisest vp to toyle anew.
By thy meanes women of their rest are bard,
Thou setst their labouring hands to spin and card.
All could I beare, but that the wench should rise
Who can endure saue him with whom none lyes?
How oft wisht I night would not giue thee place,
Nor morning starres shunne thy vprising face. (I. 13. 1–28)

The poet who can translate like this, whose feeling for verse-movement (for instance) can produce lines as sensitive as the first couplet, does not need our indulgence; but his works might as well be buried with him if they do not secure and promote our delight.

9

'HERO AND LEANDER'

PEOPLE read this poem very differently, and so, probably,
does any one reader who goes to it more than once. For
some, and some times, it has provided what they might
call a rich poetic feast, meaning something generally
considered old-fashioned, with careless raptures in it and
realms of gold. For others the outstanding delight has been
the enjoyment of a pagan romp with aesthetic and possibly
Promethean justification. In contrast to these full-blooded
pleasures, the poem has also afforded appreciation of a more
austere kind. Sophistication, wit, irony and detachment
have been diagnosed, and these too have appeared to be the
'essential' *Hero and Leander*. What everybody seems to
agree about is that it should not be taken too seriously.
'Written in a mood of dalliance' (Ellis-Fermor), in 'a form
of humour that is largely whimsy' (Kocher), its 'sole
business was to make holiday from all facts and all morals'
(C. S. Lewis): the poem is a charmer and Marlowe has
taken a turn for the better. This impression is the outcome
of many readings by many people, yet I think it is at best a
half-truth and at worst (whatever the intention) a belittling
misrepresentation.

The *pace* of reading probably counts for a great deal. The
natural pace may seem to be a very brisk one, set by the
quick, often jaunty, progression of the couplets. But
reading sensitively, it soon becomes apparent that the eye
does not by any means satisfy the inner ear. In eighteenth-
century couplets, the eye will usually do this: there is no
necessity to read aloud to make them sound right. With

Marlowe, and with others of his age, it is not so much that the couplets are inferior as that a different kind of reading is expected, involving either the actual or the inner voice. A line that in print seems flat is often a different thing altogether when read at the slower pace of a reading aloud or a reading aloud-within-oneself. For example:

> Thence flew Loue's arrow with the golden head,
> And thus *Leander* was enamoured.　　　　(I. 161–2)

One needs to get the 'tune' of this: it is not, like Pope's or Dryden's couplets, provided with verbal devices, a balance of syllables, letters or ideas, easing the eye into a ready appreciation of its neatness. Marlowe's neatness has its own subtlety, but the technique is different. It is rather that of the dramatist who expects his actor-reader to make the right pauses and inflections and to command adequate flexibility of tone and movement. As the reader says it over inside himself the tune comes: in the first line a strong unchecked movement upwards with the heroic tone faintly mocked somewhere in its harmonies; and in the second, a cool, factual tone, the movement held in check by a pause after 'thus' and coming down to earth with an unromantic bump to the tune of 'he's had it'. This really is the essential Marlovian music and already it begins to set deeper tones sounding. That last phrase describing the movement of the second line was in fact cribbed from an essay by A. P. Rossiter on Brueghel's 'Fall of Icarus'. Icarus, the Overreacher, the emblem of Faustus, symbolises much in Marlowe; and these lines, so ingenuous in appearance, do, when felt or heard properly, begin to resonate with some depth. This is true of the poem as a whole. Read so that the tune of lines can be realised, rather than at the more unreflecting pace of a forward-pressing narrative like *Don Juan*, it speaks with a distinction that begins to command stronger feelings and more subtle interests. Terms like 'dalliance', 'whimsy and 'holiday' then begin to seem less apt.

In his *Apology* of 1922, Hardy says that some of his poems have been read as misfires because they have raised the smile they were intended to raise. The tone and intention are often very delicately intimated, and we must be able to divine them 'without half a whisper': it is a problem of what he calls 'right note-catching'. *Hero and Leander* involves us in this exercise to an unusual degree. Its tones are constantly shifting. They can move from the heroic and romantic to mock-heroic and burlesque; from an oddly savage irony to warmth and sympathy; from flippancy to seriousness and back again. We recognise this much more easily on second reading than on first, because we plough back into our reading of the earlier parts the knowledge of a subtlety which is more apparent later on. Later in the poem, for instance, deflation is ruthlessly and unmistakably at work, and having seen that, we recognise the technique active in places where at first we no more than faintly suspected it. Yet a responsive first reading ought to be possible, for, right from the opening lines, there is sufficient counterplay of tones and swiftness of shift to warn us that 'right note-catching' is going to require some liveliness of mind:

> On *Hellespont* guiltie of True-loues blood,
> In view and opposit two citties stood.
> Seaborderers, disioin'd by *Neptunes* might:
> The one *Abydos*, the other *Sestos* hight.

The tone of the first line is heroic and portentous, while the second is cool and factual. The third line reinforces the first, as the fourth reinforces the second. Neat, trim, cool fact, clipped and antithetical, is paired in the unit of the couplet with tragical pomp, decked out in the solemnities of personification and myth. The curious pair is typical of the curious poem. The heroic is summoned, paraded and pricked—here quite lightly, without savagery, and in the normal impudent manner of mock-heroic; but it is not always so.

Can we, for instance, with any certainty discern what Marlowe is about in his description of Hero:

> . . . *Hero* the faire,
> Whom young *Apollo* courted for her haire,
> And offred as a dower his burning throne,
> Where she should sit for men to gaze vpon.
> The outside of her garments were of lawne,
> The lining purple silke, with guilt starres drawne,
> Her wide sleeues greene, and bordered with a groue,
> Where *Venus* in her naked glory stroue,
> To please the carelesse and disdainefull eies
> Of proud *Adonis* that before her lies.
> Her kirtle blew, whereon was many a staine,
> Made with the blood of wretched Louers slaine.
> Vpon her head she ware a myrtle wreath,
> From whence her vaile reacht to the ground beneath.
> Her vaile was artificiall flowers and leaues,
> Whose workmanship both man and beast deceaues.
> Many would praise the sweet smell as she past,
> When t'was the odour which her breath foorth cast,
> And there for honie bees haue sought in vaine,
> And beat from thence, haue lighted there againe.
> About her necke hung chaines of peble stone,
> Which lightned by her necke, like Diamonds shone.
> She ware no gloues, for neither sunne nor wind
> Would burne or parch her hands, but to her mind,
> Or warm or coole them, for they tooke delite
> To play vpon those hands, they were so white.
> Buskins of shels all siluered vsed she,
> And brancht with blushing corall to the knee;
> Where sparrowes pearcht, of hollow pearle and gold,
> Such as the world would woonder to behold:
> Those with sweet water oft her handmaid fils,
> Which as shee went would cherupe through the bils.
> Some say, for her the fairest *Cupid* pyn'd,

And looking in her face, was strooken blind.
But this is true, so like was one the other,
As he imagyn'd *Hero* was his mother.
And oftentimes into her bosome flew,
About her naked necke his bare armes threw,
And laid his childish head vpon her brest,
And with still panting rockt, there tooke his rest.
So louely faire was *Hero, Venus* Nun,
As Nature wept, thinking she was vndone;
Because she tooke more from her than she left,
And of such wondrous beautie her bereft:
Therefore in signe her treasure suffred wracke,
Since *Heroes* time, hath halfe the world beene blacke. (5-50)

All the glamour of a rare beauty is evoked, in tones not unlike the wonder of Enobarbus describing Cleopatra in her barge. In both, the magic of perfumes, colours and textures does most of the work. But Enobarbus says that her own person 'beggerd all discription' and having said so does not try to describe it. We draw close to Hero, however; in fact, quite suddenly and oddly close. We see her as a figure, somewhat remote and beautifully clothed; then we are at her mouth. With the honey-sucking bees we are suddenly intimate with the odour of her breath: the bees who 'beat from thence, haue lighted there againe'. The description works to a large extent within a convention. It is the convention of romantic hyperbole, as found in the madrigal lyrics, and all the details, down to the bees have their place in it:

> Sweet hony sucking Bees,
> Why doe you still
> Surfet on Roses,
> Pincks and Violets?
> ... Ah, make your flight
> To *Melisuauiaes* lips:
> There may you reuell
> In Ambrosian cheere.

There, in Wilbye's madrigal, is the pretty convention
working normally. In a Canzonet of Morley's, we hear how
'Laura, gentle and fair, alas hath slain me', and if Laura
had a 'kirtle blew' it might very well have been stained
with the blood of the fallen. Though, as we say this, the
query does arise: has one, in fact, seen such a detail in these
lyrics? Has not Marlowe, in fact, sent the conventional
hyperbole one stage further that it is usually made to go?
'Dressed to kill', we say, perpetuating the convention, but
it is surely a satirist, rather than rhapsodist, who thus
adorns his heroine with bloodstains, symbolic or not (and
the point has been gravely argued). Similarly, in the lines
about the breath and the bees, the whole passage is on the
verge of absurdity, and with the fourth line—'And beat
from thence [the mouth], haue lighted there again'—the
convention is extended just far enough to see it topple over
into farce. If the honey-sucking bees had stung Melisuavia,
it would have been, so to speak, bad for the convention.
Marlowe does not go as far as that, but he has, whether
knowingly or not, with the first touch of realism deflated
the romantic hyperbole.

This is to assume that the lines are raising the smile they
are intended to raise, but of course they could be misfires.
So much in the description is straightforwardly beautiful,
idyllic and conventional that one must wonder. Yet surely
the last item listed among Hero's personal effects—the
quaint device of water-filled sparrows who cheruped around
the knees 'as she went'—carries the pretty femininity of the
picture to a point where it is likely to stimulate masculine
laughter at its expense. Moreover, what follows can only
provoke more of the same kind, for Cupid, on an admittedly pretty excuse (he thought Hero was his mother), flew
into her bosom, 'And with still panting rockt, there took
his rest.' (44). Next, the equivocal epithet '*Venus* Nun'

(virgin or whore?) is bestowed on Hero and the passage ends with a playful though learned *reductio ad absurdum* of the whole romantic convention. There seems to be no question that a subtle, independent mind is involved; and even at this stage, for all the freshness and beauty as well as the sunny charm of these innocent-seeming couplets, one senses that there is somewhere at work a spirit that denies, or undermines, or 'gets at'. Yet this is not at all in the normal manner of the satirist, with his programme of demolition and formalised attitudes, but rather a part of a complex sensibility whose feelings, over a wide range and with varied emphasis and direction, are engaged in his work.

Such an undermining spirit, however, is notably absent from the next passage. In this, the description of lovely woman is matched by a portrait of perfect young manhood. One might well have expected some irony at the expense of muscle bound virility but, so far from this, the ideal is presented unspoiled and with a good deal of relish. Marlowe is still working in a convention, but we find nothing ridiculous or deflatory. He presumably likes what he is writing about:

> His bodie was as straight as *Circes* wand,
> *Ioue* might have sipt out *Nectar* from his hand.
> Euen as delicious meat is to the tast,
> So was his necke in touching, and surpast
> The white of *Pelops* shoulder. I could tell ye,
> How smooth his brest was, & how white his bellie,
> And whose immortall fingars did imprint
> That hauenly path, with many a curious dint,
> That runs along his backe . . .   (61–9)

In spite of the intimate bodily detail, the description is still statuesque, sculpted closely on classical models and removed only occasionally from the heroic-conventional:

> I could tell ye,
> How smooth his brest was, and how white his bellie.

The sly, lustful effect here is reinforced by the slower pace of monosyllables ('I could tell ye'), as the non-heroic tone is by the remarkable rhyme. An epigrammatic reference to the Narcissus myth also acts as a leaven, a flippancy in a conducted tour of the glories that were Greece:

> Those orient cheekes and lippes, exceeding his
> That leapt into the water for a kis
> Of his owne shadow, and despising many,
> Died ere he could enioy the loue of any. (73–6)

This is like lines two and four of the poem (and much in the Ovid *Elegies*), neat, smart, common-sensish in effect, an anticipation in tone if not technique of the Augustan couplet. Lastly, at the end of the section, after all the ideal statuary, the mythology and the magic, comes a touch of normal workaday realism in the observation of Leander's friends:

> *Leander,* thou art made for amorous play:
> Why art thou not in loue, and lou'd of all?
> Though thou be faire, yet be not thine owne thrall.
>
> (I. 88–90)

The natural, familiar ring of this contrasts with the artifice of the portraits and prepares us for the opening of the story when these portraits will come to life.

If the first ninety lines are like a prelude to the opera to come, the next fifty or so are like the opening chorus, and here indeed the holiday mood is dominant and exuberant:

> For euerie street like to a Firmament
> Glistered with breathing stars, who where they went,
> Frighted the melancholie earth, which deem'd
> Eternall heauen to burne, for so it seem'd,
> As if another *Phaeton* had got
> The guidance of the sunnes rich chariot.
> But far aboue the loueliest *Hero* shin'd,
> And stole away th'inchaunted gazers mind. (97–104)

The passage is wonderfully lit—'glistered', 'burne', 'shin'd', and a few lines later 'crown'd with blazing light'; and the images, Tamburlaine and Dido-like, are of vast spaces and on a great scale—'a firmament', 'stars', 'earth', 'heaven', 'the sun'. This is surely the Marlowe we value: the poetry which has no place in *The Jew of Malta* and *Edward II*. That it should be here in *Hero and Leander* successfully combined with qualities of irony and detachment which are in some ways its negation, is another of the poem's wonders. Even here enthusiasm shifts into amusement: hyperbole overplays itself by ever so little, and the fantasy-world is somehow contained and placed by the development of tone into mock-heroic. At times everything is straightforward:

> But far aboue the loueliest *Hero* shin'd
> And stole away th'inchaunted gazers mind.   (103–4)

This may call to mind lines like

> Belinda smil'd and all the world was gay,

for Marlowe is here writing simply in the convention which Pope was to satirise. But a little later on, we read:

> So at her presence all surpris'd and tooken,
> Await the sentence of her scornfull eies:
> He whom she favours liues, the other dies.   (122–4)

Here Marlowe is himself beginning to suggest the tone, technique and attitude of *The Rape of the Lock*.

These three closely related aspects—tone, technique and attitude—are the concern of this essay. In making comparison with *The Rape of the Lock* one notes how readily the definite article and singular noun can be used of that poem: 'the tone'. To talk of 'the tone' of *Hero and Leander* one would have to be confident that a very great range of tones were simultaneously being brought to mind. And until this is achieved it is no use thinking that one can talk sensibly about attitude. Many years ago Una Ellis-Fermor[1] wrote of Marlowe and this poem: 'the tone is an invaluable index of his frame of mind'. But just how far she was from catching 'the tone' one can judge from the rest of the sentence: 'Limited though the scope is, there is Hellenic security and repose in the mood that dictates it, and though it deliberately abstains from serious or profound treatment of the theme and so tells us little of his thought, the tone is a valuable index of his frame of mind'. Apart from the last clause, everything in the sentence is at least highly questionable, but the most extraordinary of its contents, I think, is its attributing to the poem a mood of 'security and repose'. It would be hard to find terms which give a less helpful idea of 'the tone' that is in turn to tell us something of the author's 'frame of mind'. Again, having *The Rape of the Lock* in mind helps to bring home the wrongness of such a reading. The tone of *Hero and Leander* encompasses many extremes: tenderness and ruthlessness, romantic luxuriance and a clipped, ironic detachment. 'Limited though the scope is' surely involves a peculiarly unappreciative assessment. Marlowe subjects his Hero to an exposure which makes one see Pope's treatment of Belinda as a marvel of propriety and moderation; yet at the same time Hero is a woman made to live and command sympathy in a way that Belinda never begins to. It is not, of course, Pope's purpose that she should, but the *breadth* of Marlowe's scope is what impresses us in the comparison with a poem about which Miss Ellis-Fermor's sentence could with some justice have been written. For instance, 'security and repose' are terms a good deal more applicable to Pope's firmness and centrality of judgment. One might compare the use of mock-heroic in the poems,

[1] *Christopher Marlowe* (1927).

taking this as an index of the security of judgment or frame of mind. Its function in *The Rape of the Lock* has been well defined by Norman Callan: it is 'to establish a scale of values whose extreme limits are epic sublimity and human pettiness, and whose point of equilibrium is the "good sense" which conditions the outlook, social, moral and artistic of the period'.[1] In *Hero* it is 'epic sublimity' itself which is being undermined, a romantic and heroic convention (itself with roots in optimism and a sense of human dignity) which is being assailed by comic deflation. In this process I see no security, much less repose, for these have been Marlowe's own conventions, and still in the same poem partially are. In Pope's clear scale of values there *is* security, and in the 'point of equilibrium' there is repose. If in Marlowe we can find any such point it is in nothing so cautious and, after all, commonplace as the common sense of the grave Clarissa. For Marlowe the golden mean would be mean indeed and not particularly golden. What, in this poem, he gives us as a positive is something (to use Hopkins's phrase) 'lovelier, more dangerous'. The only point of repose is in the moment of sexual fulfilment. It comes with love, a force which itself is unquiet, insecure, predatory, and glorious. The final attitude to this dangerous element seems, in fact, to be one associated with Conrad's Marlow (and not inappropriate to the tragedy of Leander): 'In the destructive element immerse'.

The difference between the two poems is, clearly, profound; as great as the difference between the men and the periods they represent. That Miss Ellis-Fermor's sentence should apply more justly to Pope's poem only shows how wide of the mark it is as a description of Marlowe's. Yet it is typical of much that has been written and for that reason I have fixed on it here. Not the least typical part of it

[1] *Pelican Guide to English Literature*, vol. 4, p. 260.

is the notion that the poem 'abstains from serious or profound treatment of the theme'. By 'the theme' is probably meant 'the story', to which we now return; themes emerge, however, and neither theme nor narrative abstains from profundity with half the success of the criticism which thus characterises them.

It is at the feast of Adonis that Hero and Leander meet. In Venus' temple, against a background of murals showing

> the gods in sundrie shapes,
> Committing headdie ryots, incest, rapes   (143-4)

Hero is sacrificing at the altar,

> vailing her eie-lids close,
> And modestly they opened as she rose.   (159-60)

It is a pretty picture, and what is stressed is the pretty decorum: love is going to make havoc of it. Hero's maidenly propriety of conduct and principle is even here, subtly, seen as a joke. The whole world is so much against such austerity: the gods themselves go to it pell-mell, omnipotent, all restraint and dignity thrown to the winds.

> *Ioue* slylie stealing from his sisters bed,
> To dallie with *Idalian Ganimed*,
> And for his loue *Europa* bellowing loud,
> And tumbling with the Rainbow in a cloud.
>
>   (147-50)

Against the abandonment of this promiscuity and the exuberant farce of this tumbling and bellowing, Hero strives to preserve chastity, decorum, self-government and self-respect. But she reckons without the power of love, of which she herself is the agent. From her modest eyes there

> flew Loues arrow with the golden head,
> And thus *Leander* was enamoured.   (161-2)

The glib neatness of the rhyme and the devastating ease and

simplicity of the process suggest a miraculous clock-work:
a sort of magic puppetry, powerful over these two proud,
perfect and unsuspecting human beings.

   This trivial yet tremendous little drama provokes a short
generalising passage where narrative stops and the author
speaks as chorus. Again it seems possible to read the first
couplet in two quite different ways, and which way you take
it probably depends on discrimination the fineness of a hair's
breadth. By one reading it is unimportant and merely
conventional. The tone is then lightly sententious and
there is little real feeling. By the other, it marks the poem's
first dip into overt seriousness; the lines matter personally
and the tone has some urgency and depth about it.

> It lies not in our power to loue, or hate,
> For will in vs is ouer-rul'd by fate.
> When two are stript long ere the course begin,
> We wish that one should loose, the other win;
> And one especiallie doe we affect
> Of two gold Ingots like in each respect.
> The reason no man knowes, let it suffise,
> What we behold is censur'd by our eies.
> Where both deliberat, the loue is slight,
> Who euer lov'd, that lov'd not at first sight? (167–76)

The first reading, treating the lines lightly but learnedly,
says the following:

(1) this is only a versification of a passage from Casti-
glione:

> And forsomuch as our mindes are very apte to love and to
> hate: as in the sightes of combates and games and in all other
> kinde of contencion one with an other, it is seene that the
> lookers on many times beare affeccion without any manifest
> cause why, unto one of the two parties, with a gredy desire to
> have him get the victorie, and the other to have the overthrow.[1]

---

[1] *Cortegiano,* tr. Hoby (1561); parallel first noted by Raleigh in his Preface to
Tudor Translations Edition (1900).

(2) we must not get too excited about 'will in vs is ouerrul'd by fate', because 'in the light of the first line, "will" is here to be interpreted in its narrower Elizabethan sense of amorous desire, or its opposite . . . (for) if it is to be taken in its naked simplicity, and in its natural interpretation today, it is the negation of the dominant spirit of Marlovian drama'.[1]

The other reading, taking the lines seriously, is more personal and intuitive. It depends in the first place on a feeling that the tone deepens at this point where a crisis in the narrative provokes that kind of commentary, especially in a writer whose manner at other times is so un-sententious and non-abstract. This feeling takes support from the fact that the first couplet is on any interpretation a very remarkable one to have found Marlowe writing. Even accepting Dr Boas's contention that 'will' means 'love or hate' and no more, the idea still cuts away a major part of the powers attributable to 'will' in the general sense. In a Marlowe, whose dramas originate to a great extent in the passionate wills of people, this notion of a power over-ruling will in such important departments must be one that sets resonating a great deal that is fundamental in his thought and feeling. Finally, the immediate and the larger contexts lend the lines a weight which supports a serious reading. The 'force and virtue' operate upon the will, the comedy of Leander's situation being that this whole thing has happened to him without reference to his will; and, as the poem develops, the light on Hero focuses more and more strongly to show a divided will, or a force which works upon her, over-ruling the control which her other 'will' still strongly urges upon her. (The assurance that 'will in vs is ouer-rul'd by fate' is one which may well have come bitterly to the author of *Tamburlaine*. But (in its

[1] F. S. Boas, *op. cit.*, p. 230.

larger sense) it has been realised before this: tragically in
Faustus and depressingly in *Edward II*. In *Hero and Leander*
the affirmation reads to me as a serious one, even though the
illustrations (the runners and the ingots) are trivial, the
sentiments in themselves commonplace; and even though
the context is partly comic.

These lines are also the bridge by which humanity is
admitted to the poem. From dealing with statues and con-
vention-figures we come quite warmly and intimately to
the centre of their nerves and hearts. The Ovidian comedy
of lovers' subterfuges assumes an additional sophistication in that the two lovers whom we are observing are such
novices. We watch them play all the old games in what is a
brave new world to them:

> He kneel'd, but vnto her deuoutly praid;
> Chast *Hero* to her selfe thus softly said:
> Were I the Saint hee worships, I would heare him,
> And as shee spake those words, came somewhat nere him.
> He started vp, she blusht as one asham'd;
> Wherewith *Leander* much more was inflam'd.
> He toucht her hand; in touching it she trembled,
> *Loue deepely grounded, hardly is dissembled.*
> These louers parled by the touch of hands,
> True loue is mute, and oft amazed stands.　　　(177–86)

The poem is to focus constantly on this partly comic
tension between Hero's official and private selves, between
natural 'will' and the conscientious sense of propriety in-
culcated by society and religion. Marlowe's tone here is
amused and knowing, partly detached but also compassionate. We feel the strength of Hero's emotion, the strain
of her conflict and the embarrassment of it. It is this embarrassment that, throughout the poem, he reveals more
closely, I think, than any other poet has done.

The comedy of love is presented with shrewd, humorous

perception. In it Marlowe is sometimes, as Dr M. C. Bradbrook says, 'triumphantly on the side of the gods', and at
other times compassionately on the side of the mortals.
But the sense of humour does not kill the sense of wonder.
Having come so close, seeing the touching hands and feeling
with the trembling nerves, he steps back, senses the magic, and
marvels at this 'fair encounter of two most rare affections':

> Thus while dum signs their yeelding harts entangled,
> The aire with sparkes of liuing fire was spangled,
> And night deepe drencht in mystie *Acheron*
> Heau'd vp her head, and halfe the world vpon
> Breath'd darknesse forth . . .   (187–91)

The word 'glamour', we learn, had its origins in magic,
and here its modern romantic connotations and magic
origin meet. This is the poet 'knowing his magician's
business'. The startlingly bold image of night, so characteristic in the vigour and placing of the verb, presents a
picture vivid, mysterious and vast as Goya's *Giant*.

But however marvellous when placed like this against the
heavens and eternity, these romantic affairs have to be
played out in some comparatively prosaic here-and-now.
So we come back to earth and see that Leander has found
his tongue. He prays to be heard and that his words may
take effect, the purpose being rather less altruistic than he
tries to make it sound. The argument grows bolder as it
proceeds, and it eventually appears that Hero, in basing her
life on 'this idol' termed Virginity, is being a very silly girl
indeed. Leander's text is *carpe diem* and his speech has its
place in a long and distinguished line with Comus at the head:

> Like vntun'd golden strings all women are,
> Which long time lie vntouch'd, will harshly iarre.
> Vessels of Brasse oft handl'd, brightly shine,
> What difference betwixt the richest mine,
> And basest mold, but vse?   (229–33)

He pleads expertly, working by flattery, reference to authority ('our reuerend fathers say'), professions (Mark Antony-like) of guilelessness; and then, after all the show of high-minded logic, by appeal to self-interest on the most worldly basis—fear of what people will say (he is in fact resorting to the 'honourable logic' of Joseph Surface and if Hero were as clear-headed as Lady Teazle she would no doubt retort with her: 'So, so; then I perceive your prescription is, that I must sin in my own defence, and part with my virtue to preserve my reputation'). Leander is also suiting his philosophy to the occasion in that his present views contrast ironically with what we have heard of his life up to now. Marlowe takes a Chaucerian pleasure in the rhetorical exercise, and Leander argues the Wife of Bath's case without her experience: 'Virginitie . . . compar'd with marriage, had you tried them both', he begins, shaking his wise young head, even managing the suggestion that after a reasonable trial of the second you could, if you really wanted, return to the first.

But Leander is not the only 'bold sophister' at work here. For the climax of the speech Marlowe launches this attack on the doctrine of virginity:

> This idoll which you terme *Virginitie*,
> Is neither essence subiect to the eie,
> No, nor to any one exterior sence,
> Nor hath it any place of residence,
> Nor is't of earth or mold celestiall,
> Or capable of any forme at all.
> Of that which hath no being doe not boast,
> Things that are not at all are neuer lost. (269–76)

Harry Levin[1] comments on these lines: 'The asceticism professed by the Middle Ages, the Christian ideal of Chastity, was enshrined in the cult of the Virgin Queen and

[1] *The Overreacher*, p. 37.

glorified in such figures as Spenser's Britomart. In attacking
Hero's virginity as an "idoll", he was therefore com-
mitting lèse-majesté as well as undermining the constraints
of monasticism.' The attack may be even a little more
crafty than this; and the enemy is probably neither monasticism (dead and done for) nor the ageing Gloriana on her ever
more uneasy throne, but God. Leander's ultimate count
against the worship of virginity is that the object simply
does not exist. No one has seen it, no hand has touched it,
it has no form: therefore 'of that which hath no being do
not boast'. The argument is put on such a broad materialist
basis that it displaces all religious 'idols' as readily as it
does virginity, and even goes further to suggest that, if you
stopped pretending it did exist, you wouldn't feel the loss.
The thing is, of course, a game: Marlowe is playing devil's
advocate. Later Milton was to use similar, though rather
better, persuasions in *Comus* without half such drastically
materialist implications (and allotted firmly to a wicked
enchanter rather than to a nice young man). But the zest
of judicious blasphemy marked much of Marlowe's work,
and probably still more of his life.

Leander now begins, like Chaucer's Troilus, to 'mak it
tough'. For a moment his speech is almost that of the
stern schoolmaster:

> Perhaps, thy sacred Priesthood makes thee loath:
> Tell me, to whom mad'st thou that heedlesse oath?
>
> (293–4)

And Hero's reply comes tearfully, very like the distressed
schoolgirl:

> To *Venus*, answered shee, and as shee spake
> Foorth from those two tralucent cesternes brake
> A streame of liquid pearle, which downe her face
> Made milk-white paths, whereon the gods might trace
> To *Ioues* high court. (295–9)

Hyperbole has returned, in its most exaggerated form: offered straightforwardly, however, perhaps atoning in its praise of Hero for having laughed at those two sad mincing words of reply accompanied by the two great self-pitying tears.

Leander continues to play Comus and as he is encouraged to 'quickly re-enforce his speech', so the amusement quickens, something growing with it which is ultimately to kill the comedy and turn the poem into something else. One observes for the first time a cynicism in the knowingness:

> Women are woon when they begin to iarre. (332)

There is the first of the characteristically cruel metaphors:

> Thus hauing swallow'd *Cupids* golden hooke,
> The more she striv'd, the deeper was she strooke. (333–4)

The comedy begins to depend more on a kind of humiliation. Hero's little subterfuges are all laid out and seen through:

> Yet euilly faining anger, stroue she still,
> And would be thought to graunt against her will. (335–6)

The wooing bases some of its appeal on the proper pride which is to be brought so low:

> Thee as a holy Idiot doth she scorne, (303)

echoed by:

> Faire fooles delight to be accounted nice. (326)

For the first time, as the action becomes impassioned, the comedy becomes farcical:

> With that *Leander* stoopt, to haue imbrac'd her,
> But from his spreading armes away she cast her. (341–2)

Hero's tongue betrays her:

> For vnawares (*Come thither*) from her slipt. (358)

Humiliation and shame are attendant on the betrayal:

> And sodainly her former colour chang'd,
> And here and there her eies through anger rang'd. (359–60)

Hero's turbulence is matched by Cupid's violence. He, 'all deepe enrag'd',

> beats downe her praiers with his wings. (369)

So the poem comes to its first climax, as to its end, in 'anguish, shame and rage'. In the bridge passage leading to the mythological interlude (370–5), what was serious and real has become more comically detached and the expression correspondingly more stylised. But while the human drama is being played out before us, we are insensitive if our amusement is not held in check by something almost fiercely serious within the verse. And we do Marlowe an injustice if we miss the compassion expressed in these lines and even inherent in the fierceness:

> And like a planet, moouing seuerall waies,
> At one selfe instant, she poore soule assaies,
> Louing, not to loue at all, and euerie part
> Stroue to resist the motions of her hart. (361–4)

There follows an interlude in the form of a rather complicated mythological narrative. Cupid, seeing Hero's tears, eventually comes to be sorry for what he has done and visits the Destinies to at least secure a happy outcome for the lovers. But the Destinies hated Cupid: 'Harken a while,' says Marlowe, 'and I will tell you why'. It all began when Mercury fell in love with a girl who would not have him. She was ambitious, however, and asked her lover for a draught of Nectar, which Mercury had to steal from Jove. Jove was very angry when this was done and banished him from heaven. He complained to Cupid and Cupid took his side, causing the Destinies to fall in love with him. With their aid, he (Mercury) dislodged Jove from heaven and put Saturn in his place. But having secured his end, he neglected the Destinies, and they, frustrated and furious, once again reversed the order of things. Jove returned to Elysium, Mercury (the scholar-god) was condemned to perpetual poverty, and the Destinies will now do all they can to annoy Cupid. So the outlook is black for Hero and Leander.

At a first reading the interlude probably looks flagrantly irrelevant, as to F. S. Boas it is. But some years before Boas's book, Dr Bradbrook had pointed out that 'the story of the Destinies' love for Cupid is a burlesque illustration of the same theme, not a digression', the theme being the irresistibility and the cruelty of love. Obviously it is a digression from the main story, but it is like a musical interlude, an *entr'acte* in which one recognises adaptations and developments of themes heard in the first act and to be heard again in the second. There is immediately apparent a likeness of manner. Knowing, sophisticated comedy is again curiously mixed with farce:

> Herewith he stayd his furie, and began
> To give her leaue to rise; away she ran,
> After went *Mercurie*, who vs'd such cunning,
> As she to heare his tale, left off her running. (415–18)

One recognises the characteristic stuff of the poem in Jove's indignant fury ('he inly stormed'), Mercury's scorn of the Destinies, their frustrated love, anguish, shame and rage. One can see that love is treated as in the rest of the work. But more than this, there are likenesses to the conflicts within and around Hero: 'within' in as far as the story concerns duty against inclination; 'around' in as far as it is seen as will versus fate. The interlude tells of conflict

with Mercury and Cupid on one side and Jove and the
Destinies ('the Sterne nymphs') on the other. So the myth
externalises Hero's inner conflict, and perhaps does something to universalise it. The gods representing different
aspects of life, the myth can be taken to allegorise what the
author sees as a fundamental conflict in the nature of things.
Here the gods range themselves as, on the one hand, full
of love, pleasure, grace, learning, heroism (Mercury, the
reign of Saturn, Cupid as instrument); on the other, stern,
frustrated, furious and tyrannical (Jove, the Destinies). The
conflict between these is an allegory not simply of their
conflict in Hero but of the tension of 'contraries' throughout nature.' It is true that the expression is light in tone and
not very emotional or personal, except possibly in the lines
about poor scholars, and even there it is rueful-realistic
rather than cynical-bitter. But every proposition and al-
legorised attitude certainly reads as the *outcome* of deep
thought and feeling. It may be sufficient to instance the
lines:

> And fruitfull wits that in aspiring are,
> Shall discontent run into regions farre. (477–8)

The emotional and intellectual stress behind that smoothly
regretful couplet constitutes a whole history.

The interlude ends, the fairy-tale gracefully rounded off.
The opening of Sestiad II now violently brings us back to
the story. The snatch from one to the other calls to mind
Eliot's term 'savage' used of Marlovian farce. It is a kind
of 'attack' in the literary sense, which is, however, uniquely
of this work, not merely the energetic plunge of the stylist.

The first couplet, completely farcical, has the ludicrous,
jerky, twice-the-speed movement of an early film:

> By this, sad *Hero*, with loue vnacquainted,
> Viewing *Leanders* face, fell downe and fainted. (II. 1–2)

The feminine endings help (perhaps it is that a single rhyme in a couplet is neat and tidy, the perfect rounding with its quasi-inevitability for an epigram; whereas a double rhyme draws such attention to 'the jingling sound of like endings' that it is difficult to take anything it says seriously). In the second couplet, the poet's-eye-camera takes a closer shot:

> He kist her, and breath'd life into her lips.

Then the next thing seen is the next-thing-but-one that happens. You miss a shot, and the juxtaposition of shots one and three is comic:

> He kist her, and breath'd life into her lips,
> Wherewith as one displeas'd, away she trips.   (II. 3–4)

The technique becomes more sober after this, but the comedy is brilliantly maintained. Hero drops her fan,

> Thinking to traine *Leander* therewithall.
> He being a nouice, knew not what she meant,
> But stayd, and after her a letter sent.   (II. 12–14)

Rhyme will often give the suggestion of inevitability or clockwork. So we smile at the novice missing the first gambit but hitting freshly on the inevitable and equally obvious alternative. Again we share in the amused, detached observation of two individuals moving freshly and with bewilderment, embarrassment and rapture along a route which is so well-worn. Moreover, they seem to themselves to be at one point asserting their will, or at another to be having a good idea; but the exercise of will is illusory, the struggle futile, and the explorations of the novice lead, for the sophisticated observer, to a discovery of the obvious. Yet the tone is never world-weary and the responsiveness is always rich and lively.

The second of the love scenes begins with a rapturous 'O' prefacing a straightforward description of an ecstatic meeting. But as the struggle recommences in Hero, so the

account resumes its sharp and intimately observant character. Hero's will-to-virtue leads only to her throwing her
body upon Leander 'like light *Salmacis*', and the further
irony is explicit in:

> the more she striued,
> The more a gentle pleasing heat reuiued.　　(67–8)

Later the verse takes on a more serious tone. Again the
management of couplets shows considerable mastery:

> Iewels being lost are found againe, this neuer;
> T'is lost but once, and once lost, lost for euer.　(85–6)

But in spite of the neatness and the feminine rhymes, there
is no flippancy in this. Marlowe may not be speaking in his
own voice when he calls chastity 'this inestimable gemme'
but he is saying that to Hero it *was* precious, so no wonder
('no marvell then') she held on, seeing (he adds grimly)
that the loss is irreparable.

Between this love scene and the third, which is the
climax of the poem, come two episodes. The first shows
Leander at home. Irony and paradox in the expression,
frustration and pride in the experience, are features of these
robust and highly characteristic lines. The second episode
calls for a discussion of tone and intention. Fun and
seriousness are again strangely mixed. Leander is observed
with that humour and detachment with which Chaucer
sees his lovers in *The Knight's Tale*. The fanciful world of
romantic hyperbole is invoked:

> [he] pray'd the narrow toyling *Hellespont*
> To part in twaine, that hee might come and go.　(150–51)

But this is opposed, with all the logic of rhyme, by the facts
of the case:

> But still the rising billowes answered no.　　(152)

Then comes another double-quick, silent-film movement, burlesquing the celebrated act in a triumphantly neat couplet:

> With that he stript him to the yu'rie skin
> And crying, Loue I come, leapt liuely in.   (153–4)

Hyperbole then takes charge in a comic fairy-tale world where the subject is not of similar innocence. The old Marlovian imagination plays unchecked for five lines, as the mermaids, with fine humanistic pride

> . . . tooke great pleasure
> To spurne in carelesse sort the shipwracke treasure.
>   (163–4)

With the introduction of Neptune, the pantomime quickens. The old man intends to make the most of so attractive a visitor to his realm. He promptly and vigorously involves himself with the swimmer so that Leander's progress is impeded. The sudden juxtaposition of common-sense reality ('for vnder water he was almost dead') makes it doubly ludicrous. The hero is in an absurd situation as Neptune 'heau'd him up'; and the god, 'smiling wantonly', also cuts a ridiculous figure. Leander is aghast at this monstrous irrelevance to his purposes with its infuriatingly gratuitous addition to his already considerable difficulties. 'You are deceau'd, I am no woman I' he cries out. But 'thereat smilde *Neptune*'.

What begins as pantomime, however, ends as something different. The wicked old man, for all his sophisticated smiling, makes no headway and, a grotesque addition, joins the procession of folk frustrated—the poem is full of them. The ungodlike recalling of the mace the moment it had left his hand is paid for by the humiliating cartoon-like comedy of its hitting him as it returns. But this humiliation arouses pity in Leander:

When this fresh bleeding wound *Leander* viewd,
His colour went and came, as if he rewd
The greefe which *Neptune* felt.   (213–15)

This makes Neptune think that he is loved after all and so
he tries what gifts will do. It is a pathetically faithful
allegory. Or rather, it is a presentation in mythological
terms and pantomime style of the nightmare intrusion of
the homosexual into a normal man's life. It includes the
kindness that he may exercise if he is a good man:

> In gentle brests,
> Relenting thoughts, remorse and pittie rests.
> And who haue hard hearts, and obdurat minds,
> But vicious, harebraind, and illit'rat hinds?   (215–18)

It implies also a sympathy with the homosexual's frustrated,
hopeful, importunate and often ludicrous state:

> Loue is too full of faith, too credulous,
> With follie and false hope deluding vs.   (221–2)

The love that provokes that sympathetic and serious
generalisation is the absurd Neptune's.[1]

The episode has often been seen as another irrelevance
('Then through sheer pleasure in movement and freedom
his fancy spins out several long digressions in no wise
germane to the plot'—Kocher) and has also been criticised
on other scores. L. C. Martin writes: 'the trivial incident
of Neptune's courtship of Leander in Sestiad II calls aloud
for excision or re-casting, not perhaps on moral grounds
adduced by Professor Legouis, for the gods are notoriously
superior to human ethical codes, but because this account
of Neptune's heavy enticements and ludicrous discomfiture

[1] Rosamund Tuve in *Elizabethan and Metaphysical Imagery* suggests that as 'the
substitution of the physical ocean for Neptune was as natural as breathing to any
Elizabethan, we can re-read the images as convincing, and accurate description of
the caressing flow of the water' (p. 157). This may be true of the first lines of the
episode, but the trope—if such it originally is—develops an interest of itself. The
images and symbols here have more life than any amorous water and the interest
is clearly with them.

is aesthetically inept'.[1] F. L. Lucas dismisses it with the remark that Marlowe 'could not resist parading his own homosexuality'.[2]

But 'ludicrous discomfiture', so far from being 'aesthetically inept', is an element at the heart of the whole poem. From the very beginning we hear the motif of lovers frustrated, played scherzando; and it links with the other dominant motif, again partly comic, of love's indignity and cruelty. One of the first incidental images shows Venus doing her best to entice a mortifyingly unresponsive Adonis. Another in the series—for this is a medallion-like technique, as in the murals of Venus' temple—is Narcissus:

> That leapt into the water for a kis
> Of his owne shadow, and despising many,
> Died ere he could enioy the loue of any.   (I. 74-76)

Then come the victims of Hero's charms, Hero now seen as a forerunner of Zuleika Dobson.

> He whom she fauours liues, the other dies.
> There might you see one sigh, another rage,
> And some (their violent passions to asswage)
> Compile sharpe satyrs, but alas too late,
> For faithfull loue will never turn to hate.   (I. 124-8)

These unfortunates are frustrated, that is, in the very act of easing their frustration. The gods too join the line:

> Blood-quaffing *Mars* heuing the yron net
> Which limping *Vulcan* and his *Cyclops* set . . .
> *Syluanus* weeping for the louely boy
> That now is turn'd into a *Cypres* tree. (I. 151-2; 154-5)

The frustrated Destinies, the scornful maid, the debonair Mercury, follow; and later 'chast *Diana*, when *Acteon* spyde her'. Neptune has his place among them: the old man of the sea having himself swallowed Cupid's golden hook, his

[1] *Op. cit.,* p. 70.

[2] Introduction to his translation of Musaeus' poem '*Hero and Leander*' (1949).

'ludicrous discomfiture' is no more 'aesthetically inept' than that of Hero herself.

Now begins the last movement of the poem. Attention reverts to Hero and her 'longing heart'. In the strange masculine exposure of the girl's predicament there is a sort of brutality; even in what Dr Bradbrook calls 'those delightful lines'

> Seeing a naked man, she scriecht for feare,
> Such sights as this to tender maids are rare. (II. 237–8)

Marlowe spares nothing: her very gladness betrays her like drunkenness. Her emotions chase each other in quick succession: longing, joy, drunken gladness, shock, fear. After the irony of Hero's taking 'refuge' in her bed, however, the laughter turns to Leander. He sits on the bed 'all feeble, faint and wan', remote indeed from the heroic ideal. His little speech is all sweet reasonableness. Again the rhyme does something to reinforce the 'logic':

> This head was beat with manie a churlish billow,
> And therefore let it rest vpon thy pillow. (251–2)

It is the only possible rhyme: the justice of the 'therefore', the automatic rightness of the claim, are comically emphasised. The plea succeeds, but only because Hero is 'affrighted'. Then, as 'overcome with shame' she dives down, occurs the startlingly realistic 'tent' action:

> as her siluer body downeward went,
> With both her hands she made the bed a tent,
> And in her owne mind thought her selfe secure,
> O'recast with dim and darksome couerture. (263–6)

The neatness of expression, the irony of Hero's struthious assurance of security, the physical absurdity of the situation, all make against any sort of romantic seriousness. But the farcical is moderated, and the light tone deepens at the line

> And euerie kisse to her was as a charme. (283)

This is quite serious, and it suggests a recognition that preliminaries in love may be funny, but that the rest is not for laughter. There is sympathy and no derision in 'poore sillie maiden'. This crucial moment in Hero's life is gathered up into one of the most memorable and deeply-meant couplets in the poem:

> Loue is not ful of pittie (as men say)
> But deaffe and cruell, where he meanes to pray. (287–8)

The imaginative effort goes further and produces a simile of remarkable cruelty, violence and tenderness:

> Euen as a bird, which in our hands we wring,
> Foorth plungeth, and oft flutters with her wing,
> She trembling stroue.　　　　　　　　　(289–91)

Even this trembling strife, such is the irony of things, stimulates erotic feeling. There follows then a last exposure of the struggle, and a cynical generalisation, ruthlessly disallowing any tendency we may have to sentimentalise the occasion:

> Treason was in her thought,
> And cunningly to yeeld her selfe she sought.
> Seeming not woon, yet woon she was at length,
> In such warres women vse but halfe their strength. (293–6)

These lines were quoted by Dr M. C. Bradbrook, in an essay published in *Scrutiny* many years ago,[1] and compared with a passage in *Troilus and Criseyde*:

> This Troilus in armes gan hir streyne,
> And seyde, 'O sweete, as ever mote I goon,
> Now be ye caught, now is ther but we tweyne;
> Now yeldeth yow, for other boot is noon.'
> To that Criseyde answerde thus anoon,
> 'Ne hadde I er now, my swete herte dere,
> Ben yolde, y wis, I were not now here!' (III. st. 173)

[1] 'Hero and Leander', *Scrutiny*, II, 1 (1933).

Dr Bradbrook was arguing that people still appeared to think of *Hero and Leander* as if it were a romance like *Venus and Adonis* or even *The Eve of St Agnes*, whereas it is really a detached and sophisticated comedy far closer to the spirit and manner of Chaucer. This essay emerged from a fresh, independent reading, and it still seems to me the best study of the poem. It makes an interesting comparison with what Una Ellis-Fermor wrote; here two critics, writing within a few years of each other about a poem they both admire, come armed with such different critical approaches that they might almost be reading two different works. Where Miss Ellis-Fermor had talked of simplicity, Dr Bradbrook had found subtlety; and where the other had enjoyed the 'heavy ornament and rich irrelevant imagery', Dr Bradbrook recommended the 'power in selection and arrangement of material'. She also found 'exuberance', 'exaltancy' and 'exhilaration', where Miss Ellis-Fermor had found an 'enervating enchantment'. Miss Ellis-Fermor's Marlowe is (here) often, one suspects, a beruffed, lotos-eating Swinburne: 'there are no tears in his joy and his song is sweet without sadness'. Dr Bradbrook's essay was a corrective and a stimulus; but if the comparison with Chaucer was what was wanted then, it is the contrast that needs stressing now.

There is a fierceness and destructiveness about *Hero and Leander* which is utterly unChaucerian. Charm and decorum are everywhere in Chaucer's love scene. In Marlowe there is embarrassment, fear, conflict and farce. Hero is divided, betrayed by herself ('treason was in her thought'), put to absurd shifts, subject to a sort of sexual brutality ('Euen as a bird, which in our hands we wring, Foorth plungeth'). The end of the second Sestiad is almost savagely Marlovian (not remote even from 'We sawe *Cassandra* sprauling in the streetes'), and it has nothing to do with Chaucer. Even in the early parts of the poem the comparison is only partly valid. Dr Bradbrook says that Hero's 'slyness in "coming somewhat nigh" Leander, her "come thither" (which invitation slips out "unawares"), her final attempt to "train" him by dropping her fan as she goes . . . are not the coquetries of a Cressida but the delicacies of a Criseyde'. In fact, they are not either: they are the confusions, naïvetés and self-betrayals of Marlowe's Hero. And Marlowe's Hero is a woman being, amongst other things, *exposed*, with a ruthlessness unknown to Chaucer and probably, in spite of the coexisting sympathy, quite antipathetic to him.

Hero and Leander is then, I think, not such a *pleasant* poem as Dr Bradbrook's essay with its Chaucerian comparison makes of it. Parts of it are entirely delightful, but there is something beyond this of which Dr Bradbrook gives little more inkling than Miss Ellis-Fermor. Apart from the difference in prose style, she might almost have written with Ellis-Fermor that 'the sunlight is unbroken' and spoken of 'the warm serenity of the mood'. This is to abstract from the poem light, beauty and love, and to ignore those other key-terms: night, 'follie and false hope', 'deaffe and cruell', 'anguish, shame and rage'. It is, after all, a curious Marlowe that emerges from such a reading. Dr Bradbrook does find characteristic Marlovian insolence in taking 'a notorious tragedy as basis for a comedy'[1]. But the insolence presented there seems comparatively pointless, almost gratuitously naughty; the real 'attack' of the spirit is deeper than that.

In the last forty lines of the poem, which remain to be discussed, the force and individuality are felt at their most intense concentration. In the moment of sexual fulfilment the poem finds its single point of repose. The male

[1] *Shakespeare and Elizabethan Poetry* (Cambridge, 1951).

experience is described with fervour and no cynicism; almost with awe. Hero's rapture is uninhibited at last, but for a very short time. Her joy mingles with regret that day must come, that the happiness is impermanent, and soon her embarrassment returns to be exposed again. The exposure of embarrassment is followed by a farce which exceeds all the previous pantomime:

> as her naked feet were whipping out,
> He on the suddaine cling'd her so about,
> That Meremaid-like vnto the floore she slid,
> One halfe appear'd, the other halfe was hid. (313–16)

The whole passage, as it continues, represents in one sense extreme, ultimate humiliation, yet contains the most beautiful and moving picture of Hero in the book:

> Thus neere the bed she blushing stood vpright,
> And from her countenance behold ye might
> A kind of twilight breake, which through the heare,
> As from an orient cloud, glymse here and there. (317–30)

Hero is now in the power of her lover's passion, and the energy and speed of the coda enact musically the rush of emotion. The last eight lines move in one powerful rush gathering momentum in time with day's car and night's carriage, turning the last, fierce corner to the finishing point with the daring exhilaration of the ruthless and emphatic 'dang'd'. Night, 'mockt' or humiliated, is 'o're-come with anguish, shame and rage': the terms tie up a great many strands in the poem. Along with them goes repulsion after the lovers' joy—'loathsome', 'ugly' applied to night which throughout the poem is identified with love: this all asserts the destructive, violent, ruthless spirit which lurks throughout; and it also reasserts the sense, always present in the poem, that there is a destructive, painful element strong in the love which is nevertheless the best thing which life offers to man.

Part IV

10

CONCLUSION

'THE RIPEST FRUIT of all in the interpretation of any literary figure is the attainment of some comprehensive and unified view of his nature in its relations with his work.'[1] The ends are fine but the means suspect, for the writings, says Kocher, should be studied 'only secondarily as works of art, and primarily as mirrors of the thought, learning and character of their creator.'[2] This is a familiar programme but it involves a drastic short cut with consequent loss and distortion. Marlowe *wrote* 'separate works of art'. To be interested in them 'only secondarily' for what they are cannot be the way to find out the truth about them. The 'thought, character and learning' are expressed in the art— that is, the drama and the poetry—and if one wants to know them it can only be through the kinds of reading appropriate to those arts. Going to the works in search of these things ('thought, character and learning'), we may well find much that is of interest; but 'the ripest fruit of all' will have proved elusive, whether it is defined in Kocher's terms or in terms which also introduce some idea of the pleasures of poetry.

It is possible indeed that the ripest fruit is still left on the tree when all the debate about free thought or orthodoxy, subjective or objective heroes and so forth, has passed over. Does one gather from those discussions (*in toto*) something that can be called a riper or more abundant yield than from

---

[1] P. H. Kocher, *op. cit.*, pp. 6–7.   [2] *Ibid.*, p. 3.

a reading of Marlowe which leaves one in full *possession* of lines and passages:

> Heauen enuious of our ioyes is waxen pale,
> And when we whisper, then the starres fall downe,
> To be partakers of our honey talke.
>
> (Dido, 1258–60)
>
> For in his lookes I see eternitie,
> And heele make me immortall with a kisse.
>
> (Dido, 1328–9)
>
> If it were made for man, twas made for me:
> I wil renounce this magicke, and repent.
>
> (Faustus, 621–2)
>
> So when this worlds compounded vnion breakes,
> Time ends and to old *Chaos* all things turne;
> Confused stars shal meete, celestiall fire
> Fleete on the flouds . . .
>
> (Lucan, 73–6)

'Possession' of this kind is fragmentary (and therefore unsatisfactory, 'unripe'), but such a random harvest is of value and brings its owner closer to the 'nature' of the poet than much systematic inquiry will do. Through such passages he is far more likely to know Chapman's Marlowe

> whose liuing subject stood
> Vp to the chin in the Pyerean flood.
>
> (Hero, Third Sestiad, 189–90)

This is the Marlowe most constantly disregarded in thought-mongering critical processes: the best fruits tend to pass untasted while we hunt around for sniping references to the Bible or first-hand knowledge of Machiavelli.

But the main point is that only by a reading which is responsive to the poetry and drama as such can one hope to come near the 'comprehensive and unified view' which it is certainly very desirable to have. This is true of large things (the grasp of a play's organisation, the view of life it offers, or the conflict it expresses) and of small. To have

within oneself the opening of the Thirteenth *Elegy*, for
example:

> Now ore the sea from her old Loue comes she
> That drawes the day from heauens cold axletree

means feeling, whether consciously or not, the music of
the long vowels and assonances (sea, she, tree; ore, drawes);
and feeling it through the particular word-order as the
gradual approach of dawn, with a romantic sense of wonder
and magic perhaps warming itself to life by the eroticism
of the myth. Having these lines in this sort of possession
is to know a Marlowe capable, however fitfully, of tenderness; and one cannot know the poet without giving him
this sort of reading. It is the *primary* need, because if the
priorities are reversed, we abstract from an author not so
much what he has to give as what we are interested in
finding. The process has its own reward but it is unlikely
to achieve with real completeness or justness of proportion
that comprehensive view of the poet's nature which was
the given aim.

With Marlowe more than with most authors one feels an
urge to connect, trace a development and see the man in
the work. The works themselves prompt these interests in
many ways, but it is also true that the (sometimes doubtful)
facts of Marlowe's biography have stimulated them further.
At this point, as Kocher says, one meets with famous
interpretative crossroads.

Critics and others will sometimes say what a good thing
it is that we know as little as we do about Shakespeare's
life. As a corollary it might be thought a pity that we know
so much about Marlowe's. Facts about Shakespeare are
relatively unexciting, so the temptation to interpret his
works in the light of his biography has been minimal. With
Marlowe, the facts involve quarrels, imprisonment, sudden

death and a fair variety of colourful ideas and practices; together with the theories based on them, these have had a notable effect on the way he is read. For a hundred years now, most readers have come to the texts with some prior knowledge: knowing or believing that he 'died swearing', or that he was generally speaking an angry young Elizabethan who represented his age with 'the swelling bombast of a bragging blank verse' and the confident strut of the 'aspiring mind' which it expressed. No portrait of Marlowe enlivens the editions of his works, but no poet has the public image of his character more vividly imposed on the words he wrote.

This is regrettable in several respects. For one thing, the works gain a false glamour. The poetry, often brilliant in itself, has its colour intensified (and perhaps changed) by its author's reputation as a colourful man. A piece of daring criticism or free-thought is diagnosed in a passage which would have appeared unremarkable enough had the critic not known of Marlowe's reputation as an atheist. The danger of 'reading in' is apparent. But more insidious are the processes of reaction to this. Dutifully on guard against the romantic and subjective, we may in fact be exercising our scepticism on a perfectly valid and probably useful finding. A similar and rather more crucial dilemma meets us in any consideration of Marlowe's heroes. Because we have a picture of Christopher Marlowe as rebellious in spirit and turbulent in life, we may be inclined to suppose that he created Tamburlaine and Faustus in his own image; or at least to assume that he is involved with them in a way unlike Shakespeare's involvement with, say, Henry V and Othello. This is natural and may indeed be correct. On the other hand, it may prejudice one's idea of Marlowe's attitude to his heroes and so distort the whole understanding of his work. Some critics believe that it has in fact done so, and they urge that we should credit Marlowe as we do other playwrights with the ability to create character objectively. This too is very reasonable. The first view is called 'romantic', and I suppose the description is just, though it often goes with the possibly unjust assumption that the epithet is itself sufficient to demonstrate an absurdity. The second is called 'modern' and by a similarly rash assumption the epithet is supposed to guarantee rightness.

The division between recent critics can probably be seen at its widest in the work of Kocher on the one hand and Battenhouses's study of *Tamburlaine* on the other. Kocher believes in the biographical evidence pointing to Marlowe's unorthodoxy. In particular, he takes the Baines note seriously as a summary of Marlowe's attack on religion and a key to his essential thought. He also sees *Tamburlaine* as a daring, anti-Christian play and *The Jew of Malta* as another strong criticism. To Battenhouse *Tamburlaine* is 'one of the most grandly moral spectacles in the whole realm of English drama'. Marlowe is seen as dramatising, objectively, a man of degenerate inspiration, whose sinful ambition incurs its full and proper nemesis.

Now although Battenhouse is ranged among critics of the 'objective' school, we find that the biographical evidence weighs with him too and that he simply gives an interpretation which is the opposite of Kocher's. He does not believe the accusations of unorthodoxy and he stresses the argument that men like Raleigh and Chapman who had some association with Marlowe were devoutly religious and often stern moralists. Both critics have in fact come to the work from the biography. Kocher says: 'The *first* obligation of a study of the mind of Marlowe is to interpret all available biographical evidence of his thought. The extant plays and poems are *next* to be interpreted' (my italics). Similarly, Battenhouse's starting-point, he tells us, was 'the vexing problem of Marlowe's "atheism"'. He could not square the Marlowe of Kyd's and Baines's accusations with 'the Marlowe who studied Divinity at Cambridge and whose loyalty to her Majesty's religion was vouched for by the Privy Council'. Why this should have been a 'vexing problem' is not clear, but evidently it was and Professor Battenhouse solved it to his own satisfaction, presenting a Marlowe who would do the Divinity School credit, and who applied the standards of Her Majesty's religion most conventionally in the very play where his unorthodoxy had been thought most apparent.

The division, then, between the 'romantic' and the 'modern' critic here appears to be a matter of different conclusions rather than of critical method. Both studies of *Tamburlaine* are based on what is, in its literal sense, a prejudice: an idea about the *man* derived from biographical research. The method is very similar: Kocher quotes unorthodox thinkers to support his theory about the Baines note; Battenhouse quotes orthodox moralists to support his interpretation of *Tamburlaine*.

The whole procedure is surely extremely misguided. The perversity of Battenhouse's conclusions only demonstrates the wrongness of Kocher's critical priorities and procedures. Biographical interests *must* be subordinated especially when the available evidence is as incomplete as here. This is not to say the evidence should be ignored or that one should refrain from drawing tentative conclusions from it. I think, for instance, that the evidence of unorthodoxy is strong, and that it does often align itself with the writings. I think too that while the volume on our shelves which we call Marlowe matters primarily because of the quality of the individual works, it matters still more (and more than is true of most poets) when the works are related to each other and to the author's life. But such an act of relating must be one's last and not one's first undertaking.

So much arguing of critical doctrine may be found hard to forgive but I must take it a little further. If Kocher's study of *Tamburlaine* is sounder than that of Battenhouse, it is in the first place because his biographical preconceptions lead him in less eccentric paths and then because out of his own insight and scholarship he raises and discusses a great deal that is of interest. But it is in spite of rather than because of the critical method involved. This is what makes him say of *Hero and Leander* that 'it has the air of being an interlude' and of *Edward II* that it marks a satisfactory stage in a progress towards normality. For he has a thesis about Marlowe in which *Hero and Leander* has no important place; and as the thesis brings a departmental interest to bear he is not much bothered by the quality of writing in *Edward II*. The 'thesis-method' here falsifies as it does in Battenhouse, when the idea which he is working out seems to cut him off from a proper reading ('as a separate work of art') of the work he is ostensibly studying. In both writers, the method defeats its own ultimate purpose.

Battenhouse, for example, seeking to establish the truth about *Tamburlaine*, makes a comparison with *Selimus*, the play published in 1594 and attributed by Grosart to Greene who died in 1592. This has its place in the argument, because only the first part of what was presumably two plays survives. Like *Tamburlaine* it follows the career of a tyrant, and as with Marlowe, Part I comes to a close with nothing to mar his bliss. The second part would no doubt have brought retribution and the whole work is seen as being within that category of moral drama of which *Tamburlaine* is supposed to be the shining example. The parallel with Marlovian drama is represented as being very close, and it certainly is true that there are striking resemblances. Selim's first speech catches the Marlovian note:

> Now *Selimus*, consider who thou art

This is the tone of the self-conscious Marlovian figure whose drama is about to begin. His philosophy is materialist and cynical, recalling the statements attributed to Marlowe himself in the Baines note:

> Then some sage men, aboue the vulgar wise,
> Knowing that laws could not in quiet dwell
> Unless they were observed, did first devise
> The name of Gods, religion, heaven, and hell,
> And 'gan of pains, and feign'd rewards, to tell:
> Pains for those men which did neglect the law,
> Rewards, for those that lived in quiet awe.
> Whereas indeed, they were mere fictions,
> And if they were not, *Selim* thinks they were;
> And these religious observations,
> Only bug-bears to keep the world in fear,
> And make men quietly a yoke to bear.   (330–41)

There can be no doubt that the play is in some way related to Marlowe, but when one starts to compare, the differences are as striking as the resemblances and a good deal more significant. *Selimus* begins, for instance, with the presentation of a weak king; so does *Tamburlaine*. But the old Emperor of Turkey in *Selimus* is dignified and respected, weak only through age, whereas in *Tamburlaine* Mycetes is a figure of fun. When the first loses his crown we are meant to feel it as monstrous and unnatural; when the second loses his it is made to seem natural and right. The Emperor commands pity and respect; Mycetes only mirth and contempt. This is typical. The characters who stand against Selim are accorded some status. Corcut, the peaceable scholar, is a respected figure, and his death is another tragedy. The only peace-loving men in *Tamburlaine* are fools, cowards and degenerates. In *Selimus* the victims are allowed speech which matches Selim's own; in *Tamburlaine* the power over words goes with the power over men— Tamburlaine, at the top of the scale, has it, and Mycetes, at the bottom, is as ineffective in speech as in everything else (he, we remember, speaks the line 'Accurst be he that first inuented war' and it is clearly there for a laugh). The progress of tyranny in *Selimus* is seen as the vile accomplishment of a self-declared exponent of evil, and it is utterly unlike Tamburlaine's, who draws men and women to him by strength of personality and whose enemies are (usually) weaklings, overblown, pompous creatures, or at any rate no better, morally, than himself. The play might in fact have been written as a commentary on *Tamburlaine*, showing the path of the conqueror as unequivocally evil by allowing plenty of weight to the 'opposition', not glamorising the 'scourge' and not underplaying his strength of character either. Parallel lines and situations mean nothing of themselves. If a reading of *Selimus* brings the truth about *Tamburlaine* any nearer, it is because there is every dramatic and poetic pointer to the intention's being different and so the resemblance only serves to emphasise the contrast. To see this difference involves reading the plays as poetic drama where attitudes are determined by poetic and dramatic means—the only means by which you can judge whether any convention diagnosed is being used in the normal way or its opposite. It also involves recognising the unorthodoxy of Marlowe's play and the wrongness of Battenhouse in his dealings with it. *And* it means renouncing as untrustworthy the kind of method that begins with biography and then searches literature for 'thought, learning and character', 'only secondarily' (which usually means never at all) treating poetry and drama as the works of art they essentially are.

345

But what Marlowe, in a view made 'comprehensive and unified', emerges from the kind of reading obliquely commended in these strictures (and therefore, the reader must presume, attempted in this book)? It is an intimidating question. If in the study of a classic we are coming to know 'the precious life-blood of a master spirit', it is one thing to follow and try to describe its flow and another to take this and that drop of it and cry 'Here is the master spirit, here is the quintessence'. Yet, as Kocher says, we often hope to attain such an end, and if it were ever attainable it might well be 'the ripest fruit'.

As one looks over Marlowe's work, perhaps the most striking thing of all is the range of it and the changes there are within it. Individuality is preserved: there is no mistaking Marlowe's voice in any of his works. But there never was an author less static, less possible to represent as being 'held' or contained in any single place. Between *Tamburlaine* and *Edward II* there is a whole world of difference; or between *Tamburlaine* and the Ovid translations or *Hero and Leander*. The difference is not that *Tamburlaine* tells of strength and success while *Edward* tells of weakness and failure, but that corresponding to these contrasts between the raw materials there is an extraordinary change of style—which is no 'mere' literary matter but the symptom of a revolution in attitude and sensibility. Nor is it much less surprising that the man whose creative energies are best known for having brought into the theatre (and so into effective life) the 'mighty line', the blank verse of Shakespeare's perfecting, was also an early experimenter in the heroic couplet of Pope's perfecting, the verse form most remote from that of *Tamburlaine*. Going with this too are remarkable contrasts of mind: one cultivating a sharp, critical humour which is oddly destructive of the rapt high-seriousness and idealism that marks the other.

One would like, of course, to be able to trace Marlowe's development chronologically and follow the stages of such change. The dates of only three works are known with reasonable certainty, however: these are *Tamburlaine*, *The Jew of Malta* and *Edward II*. In spite of much hard labour, the date of *Faustus* is still an open question, and for the poems and *Dido* we have to go entirely on internal evidence. As a hypothesis let us suppose for a moment that the works were written in the same order as they appear in the chapters of this book (as is not out of the question); it is then at least possible to trace a likely development between *Tamburlaine*, *Doctor Faustus*, *The Jew of Malta* and *Edward II*. Miss Mahood has done so very convincingly in 'Poetry and Humanism'.[1] She claims that in these tragedies 'the whole story of Renaissance humanism is told', its worship of life and pride in humanity suffering gradual diminution and impoverishment until 'man abdicates from the humanist throne' and death seems to come as a release. 'A similar intellectual process', she writes, 'is reflected in the half-century of Elizabethan and Jacobean drama as a whole. But Marlowe's acumen made it possible for him to diagnose and describe the times' disease in the half-dozen or so years between the first part of *Tamburlaine* and *Edward II*' (p. 55). One might question some of the assumptions here (so much objectivity is posited and it seems no more certain than that Marlowe was himself a symptom of the times' disease), but the basic points surely tell a remarkable truth.

Miss Mahood argues chiefly from the characterisation of the protagonists and the significance of the episodes they pass through. But change affects the whole sensibility and is felt in every form its expression takes: in action, presentation of men, and in the kind of language they use, its

---

[1] The essay is now included in the paper-back *Elizabethan Drama* (*Modern Essays in Criticism*), ed. R. J. Kaufmann (1961).

imagery, tone and energy. So Tamburlaine moves against a background of the whole creation. The world is his parade ground and a special kind of heaven his dwelling place:

> with our Sun-bright armour as we march,
> Weel chase the Stars from heauen . . .   (620–21)

As he himself is 'in euery part proportioned like the man, Should make the world subdued to *Tamburlaine*', so is the world of an exciting scope and glamour proportioned to its master. The 'high astounding term' and the 'aspiring mind' are as one: hyperbole, with its thrust and exhilaration, is the very stuff of the drama. The fortunes of Faustus are also set against a vast background. 'All things that mooue between the quiet poles' seem to be wonderfully within his grasp. India, America, the Oceans, have their unknown treasures; 'the massie entrails of the earth', the unlimitable kingdom of perpetual night, the firmament where Christ's blood streams, are still properties of the imagination in this play. But during its course the world and its possibilities shrink: the grand tour encompasses it and brings little of the expected profit and delight. Time and place constrict and limit, and so does heavenly power, so that Faustus, whose pride in human status speaks in his wonder at whatever might stretch 'as farre as doth the minde of man', is driven to will desperately that he might become a 'creature wanting soul' or to forfeit all individuality as a drop of water, the least of created things. But he still has his dignity and when the crooked branch is cut it is still felt as tragedy. The shrinkage goes further in *The Jew of Malta*. The world, the Mediterranean, the island, the city, the little room: it is like an inversion of the addresses children write in their books. Instead of opening out, everything is contracting. The world was Tamburlaine's kingdom; over Europe Faustus cast his shoe; the Mediterranean is Barabas' washpot.

The sun, stars and heaven have disappeared altogether. Man has shrunk also. Tamburlaine was a soldier and Faustus a scholar and both had the souls of poets; but Barabas is a bottle-nosed millionaire whose person and language undermine heroic hyperbole and strip it of all dignity. *Faustus*, with its irresolutions and tension, can at least seem to voice a position like Sir John Davies's:

> I know myselfe a MAN
> Which is a *proud*, and yet a *wretched* thing.

But the man in Barabas is perverted into monster and in his indignity only a very little of the proud is left him. There remain zest and humour, and a superiority to those around. In *Edward II* these too are gone. The relish for creation, or indeed any sense of its existence, has been abandoned. In this play if man is proud it is pathetic to observe, for generally he is wretched. In Edward the species is humiliated first by the exposure of a weak, wilful and selfish nature and then by sufferings: merciless disappointments, petty indignities, and a gross and cruel death. The depression of all this is not transcended either by heroism or by the presence of a compassionate moral sense. Tamburlaine, moreover, was the apex of a human pyramid which also contained strong human beings like Theridamas and Callapine, or Zenocrate and Olimpia; Faustus moved among eager students and had a servant whose humour was kindly and likeable; Barabas was pitted against mean hypocrites, but even here there was Abigail and a sort of humorous vitality in the trio of supporting rogues. Edward II, however, inhabits a world of petty, striving wills shut within their narrow selves; and the only vitality of character or language is the snapping animosity of mangy, undernourished dogs. In the end, the infinite space that Tamburlaine counted himself lord of has shrunk to the little room of Edward's dungeon 'wherein the filthe of all the castell falles'. Kingship which was more glorious than godhead is washed in puddle water and forcibly shaved. Death, which to Tamburlaine brought promise of a still intenser light by which the soul should 'pierce through the coffin and the sheet of gold', finds Edward in mire and darkness, and means extinction. The wheel has come half-circle; the pointing seemed upwards, the movement was all downwards, and after *Edward II* one feels that a great resurgence of energy would be needed to set it again in motion.

This oversimplifies, as attempts at 'unified and com-prehensive views' tend to do. It does not mention excep-tions in its generalising about *Edward II*, and it suggests a single- (and simple-) minded enthusiasm in *Tamburlaine*, so ignoring what in the earlier chapter is called the 'debate' element. An attempt to *explain* the development outlined probably needs to start with this conflict which one feels to be never far below the surface in that apparently stable and unified play.

Tamburlaine's greatness is, I think, overwhelmingly affirmed, but it is constantly in question. His emergence into the world is felt as an incalculable disturbance of equilibrium:

> Euen as when windy exhalations,
> Fighting for passage, tilt within the earth. (1 : 246–7)

This is exciting and dynamic, but the ambiguity of it is expressed in Ortygius' bewildered 'What God or Feend . . . Whether from earth, or hell, or heauen he grow'. In the face of all the dramatised opposition, Tamburlaine wins the debate, and it seems essential to Marlowe that he should. For all the imaginative effort and fervour have gone into his creation: the wonder of his person and the magnificence of his speech. Moreover, he embodies something which is in the nature of a religion: God is always felt as a presence in the play, but as the antithesis of the Christian God. He is an inexorable God of power who offers his creation to the being most like himself. He expresses himself through a dynamic, warring Nature, where only the fit survive and where there are prizes of infinite magnitude and beauty for the fittest. I think such creative fervour goes into this, while such scorn so often attends any negation of it, that one *must* sense an unusual kind of personal involvement. It is also, I think, very clear that this is not a vision that can be held for long, granted any play of critical intelligence or moral or religious scruple; and enough of all these is already there in the two parts of the play to make it almost certain that they will grow in power and destroy the vision.

The vision further depends on a doctrine of the will, for which the aspiring mind is an emotionally-toned phrase. The conviction that, given free expression, 'will' submits to the brutish in man is common, and to the conventional moralist Tamburlaine demonstrates it. But if this soaring, vital energy is to be held in check, the constriction can only be *bitterly* acknowledged by one whose mind had been so lit by the conception of a free stretch and range of spirit. Once admit the untrustworthiness of will, the need to control it follows; and the claim of religion to have divine sanction for such control is then to be reckoned with. For the 'aspiring mind' begins to look like original sin in especially large doses. Now the whole weight of traditional belief makes itself felt: after sin the Judgment, and after the Judgment damnation. When the infected will is seconded by an erected wit, sceptical intelligence may say 'bugbears and hobgoblins'; but centuries of faith will whisper of devils who wait to tear the godless piecemeal. This is what is dramatised in *Doctor Faustus*.

The will to 'settle', 'begin' and 'be' chafes against an ordinary featureless drift, living and half-living, restricted by the paltry routine of this or that profession; and particularly against the dead weight of a determinism which mocks the energy of your 'free' plunge:

> What doctrine call you this, *Che sera, sera*? (75)

This sense of inevitability is present throughout and is recognised explicitly in the end:

> You starres that raignd at my natiuitie,
> Whose influence hath alotted death and hel. (1443–4)

Even when Faustus seemed to be exercising his will most powerfully he was deluded, for his conjuring speeches raised Mephastophilis only *per accidens*: the state of his being was the real, and involuntary, cause.

It is above all this sense of man's captivity that makes the tragedy in *Faustus*. It is true, of course, that we are made to see Faustus as sinful; all the explicit commentary, and much of the more subtle dramatic working enforces this. But all the imaginative feeling goes into Faustus' plight, and the force of the morality is a depressing sense that God will always cramp man's style, that excitement, freedom and power are not for him, and that if he stands too proudly on his own feet Heaven and Hell between them will pound the life out of him.

Again there seems to be a personal involvement; for Faustus' excitement and more remarkably his instability, the sudden about-turns of attitude, are Marlovian characteristics. The same impulsiveness is marked in *Dido* and the poems, and in a sense the seesaw motion of debate between Heaven and Hell inside and outside Faustus continues the to-and-fro of debate in *Tamburlaine*. Moreover the biographical evidence points on the whole to Marlowe's own unorthodoxy, and it is absurd to shut one's eyes to possible connections with the plight of his protagonist. However bold Marlowe may have been in 'whatsoever company', the play suggests that he knew all about an atheist's secret fears: 'concede me but the merest chance Doubt may be wrong', says Browning's Bishop Blougram, 'there's judgment, life to come'. Blougram also says:

No, when the fight begins within himself,
A man's worth something. God stoops o'er his head,
Satan looks up between his feet—both tug—
He's left, himself, i' the middle: the soul wakes
And grows.[1]

But Marlowe was not a Victorian spiritual hearty. He had seen man as a creature with space to walk in; or to fly; certainly to 'be'. But now between the upper and nether millstones he is squeezed into narrowness. He is so much less the man—and he shrinks, not grows.

It might have been clear, even from *Tamburlaine*, what would fill the vacuum if the vision failed. It will not be an increased sense of beauty, for all beauty in *Tamburlaine* is seen in or through him and his speeches; and in *Faustus* beauty lies in forbidden imagination or in the damning loveliness of Helen. The other form which Marlowe's energy takes is destructive. Pride in strength goes with scorn of weakness. The sadistic energy which finds scope in *Tamburlaine* also nourishes a hard humour of discomfiture; and as man and his world shrink in Marlowe's presentation, this is what grows. So in *The Jew of Malta* the gradual change to farce comes as the fitting way to present a cheapened world and ludicrous people. The protagonist is a sort of debased Tamburlaine who makes amusing rings round establishment-squares and then provides the most extreme spectacle of ludicrous discomfiture himself. Death is usually the best joke of all; even the pathos of Abigail's

[1] *Bishop Blougram's Apology*, 697–701.

death is, as Harry Levin says, 'undercut by the cynical dictum of her confessor'. An off-stage execution offers opportunities for humour and they are not neglected: 'I neuer knew a man take his death so patiently as this Fryar; he was ready to leape off e're the halter was about his necke; and when the Hangman had put on his Hempen Tippett, he made such haste to his prayers, as if hee had had another Cure to serue.' (1738–42) No doubt this sort of chattering brutality was common enough in Elizabethan times, as in Roman, but it is all perfectly in key with the rest of the play. With this goes a comedy of deflation. Tamburlaine's language and person had matched each other; with Barabas there is an absurd incongruity. 'But stay, what starre shines yonder in the East' (680): Romeo's language in Barabas' lips (presumably by anticipation), while the approaching beloved is his daughter with the money-bags. So, in its context, is the tender poetry of the lark singing over her young a ludicrous debasement of the lyricism it appropriates. When the delicacies of 'Come live with me and be my love' are offered by a low comic to a punk they also lose dignity. Perhaps the 'high astounding term' trembled on the verge of conscious farce even in 'Holla, ye pampered Iades of *Asia*'. Certainly it is exactly the sort of thing in which the writer surfeits while composing. Having done it, forcing the ideal and the medium to their utmost limits, there is no further to go: and there is in *Tamburlaine* an occasional sense of strain. At any rate, in *The Jew of Malta* language takes some undignified tumbles along with mankind and his cheap, farcical world.

The world of *Edward II* is certainly not farcical; and, however nasty, it is not exactly cheap, if that suggests something tawdry and meretricious. But of course it is the fun of the farce and the colour of the vulgarity that have preserved life in *The Jew of Malta*. There is a sort of intoxication even in that play: the quick-moving shifts of situation all offering some dramatic extravagance to be manipulated by the unpredictable ingenuity of Barabas. Let that excitement simmer down and then look with sobriety at the bickering, humiliating little world of Malta —or England—and all is set for *Edward II*.

Some such line of development seems to be implied by the existence of these plays. *Faustus* may, of course, come as the last and not the second; if so it would mark an upward movement from *Edward II* for the whole sensibility is more alive and the interests are altogether wider and more outward-looking. 'Man's mounting spirit in his bone-house, mean house dwells': both plays carry this feeling, though in *Faustus* the passion and dignity of tragedy redeem that depression which sets over the pettiness of action or mere passiveness of endurance in *Edward II*. But in every aspect of the writing, *Faustus* is much more close to *Tamburlaine* than to *Edward II*. As Miss Mahood says, 'Pride in man's potentialities is swiftly reversed to despair at his limitations . . . and in the absence of conclusive evidence for a late date of *Doctor Faustus*, this natural kinship of the two states of mind suggests that the play was the successor to *Tamburlaine*.'[1]

Whatever the sequence of these plays, the range is extraordinary, and the poems extend it. These (the translations and *Hero and Leander*) cannot be dated with any certainty at all; neither can *Dido, Queen of Carthage*. The Ovid translations are usually thought to be early Cambridge work because the Latin is faulty, but then of course they might be late, the Latin having rusted. Lucan's First Book is usually taken to be late because the verse is technically mature; but in line-for-line translation one may well be driven to more flexibility than in original composition.

---

[1] *Poetry and Humanism*, p. 66.

Hero and Leander is generally reckoned as the last work because Marlowe did not bring the story to its conclusion; but perhaps he didn't intend to, or perhaps the poem had long lain unfinished. *Dido* is considered both early and late,[1] written first among the plays but probably revised years later; and this at least seems a likely explanation of the unevenness, though much of its best verse bears a close resemblance to the Marlowe of *Tamburlaine* rather than of any other play. If *Edward II* is the latest of the dramatic works, there followed at least two years in which Marlowe wrote no surviving play.[2] It may have seemed that *Edward II* marked a dead end: certainly that particular chord drawn across the circle of human experience is completed with it. Some critics have seen reality opening up for the Marlowe of *The Jew of Malta* and *Edward II* to compensate for the loss of idealism; but the particular nature of that reality has so little to offer a poet that Marlowe may well have turned from it as stultifying. What, then, of the remaining years? He may have had plenty to do as a Roaring Boy about town or as a government agent. Or his interests may have turned to the criticism of religion as Kyd, Baines and the rumours of an atheist book or lecture suggest. But he was remembered as a poet, and I should be surprised if *Hero and Leander*, at any rate, were not written during this time. For so much in the sensibility displayed there seems to forbid a *Tamburlaine* (there is much too critical a sense of proportion) as much as an *Edward* (there is too much humour, warmth

---

[1] See also 'Evidence for Dating Marlowe's Tragedy of Dido' by T. M. Pearce included in *Studies in the English Renaissance* (1959). Mr Pearce presents lines which resemble others by Kyd and suggests that the period when Kyd was likely to have had most influence over Marlowe was the late spring or early summer of 1591 when they were writing companions serving a single patron and his company of players. It is difficult to judge here, but on the whole I think that the influence shown in these quotations is not so marked as to indicate a closer contact than was likely to have existed between the two dramatists at any time.

[2] *The Massacre at Paris* has been left out of consideration in this chapter, the incomplete text providing unsure basis for comment here.

and enchantment). But nor do the translations look like juvenilia: the Ovid is for one thing remarkably close to *Hero* and both translations are the works of a skilled and practised versifier. I can understand that at a time when inspiration flags, a poet might turn to translation, to keep his hand in and to make some money. Could it be that after *Edward II* Marlowe warmed himself back to life with his Lucan and Ovid, and that out of this new life came *Hero* and the revised *Dido*? But such speculation is probably idle, and there is the solid merit of the works before us.

Dido, Ovid and *Hero and Leander* form a group of love poems which cover almost as wide a range in their own field as the main sequence of plays in theirs. In all of these, love is exalted with a shining fervour and thrust, rare even among Elizabethan poets; but in none is the attitude simply that. Here too is the characteristic diversity and conflict. In *Dido* the glory of love in the woman's soul and the magnificence of its enactment filling earth and heaven with wonder and value are presented powerfully enough to make *Antony and Cleopatra* the obvious comparison. But love is also one of the world's 'ticements'. Along with downy beds and sugar comfits, it may be a weak degeneracy from the true business of a man. He knows another reality and looks towards the sea and another world. Whatever the failures in *Dido*, the classic conflict has much of the vast area of emotion which it opens up seized on by Marlowe with a freshness and depth of mind that make it a precious work in the canon; he cannot rise to the tragedy, but many of the acute pleasures and pains of love are dramatised with fidelity and imagination. The Ovid translations also cover a greater range than is usually acknowledged, for they can be tender or rapturous, flippant or brutal, charming or cynical; and whether for Ovid real love had any part in his poetic business, for Marlowe there is a realistic, often colloquial eroticism which is the product of no mere literary convention. But more than the variety within the volume, the remarkable thing here is the extension these translations make in the range of Marlowe's poetry. The humour and lightness of tone are part of it; but more important is the effect the form must have, imposing its discipline, drawing towards grace and point, antithetical neatness and a compact self-sufficiency in the couplet. Marlowe attained these Augustan virtues only fitfully, but the attempt is remarkable and so is the extent of its success. The pursuit of love as an ingenious and absorbing game is also an aspect of the matter seen little in *Dido* and with all its un-Laurentian irreverence it presents much that is common experience. That an engagement with comedy was to Marlowe's benefit is certain: the delight of *Hero and Leander* is one sign of it. Here in wonderfully assured couplets the sophisticated comedy, with beautiful novices for its actors, is played against a background touched by the magic of their strange sensations:

> Thus while dum signs their yeelding harts entangled,
> The aire with sparkes of liuing fire was spangled,
> And night deepe drencht in mystie *Acheron*
> Heau'd vp her head, and halfe the world vpon
> Breath'd darknesse forth. (I. 187–91)

The nervous tenderness, the absurdities of the pursuit, the embarrassments and affronts to dignity, the hard, predatory will, the infinite resources of passion, the wonder of its fulfilment and the new beauty it creates: all these are in the poem, and again an extraordinary breadth is there to be recognised.

All of this is as it were to *chart* Marlowe, with horizontals (say) to represent love (degeneration—apotheosis; destruction—fulfilment), God (submission—defiance; dynamic—repressive), the nature of man (god—worm) and his environment (brilliant—drab; infinity—a nutshell). But this is not Marlowe, and even if we draw in a number of verticals the square will not have him; ultimately it is to the lines on his own pages that we have to return. But the verticals, or the range of his own apparent temperament, would also lead us from bright day to ugly night—or from a free, open enthusiasm for beauty and energy, to a hard and narrow destructiveness. Even in *Hero and Leander* this dark side is present. Hero's modesty is exposed with a kind of pleasure in the discomfiture that is not a simple thing like Fielding's upturning of Sophia Western,[1] but is insistent and sometimes explicitly cruel:

> Thus hauing swallow'd *Cupids* golden hooke,
> The more she striv'd, the deeper was she strooke. (I. 333–4)

The neat, jaunty couplet should not persuade us that Marlowe does not mean what he says.

> Euen as a bird, which in our hands we wring
> Foorth plungeth, and oft flutters with her wing,
> She trembling stroue.   (II. 289–91)

Here the cruel image is attended by some compassion, but this element, strong in the poem, of an attraction towards dignity or independence violated, makes of it something very unlike the Chaucerian comedy with which it is some-

---

[1] Chapman seems to have had some sense of this. In his continuation he says he has refrained from following Hero at the point where Marlowe left her:

> Astonisht *Hero*, whose most wished view
> I thus long haue forborne, because I left her
> So out of countnance, and her spirits bereft her.
> *To looke of one abasht is impudence,*
> *When of sleight faults he hath too deepe a sence.*   (III. 170–74)

Chapman is concerned to assert 'Ceremonie', insisting on the poverty of 'svbstance without rites', and for his own narration he says 'I faile if it prophane your daintiest eare'. This is a conventional scruple, but the 'impudence' recognised is accurately observed: 'to looke of one abasht' is what Marlowe has been constantly doing. Chapman is not on the face of it reproving his predecessor, for I take it that his last lines mean: 'if one is the sort of person who is put out by a trivial impropriety then this will seem an immodesty'. Even so, he makes it clear by his own principles and practice that he sympathises with the propriety he doesn't want to offend.

times compared. We are often aware of a cynical knowingness, and a laughter of belittlement in the sometimes
farcical comedy. Dignity is undercut again and again, and
there is something even *self-destructive* in this.

> It lies not in our power to loue or hate,
> For will in vs is ouer-rul'd by fate.   (I. 167–8)

Whether 'will' is interpreted in the broader or narrower
sense, the couplet still speaks with weight, coming from a
man whose plays are so much concerned with will and
which began with such proud expression of it. But as
heroic hyperbole is pricked in *The Jew of Malta* so is romantic
hyperbole in *Hero*. The deflation touches Marlowe's own
poetic practice, though with the quick shifts of tone such
deflation is intermittent (often juxtaposed with hyperbole
'played straight' and within a normal romantic convention).
But destructiveness and cruelty are never far absent in
Marlowe. The kinship with Lucan tells of it, and so does
the additional violence of expression in the Ovid translations or even the tone of ridicule involved in Cupid's play
with the Nurse. The laughter which accompanies death or
mutilation in *The Jew of Malta* and *The Massacre at Paris*, the
petty humiliation of Edward II, the queen's oration cut off
in mid-flight, the caged Bajazet offered meat like a dog and
taunted with his condition and his wife's: all, and so much
more, are manifestations of a taste for humiliation that is
generally very repellent in Marlowe. It is the touch we see
in Aeneas' tale of Troy, where 'a Greekish lad . . . with
steele Pol-axes' dashes out the brains of an old man who
kneels for mercy; or where Priam is 'raised vp' by Pyrrhus'
falchion point and Hecuba 'puld by the heeles And
swong . . . howlling in the emptie ayre'; or where

> We sawe *Cassandra* sprauling in the streetes.   (569)

The characteristic is not likeable, but it *is* interesting. With so many elements in this passionate and unstable poet it seems to make for an interesting condition, rarely for a completely happy achievement. 'Nothing is finer for the purposes of great productions than a very gradual ripening of the intellectual powers', wrote Keats.[1] In Shakespeare one sees just such a process; so that in the *Henry VI* plays, for instance, one is aware of immaturity but also of a growing mind. The language testifies to wide, objective interests and an exploratory will to understand. With Marlowe it is different. Sudden brilliances, strong, passionately held positions, sudden about-turns, a language which derives its energy from something internal, visionary or literary, a sensibility which aspires to beauty and attains it and which also expresses itself in a kind of sniping, belittling harshness: these are not the conditions of steady growth and great production. Not, at least, if we save that term 'great' for Shakespeare and a few others who can speak to us from a position of centrality: with creative power and acute insight, and also a balance and rightness of judgment. At any other level the term would be hard to refuse to Marlowe, for remarkable and lasting things were done during the few years of his productive life.

We cannot judge him with any finality, partly because great writers tend to exceed our grasp whatever we think to the contrary. Also because there are considerable gaps in our knowledge. We know just enough about his life to make us feel we know everything; and his works come to us sometimes in bad texts, almost certainly incomplete. He may indeed have written the anonymous works sometimes attributed to him. Whatever play it was in which 'Mars did mate the Carthaginians' might have altered all our ideas about his development; the 'Marlo' which the

[1] To George and Thomas Keats, 23 January 1818.

conscientious Mr Fineaux of Dover learned by heart may have been all air and fire; and if he wrote a play with a 'mad Priest of the Sun' in it it may have been the best of all. Indeed if Marlowe were to see the extant body of work by which he is remembered, he might well wonder what all the fuss was about. And no doubt he would be very surprised by our answers.

APPENDIX I

The Baines Note

A note containing the opinion of one Christopher Marly Concerning his damnable Iudgment of Religion, and scorn of Gods word.

That the Indians and many Authors of antiquity have assuredly written of above 16 thousand yeares agone wheras Adam is proved to haue liued within 6 thowsand yeares.

He affirmeth that Moyses was but a Jugler & that one Heriots being Sir W Raleighs man Can do more than he.

That Moyses made the Iews to travell xl yeares in the wildernes (which Journey might have bin done in lesse then one yeare) ere they Came to the promised land to thintent that those who were priuy to most of his subtilties might perish and so an everlasting superstition Remain in the hartes of the people.

That the first beginning of Religioun was only to keep men in awe.

That it was an easy matter for Moyses being brought up in all the artes of the Egiptians to abuse the Iewes being a rude and grosse people.

That Christ was a bastard and his mother dishonest.

That he was the sonne of a Carpenter and that if the Iewes among whome he was borne did Crucify him theie best knew him and whence he Came.

That Christ deserued better to dy than Barrabas and that the Iewes made a good Choise, though Barrabas were both a thief and a murtherer.

That if there be any god or any good Religion, then it is in the papistes because the service of god is performed with more Cerimonies, as Eleuation of the mass, organs, singing men, Shauen Crownes & etc. That all protestantes are Hypocriticall asses.

That if he were put to write a new Religion, he would undertake both a more Exellent and Admirable methode and that all the new testament is filthily written.

363

That the women of Samaria & her sister were whores & that Christ knew them dishonestly.

That St John the Evangelist was bedfellow to Christ and leaned alwaies in his bosome, that he vsed him as the sinners of Sodoma.

That all they that love not tobacco & Boyes were fooles.

That all the apostles were fishermen and base fellowes neyther of wit nor worth, that Paull only had wit but he was a timerous fellow in bidding men to be subiect to magistrates against his Conscience.

That he had as good Right to Coine as the Queen of England and that he was aquainted with one Poole a prisoner in Newgate who hath greate skill in mixture of mettals and hauing learned some thinges of him he ment through help of a Cunninge stamp maker to Coin ffrench Crownes pistoletes and English shillinges.

That if Christ would have instituted the sacrament with more Ceremoniall Reverence it would have bin had in more admiration, that it would haue bin much better being administered in a Tobacco pipe.

That the Angel Gabriell was baud to the holy ghost, because he brought the salutation to Mary.

That on Ric Cholmley hath Confessed that he was perswaded by Marloe's Reasons to become an Atheist.

These things, with many other shall by good and honest witnes be aproved to be his opinions and Comon Speeches and that this Marlow doth not only hould them himself, but almost into euery Company he Cometh he perswades men to Atheism, willing them not to be afeard of bugbeares and hobgoblins, and utterly scorning both god and his ministers as I Richard Baines will Iustify & approue both by mine oth and the testimony of many honest men, and almost al men with whome he hath Conversed any time will testify the same, and as I think all men in Christianity ought to indeuor that the mouth of so dangerous a member may be stopped, he saieth likewise that he hath quoted a number of Contrarieties oute of the Scripture which he hath giuen to some great men who in Convenient time shalbe named. When these thinges shalbe Called in question the witnes shalbe produced.

Richard Baines

APPENDIX II

'Dr Faustus': the Diabolonian Interpretation

Erich Heller gave three broadcast talks early in 1962 on the Faust story and its treatment in European literature. The chapter on 'Doctor Faustus' in this book had then been written and I could not find a convenient place to insert any comments on what Heller said about Marlowe's play, which was the centre of his first talk (printed in *The Listener*, 11 January, 1962). Briefly his interpretation held that the 'official' morality of the fable is belied in Marlowe by the deeper, rebellious morality of the poetry. There is 'an incongruity between the mind of its language and the mind of its action'. All the vitality has gone into the poetry of aspiration, and 'the sensibility of the writer is in a state of flagrant insurrection against the opinions of his fable'.

Ten years before this, Nicholas Brooke had developed a similar line of thought in an interesting study of 'Faustus' in *The Cambridge Journal* (V. ii, 1952). Brooke sees the same 'incongruity' and takes it to be fully conscious. Marlowe's 'adoption of Morality form must be seen as deliberate misuse of popular old-fashioned material'. The 'misuse' involves a reversal of normal Morality values, having these as it were painted over a diabolonian Morality which shows through clearly enough for all who have eyes to see. According to this, Faustus' 'temptation, his weakness, is in offers of repentance . . . Heaven is the subjection of self, Hell in this sense is the assertion of self . . . the formulation of Marlowe's philosophical position is that man has certain over-riding desires where realisation is denied by any form of servitude, and the order of God is, as Milton's Satan observed, an order of servitude'.

Heller and Brooke both seem to me to be indulging a wish and presenting the play that probably most readers would *like* Marlowe to have written. Heller writes: 'the truth of the poetic imagination gives the lie to the religious assertiveness of the

plot'. But religion asserts itself in many deeply impressive lines
of poetry:

> Why this is hel, nor am I out of it:
> Thinkst thou that I who saw the face of God,
> And tasted the eternal ioyes of heauen,
> Am not tormented with ten thousand hels,
> In being depriv'd of euerlasting blisse? (312–16)

What is dramatised with the most intense poetic imagination is
moreover not the aspiration, which only occasionally has the
thrust and conviction of *Tamburlaine*, but the agony of guilt and
loss:

> See see where Christs blood streames in the firmament.
> One drop would saue my soule, halfe a drop, ah my Christ.
> Ah rend not my heart for naming of my Christ. (1432–4)

The guilt which speaks with such agony pays homage to the
morality it has flouted. Marlowe himself may well have come to
accept this limiting power of God over the aspiring will only
with the utmost bitterness; hence the strong element of pity and
sympathy with mankind who have to submit to these limitations.
The state of mind which the play expresses is not a simple thing,
but on balance it is weighted to accept Faustus as sinful and his
fate as inevitable. The tragedy is a double one: that the promising
branch should have grown crooked, and that the nature of its
conditions of life should prevent the exciting, free growth that
imagination could envisage. But the whole organisation of the
play (not merely the re-telling of the fable) expresses a bitter
acceptance of the tragedy rather than a rebellious disowning of it.
'Who speaks of Faustus' sin?' asks Heller. 'The plot, but not
the poetry.' But this simply is not true:

> . . . glutted now with learnings golden gifts,
> He surffets vpon cursed Negromancy.
> Nothing so sweete as magicke is to him
> Which he preferres before his chiefest blisse,
> And this the man that in his study sits. (24–8)

What the poetry enforces here is that the preference is a wrong
one and carries its retribution with it. The harshness of the

second line contrasts with the easy, oily smoothness of the first. In the first we slither down the well-oiled road to damnation and in the second can already hear hell call with a roaring voice for its victim. One could give many other examples: the poetry *does* speak of Faustus' sin. Heller gives only three quotations from Marlowe to back his assertions about what the poetry does —and two of these are from *Tamburlaine*. He seems to assume that Marlowe's mind in the two plays is in very much the same state, which I think it is not. And although he gave a very sharp rap to a correspondent who questioned his use of the one line with which he supported his statement about the poetry (the correspondent was represented as being tiresomely simple-minded and obtuse), it seems to me that his own reading of Faustus' early speeches can have made little of the character Marlowe is creating in them. Will, imagination and energy are only one side; on the other is a reckless, unintelligent selfishness, which the play goes on to show up (in its poetry as well as its plot) as immature and disastrous.

For Nicholas Brooke's idea that Marlowe is deliberately mis-using Morality form and satirising it, I can see no evidence at all (much as one would like to see it). The Morality Play simply offered the form in which Marlowe could externalise the struggle that he saw and found interesting in the Faust story. Brooke says, for instance, that Mephastophilis' reply to Faustus' question about the Fall, is an ironical one:

> *Fau.* How comes it then that he is prince of diuels?
> *Me.* O by aspiring pride and insolence,
>   For which God threw him from the face of heauen.
>
> (302–4)

There is probably a sullen resentfulness about the tone, but the kind of irony which involves a criticism is quite forbidden by the context (unless one wants to make 'Thinkst thou that I who saw the face of God . . .' ironical too—and one may well *want* to, but that is hardly a valid reason).

The idea that Faustus' real sin lies in his defection from evil, his 'offers of repentence', is also attractive and, I think, equally perverse. Behind the development of this in Brooke's essay is most likely a particularly perverse page of *Seven Types of*

Ambiguity (Penguin edition, p. 206). In this Empson quotes the last lines of Faustus' final soliloquy:

> My God, my God, looke not so fierce on me:
> Adders, and Serpents, let me breathe a while:
> Vgly hell gape not, come not *Lucifer*,
> Ile burne my bookes, ah *Mephastophilis*.   (1474–7)

He holds that there is an ambiguity here because as no emphasis falls on the negatives, 'the main meaning is a shuddering acceptance'. 'Vgly hell gape not' is not 'a direct imperative, like "stop gaping there", and it is evident that with the last two words he has abandoned the effort to organise his preferences, and is falling to the devil like a tired child'. I do not think this is evident at all. Nor does it follow that, where there is no stress on a negative, the speaker is really meaning the opposite of what he says. 'Behind this', says Empson, 'there is also a demand for the final intellectual curiosity, at whatever cost, to be satisfied:

> *Let* Ugly Hell gape, *show* me Lucifer;

so that perhaps, behind all his terror, it is for this reason that he is willing to abandon his learning, that he is going to a world where knowledge is immediate, and in those flames his *books* will be no longer required.' But this diagnosis of an ambiguity is based on what I think to be the unwarrantable assumption that there is no stress on the negatives. Empson says that 'as a matter of scansion' there is none; and 'a matter of scansion' is made to sound authoritative and certain as 'a matter of fact'. But here is a critic who takes no 'fact' on simple trust, and he might have thought twice about the scansion. Text-book scansion sees a decasyllabic line and looks around for five stresses. But Marlowe wasn't a text-book poet or dramatist. His work contains many lines which, spoken naturally and expressively, do not obey the laws of scansion, and I think the line that Empson is talking about is one of them. The monosyllables are all there, a powerful armoury, to be rapped out for all they are worth. The actor who throws away his *nots* does not know his business. The monosyllables enforce the effort Faustus is making to thrust away from him at this last moment the horror which is about to overwhelm him (and, of course, even if one prefers a text-book reading to a dramatic one, there are still plenty of *nots* to make up in number what they lack in stress). The lines of thought sketched or worked out by these critics do have a real basis. It is partly a biographical one no doubt, but it is also a matter of the just observation of unorthodoxy, a fierce spirit and a complicated, 'ambiguous' or unstable sensibility expressed in the works. It then, I believe, misleads by suggesting what Marlowe *might* possibly have done, what with a little cleverness he can be seen as actually doing. Then a theory takes charge and the real weights and balances of the work itself get distorted. The direction the theory takes here is the opposite of the direction in which Battenhouse's theory about *Tamburlaine* takes him. But both of these unorthodox interpretations seem to me to be very mistaken.

NOTE. Erich Heller's broadcast talks are now reprinted in *The Artist's Journey into the Interior* (New York, 1965). The objections raised in this Appendix are discussed at length in a footnote, pp. 11–15.

APPENDIX III

Two Translations of Ovid (Book I Elegy 15) Compared

Marlowe's translation

Enuie why carpest thou my time is spent so ill,
And termst my workes fruites of an idle quill?
Or that vnlike the line from whence I come,[1]
Warres dustie honours are refusd being yong?
Nor that I study not the brawling lawes,
Nor set my voyce to sale in euery cause?
Thy scope is mortall, mine eternall fame,
That all the world may euer chaunt my name.
Homer shall liue while *Tenedos* stands and *Ide*,
Or into Sea swift *Simois* doth slide.
Ascreus liues, while grapes with new wine swell,
Or men with crooked Sickles corne downe fell.
The world shall of *Callimachus* euer speake,
His Arte excelld, although his witte was weake.
For euer lasts high *Sophocles* proud vaine,
With Sunne and Moone *Aratus* shall remaine.
While bond-men cheate, fathers hard, bawds whorish,
And strumpets flatter, shall *Menander* flourish.
Rude *Ennius*, and *Plautus* full of witt,
Are both in fames eternall legend writt.
What age of *Varroes* name shall not be tolde,
And *Iasons Argos* and the fleece of golde?
Loftie *Lucretius* shall liue that howre,
That nature shall dissolue this earthly bower.
Aeneas warre, and *Tityrus* shall be read,
While *Rome* of all the conquered world is head.
Till *Cupids* Bowe and fiery Shafts be broken,
Thy verses sweet *Tibullus* shalbe spoken.

---

[1] No doubt Dyce was right in his conjecture that 'come' is a misprint, and that sprung' (as in Jonson's version) should be substituted.

And *Gallus* shall be knowne from East to West,
So shall *Licoris* whom he loued best.
Therefore when Flint and Iron weare away,
Verse is immortall, and shall nere decay.
To verse let Kings giue place, and Kingly showes,
And bankes ore which gold-bearing *Tagus* flowes.
Let base conceipted witts admire vilde things,
Faire *Phoebus* lead me to the Muses springs.
About my head be quiuering mirtle wound,
And in sad louers heads let me be found.
The liuing, not the dead can enuie bite,
For after death all men receiue their right.
Then though death rakes my bones in funerall fire,
Ile liue, and as he puls me downe mount higher.

The same by B.I.
Enuie, why twitst thou me, my Time's spent ill?
And call'st my verse fruites of an idle quill?
Or that (vnlike the line from whence I sprong)
Wars dustie honors I pursue not young?
Or that I studie not the tedious lawes;
And prostitute my voyce in euery cause?
Thy scope is mortall; mine eternall Fame,
Which through the world shall euer chaunt my name.
Homer will liue, whil'st *Tenedos* stands, and *Ide*,
Or to the sea, fleete *Simoïs* doth slide:
And so shall *Hesiod* too, while vines doe beare,
Or crooked sickles crop the ripened eare,
Callimachus, though in Inuention lowe,
Shall still be sung, since he in Arte doth flowe.
No losse shall come to *Sophocles* proud vaine,
With Sunne and Moone, *Aratus* shall remaine.
Whil'st Slaues be false, Fathers hard, & Bauds be whorish
Whilst Harlots flatter, shall *Menander* florish.
Ennius, though rude, and *Accius* high-reard straine,
A fresh applause in euery age shall gaine.
Of *Varro's* name, what eare shall not be tolde?
Of *Iasons Argo*? and the *Fleece* of *golde*?
Then shall *Lucretius* loftie numbers die,

When Earth, and Seas in fire and flames shall frie.
Titirus, Tillage, *Æney* shall be read,
Whilst *Rome* of all the conquer'd world is head.
Till *Cupids* fires be out, and his bowe broken,
Thy verses (neate *Tibullus*) shall be spoken.
Our *Gallus* shall be knowne from East to west:
So shall *Licoris,* whom he now loues best.
The suffering Plough-share or the flint may weare:
But heauenly *Poësie* no death can feare.
Kings shall giue place to it, and Kingly showes,
The bankes ore which gold-bearing *Tagus* flowes.
Kneele hindes to trash: me let bright Phœbus swell,
With cups full flowing from the *Muses* well.
The frost-drad myrtle shall impale my head,
And of sad louers Ile be often read.
"Enuy the liuing, not the dead, doth bite.
"For after death all men receiue their right.
Then when this body falls in funeral fire,
My name shall liue, and my best part aspire.

Chapter 6, especially in its opening and conclusion, no longer represents the balance of my judgment on *Edward II*. I had long suspected that critics were right in saying that it undervalued certain elements in the play, though even as I re-read with these things in mind, I could not see where its features were other than what was described there. The revelation came very powerfully through Toby Robertson's production with the Prospect Theatre Company, first at the Edinburgh Festival of 1969, and eventually at the Piccadilly Theatre, where I saw it in 1970. The play emerged as having a dramatic tension (superbly created and maintained by intense acting and sheer speed and efficiency of production) that did much to compensate for the 'poetic thinness', and also a greater strength in its 'positives' than had ever been apparent in reading or in previous theatrical productions that I had known. As sympathies became passionately engaged, so a genuine and intense problem-play came into existence. On one hand is the scale of values suggested in the phrases of Douglas Cole ('the pain of loss, the irony of human aspirations, the root of evil in the will of man'), firmly invoked as the basis of a civilised moral judgment; on the other, the negating concepts are set up, somewhere very near the centre of sensibility, for they attack what we call the heart. If 'the pain of loss' is great, that pain is implicit testimony to the joy of possession; if there is irony in human aspiration, there is also vision and excitement, which the irony may smile upon sourly but which it can kill only with itself (for irony is parasitical and feeds on what it may destroy); and if the will of man is labelled as simply evil, then all the questioning, sceptical and liberal side of humanity rises up to say with the Wife of Bath: 'The experience woot wel it is noght so'. And then to add, with more moderation, 'at least no wholly so'. For though the play may be seen as enforcing, by the tale it tells, a view of life which implicitly commends traditional Christian and classical virtues of restraint, discipline and moderation, yet such positives as have effective dramatic power are quite other: the strongest is the passionate loyalty of a man for his male lover, the others are the vision of a coloured, permissive enchantment which might raise a leaden court to excitement and a quickened sense of beauty, and an aspiring pride which will go to death as an adventure to discover 'countries yet unknown'. Somewhere between these two ways of observation and judgment, the wretched people of this play strive, triumph, suffer and have their being. Perhaps this wretchedness is due to their erected wills and wits, and peace could come only in concord with the will of God; perhaps the wit and the will know of joys which God and the social order combine to frustrate. Both possibilities were called to mind as one watched this production. Choice of judgment can hardly have existed as an admissably conscious possibility for a god-fearing Elizabethan, but Marlowe forces choice upon him to the highest extent conceivable under the circumstances in which the Elizabethan theatre functioned. What seemed to emerge from this stage production was that Marlowe (again ahead of his time) had in fact written a problem play, more akin in genre to *Measure for Measure* or *Troilus and Cressida* than to *Richard II* or other chronicle plays. *Quod me nutrit me destruit*: the sentence in the Corpus Christi portrait (of a young man of Marlowe's age who possibly might be Marlowe) is true of all the characters. But the text inevitably suggests its own reversal: the destructive element also nourishes. If Mortimer and Gaveston have any fleeting greatness it is through the energy of pride that feeds on will. Edward certainly has a time of greatness, and it is a destructive love which creates it in him: we see the weakling become a man ('Edward this day hath crowned him king anew') and the force which has nourished his growth is the tragically frustrated homosexual love which is also his destroyer.

SELECTED BIBLIOGRAPHY

1. Editions of Marlowe's Works

The Works and Life of Christopher Marlowe. General editor: R. H. Case. 6 vols, London, 1930–3 ('Life of Marlowe' and *Dido, Queen of Carthage,* ed. C. F. Tucker Brooke, 1930; *Tamburlaine,* ed. U. Ellis-Fermor, 1930; *The Jew of Malta* and *The Massacre at Paris,* ed. H. S. Bennett, 1931; *Poems,* ed. L. C. Martin, 1931; *Doctor Faustus,* ed. F. S. Boas, 1932; *Edward II,* ed. H. B. Charlton and R. D. Waller, 1933. Rev. F. N. Lees, 1955).

'The Revels Plays': *Doctor Faustus,* ed. J. D. Jump, 1962; *Dido, Queen of Carthage* and *The Massacre at Paris,* ed. H. J. Oliver, 1968; *Poems,* ed. Millar Maclure, 1968.

'The New Mermaids': *Doctor Faustus,* ed. R. Gill, 1965; *The Jew of Malta,* ed. T. W. Craik, 1966; *Edward II,* ed. M. Merchant, 1967.

'Regent's Renaissance Drama Series': *Tamburlaine,* ed. J. D. Jump, 1965; *The Jew of Malta,* ed. R. W. Van Fossen, 1965.

The Works of Christopher Marlowe, ed. C. F. Tucker Brooke. Oxford, 1910.

The Plays of Christopher Marlowe, ed. L. Kirschbaum. Cleveland, 1962.

Christopher Marlowe: The Complete Plays, ed. J. B. Steane (Penguin English Library). London, 1969.

Marlowe's 'Doctor Faustus' 1604–1616: Parallel Texts, ed. W. W. Greg. Oxford, 1950.

The Tragical History of the Life and Death of Doctor Faustus: A Conjectural Reconstruction, ed. W. W. Greg. Oxford, 1950.

Tamburlaine the Great: an Acting Version, ed. T. Guthrie and D. Wolfit. London, 1951.

2. Books on Marlowe

Bakeless, J. *Christopher Marlowe.* London, 1938.
    The Tragicall History of Christopher Marlowe. 2 vols. Cambridge, Mass., 1942.
Battenhouse, R. *Marlowe's Tamburlaine: a Study in Renaissance Moral Philosophy.* Nashville, 1941; reprinted 1964.
Boas, F. S. *Christopher Marlowe: A Biographical and Critical Study.* Oxford, 1940.
Cole, D. *Suffering and Evil in the Plays of Christopher Marlowe.* Princeton, 1962.
Eccles, M. *Marlowe in London.* Cambridge, Mass., 1934.
Ellis-Fermor, U. *Christopher Marlowe.* London, 1927.
Henderson, P. *Marlowe* ('Men and Books'). London, 1952.
Hotson, J. L. *The Death of Christopher Marlowe.* London, 1925.
Kocher, P. H. *Christopher Marlowe: a Study of his Thought, Learning and Character.* N. Carolina, 1946.
Levin, H. *The Overreacher: a Study of Christopher Marlowe.* Cambridge, Mass., 1952.
Poirier, M. *Christopher Marlowe.* London, 1951.
Rowse, A. L. *Christopher Marlowe: A Biography.* London, 1964.
Waight, A. D., and Stern. *In Search of Christopher Marlowe.* London, 1965.
Wilson, F. P. *Marlowe and the Early Shakespeare.* Oxford, 1953.

3. Collected Essays

Marlowe: A Collection of Critical Essays, ed. C. Leech ('Twentieth Century Views'). New Jersey, 1964.

SELECTED BIBLIOGRAPHY

Tulane Drama Review (Marlowe Issue), VIII, 4. 1964.
Christopher Marlowe: Doctor Faustus: Text and Major Criticism, ed. I. Ribner. New York, 1966.
Christopher Marlowe, ed. B. Morris ('Mermaid Critical Commentaries'). London, 1968.
Critics on Marlowe: readings in literary criticism, ed. J. O'Neill. London, 1969.
Twentieth Century Interpretations of 'Doctor Faustus', ed. W. Farnham. New Jersey, 1969.
Doctor Faustus ('Casebook Series'), ed. J. D. Jump. London, 1969.

4. Essays and Studies

a) 'Dido, Queen of Carthage'

Pearce, T. M. 'Evidence for Dating Marlowe's *Tragedy of Dido*'. *Studies in the English Renaissance Drama*, 1959.
Rousseau, G. S. 'Marlowe's *Dido* and a Rhetoric of Love'. *English Miscellany*, 19. 1968.
(See also Introduction to H. J. Oliver's edition as above.)

b) 'Tamburlaine'

Armstrong, W. A. *Marlowe's Tamburlaine: the Image and the Stage*. Hull, 1966.
Duthie, G. I. 'The Dramatic Structure of Marlowe's *Tamburlaine the Great*' Pts. I. and II'. *English Studies*, I. 1948.
Fiedler, F. B. *Tamburlaine. Part I and its audience*. Florida, 1962.
Gardner, H. L. 'The Second Part of *Tamburlaine the Great*'. *Modern Language Review*, 37. 1942.
Smith, H. '*Tamburlaine* and the Renaissance'. *Elizabethan Studies*, University of Colorado Studies, Series B, II, 4. 1945.
Spence, L. '*Tamburlaine* and Marlowe'. *Publications of the Modern Language Association of America*, XLII. 1927.
Wyler, S. 'Marlowe's Technique of Communicating with his Audience, as seen in his *Tamburlaine* Pt I'. *English Studies*, 48. 1967.

c) 'Doctor Faustus'

Bowers, F. 'The Text of Marlowe's *Faustus*'. *Modern Philology*, XLIX. 1951–2.
Bradbrook, M. C. 'Marlowe's *Doctor Faustus* and the Eldritch Tradition'. *Essays on Shakespeare and Elizabethan Drama in Honor of H. Craig*, ed. R. Hosley. Columbia, Missouri, 1963.
Brooke, N. 'The Moral Tragedy of *Doctor Faustus*'. *Cambridge Journal*. 1952.
Campbell, L. B. '*Doctor Faustus*: a Case of Conscience'. *Publications of the Modern Language Association of America*, LXVII. 1952.
Davidson, C. 'Doctor Faustus of Wittenberg'. *Studies in Philology*, LIX. 1962.
Frye, R. M. 'Marlowe's *Doctor Faustus*: the Repudiation of Humanity'. *South Atlantic Quarterly*, LV, 3. 1956.
Gardner, H. L. 'The Tragedy of Damnation'. *Elizabethan Drama*, ed. Kaufman. New York, 1961.
Greg, W. W. 'The Damnation of Faustus'. *Modern Language Review*, XLI. 1946.
Heller, E. 'Faustus' Damnation: the Morality of Knowledge'. *Listener*, 11 January, 1962. Reprinted with additions in *The Artist's Journey into the Interior*. New York, 1965.
Jenkins, H. Review of Greg's edition of *Doctor Faustus*. *Modern Language Review*, XLVI. 1951.
Kaula, D. 'Time and the Timeless in *Doctor Faustus*'. *College English*, XXII. 1960.

SELECTED BIBLIOGRAPHY

Kocher, P. H. 'The Witchcraft Basis in Marlowe's *Faustus*'. *Modern Philology*, XXXVIII. 1940.

'Nashe's Authorship of the Prose Scenes in *Faustus*'. *Modern Language Quarterly*, III. 1942.

'The Early Date for Marlowe's *Faustus*'. *Modern Language Notes*, LVIII. 1943.

McCloskey, J. C. 'The Theme of Despair in Marlowe's *Faustus*'. *College English*, IV. 1942.

McCullen, J. T. '*Doctor Faustus* and Renaissance Learning'. *Modern Language Review*, LI. 1956.

Ornstein, R. 'The Comic Synthesis in *Doctor Faustus*'. *Journal of English Literary History*, XXII. 1955.

Palmer, D. J. 'Magic and Poetry in *Doctor Faustus*'. *Critical Quarterly*, VI. 1964. Reprinted in *Doctor Faustus, Text and Major Criticism* ed. Ribner, 1966.

Sachs, A. 'The Religious Despair of Doctor Faustus'. *Journal of English and Germanic Philology*, LXIII. 1964.

Simpson, P. 'The 1604 Text of Marlowe's *Doctor Faustus*'. *Essays and Studies*, VII. 1921.

Smidt, K. 'Two Aspects of Despair in Elizabethan Tragedy'. *English Studies*, L, 3. 1969.

Smith, J. 'Marlowe's *Doctor Faustus*'. *Scrutiny*, VIII, 1. 1939.

Smith, W. D. 'The Nature of Evil in *Doctor Faustus*'. *Modern Language Review*, I.X. 1965.

Westlund, J. 'The Orthodox Christian Framework of Marlowe's *Faustus*'. *Studies in English Literature*, III. 1963.

Zimansky, C. A. 'Marlowe's *Faustus*: the Date again'. *Philological Quarterly*, XLI. 1962.

d) '*The Jew of Malta*'

Andrea, A. D. 'Marlowe's Prologue to *The Jew of Malta*'. *Mediaeval and Renaissance Studies*, V. 1960.

Babb, H. S. 'Policy in Marlowe's *Jew of Malta*'. *Journal of English Literary History*, XXIV. 1957.

Currie, R. A. 'Marlowe's *Jew of Malta*'. McGill University thesis, 1951.

Hunter, G. K. 'The Theology of Marlowe's *Jew of Malta*'. *Journal of the Warburg and Courtauld Institutes*, XXVII. 1964.

Kirschbaum, L. 'Some Light on Marlowe's *Jew of Malta*'. *Modern Language Quarterly*, VII. 1946.

Maxwell, J. C. 'How Bad is the Text of *The Jew of Malta*'? *Modern Language Review*, XLVIII. 1953.

e) '*Edward II*'

Fricker, R. 'The Dramatic Structure of *Edward II*'. *English Studies*, XXXIV. 1953.

Leech, C. 'Marlowe's *Edward II*: Power and Suffering'. *Critical Quarterly*, I, 3. 1959.

Mills, L. J. 'The Meaning of *Edward II*'. *Modern Philology*, XXXII. 1934.

Sunesen, B. 'Marlowe and the Dumb Show'. *English Studies*, XXXV.

f) '*The Massacre at Paris*'

Kocher, P. H. 'François Hotman and Marlowe's *The Massacre at Paris*'. *Publications of the Modern Language Association of America*, LVI. 1941.

'Contemporary Pamphlet Backgrounds for Marlowe's *The Massacre at Paris*'. *Modern Language Quarterly*, VIII. 1947.

g) *Translations*

Gill, R. *Snakes leape by Verse.* 'Mermaid Critical Commentaries', ed. Morris. London, 1968.

Jacobsen, E. *Translation a traditional craft, an introductory Sketch with a study of Marlowe's Elegies.* Copenhagen, 1958.

(See also Introduction to M. Maclure's edition of *The Poems*, 'Revel Plays', 1968.)

h) *'Hero and Leander'*

Baldwin, T. W. 'Marlowe's Musaeus'. *Journal of English and Germanic Philology*, Oct. 1955.

Bradbrook, M. C. *'Hero and Leander'. Scrutiny*, II, 1. 1933.

Bush, D. 'Notes on *Hero and Leander'. Publications of the Modern Language Association of America*, XLIV. 1929.

Fraser, R. A. 'The Art of *Hero and Leander'. Journal of English and Germanic Philology*, Oct. 1958.

Knowlton, E. C. 'The Origin of the Closed Couplet in English Poetry'. *Nation*, 30 July 1914.

Lewis, C. S. *Hero and Leander.* British Academy Lecture, 1952.

Miller, P. W. 'A Function of Myth in Marlowe's *Hero and Leander'. Studies in Philology*, April 1953.

Williams, M. T. 'The Temptations in Marlowe's *Hero and Leander'. Modern Language Quarterly*, Sept. 1955.

i) *Other subjects*

Brooke, C. F. T. 'The Marlowe Canon'. *Publications of the Modern Language Association of America*, XVII. 1922.

Brooke, N. 'Marlowe a Provocative Agent in Shakespeare's Early Plays'. *Shakespeare Survey*, 14. 1961.

'Marlowe the Dramatist'. *Elizabethan Theatre*, 'Stratford-upon-Avon Studies', 9. 1966.

Eliot, T. S. 'Notes on the Blank Verse of Christopher Marlowe' (1919). Reprinted in *The Sacred Wood* (1920), and *Selected Essays*. London, 1932.

Empson, W. 'Two Proper Crimes' (review of Kocher's *Marlowe*). *Nation*, CLXIII. 1946.

Gruninger, H. W. 'Brecht and Marlowe'. *Comparative Literature*, XXI, 3. 1969. (See also essay on this subject in the 'Mermaid Critical Commentaries', ed. Morris.)

Johnson, F. R. 'Marlowe's Astronomy and Renaissance Skepticism'. *Journal of English Literary History*, XIII. 1946.

Leech, C. 'Marlowe's Humour'. *Essays on Shakespeare and Elizabethan Drama in Honor of H. Craig.* Columbia, Missouri, 1963. Reprinted in *Marlowe: Twentieth Century Views*. 1964.

Mahood, M. M. 'Marlowe's Heroes'. *Poetry and Humanism.* London, 1950. Reprinted in *Elizabethan Drama*, ed. Kaufman, 1961.

Maxwell, J. C. 'The Plays of Christopher Marlowe'. *Pelican Guide to English Literature*, vol. II. 1955.

Muir, K. 'The Chronology of Marlowe's Plays'. *Proceedings of the Leeds Philosophical and Literary Society*, V. 1943.

Praz, M. 'Christopher Marlowe'. *English Studies*, XIII. 1931.

Ribner, I. 'Marlowe and Machiavelli'. *Comparative Literature*, 6. 1954.

'Marlowe and Shakespeare'. *Shakespeare Quarterly*, XV. 1964.

Seaton, E. 'Marlowe and his Authorities'. *Times Literary Supplement*, 16 June 1921.

'Marlowe's Map'. *Essays and Studies*, x. 1924.
'Fresh Sources for Marlowe'. *Review of English Studies*, v, 1929.
'Marlowe, Robert Poley, and the Tippings'. *Review of English Studies*, v, 1929.
'Marlowe's Light Reading'. *Elizabethan and Jacobean Studies presented to F. P. Wilson*. Oxford, 1959.
Tannenbaum, S. A. *The Assassination of Christopher Marlowe*. New York, 1928.
Urry, W. 'Marlowe and Canterbury'. *Times Literary Supplement*, 13 February 1964.

5. Books and Collected Essays containing work on Marlowe

Bevington, D. M. *From Mankind to Marlowe: the growth of Structure in the Popular Drama of Tudor England*. Harvard, 1962.
Bradbrook, M. C. *Themes and Conventions of Elizabethan Tragedy*. Cambridge, 1935. *The School of Night*. Cambridge, 1936.
Clemen, W. *English Tragedy before Shakespeare: the Development of Dramatic Speech*. Heidelberg, 1955; London, 1961.
Ellis-Fermor, U. *The Frontiers of Drama*. London, 1945.
Empson, W. *Seven Types of Ambiguity*. London, 1931.
Gardner, H. *A Reading of 'Paradise Lost'*. Oxford, 1965. (Contains the essay 'Milton's Satan and the Theme of Damnation', from *Essays and Studies*, 1948.)
Hosley, R. (ed.) *Essays on Shakespeare and Elizabethan Drama in Honor of H. Craig*. Columbia, Missouri, 1963.
Kaufman, R. J. (ed.). *Elizabethan Drama*. Oxford, 1961.
Knights, L. C. *Further Explorations*. London, 1965.
Lewis, C. S. *English Literature in the Sixteenth Century, Excluding Drama*. Oxford, 1954.
Rabhin, N. (ed.) *Reinterpretations of Elizabethan Drama*. Columbia, 1969.
Ribner, I. *The English History Play in the Age of Shakespeare*. Princeton, 1957.
Santayana, G. *Three Philosophical Poets: Lucretius, Dante, and Goethe*. Cambridge, Mass., 1910.
Saunders, W. *The Dramatist and the Received Idea*. Cambridge, 1968.
Sewall, R. B. *The Vision of Tragedy*. New Haven, 1959.
Spivack, B. *Shakespeare and the Allegory of Evil: The History of a Metaphor in Relation to his Major Villains*. New York, 1958.
Waith, E. M. *The Herculean Hero in Marlowe, Chapman, Shakespeare and Dryden*. Columbia, 1962.

6. Reference

Crawford, C. *The Marlowe Concordance*. 5 vols. Louvain, 1911–32; reprint 2 vols, 1963.
Johnson, R. C. *Elizabethan Bibliographies Supplements*, 6 (Marlowe, 1946–65), 1967.
Tannenbaum, S. A. *Marlowe: A Concise Bibliography*. New York, 1937. Supplement, 1947.

INDEX

INDEX